WITH WALT WHITMAN IN CAMDEN

September 15, 1889–July 6, 1890

6

Horace L. Traubel in 1916
Pen-and-ink sketch from a photograph.

WITH WALT WHITMAN IN CAMDEN

September 15, 1889–July 6, 1890

6

———

By HORACE TRAUBEL

Edited by

GERTRUDE TRAUBEL

WILLIAM WHITE

SOUTHERN ILLINOIS UNIVERSITY PRESS

CARBONDALE AND EDWARDSVILLE

Library of Congress Cataloging in Publication Data (Revised)

Traubel, Horace, 1858–1919.
  With Walt Whitman in Camden.

    Vol. 4 edited by Sculley Bradley; v. 5 edited by
Gertrude Traubel; v. 6 edited by Gertrude Traubel and
William White.
    Vol. 2 has imprint: New York : D. Appleton;
v. 3: New York : M. Kennerley; v. 4: Philadelphia :
University of Pennsylvania Press; v. 5: Carbondale :
Southern Illinois University Press.
    Includes indexes.
    1. Whitman, Walt, 1819–1892—Biography. 2. Poets,
American—19th century—Biography. I. Bradley, Sculley.
II. Traubel, Gertrude. III. White, William, 1910–.
IV. Title.
PS3232.T7   811'.3 [B]   8–5603
ISBN 0–8093–1047–3 (v.6)   AACR2

PREFACE

Because this sixth volume of Horace Traubel's *With Walt Whitman in Camden* will most likely be used by those who know the preceding five volumes, published in 1906, 1908, 1914, 1953, and 1964, not much need be added to what Horace Traubel wrote "To Readers" in 1906 (reprinted in Volume 4) and to Sculley Bradley's Introduction to Volume 4 in 1953.

In Volumes 2 and 3, instead of writing a Preface, Traubel only quoted remarks Whitman made to him, the most pertinent of which is worth repeating: "I want you to be in possession of data which will equip you after I am gone for making statements, that sort of thing, when necessary. I can't sit down offhand and dictate the story to you, but I can talk with you and give you the documentary evidence here and there, adding a little every day, so as to finally graduate you for the job."

So in the poet's own words, as recorded by his dutiful friend, what we have here in these conversations with Whitman in his last few years in Camden are data, statements, and documentary evidence for the biographer to do his job, or for the reader to know more about the man who created *Leaves of Grass*.

Both Horace Traubel's wife, Anne Montgomerie Traubel, and his daughter, Gertrude Traubel, had considerable respect for the unpublished material left in their hands; thus out of concern for this and in the tradition of current editorial practice, I have made almost no alterations in the text—I have "edited" as little as possible, though obvious typists' errors have been silently corrected, as Traubel would have done if he had seen this volume through the press. Typographically and in format and design Volume 6 follows the earlier volumes.

Most of the transcribing and editing had already been done by Gertrude Traubel, whose illness prevented her from completing the task. Charles E. Feinberg, whose collection of Whitman materials is in the Library of Congress, and whose generosity in connection with Walt Whitman endeavors—including the present one—has become legendary, has asked me to see Volume 6 and succeeding volumes of *With Walt Whitman in Camden* through the press as a reference tool of the greatest importance to Whitman scholarship.

Franklin Village, Michigan   WILLIAM WHITE
6 October 1981

CONTENTS

ILLUSTRATIONS CONTAINED
IN THIS VOLUME

LETTERS CONTAINED
IN THIS VOLUME

WITH WALT WHITMAN IN CAMDEN

Sunday, September 15, 1889
and
Monday, September 16, 1889

Not in at W.'s. On the 15th was at Logan—on the 16th detained for settlement at the Bank up to too late an hour to stop in. But learn W. has spent several bad days. Did not go to Harned's on Sunday, though H[arned] stopped in to see W. Notice of [Edwin] Arnold's visit to him 3 of our papers Sunday—Press, Times and Record—perhaps others—these all I saw. Had to confer with Clifford Sunday about his changes in the book.

Tuesday, September 17, 1889

8.10 P.M. W. in his room. It rained hard. Found him reading Stedman's "Literature." Did not look well—nor was he. "I am not having a good time of it these days—not at all." Asking: "It still storms? We do not get out this weather." Then further: "Where have you been? We have wondered what came of you." Referred to Press of Sunday: "It was a silly piece—absolutely silly—and lying, too. The Times article— did you see that?—was better. I have sent papers up to Bucke. That man Green was the most unwelcome reporter I ever had call on me. I told you so at the time. We might forgive a little knavishness, but silliness!—it is damnable! The

WITH WALT WHITMAN IN CAMDEN

Times man tells several brazen lies—yet gets more the truth than this other fellow." Did he use that word "soft-sawder-ing?" "No indeed—did not even think it. It is utterly silly, the whole invention. The man's name in this case is very signifi-cant of the man himself—he is Green enough. I hope never to see him about here again. I shall tell Talcott Williams that if he ever has occasion to send a man over here, he should take care not to have it this one." He did "not wonder that people" thought the report a "burlesque." As to the darkness of his hallway and Arnold's stumbling: "That is the reporter's own version—he came up, perhaps stumbled: then he puts Arnold in his place."

Afterwards he reminded me: "I have had a letter from Tom Donaldson. He writes of an accident—an accident to his arm—his right arm. The letter seems as if written under re-straint—he says he writes with his left hand. I was glad Tom said he would soon be over and bring the Irving money along with him—not that I am in any way troubled about the money, but for my wish that it might be acknowledged to Irving—a point probably long due."

I took a look through his old bulgy scrap-book to-night—full—choked—with magazine pages, newspaper extracts, written (the text everywhere scored, marked, commented on) pieces (copied, original)—"the origins, beginnings, if not whole of Leaves of Grass—just there," W. says. A precious volume, which he reads daily, almost. Speaking of the Mod-jeska–Booth combination, W. declared: "Of Modjeska person-ally I have nothing to say—she is a delightful true woman: but the Modjeska of the stage I do not fancy." W. received what he calls "one of my funny notes" a while ago. A young man in Richmond, "a Southern boy"—writes a novel—says publishers refuse it because it shocks" etc. Asks W. to read it—it is only 109 pp. legal cap! Of course W. never answered. "I left down on the table in the front room," he said—"a package for you—the pictures I wish mounted—photos—300 of them—and instructions inside." I received at last the Liberty extras so wanted. McKay will include Symonds' letter provided we provide for composition—he to furnish other extras, paper, printing, etc. W. expressed astonishment at the charge—also at McKay's resolution to charge Gilder for alterations. "I think we might do that much for Gilder: it was kind enough of him to come on—to be here—to speak at all." Still Dave's was "purely the commercial view" and we had "to excuse it by that consideration." Returned me Forum containing Gosse's piece. The pictures in package totalled 300— 4 kinds—butterfly, Sarony, Centennial Edition photo and Lear pictures.

Wednesday, September 18, 1889

7:30 P.M. W. in parlor, with a little girl sitting at the opposite window. W. introduced her to me in the dark: in a little while she went back to Mrs. Davis in the kitchen, evidently not interested in our talk. W. asked me: "Does it show any more inclination to clear off? I seemed to sniff the air of something tonight, but later it came as cloudy as ever." I referred to the magnificence of the golden sunset as I had seen it from the boat. "Ah!" he exclaimed, "that must have been the glint I perceived—the influence I caught—in the early evening." And then he added: "No—I am not extra well—only so-so!" I had left at the house for him in the forenoon copies of Liberty. He remarked: "Yes, I got them—sent 3 or 4 of them off at once today—one to Mrs. O'Connor, not knowing if she already had a copy—one to Doctor—one to that dear friend of William's who is also my dear friend—who is in the revenue service there in California. I could easily use other copies." And after a pause: "Already I have an idea I discern a faint

3

glint, glimmer, growing, of reviving interest in William. It will come more and more."

We discussed the first edition of Leaves of Grass. The Glasgow copy I brought last week he had already forgotten. "Did I sign it? It was already passed out of mind!" he remarked. Yet the old things he remembers with perfect clearness—as that of Cliff Riggs, whom I met on the Logan train the other night and who asked me to find out from W. if he remembered a young man who came to him from Sinnickson Chew about 1880 for a copy or more of L. of G. for Edmund Clarence Stedman and of whom W. instantly asked on my doing so: "Was he a printer boy—tall, slim, bright—very tall?"—indicating absolute remembrance. "Oh, yes! I remember him well, though I did not know he got the book for Stedman. Of course, matters of moment still make the wonted impression, but the minor details are apt to go." He went on to describe the first edition. "It was in green back—dark green—mottled—rough—large gilt letters." Tom had spoken of getting—or trying to get—a first edition. W. appealed: "Tell him not to—tell him it's not worth while—not worth the powder. I don't know what a fellow can want with it—it costs 20 dollars—I think that is the price. If Bucke got one for less—I think he did—he got it at a discount. Yes, yes—tell Tom not to. It is held at a ridiculous figure. Why, I should think a fellow would want the last book—the last edition—the full edition—complete. Doctor, along with other things, is a curio hunter, anyhow—and I greatly encourage, humor, it in him, too—send him all sorts of scraps I think he would count of value. Having committed himself to this thing,—us—he works it for all its worth—must have things, de novo."

He asked me—"You have read 'Leaves of Grass' Imprints? the little book before the war? I came across a copy today—and for fear you had not seen it, I put it here in this envelope for you"—reaching to table and taking from it a bulky big envelope marked

4

"'Leaves of Grass Imprints'
1860

O'Connor's Criticism
in 1866

the Burns Monument
in Rome

return to W.W. without
fail"—

Added—"I put in the other pieces, knowing you are interested in old things—in new, too: for there's not only the O'Connor piece but another, from the Boston Transcript—written by Chamberlain—a good friend there of Leaves of Grass. It is about Bruno—it seems somebody over in Italy forwarded him photographs of the monument. The event has been in every way a success." I suggested laughingly: "In spite of the Pope and the Cardinal?" And he responded: "Yes indeed—I was going to say, in part because of them—on the ground that none of the greatest men—discoverers, leaders—but had to pass through the ordeal of the Popes, Cardinals, such: the squirming, hissing, squealing, howling, anathematizingness, of Popes and Cardinals belong—set the event off, in fact. All the great fellows realized it—even Columbus had to be handcuffed, died in poverty."

He inquired later: "What have you done about the Symonds letter?" When I explained that McKay would not pay the cost of composition but would pay all others, he said: "Well, if we have to do that we might do more—I have been thinking over something to propose—not for anything written for me—but matter of some sort or other that might fitly go in as an appendix." Then he turned more definitely to Symonds. "The significance of the Symonds letter is in Symonds himself." I gave him my conclusions—that S. made three overwhelming statements—that L. of G. was the greatest single volume ever written—S. excepting only the Bible, which is a literature, not the work of one person—that W. was the emancipator of literature and life (quote "Academical culture") and in closing, signed himself a disciple. W. again: "Symonds stands high—is the greatest of Greekists—in the spirit at the very top, in the letter almost as high—classicist of classicists, among all men in England in our day—so I have understood. When you get the matter in type, can't you get me an extra proof of it?" He had "not got hold of the points definitely, clearly" the other night when I read. "This deafness stands badly in my way—and worse, it seems to be growing and growing."

I left photographs with mounter today and am promised them finished in a week, price 4 cents per copy, as before—even though the card requires to be larger. W. laughed about the envelope man, and said of him—"He knows how to charge as well as how to make an envelope." Comparing Press editorial today on Arnold with the interview report, W. called the former "more respectable."

Thursday, September 19, 1889

7.30 P.M. W. in his bed-room, reading Stedman's big book. I told him I had read the O'Connor review of L. of G. and when I called it "a remarkable article," he said himself: "Yes indeed—it is a remarkable article. I doubt if, aside from the Times file copies, there is another copy extant aside from mine. I doubt if Dr. Bucke has one, or ever heard of it. William must have written many things of the sort of which I never heard. Whether Nellie knew of them all—kept copies—the run of them, is something I could not say." I remarked: "There's no one in America writing such book reviews today"—and he quickly, energetically, in raised tones, assented: "No—not one: even the fellows like Gilder, Stedman, good as they are, do no such work as that—none of them. They could not do it in the first place—then, they would not if they could." I said: "O'Connor's sympathy for other writers is everywhere palpable." W. then: "It is! It is! His was the most catholic mind I knew—a mind catholic in the large generic sense of that word—a democrat of democrats—above all, a lover of freedom—freedom of mind—especially of literary freedom: oh! how all-inclusive was his judgment of writers—poets, all!" I said further: "His sympathy is everywhere. While he leaves no one in doubt of his espousal of you, he puts up no bar against any other. It is as if he took us to the stars: it is unmistakable which star he is pointing out to us; yet he in no way objects to our seeing the others and putting what value we choose upon them." W.'s face was radiant: I know he fully entered into my idea—indeed endorsed it. "Every line, word, is true!" he exclaimed, "every line, word—intuitively grasping him. It is all exactly as you say!"

He referred to Dr. True's letter that Clifford had brought down. "I receive many queer letters—a couple of weeks ago there was one from an Englishman—he signed himself a priest—it was very gushing, very. Yes, I have received love letters—many of them—especially years ago—plenty—even now, having one occasionally." As we sat there, Ed came in with a letter from Bucke, which W. read aloud. An allusion to me and the book greatly excited W.'s laughter. Bucke asked if I was one of the everlastings, like Willie Gurd &c. W. said: "My first impulse would have been to get mad at the delay; but as you say, when I see the dishes our delay has brought to the feast, I am satisfied—more than satisfied." We discussed my idea of closing the volume with a paragraph from Sarrazin. W. took hold at once. "I will see what comes to me tonight and tomorrow about the matter—probably something will be aroused—I am pretty sure it will." I had taken him proofs of the Symonds letter, and left it with him. "Now I will get a sufficient taste of it," he remarked. Spoke of the Sarrazin piece—thought he would get Morris and me "to spend an hour or so marking a copy of Leaves of Grass for me"—and

7

our marks "must be in blue pencil"—and he started forthwith to give me a part of his blue pencil, until I objected and he was satisfied.

W. immensely amused over two new brilliants given me by Clifford: one of a man who spoke of Goethe as "the Edwin P. Whipple of Germany" and the other of a remark he overheard in a parlor from Dan Dawson (in re Walt Whitman) "if he's a poet, then I'm no poet." Greatly curious about my meeting with Franz Vetta (Louis Neumayer) today—and questioned me explicitly. Had not been extra well. Keeps to his own room. I advised him to build a fire to take the chill off the room. He said: "I have been thinking of that myself." Shows inclination to stay more indoors. Makes no suggestion even of going out. Ed said as I left that he wished "to take a walk"— so, as I was bound Philadelphia-ward, walked with me to the ferry. On the way told me of his resolve to go back to Canada Oct. 20. Had engaged with a veterinary surgeon to go with him on that date. This rather staggered me, as experience has shown how difficult it is to get a nurse for W. who combines qualities we desire and those which commend him to W.

Friday, September 20, 1889

5:30 P.M. I found W. in his room just eating his dinner. He sat eating and talking during nearly the whole time of my stay. At one point said: "I think this is the heartiest meal I have eaten in a fortnight." Because he was extra well? "No—not that—but this corn"—munching a little for an instant—"This corn is the cause of it and you can put it down in your notes." Laughingly: "I remember when Sidney was here—he took lots of notes—always had his pencil ready—and I would say to him—put this down—that down. Now you put down for me—say that Walt Whitman likes nothing on this earth in the way of eating better than good, genuine, sweet corn. Mrs. Davis gets a good batch now and then—knows just how to

8

prepare it for me—to suit me." Mrs. Davis came into the room with a little baby—"This is Mrs. Williams'—she is going—I thought I would bring it in for you to see." W. was radiant, instantly—took up the towel, wiped his lips and hands. "O the dear! the dear! Why, it is pretty, too—almost the prettiest I ever seed. Why, I must up and take it—it has been a long time since I held a youngster like that in my arms"—reached out for it—took it—kissed it. The baby (only 3 weeks old) crying instantly—Mrs. D. hurrying with it from the room and W. exclaiming—"Oh! it is afraid of me! it's afraid of the critter—afraid I'll eat it up!" I advised him to have a little fire in his room. "I have been thinking that myself," he replied, "especially if this chill keeps up."

I brought him copies of the picture-envelopes, now finished, which he examined. "It is a noble, genuine job," he said at once, "though this red silk—I don't know about it—I prepared the yellow" &c. Put his hand in his vest pocket—gave me a 10 dollar bill. "Pay him out of this," he said, "he is a stranger—don't know us—we must treat him well." "I shall send but a few of them away at a time—for the present a very few" &c. Said: "I have read Symonds' letter, now I have the point of it. It is grand—grand!" And he said later on: "I must send him a copy of the big book. I have not done it—should have done it long ago."

Near by a copy of Poet-Lore containing H. S. Morris' paper on Browning. Said W.: "I saw it there—looked into it a little—did not read it, however. Horace, there must certainly be something in Browning that the young fellows take hold of him—something—perhaps a great deal. A young Englishman recently told me, the young fellows over there were leaving Tennyson and taking up with Browning—with Browning." Then after a pause—"and one other—Walt Whitman." I asked: "Was it Arnold?" "No—not Arnold—another—Herbert." And then: "But they don't know: so many of my friends think I make too much of Tennyson—but no—no—I do not—

9

I am sure of my ground—I take Tennyson the native, in the rough, for basic uses, origins—and I see him large because I see *him*." I asked: "O'Connor never reproached you on that score?" "No—no indeed. O'Connor was one who knew, himself, of these things. But there are many of my friends—and fond friends—who do not understand it"—here he laughed— "do not understand my preference. But neither do some of my friends understand my love for the prairies—my statement, insistence, that the prairies typify America—our land—these States—democracy—freedom, expanse, vista, magnificence, sweep, hospitality. But I understand why I make my claim—I know—I see its justification—its necessity. I have been on the prairies by day, by night—have seen the great, vast spaces spreading out before me—often the stars overhead—then the sun. I would look from car-windows— and to me it was a revelation, even a glory—a magnificent spiritual drama, lesson." He spoke with great feeling. I had with me a copy of the Magazine of Art, containing a paper (illustrated) on Millet, by David Croal Thompson, which W. asked me to leave with him. He put on his glasses and took a great interest in the pictures. "There's the Sower—there's the Angelus, too—that is the picture some of the fellows over there think too much is thought of, paid for." I said: "Perhaps—but in a sense, they're not up to him." W. exclaiming: "That's it!—they're not up to him—nor for long will be. It takes a long time to get up to him—to the likes of such a man. Yet, even in his life, just before he died, there were those astonishing prices."

Seeing papers in my hand, and learning they were last Sunday's Press and Times—he referred emphatically to the man Green again. "That Press reporter was vulgar—a liar—a most unfit, unprepossessing man—to me absolutely disgusting. His description of the visit of Arnold was grotesque, in fact. I was down-stairs with Arnold—sat at the front window, as you have hundreds of times seen me—there was no excitement—no looker-on. That touch, about the neighbors, was the touch of the vulgarian—thinking it would be a bright stroke to represent the neighborhood all out. Yet I venture to say there was not a single person abroad for the purpose given—not a person. Indeed, the American character itself is my backer—for an American as a rule does no such gazing, impertinently—what not, they might take furtive glances, but that would be all. This man Green made a great enemy of Mrs. Davis that day he came—I don't know what he said— or whether it was only some action at the door—but whatever, she was aroused and indignant." He handed me a copy of the N.Y. Herald of Saturday last—containing a Washington interview with Arnold—"before his coming here." A reference in it to W. W. W. added: "I suppose he is in Boston now. He is to lecture there—speak—at the college, I think—on the Mahabharata—something of that character."

I told him of an opportunity I had to sell a complete Whitman for 5 dollars, if he chose—and he laughingly reflected: "Well—as the tradesman says, we'd better let it go at that price—as trade is dull, and our stock languishes, we'd better do what we can to deal it out! Of course they'll all distribute by and by, when we are dead—but we may just as well have some of the glory, the fun, now!" When I started up to leave, he called me back and advised me how to adjust my various papers so as most easily to manage with them in walking— "You see, I am as stiff in that point as old A. T. Stewart with his string. He expostulated with a boy who was using too much string for an 80 dollar sale." I said: "He was given but little string when he died," and W. in a laughing way—"True enough—but as much as he deserved." Fixed up my Gutekunst picture for me as I waited. Wrote his own name and "taken from life" with date. "I was going to put your name there with my own—but did not do it; unless you think so, I'll not do it." And so I did not insist, I took the picture as it was. He spoke of Gilchrist's having been over last night. "He

11

comes quite frequently nowadays—often stays long." Had followed up my proposition of last night for a piece out of the Sarrazin essay to close the book. Copied off several manuscript pages and indited an advertisement of his books. In a blue envelope—inscribed—

"Excerpt f'm Gabriel Sarrazin
to fill out Horace's book
(correct and bring proof)"

Said: "Doctor always speaks of it as 'Horace's book.'"

Saturday, September 21, 1889

8 P.M. W. in his room. Had not got out today. Started a fire,—the wood had a fine, memoried odor, as of the hazardous days last winter. The envelopes had come over as directed by me—made a big bundle, and stood on the floor there—I was amused by the line—"Don't crush." I gave him the receipt, which he put on the table, and will probably utterly lose in the litter. He had been writing in his note-book, which laid open on the table. On my entrance was reading a newspaper. Started a considerable hunt for a copy of the Transcript. "It contains something about Bruno which perhaps you will like to see. I don't think it interesting—not at all—dry, rather. Yet you may see more than I do. A column or so, letters—marked with a blue pencil." Then reflected: "It is a surprise, somewhat, that the Popes, Cardinals, bigots, don't know better than to slap Bruno in the face. I, for my part, rejoice in the opposition—in the whole turmoil—it evokes declarations from the other side—radical utterances. Here is one of the Transcript writers delivering tremendous blows. Would he, if the Pope hadn't come out with such a display? I do not know much about Bruno—not much in a definite, particular way—but the men who cluster about him—they're enough for me." I had heard a Catholic say today of Bruno: "Why! he's an infidel!" and this greatly amused W. "Yes—he

was—and so were all the great men—they had to be. But 'infidel' don't hurt—we are all infidels enough to the Catholic Church—to other churches, too, for that matter. The Pope has issued a little document, I suppose, about two inches,—on Bruno—and the first disposition of every Catholic will be, to get up a great hurrah, enthusiasm, glow, over it—boost the Pope, his Cardinals. But psha! we don't care for the Catholics—undoubtedly things will come about entirely as is best in the long run."

Had read the Millet piece in the Magazine of Art, which he returned to me. As to the portrait there of M., done "by himself" W. "liked it much." And "the whole article was of great interest" though not new in its treatment. Referred to Kennedy. "He has a vacation—will probably go off somewhere—I don't know where. I wonder if he'll get down this way?—perhaps—perhaps." And when I said: "He deserves a vacation—he works very hard." W. said: "Indeed he does—he does" (pronouncing as if spelled d-u-e-s). Adding after a pause: "I have known half a dozen fellows who in their time got married out of worldly considerations,—and in every case the marriage was a disappointment—a palpable failure—resulting in the way to put a man's nose—so the old expression was—nearer and harder upon the grindstone." I instanced—"for money?" And he shook his head. "I don't mean just that—have rather in mind, worldly position—ease—something in that line." And he then added: 'Rhys, when he was here, stopped with them—did not like them at all"—hesitating—"perhaps I am hardly justified in that"—pausing still again—"but I am—I am—even dislike. Kennedy looks on Ernest as essentially—first of all—a selfish nature—that he is out to gather what may be to himself, let others what others may. But this is not my view—not at all. I can realize that Ernest has the English acquisitiveness—and Lord knows! our own is great enough—and I don't see how I can object to it either."

Left with him proof of the last two pages—with which he

13

expressed himself as well-pleased. "I hardly expected you would get the proofs tonight—and it looks all right, too—seems rightly done." I told him the dollar Gilder had sent to the proofmen had been placed to G.'s credit in the office, and W. said: "I hope my 50-centses and whatnot always go direct to the men? I don't want the office between us. But then I recognize that the cases are unlike." When I told W. that probably Tom would be bringing in some of the representatives at the Unitarian Conference in Phila. next month, he said: "Let 'em come." Would read proof tomorrow and if I did not get down would send it up to the house by Ed.

Sunday, September 22, 1889

Did not see W. today. But he went over proof of Sarrazin extract, as he had promised, and sent it up to the house by Ed. Suggested that instead of "Then, Postscript" I say, "Last Words"—but I prefer my own choice and shall let it go at that. W. not out of the house the whole day.

Monday, September 23, 1889

8:10 P.M. W. in his room—staying upstairs now entirely. Reading "Waverly." Looked ruddy, but said he had not been "chipper." A couple of visitors today—women, New Yorkers, who bought copies of November Boughs. Referred to Tom's visit yesterday and to the fact that Clifford, though in Camden, did not stop in. I wrote Brinton in response to his postal, inviting him to come over to see Walt instead of eking out mere hints of his condition by correspondence. Told W., who was pleased. "I am glad you did it," he announced, "Brinton is one of our men." I asked W. about the Arnold letter to him printed in the Times. "As I told Tom—haven't I told you?—it was all news to me as to others: I never got such a letter." I said, "If it is true that Arnold said, as reported in Herald there"—I returned him the Herald sheet with the Washington interview—"that Longfellow is our greatest poet, then I give no weight to his endorsement of you." W. gave a slight laugh. "But you know, Horace, you must not predicate a man's judgment by anything you see in the papers about him. We ought to know, of all men! For you have often heard me say, it is with a newspaper man, not, 'What is the truth? What can I tell here that is true?' but, 'What is interesting, spicy?—what can I tell here that will interest, sparkle, attract?'" Repeatedly speaks of this as "the Moncure-Conwayism of journalism."

He had quite a siege hunting up Johnston's address for me in the notebook. Then later he tried to find the Sarrazin manuscript, which just the other day had been the top of the heap but now had entirely disappeared. His expressions were very amusing. He hunted—leaned over,—till his head hurt—then would sit back—then recommence. Finally relinquished. "It will turn up readily enough when I am not looking." Would take his cane, give a pile of books, &c., a knock—"make matters worse," as he said. "To-morrow, I'm sure to hit upon it somewhere."

Showed him the slip herewith, from Item last week. He laughed especially with idea of the Item getting on moral stilts—the dirtiest lyingest sheet in these parts. "Reminded him," he said, "of the old-time criticisms" in which now there seemed a lull.

Sir Edwin Arnold

It was very kind of Mr. Childs to give a dinner to Sir Edwin Arnold, but the gifted Englishman ought not to assume that we are deaf, dumb and blind, and lack understanding.

Coinciding with the New York World, we assume that Sir Edwin intended the following remarks about "Walt" Whitman in the kindest spirit to the American people: "I am more than ever convinced that he is one of the greatest of your American writers. His poetry is wonderful. Prudish people, I know, object to some of it, but there is nothing impure in it. It is the expression of a simple child of nature."

It is, perhaps, ungracious to object to what is intended to be flattering in the remark of so distinguished a visitor, but we cannot help saying that, unless Sir Edwin is acquainted only with the expurgated English edition of Whitman's poems, his compliment is a little left-handed. If it be conceded to "Walt's" admirers that the proportion of nastiness they prefer in their poetry is a matter of taste, they should at least refrain from calling those who prefer poetry without nastiness "prudish people."

There are many fairly educated people who do not find Whitman's writings poetry at all, and to whom his filth is only a source of added weariness; but those who are so constituted as to admire him will hardly, we think, indorse Sir Edwin's opinion that there is "nothing impure" in his writing. They could not easily do so, if they had read all his verses, without admitting that impurity is not a quality of dirt.

Handed me a picture of Tolstoi out of Book News—remarking my interest in him and "the strong face."

Tuesday, September 24, 1889

7.30 P.M. W. in his room. Reading paper—which he laid aside. Looked ruddy as usual, but with rather a labored expression. Not out today, or even down-stairs, as has been the case for many days now. Morris told me today of Tom White's new enthusiasm over L. of G., to him a new book. W. remarked: "We seem to be booming nowadays. What it will all come to, who can say?" Had found the Sarrazin translation. "It was on the floor—had slipped down," he laughingly said. Was exceedingly anxious I should take half of his blue pencil for Morris, but I did not. Rained. He asked about the weather. Keeps his room closed. No fire. I do not like the so-much staying at home. It smacks of the habit of last winter:

16

suggests confinement, ill air, the consequent impairment of his condition. But he is so susceptible to the cold,—his blood so sluggish—all that is therein explained. As we sat there Mrs. Davis came in and sat down. She had been off to Doylestown, visiting the old grandmother of the Fritzinger boys. W. very inquiring so she recited incidents of the visit. As to the old lady's childishness: "So her old age and sickness give signs in that way, eh?" A deep feeling in his voice. I showed him new sheets of the last pages of the book. As he examined them he said: "I see you did not take up with my suggestion, 'Last Words.'" Of course made no ado about it. Added: "I have been thinking I would have a couple of hundred of these pages struck off for myself—not now, but after the book is out. These two are—I should not say the best, but among the best, pages of the book—with the best pages, anyhow." The printer had spelled "portrayal"—p-o-u-r &c. W. laughed. "No indeed, we do not want this: this was a fashion forty years ago, but we do not make much of it this year. It is a peculiarity of printers to insist and insist. If there had been something in that page particularly needing to be seen—fixed—eluding us—he would not have seen it. That's the way." He laughed brightly as I told him Dave's first edition would be 500 copies. W.: "He ought to print more—I should say, a thousand, at least."

Brinton sends me his pamphlet discussing the aims and traits of a world-language—(Nineteenth Century Club paper). When I proposed that W. read it, he said: "Yes, indeed, read it—I shall look it over—it will interest me. I was going to ask of Brinton and the universal language, what was asked of Emerson and immortality so often: does Brinton accept the fact? I have heard of the great German philologists—the greatest, perhaps—who think the English is to be that language—become universal." I said I believed Brinton did not. W. then: "At any rate, the idea of a universal language is grand, noble—is in line with all the broad, deep, tendencies of the time—is one with our political progress—governments, free trade, solidarity—the democratic drifts, glories, of our time—the over-flowing, ever-flowing, humanities!" At another moment he said: "I had quite a long letter from Rhys today—a good one, too—written, not from London, but Wales. He seems to be bustling about—vigorous. They have been having a harp festival there in Wales—they have them, I understand—both in North and South Wales—a sort of equivalent for the Roman, Grecian games. The Welsh people are an animated, gesticulative people." But was Rhys not quiet? "Well, Ernest was practically raised in England. They call these games, Eistedfodd. I have met harpists—I remember they coached me in the pronounciation of the word, which is not as we would pronounce it, though what I could no more tell now than fly!"

Wednesday, September 25, 1889

7.30 P.M. Found W. in the kitchen, talking with Mrs. Davis. Asked me if the weather was "settled" yet—turning then laughingly to Mrs. Davis: "That is, if anything can ever be called settled—as they cannot, and best not!" Sat back in the corner, out of the draught. Ed came in with a postal shortly, which W., not having his glasses with him, found it impossible to read. I showed Morris today the Sarrazin extract in the book. He wished to know if W. had not altered it considerably. "I am sure I made it to read more smoothly than that." I now asked W.: "Did you make extensive alterations in the text?" He said at once: "No indeed—only enough to make it read smoothly!" I laughed outright. W. looked at me. "What is it?" he asked. And when I repeated to him Morris' remarks, he too laughed. "We differ about smoothness, it seems," he finally exclaimed, with another hearty laugh. Then he added—"There are a number of expressions along in the English of that piece which seem to me to be misleading—evidently too literal. Sarrazin is made in one place to say my father was a great lover of infants. John Burroughs always beautifully said my father was a lover of children—and that is right—children is the word. It is only in such ways I have undertaken to alter."

I received a letter from Mrs. O'Connor today dated Nantucket. Read to W., who was much interested and questioning. She has been ill again, but is recovered, mainly. Speaks in warm terms of my Liberty piece on O'Connor. W. very susceptible to cold. Insisted on Ed's putting the sash down, though shutters were closed. "You may catch cold," he insisted—Ed smiling meanwhile. Of course does not get out at all. I had a postal from Brinton today saying, he would be over Friday evening, probably. W. said:—"I shall be glad— very glad—to have him come. But he knows I can't see him long, don't he?—only 15 minutes or so?"

Thursday, September 26, 1889

8 P.M. W. upstairs in his bedroom, gas on, and Gilchrist there talking with him. Although his color was high enough, he did not look well, and he evidently spoke with much effort. Yet he grew interested and was free enough in gesture and phrase. Gilchrist left some 5 or 10 minutes before I did. A bundle of Harper's Weeklies on chair. His exposition poem appeared this week. Gilchrist was examining a copy of my entrance. W. asked me: "Well, Horace—what's the news?" And when I answered, "Oh! I came here to learn the news! Walt has more time for reading than the rest of us!"—he said quickly—"I have! I have! More time than I want! I envy the man out-of-doors—the boatman in the river, the carter with his team, the farmer at his plough—the active, unliterary employments!—their freedom—the elasticity they develop!" Then added for himself—"I am most interested in the French

19

elections"—G. saying—yes—he regretted the fall of Boulanger—we all liked a sensation etc. W. said: "I regret just the opposite—that he wasn't buried deeper—not that I think he as a person amounts to anything, but that what he represents, stands for, is of all things the most abhorrent, repulsive, hateful to me. My sympathies are all against him." G. explained that he knew W. was essentially right—W. proceeding—"President Carnot and his group, ministers, occupy a position in quantity—though in no other respect—analogous to our Abraham Lincoln's. The time is on, to be conservative, hold your horses, not let yourself be run away with."

Reference to Brinton's pamphlet. W. said: "I read it—read it all—and read it with great interest. Brinton refrains from stating himself positively, I notice—writes somewhat in the Captain Cuttle vein—of Captain Cuttle, who said"—here W. assumed a voice and position of vehemence—"if the ship comes safely into harbor, very well then, she is safe in harbor; if the ship goes down, very well then, too—she goes down!—it is in that spirit." Yet there was "more than that to be said," of course. "A universal language—a world language I very much doubt: the Central African will never develope into it." This replying to my question if such a language would not be developed. "But its genesis—its origin—its conception—is essentially noble—in line with all the modern tendencies that I value and cherish. Solidarity, unifying—unification! This is in fact my argument for free trade—not that it will produce so much and so much in dollars—though that too is to be said, and I feel that free trade could be justified even on that ground—but that it will break down partitions, dividing lines—lines of demarkation—bring the race together—interests not worldly alone, but on the human side—the high deep embracing spiritualities." But Gilchrist spoke of the great lesson his American experience had taught him—that we went on differentiating, in spite of talk of union with English life, etc. W. allowed it: "That is true, much else is true—then comes in another department—then enter other considerations—after differentiation, then unity, too." He dwelt upon commercial necessities. "Probably for these purposes, a system of signs—new codes—will be—will have to be—established." Talked thus vigorously for some time. Gilchrist by and by withdrew.

W. then spoke of the weather—how it interfered with his freedom of movement—kept him in-doors. I found out from the picture-mounter today that our pictures would not be done till next week. On the table a handsome blue book which I picked up. "Have you ever seen it?" W. inquired. Adding after I had remarked that it was Swinburne's Essay on Blake—"Have you any curiosity at all to read it? If you have enough to persuade you, take it along—look it through—I don't know but it would interest you. I came upon it today in looking for something else." Swinburne himself had written on the title page simply

> To
> Walt Whitman
> from
> A. C. Swinburne

and W. had added along the outer edge

> "Walt Whitman
> sent me by A C S to Washington D C. in 1870"

no more punctuation on either side than I have indicated. Beyond writing on the title page under Blake's name

> "born 20th Nov: 1757
> died   Aug: 1827 not quite 70"

W., so far as my cursory glance showed me, has not marked the book at all. A book that touches him is always marked if it is his property. He spoke of this as "much less full, elaborate—than Mrs. Gilchrist's book on Blake," but offered no further criticism.

Ed has not yet told him of his intention to go to Canada in October. I conferred with Harned this evening about a new

man and about the fund matter generally. W. showed a peculiar interest in Gilchrist's explanation of his impression of
American life—its significance—as he always does in intelligent views that are alien—that give us to see ourselves as
others see us.

Friday, September 27, 1889

8 P.M. Brinton came over just a few minutes before 8 and
we went to W.'s immediately, remaining there till the clock
struck 9. Found W. in the kitchen with Ed and Mrs. Davis.
He greeted Brinton cordially—kept his place way back in the
corner away from draught and talked a good deal of the time
freely enough. To B.'s inquiries after his health W. talked very
freely. B. expatiated on an extract from one of W.'s letters to
someone in England which he had seen in a Paris paper describing himself as a wreck. B. was chary of such belief. But
W. said "Ah! Doctor—it is true—and that is putting it mildly,
too: I am literally an old hulk—hauled up on the shore, in the
mud! The last 3 or 4 years—especially the last year—has
damaged me very badly—very." But did he not get out daily?
"Often—often—though the last week or so has not once
tempted me forth. I am a great waiter on the spirit—on
whether the spirit moves me—and if I go, if I stay, it is because I am strongly moved to the one or the other. I have all
my life observed this habit—so that now I am rather its victim
than its devotee—it may be said to have possession of me. I
can see how it has inestimable benefits—then I can see
more—can see when it is a weakness, a drawback. How
many's the argument I had on this very point with my friend
Mrs. Gilchrist, in England—in most respects the finest, cutest, most womanly woman I have ever known. She was a
great believer in deliberation—in pre-arranging things. For
instance, she had a household in England—comfortable, chil-

dren—she takes up the notion of coming to America—for several months calculates, arranges—then comes. That is what I
mean. I could never do that—my whole make-up is opposed.
As the spirit calls, so I follow—in no other way." Brinton objected that while that was a felicitous arrangement of an individual life, he did not know that it would work as a general
principle. W. assented instantly: "I can see that clearly—I realize that there is the one truth, then something more: in all
individuals there is the countervailing force—the other thing,
duly emphasized, active—that other thing weak in me beyond belief, as I know—but I am too old—now in my seventy-first year—to review my habits. I well comprehend,
however, how the constitution of the cosmos is such as to
make all such apparent failure right in the end—as I said, the
countervailing force. Mrs. Gilchrist is enforced in the way
processes of the worlds—the orbs, suns, all such work:
work—not by my method—not by the fact of to-day, but by
prearrangement: every turn prepared, provided for, not today, but thousands, tens of thousands, of years ahead. The
one force—or lack of force—is countervailed by the other."
W. then added with a laugh: "That is a part of my quarrel with
Horace here about Emerson. He will not hear to it, but I
always insist that Emersonism, legitimately followed out, always ends in weakness—takes all color out of life. Not that
this could be said of Emerson himself, because, as I point
out—as is plain to me—Emerson supplies his own antidote—
teaches his own destruction—if seen at his best. Besides, it is
more to know the actual Emerson—the corporeal, physiological Emerson—to come in contact with him, his voice,
face, manner—for I believe Emerson was greater by far than
his books." Brinton reminded W. of a time when he, B., too,
had taken me to task for my espousal of Emerson. W. saying
again: "But of course, I never will allow anything to be said
against the good Emerson—I am sturdily his defender
through thick and thin—will not hear him offended."

23

Brinton gave W. a specific account of his trip to Europe. Spoke of his Quaker ancestry. W. very curious as to the Arabian experience of the Doctor. Asked him many questions. As to their abstemious living B. was very explicit—also on the point of personal appearance etc. W. asked, "Are they still so utterly barbarous—just as you say?" and then—"And after all that is said, how are they as persons; individuals, companions?" And—"What is their amenability to civilization?" and "What manner of books or what not have they? none at all?—none?" B.'s account was full of strange detail. I could see how W. feasted on it, sitting there in the corner, saying little or nothing. After W.'s account of his breaking up, B. had protested in a rather laudatory vein. W. listened—here again said nothing. Inquired after B.'s wife—whether bettered much by her trip. The conversation developed at one point to the Bruno episode in Rome. B. gave some note of his experience—of the intense feeling grown out of the erection of the statue in Southern Europe. W. said: "That is all what we want to hear. There has been a great to-do about it in this country. I myself have rejoiced in it. It has made people ask themselves—as it made me—who is this Bruno they are kicking up such a devil of a row about—what did he do—to what extent must we all recognize him, denounce him? It is very important—very—to get even that far with such a man. There are letters to be read—or letters have been read—in all the churches about it—the Catholic Churches—deliverances by the Pope, bishops, others." B.'s recital of the outline of Bruno's life W. regarded intently—thought B.'s assertion of freedom "glorious"—and to a quotation from Spinoza he exclaimed quickly as though it had forcibly struck him—"So that is from Spinoza!" W. said at one point: "In this last year or so—perhaps more markedly still in the last six months—we have been boomed—boosted—as never in our life before. It would be hard to tell what it all amounts to—leads to." Of the dinner he said: "I was not favorable to it at the start—told the

24

boys so—sort of felt it would be what they call a 'flunk.' But somehow it proved more than a success. I suppose [it] was a surprise to us all—even to the most expectant of us." And again—"And perhaps what the dinner led to is the most important of all."

On entering W. had introduced B. to Mrs. Davis—"My friend"—he called her—and to Ed also, in a similar phrase. B. picked up a book that he saw on the table—a veterinary volume—and W. said—"That is Ed's there—he is studying it." B. thereupon speaking of a volume of his own "in my salad days" on that subject and offering to send a copy of it to Ed.— speaking of his later dislike of the horse as having risen from his early plodding farm work with one etc. Before we went W. arose and insisted on going up stairs to get B. a pamphlet "about the centenary of the Grimm brothers"—bringing it down laboriously in a few minutes with the remark—"Perhaps it may seem a trifle but it is a sort of fillip, anyhow." B. expressed a pleasure in his visit and W. reciprocated, only adding—"You find me insufferably dull, but that is the attendant of my sluggish nature and my age"—adding too as to B.'s pleasure—"I will believe it when I find you coming often." B. went with me to Harned's, who was not at home. Thence to town, talking much by the way of W. I showed him Symonds' letter which he read with astonishment and applause. Says he is writing a book on Rhythm—wants definite talk with me sometime about W.'s origins etc. in art. A fine evening, which I think we all enjoyed. W. very simple, amply communicative, yet rather letting B.'s good talk flow on than interposing as much of his own as sometimes. The night clear and heaven studded with stars.

Saturday, September 28, 1889

7.30 P.M. W. in his bed-room, light up full, talking with Harned and Hobart Clark, the Unitarian minister who

25

preaches here tomorrow. W. said right quickly after we had shaken hands: "What do you think, Horace? John Burroughs was in here to see me today—came in on a flying visit—stayed awhile—was off again. He said he was going directly home again. He wanted badly to see you, but I could not tell him where you were—I thought I knew but I didn't. I hoped some way to get you word so you could come over earlier than usual. He went to town to see Herbert on the way off. Certainly he must now be gone, though it would not be impossible for him to step in here to surprise us this very hour. He came down from Ocean Grove. Oh yes! he looks well—better than I have known him to look for a long time—and he tells me he eats well at last. You know, awhile ago, perhaps several years now, John was taken with that spasm which seems at one time or another to attack every American—the avoidance of meats—subsisting on vegetable supplies—no mutton, beef, pork—though I do not wonder at the pork—and all liquors—wines, everything. And he persisted in it, too—I think for several years—2 years or so. He got it, curious to say, of a German doctor—a cute man, able, broad, I am assured. John said when he was about leaving that he felt the premonition of one of his periodical headaches. Every 4 or 5 months he gets "a spell of this kind." Then W. turned to me again specially—"I am very sorry, Horace, you and John did not meet, but you see how it was." W. having referred to Gilchrist, Tom spoke of the mother, whereupon W. said looking towards Clark: "Both of these gentlemen know her—of her. She was my friend indeed—and a woman to know, too, like Emerson, as I have so often said, to be met personally—to be taken into actual physical contact—with voice, eye, lip, all—before fully known—known for her true greatness." Theological matters coming up. W. remarked at one instant: "The idea of the ministers seems to be, that without the theory of heaven and hell—particularly of hell—society would not be safe—things would not go on—we would collapse!" He laughed merrily. I told him I had repeated to Brinton W.'s expression some time ago that morality as he grew older, more and more relegated itself. Brinton thought it important and interesting to know this—Goethe had made a similar confession. W. rejoined, "Yes, and not only Goethe but all the fellows that amount to anything—all. I am glad to hear Brinton's own confession. That is the creed of Leaves of Grass, the in-working, through-working principle." I remarked that Brinton is more and more taken with L. of G., and W. laughed—"Well, that is what it is for, to grow into people." To which I said, "And Brinton is a good sort of a man to have it grow into!" W. then—"Sure enough!" Laughed over Brinton's idea of the literary class, that it was a cowardly one. "Likely enough" he exclaimed mischievously—"I have heard such things said!"

Tom read Clark the Symonds letter upon my recommendation. I asked if he had shown that to Burroughs, and he said—"No—I never thought of it." Communicated Brinton's high opinion of it—then the fact that B. would write a volume on poetic form, rhythm; W. saying thereto: "I should think that would be profoundly interesting, especially as coming from Brinton—yet I confess I have some qualms, at first blush. My wonder is, is Brinton the man to write a book on that subject? From what I have heard—what I have seen— Brinton would not detect rhythm by his own ear—gets it rather by other forces, agents. Not that I would in any way discount his book or whatever, in advance—only, that there are delicacies, intricacies, to be traced, followed, in such a study, which demand the finest ear—the best organized. And my doubt of Brinton would be, not that he could produce a valuable study, but that he would produce a study of topmost power—the best deliverance on the subject—exhaustive. I have a book here somewhere which it seems to me would be important in this connection—I have spoken of it before— C. C. Felton's lectures on Greek art, literature. Even if not of importance on that subject direct, of importance in itself, a book Brinton, I should think, would enjoy to read. If he has not the book, I should be glad to have him use my copy. Tell him so." Alluded to the religious discussions of the time as "mostly thorns crackling under a pot."

Harned picked up a pamphlet from the floor—poems—and W. laughed when questioned about it. "That's one of the thousand and more choice lists I get from the fledglings who write poetry, as they call it. But that's not the worst: as the boys have it, they get the drop on you sometimes with a whole manuscript, on which they want your opinion—'dear sir, I am a young man, need help—if you will only tell me' etc. etc.— something in that strain." Referred again to Edwin Arnold's letter as in the Times. "It's as new to me as to you—to any reader: yet it sounds something like, as if Jim came upon it fresh somewhere—certainly not here." As we hung around, he opened a little package Ed had brought in containing the picture from Mrs. O'Connor of William. "I sent it to her a while ago—now she sends it back. She had asked me about a picture of William to have engraved—she says she has this. I had a letter from her today—she is still at Nantucket. Yes, this picture is very fine—I always liked it." I said: "He was rather stouter when I saw him." W., "Can it be? In my time, usually thinner than this—this already is fat." Spoke with Clark about Eistedfodd—the pronunciation of the word. "I received a letter—a very interesting—even strong—one— about it—and a paper, too—from my friend Ernest Rhys— over there in England. By the by, I sent them off just this evening to Dr. Bucke. The Welsh people, as Rhys makes them out, are warm, flush,—not flamboyant—but flowing, radiant—in their poetic, musical, forms"—and so on.

Handed me a pamphlet in "Riverside Literature Series" containing some Lincoln speeches and Lowell's Essay on Lincoln. "If you think this would in any way appeal to you, Horace—you can have it—take it along. They had a piece of mine in it, which was all blundered, bad—I tore it out, sent it back, with the message that it would not do." He looked over the book—became a little doubtful. "I don't know—probably this is not the book: but it was just such a volume." As we were about to leave W. asked: "And how's the family, Tom? Is the baby come about all right?" And to the favorable response, "Good! Good!" Harned asked: "Are you coming up tomorrow, Walt?" "That remains to be seen." "I'll open a bottle of champagne for you." "That's good—the very best—inducement, to be sure." Tom then to Clark: "Walt won't eat anything at my house any more, but he'll crack a bottle of champagne with me any time. His doctor keeps pegging good advice into him." W. protested with a laugh—"No—it's not because of the admonitions of the Doctor—it's because the cookery is so tempting—I take more than I ought to." Harned expressed some doubt of the effect of champagne on himself, but W. insisted banteringly: "For me, champagne is the top of the list: then, Tom, it's to be remembered there are some people to whom good things—champagne for one—are particularly addressed—and I think I am one of those people. But whether I come up or not, I should be glad to have you come in here—both of you." Morris will have the translation ready early next week. W. "pleased" with the notion of "having it back again."

Sunday, September 29, 1889

9.40 A.M. W. just up. Had put a big brown-mixed coat on and was opening the shutter blinds. Very cheery, and looked well. Sat down and spoke with me. I wished to leave him Ashton Bell's name for inscribing in a copy of the big book. He promised to write it and send the book to my house by and by by Ed. I had the Swinburne book under my arm. He asked—"What have you there?" And when I told him he said: "You will like to examine it, as you would a curio—but it is

not much—not profound—never touches bottom, or near."
Again said: "If you are going to Germantown give my affection
and best love to Clifford"—adding as he looked out of the
window: "It appears to be a beautiful day: isn't it mild, fine?"
And then—"The clear sky—how it beams! This might be a
day to get out, after all."

Spoke of "Emersonism" as so often before. "Emersonism
finds nothing infallible enough for its test—nothing—all is
fluid, uncertain"—and then—"Let us stay on the earth," etc.
I did not linger. Ed came in with a bowl of water, in which W.
proceeded at once to bathe his hands and face. Since Dr.
Brinton's advice to Ed to take a University Veterinary course,
Ed is inclined somewhat, to stay. I have some hope of it.

Monday, September 30, 1889

8 P.M. W. in his room, reading evening mail that Ed had
just brought in. I took him the five dollars from Ashton Bell.
"I have the ninth volume of Webster's Mark Twain's Stedman's book," he said curiously, "and I like it well—like all the
later volumes better than the earlier. In this one are extracts
from O'Connor and Burroughs, and a picture of John—a good
one, too"—picking the book up from the floor, searching it,
finally pointing out portrait of J. B. "This is John, to be sure—
a little bit of pain in it—and a stoop—but they belong to
him—the picture really very like. But some of them here
beat the devil. Here, look at this—Willie Winter"—pointing
to a portrait that faced him—"He's a little damned fool anyway: this is all made up: in life, speech, profession, there's
nothing like this to him—nothing at all: this is all damned
affectation—made up for the occasion." "But there is another
face I like much—Mrs. Dodge—Mary Mapes Dodge—probably because I have always sort of liked her." Contemplated
her face—"A good one—don't you think? And then they're
most of 'em superior in this volume." Pointing to the poem

opposite—"The two Mysteries"—W. went on—"This is the poem—but the three or four or six lines of explanation that used to go along with it are indispensable. But I suppose they left 'em out 'for reasons.'" By some searching he found out the O'Connor pages. I examined them and said: "And not a word out of 'The Good Gray Poet'!" He asked, "Do you think there ought to be?" I answered, "Yes, I think they're like the lines to that poem—indispensable." He laughed—"So you think that? A part of 'The Carpenter' is here: I am a figure in that."

Referred to the possibility of Arnold's return to Philadelphia. "He said he was to come from Boston to New York. No time was set, but I am sure he said he was going west." Brinton told me more definitely today that his book on rhythm and the poetic art would be scientific—concerned most for tendencies. He had not read Felton's book—would get it out of a library. W. enlarged on general talk of Greek art—methods: "They believed in the harmonies—harmonies of character—were esthetic, yet not alone that—and moralistic, too. All through history, we find—in all ancient peoples—moralism had a part. They laid a good deal of stress on the physiological man: so do we, in a sense—in the colleges, with the gymnasiums and the like—but then this is an artificial stress—like the Unitarian faith in religion, believing in cold reason, to Spanish Roman Catholicism, which will have nothing but passion, fervor. The Greek principle was one that laid primary stress here." "They did not disdain to draw analogues from the songs of birds—harmony: human character must be many-sided—not one thing alone. They were not blind to what we call the Christian virtues—neither inclined to think the Christian virtues all in all. In such respects inferior to our typical man, some would be inclined to say—in such respects superior, others—and I would be inclined to pass with the last. They would educate the whole man. Some insist they were superior in astronomy, but I am inclined to accept that—it appears rather to me, they were inferior. They had a music—a music of their own, undoubtedly. Felton tells in his book there of some scrap that was unearthed, even from the time of Euripides, Sophocles—which he had tried—which was enough to bring the devil out of hell. But I don't think that authentic, even to begin with: there's only one out of ten million chances that it was the thing. Then the wild notion, that an old Greek piece could be rendered—be given justice,—as a modern piano tune! It is out of respect altogether!"

W. is writing a verse—"Champagne in Ice"—inspired by evident facts. A sheet he has been writing contains a list of philanthropic millionaires. Gave me a copy of the Harper's Weekly poem, printed on a slip by Curtz. "Bravo, Paris Exhibition"—he had changed to "Bravo, Paris Exposition!" and the line originally

"Add to your show, dear France"

he made—

"Add to your show before you close it, France."—

the change evidently necessitated by the time consumed in refusals of Herald and World to print the poem. Referred to Arnold again as "great on the globe-trot, like our own Americans, most of 'em, when they can." Was "pleased to know" Stedman had "made quotations from Ingersoll in the book." "Some would not have done it."

Tuesday, October 1, 1889

8.05 P.M. W. in his room, reading letters. Asked me immediately—"Did you know Harry Wroth?" And on my assent—"Did you know his brother Johnny?" he continued—adding thereupon—"This letter here on my lap is from the brother Johnny—as I knew him, a boy—now grown almost—perhaps quite a man. Harry went to Albuquerque—in New Mexico—and became something there, I should judge. The

32

Governor, the judge and the doctor are the famous men in these new places. I knew the Wroth family well here—liked them. The wife—there was a daughter too—a nice girl. The father was treasurer of the city once—got under a cloud." "This boy Johnny writes me often—I enjoy the letters, too." Then again. "And there was a note—a postal—from John Burroughs, along in this evening's mail. He said he had his headache—felt in dubious humor—went to town and right off in the train. He stopped at Herbert's, but Herbert was out. Now he is at West Park again." I alluded to Ashton Bell's early favorable reading of Leaves of Grass. W. smiled. "So you think he takes some hold? Well—I almost pity the young man (or woman) who grapples with Leaves of Grass. It is so hard a tussle."

Gave me a copy of To-Day containing an essay by Edward Carpenter. "Mrs. Kennedy—Sloane's wife—happened in to-day: came about eleven—that was one of my changes of garments." But he did not enlarge. I left with him the Sarrazin manuscript, at last finished by Morris. He examined it and was pleased. Thinks "seriously of publishing it" but does "not know where, how, as yet." He had a fire in his room, which he stirred now and then. Not looking extra well. I had been arguing with Ed to stay and take the University Veterinary course this coming winter. Explained to W., who said: "I did not know anything about his going away—he said nothing to me. But I can see the wisdom of your suggestion—how indispensable are the two hundred or more things embosomed in such an opportunity." As to department clerks at Washington: "It is a great mistake to suppose the positions all or mostly sinecures—some of the clerks work like beavers."

Wednesday, October 2, 1889

8.05 P.M. W. in kitchen, talking with Gilchrist. We stayed till a few minutes after 9—then left together. Gilchrist thinks W. benefited greatly by the good long talk. I wonder? Talked of many things—W. very free. We found his voice better even than usual. Spoke of Mrs. Kennedy. "She has not gone directly home: is junketing about a little—after a long stay in one place—keeping close to duties, all that." And then of Kennedy: "He appears to be writing a book about Whittier. He did this once before—but the Whittiereans are not satisfied with it, nor was Sloane himself—so he is to make another attempt. There is a publisher up there at Cambridge who employs Kennedy for this—pays him little or nothing yet throws out consideration, even at this, when five dollars is so important a matter to Kennedy." W. pointed to a book on the table—"Have either of you seen the 5th Reader? Harper's 5th Reader? Look at that! I am quite carried away with it! Look at that print, look at that letter on the cover—look at that paper! It is astonishing, the beauty they achieve. Oh yes! they have a poem of mine there! It has been so long since they asked I had forgotten all about it." Gilchrist queried: "I suppose they put it in without your permission?" to which—"Oh no they did not! they not only wrote me the flattering note yesterday—sent the book—but came up like a man long ago and asked my assent. I do not know who wrote yesterday's letter." I showed them a sheet of the paper Dave had selected for the book. Both liked it. W. put on his glasses and examined it critically, expressing his gratification.

Gilchrist inquired what W. knew of Henry James. W. said: "Very little—very little: I don't think I have ever met him— know I have not." G. repeated several amusing stories of James' visit to Gilder some time ago. W. then—"I thought as much. I knew and know very little of this Henry James, but of the father—the old man—I know very much more. I had a friend who was quite intimate with him. So far as I could gather James was the type of the man in his place—in the universities—a man afraid of facts,—divine facts: not to be better expressed than by the figure of a mirror—with its reflection: and the notion of the man who could be very well satisfied with that mirror—but with the fact itself—oh no! let us not talk about that—hear none of it—would rather be excused!" G. spoke of James' regret spoken somewhere that he had not seen W. personally, because a few minutes face to face clears many things. W. exclaimed—"Well—whatever he writes that is false, that, for a surety, is true." Discussed pronunciation of Symonds' name? W. argued—"I am sure it is Sim-monds. You know, it was Edward Clifford, the artist, very closely allied with Symonds—who was here and told me about it." G. said James considered London the greatest city in the world and W. exclaimed—"Well—I guess there's no doubt about that!"

Mention of Cooper—Gilchrist seemed to be very ignorant of his life and work. W. said among other things: "Cooper is way better than Hawthorne—50 percent better: something in his ways like Scott, though with less sparkle than Scott but having in common with Scott a sort of garrulity. Not that it is really garrulity in an offensive sense. I find as I grow older, I read and read the novels again, then turn to the long labored prefaces and read every word again. You are right—even these escape garrulity in its odiousness." G. had "thought Cooper's works of the Charles O'Malley order" but W. said: "No, they are not: they are not so sparkly, so brilliant, as that, but are of a solider metal." Quite detailedly he spoke of Cooper's work: "His first work was 'The Spy—no—not that—another—'Precaution,' he called it. Then there was 'The Pilot'—then the Natty Bumppo tales—all worth knowing. And still more, one that is not generally ranked as his best, yet always appealed to me—held me—fastened upon me— 'The Wept of Wish-ton-Wish,' a tale of an early New England settlement. 'The Spy' is not a great book—yet a very good one nevertheless." Described minutely 'The Wept of Wish-ton-Wish,' then: "A very good play was founded on this story many years ago—probably fifty—and it made a great impression on me, for I remember it very clearly to this day. A great French pantomimist—a Madame Celeste—a famous woman in those days—took the part of the lost girl. Her power was great—lasting." W. spoke of other writers as compared with Cooper: "It is like comparing dimes to dollars—the world seems rather to prefer quarters, dimes, to dollars but I consider Cooper greater—much greater—than Hawthorne, just as I consider Bryant—though the world will not have it so—incomparably greater than Longfellow. But such comparisons, I suppose, are not good, wherever made."

He then said: "I have received a copy of The Open Court—somebody has sent it to me—and now I think I have an idea what monism is, which I never had before. The Open Court is the great court of metaphysics, in which the fellows beat each other about, this way and that, on questions of which nobody knows anything at all." He said laughingly, "The function of the true reporter of our time is, if he can't make an interesting enough report out of the facts as he finds them, to get up facts to suit!" Spoke of Cooper as "open, free, expansive, if not as elegant as other writers known." As he used the expression "open, free, expansive," he threw his arms open wide and his body back in the chair.

Gilchrist asked W. if Talcott Williams had been over? W. answered "Yes." Had W. asked him the proposed question about the letters in The Press? W. answered first, "No—I forgot all about it—never said a word"—then asked quickly—"That would be rather a pointed question, wouldn't it?—taking unwarranted liberties, with what are perhaps professional secrets." G. said, "Talcott would be able to take care of himself." W. thereupon—"Yes—no doubt: and besides, it would really only be one priest asking another priest." A paper on the wall—pinned there—a newspaper—slipped down as he rubbed against it, and he said—"It seems to have discovered an affinity for me." Complained that Knortz did not return him the Gilchrist book: "I wrote him once about it—told him there was someone here anxious to read it—but he asked to

keep it a little while longer—so I let it go. I must write again."
I stayed longer than I intended, expecting after G. went to
give W. the samples of mounted photographs I had with me,
and proof sheet of bust for book. But finally showed them to
W. anyhow—after which G. and I went off together. Ed has
finally consented to stay and take the college course. I am to
pay his board and pay him twenty dollars per month—he to
be with W. mornings and evenings and Sundays—and to stay
all day in case of any sick turn in W. That is the agreement.
W. pleased when I told him of it tonight. "I wished it so," was
all he said, "though I have said nothing to Ed about it myself."

Thursday, October 3, 1889

8 P.M. W. in his room, reading a newspaper. "I have just
been down stairs," he said to me. We talked some time together alone—and after a while Gilchrist came in. When I
left, G. was still there.

He had enclosed several matters in an envelope for me to
attend to—and written instructions on the outside—then he
laughed, giving it to me—"Don't lose the 5-pound note: that
has a special importance to me"—I put in—"Nor the check,
for that has a special importance to Oldach"—at which he
laughed again heartily—"That is more true than many
things!" he exclaimed.

Remarked his amusement over the newspaper criticism of
Curtis for his civil service reform speech the other day in
Phila. "It makes me think of an expression I used to hear up
along Long Island when I was a boy—signifying, here are
people damning a man for the one good act of his life. But it
is easy for Harrison to have defenders—the man in power,
the party in power, power itself, emolument, office, show,
never want for friends—friends as friends of that sort go. But
what does it all amount to—a defense set on such pins?"

He spoke of what one paper calls "the All-America Congress"—of representatives [diplomats from Central and South American countries, who were welcomed to Washington by Secretary of State Blaine]. "I read Blaine's speech—read it all—liked it all—it was fine—all in the right spirit—broad—expansive—the best thing Blaine ever did. But the most wonderful thing about it all is the jaunt the delegates will make—5 thousand miles by rail, about America—the United States—never changing cars—starting from Washington—going to New England, to the West, coming back again, in the very cars that took them first. Blaine will not go with them, but he has thrown everything of good purpose in the scale for them—eased their going about—sent his men—engaged with the railroads—thrown the panoply of the government about them. I took to his little speech: it started off a little materialistically—like Colfax's speeches long ago, and Banks'—N. O. Banks'—I remember, they always measured success by so much land, goods—so many dollars—and so Blaine's speech at the start, though there was more than that to it." He said much of this over again for Gilchrist's benefit, when he came in later on. Said moreover: "No—I don't think the broadest significance of this strikes Blaine or any of them—but it is a good thing, nevertheless—it will produce its own results—good results—notwithstanding. It will not strike Harrison, surely—Harrison is the man out of all the rest of them to calculate action with reference to its political effect—no, worse than that, even—rather party than political effect. But the universe takes its road—is on and on and on—and events prosper far more than the actors believe, understand—in spite of them. It is all provided for in the inherencies of things."

Said he had had a letter from Bucke about the book. When would it come?

Touched upon Chase—"a man out of men—a trivial, damnable man,—a dangerous, handsome man. I always thought D. Ridge here on our street much resembling him—I mean

38

in form. In head, Chase was noble, almost impressive—deceptively so. Carlyle did not believe in our democracy—criticised it out of a divine disbelief, and I always welcomed his criticisms—always thought them valuable—do now: but Chase's, from the inside, were the most hateful, insidious, to be imagined. In all these things it was not the surface alone that gave importance to events, but the undercurrents, the bases: while Lincoln and Grant greatly, not them alone." War was not luck—"often it is something of the sort—a sortie, an assault, a surprise, a surrender—something of that sort—but that is not the whole story. In long-prepared transactions—in arranged, calculated, campaigns—in persevering effort, like Lincoln's, Grant's—towards a great purpose—acknowledging no defeat—there is no luck—no chance. It is like our fine macadamized roads—not the surface alone, but the underpinning—the basis—there is nearly the whole virtue: if that is bad—if the determination of the soil yields—the soil lacks it—all is lost. No one can know as I know how this applies to Lincoln: not enemies at the front alone but in the rear—everywhere—subtle, keen, unscrupulous. I was myself a New Yorker—nestled in the very bone—perhaps not heart, but brain, viscera, of the malcontent—knew it all—from what it came—what was to be expected of it—realized how dark and rapid a weapon it could be. Yet Lincoln, knowing it all, was calm in it all—persevered in his way." Such the drift of his talk.

I received a card of introduction of Prof. Huidekoper for Ed from Brinton today, who has gone to New York. W. informed me Ed had gone over, not found the professor in but found out at what hour to get at him tomorrow.

Friday, October 4, 1889

7.50 P.M. W. in his room. I took him down the bundle of mounted photos. He called it "quite a packet." As to his health—"It becomes quite a tedium, to sit here confined—I should try to get out some." Adding after a bit: "Tom was here tonight with a couple of gentlemen—one of them is to lecture on prohibition down here at the church—and it was no small addition to the tedium to have him here, lightening himself of his load of doctrine." But he laughed quietly, looking across at me, "But we survive all such things—they are a part of our growth!" I asked him whether, after the Morse head was printed, there was any other to add to the envelope. "For the present, none—at least, none till some other strikes us!" The conversation turned by his own remark: "Did you read the account of the delegates?—the trip to West Point? Not the least part of it was Sherman's little speech—the General's—it was very good." I asked: "Are not our generals anyhow advanced over those abroad—more humane—seeing better that war is only a make-shift?" He answered quickly: "Yes indeed—in that way—in many other ways: and not only the several we know—like Grant, Sherman, Sheridan, whom we always mention,—but others—many—who stood ready, only waiting the opportunity, very much resides in opportunity— no one being all told till severely tried."

Some reference to Bruno occasioned W.'s remark: "They seem to have given it up—the Church has retreated: so far as I know, the Archbishop's letter, which was ostentatiously to have been read everywhere was read nowhere. Some powerful thumb came down at the right time—some keen intellect saw the mistake in time—imposed quiet—some subtle-sensitive thumb, that can move a world. Well that it was so! I suppose we can count that as a great victory. I wondered from the first that these fellows didn't see." Of the Spanish protest that the "All-America" congress was a protection move W. said: "I can see the hand of Castelar in that protest—commend, endorse, it too. But still I would say to this congress, others like it, go on—go on—in spite of yourselves you are working for free trade, for brotherhood, for human unity!

Dear as the principle of free trade is to me—near as it is to my heart—fully as I am convinced that in it, only in it, is brotherhood, solidarity, democracy, assured—still, in the event of protection success, I would say, go on with that, too—let that try itself by high, severe standards!"

I had a letter from Mead today asking for a ten page paper on W. W. for the New England Magazine. When he heard of it, W. was much struck. "How do you explain it, Horace? as you say, it is significant. Is it because they are making such a racket about us in England, France, Germany?" I told him I proposed writing more of his later years than the early ones, and suggested using the Gutekunst picture, Mead volunteering illustrations. "Oh yes! use it, if it will do!" And when I said: "Walt Whitman at 70" was one of my suggestions of a title, he said: "Yes, that is very good—very. How would this do for a headline—'Walt Whitman at Date'"—"I can't think of another name just now," he exclaimed. To his further question—"What causes all the kindness?" I replied—that Darwin two centuries ago would have had to wait longer for justice; progress accelerates; so will the Whitman idea. He said: "That is a striking way to put it, that no doubt is one of the glories of our time." I said, "Browning asked me on a car the other day if the Herald had gone back on you." He responded: "Well—there was the Paris Exposition poem—it was declined by the Herald but met a better fate—was, as you know, in Harper's—and they paid me ten dollars for it without protest." Adding, "And I suppose the next number of the Century will contain a little piece—six lines or so." I paid fifty dollars to Oldach today, changed the 5-pound note, paid for and secured mounted photographs. W. satisfied with all. I asked if he wished a set of sheets of my own little book. "Oh yes! and then I can write Dr. Bucke positively at last that the book is practically done."

I had opened vol. 5 of the Stedman's big book at the portrait of Cooper and W. said: "Yes—I thought him a handsome man always—I saw him often—he looked like a gentleman farmer—richly dressed, yet simply—like plain Europeans we sometimes see—men of means but of native taste and sobriety. I have sometimes thought—perhaps have said—that if Cooper had had a little more of Tennyson's grim determination to be by no means led into a fight, and Tennyson had had a little of Cooper's—I don't know what to call it—it would have been better for both. Though I don't know that Tennyson is quite so much the reserved man as is sometimes reported. From things Herbert tells me, I am persuaded he likes to mix in with the people, be democratic—plain. I think he would shrink from notoriety, but not from this." Then— "Cooper was not distinctively the literary man." Of Stedman: "Stedman is under pressure there in New York. I do not altogether wonder at his coolness towards us—he is like a piece of iron that has been many times heated and now is the critical heating!" "I have told you I knew Stedman at Washington—he had my position before me. When the Secretary of the Interior cut my head off—I went over to the Attorney General's office—took Stedman's place. But of course we were good friends then. Twenty years ago—in those days— Stedman was more dandaical, as O'Connor would declare, but in the years since he has expanded greatly—thrown aside many of the old trappings." But there were no doubt fellows over there who took advantage of the Herald scrap to point out to Stedman—now what of your Walt Whitman. "They will lie—outright—we know that well enough—so that we do them no injustice." Gave me a copy of the journal called Society with its big flaring initial letter, and said, "I don't know who sends it to me. It is all frivol—frivol!" And The Open Court: "Take it along if you would like to look through it." An article there by Paul Carus on Wagner was marked. Who? W., "You mean the lead-pencillings? They are Kennedy's, I guess—the papers come from him." Talcott Williams writes me, "The workingmen's letters are printed just as they are received." W. said: "I am glad to hear that—glad to hear that

insufferable tendency of the newspaper bigots was resisted—
I rather thought it had not been."

Saturday, October 5, 1889

7.30 P.M. W. in his room—not appearing extra well, nor
feeling so—for he said: "This is one of my bad days: I have
had rather a bad spell today: I live by spells and spells." He
asked after "news"—saying, "I am told by the folks here it is
a fine night. Is it?" I read him part of a letter received today
from Lincoln Eyre in regard to the fund, W. remarking: "It
would seem that the Lord not only permits but provides us
friends at last—even lets us turn up a Jack now and then, as
they say in cards!" Said: "I really must make some struggle to
get out-of-doors—but the temptation to stay here—rest
here—settle—is very great, usually triumphant."

I see he has cut the leaves out of Bucke's black-bound annual report, pasted a sheet of white paper over the gilt letter-
ing and commenced to use it for the disposal of his scraps. It
is on the table with the "annex to the annex" (of November
Boughs) now growing bulky. He is very curious to see a copy
of the New England Magazine—proposed yesterday that I
write for one. A copy arrived anyhow today. I promised to
leave it with him in the morning on my way to Philadelphia.
He studied the sample sheet I had from Mead—dissected the
reprint of the cover—"And this," he asked—pointing to the
leafage—"is this the Mayflower or what? And this boat—is it
the boat Mayflower? It has all the form—high at both ends—
thick—even like Columbus' boats." I only stayed a few minutes.

Sunday, October 6, 1889

9.35 A.M. Stopped in on the way to Philadelphia to leave
the New England Magazine with him. He was in his room,
eating his breakfast. Laid down the towel he was using as a

napkin—took the book—commented on it: "Yes—there it is—the Old South Church—the very essence, culmination, of New England Presbyterianism, Cotton-Matherism and everything that is damnable." "But then," he added after a pause, "even these things had their place, and today they serve at least as curios, if not for more." Spoke of the morning as "an ill one" for him. "I got up rather bad, all over." Still, his color stood its own. Had been reading a Century piece about Olin Warner, the sculptor. "Do you know of him?" he asked—adding "He is a new man to me."

8.30 P.M. In for about 20 minutes with Fred May. W. talked very well, though expressing the fact that he had spent a very bad day. I introduced Fred. W. then asked—"What did you say his name was? May? Oh! that name takes you into a world of reformers, anti-slaveryists, radicals, progressists."

Remarked that Tom had not been in today.

I had with me the following extract from the Boston Herald—caught on the fly by [Joe] Fels in Boston the other day (Oct. 6, 1889).

WALT WHITMAN.
The Good Gray Poet Since His 70th Birthday.

The latest tidings from Walt Whitman are that he is now more of an invalid than ever. He is no longer able to drive out, his legs having failed him so that he cannot get in and out of a carriage. On pleasant days, however, he goes out in a wheel-chair, and passes considerable time on the river bank enjoying the air and scenery. He is carefully attended by a male nurse, sent by his friend Dr. Bucke of London, Ont. The nurse is a strong and sympathetic young Canadian, and the expense is met by a number of Whitman's friends, who make monthly contributions for the purpose. Mr. Horace L. Traubel, a young gentleman of Camden, who has been of great service to the venerable poet, is looking after the matter.

Whitman now no longer sits in the front room on the ground floor of his humble house on Mickle Street, where his face at the

open window in mild weather has long been a familiar sight to pass-
ers, and whence he was wont to pass a cheery word with neighbors,
or with the children in the street, who were much attached to him.
He keeps chiefly to his room on the second floor, where he sits,
surrounded by a pile of books and papers, strewn confusedly
around, doing a little desultory reading now and then. He receives
calls from numerous friends and admirers, many strangers from Europe coming to pay their tributes of esteem; among the recent ones
was Sir Edwin Arnold, who, like Tennyson and many other distinguished men of letters in Great Britain, has a profound admiration
for Whitman, and did him the honor of paying him the second visit
which he made in the United States, his call upon the President, as
the head of the American nation, being the first.

The poet also does a little writing when the mood seizes him,
and keeps up a correspondence with some of his friends, chiefly by
means of postal cards, upon which he jots down fragmentary
thoughts without formality. His handwriting is as firm and vigorous
as ever, showing no trace of infirmity. Among those with whom he
keeps in regular correspondence is Mr. W. Sloane Kennedy of Belmont, who has written several critical essays on Whitman, which
are soon to be issued in book form, together with a concordance of
his poems and a list of the various articles and essays which have
been written on Whitman that show that he has been more the
subject of literary discussion than any poet of this century since
Goethe.

The proceedings at the banquet in Camden last May, at which
Whitman's friends celebrated his 70th birthday, are to be published
in a little memorial volume by a committee appointed for the purpose, Mr. Traubel being in charge. Whitman calls it "Traubel's dinner book."

Still another edition of Whitman's poems has appeared in the
shape of a most attractive issue of "Leaves of Grass" with the addition of "Sands at Seventy" and "A Backward Glance O'er Travel'd
Roads." It makes a dainty looking small volume, bound in pocket-
book shape, with fine dark green leather. The edges are gilt, and
there is a receptacle for keeping scraps and memoranda. The following characteristic words on the title page tells its story:

WITH WALT WHITMAN IN CAMDEN

May 31, 1889.

Today, finishing my 70th year, the fancy comes for celebrating it by a special, complete final utterance, in one handy volume of "L. of G." with their "Annex" and "Backward Glance," and for stamping and sprinkling all with portraits and facial photos, such as they actually were, taken from life, different stages. Doubtless, anyhow, the volume is more a PERSON than a book. And for testimony to all (and good measure), I here with pen and ink append my name.

WALT WHITMAN.

The edition is limited to 300 copies only, and the volumes, which are sold at $5 each, may be obtained by sending direct to the poet, 328 Mickle street, Camden, N.J. The autograph, together with [missing] number of copies make them particularly valuable to bibliophiles as well as the friends of Whitman.

Gave it to W. who said, "Will you leave this with me, or do you wish me to read it now?" He read it at once, putting on his glasses and saying when done, in answer to my question, "Yes—it is wonderfully accurate—every word of it—a marvel of newspapery. Baxter certainly typifies the ideal reporter. I have been very fond of saying that Emerson redeems the whole literary guild—the man himself—out of the fact of what he was; and so I may say of Baxter, he redeems the whole tribe of reporters. I read his article on Edward Bellamy in the New England Magazine there. He is very radical—progressive, he is enthusiastic over Bellamy's book, I knew this in fact when he was here—he was warm to espouse it. But no—no—no—we are not going to be reformed in this way, by parcels—not by Henry Georgian Socialism, Anarchism, Schools—any one agency. Our human nature is like the weather—it comes from all quarters—and while all these suggestions, reforms, doctrines, may help, certainly belong, no one of them can do the business for us. It is too long a story. The great feature is, everybody is occupied with it nowadays—even the millionaires, who if they have a few millions at death, leave a little of it—a million or so for ameliorative

46

purposes." May expressed some surprise that W. read the newspaper clippings so easily. But W. himself said: "My sight, like my hearing, is gradually going: I feel it from time to time markedly."

He turned to me suddenly: "Your article, Horace, if it fills 10 pages in the Magazine, will have to be 8500 words—I counted a page today—got at it that way." I laughed at the idea and he added—"That is an old habit—I have done it before—it is the only absolute measurement." Then he continued—"I freely give my consent to the use of the Gutekunst portrait if you care to use that. I would suggest that you have it printed on a sheet by itself." He also had a photograph of the house he said I might use. "I shall doubtless have a little piece in the next number of the Century—a few lines," he remarked, "and so we appear to be booming everywhere in unexpected ways."

May said something about reading W.'s book—W. asking him then curiously—"Well—could you take hold of it? Was it clear sailing? Could you make anything of it?" Said he had read Coquelin's Century paper on Molière and Shakespeare. "It is very interesting—very smart—but there's an end: it is not profound—he does not send his plummet very deep."

Ed told me he finally had decided to go to Canada. Saw Huidekoper, but was not satisfied, also fears uncertainty of tenure here.

Monday, October 7, 1889

7.30 P.M. W. in his own room—the wood-fire burning lustily, and the air one of comfort. He asked me immediately—"Is it too warm? How is it out-of-doors?" Had been reading the Century. Did not look, nor was he, well. Some Boston girl writes me a long letter for W.'s autograph—almost pathetic in its exhortation. I gave it to W., with the return stamped envelope. He addressed it mock-seriously—"Mr. Stamp—I am very much afraid I shall confiscate you and consign the rest of you to the fire." I said—"I'm afraid you will, too." W. then—"How well—how good a hand—Miss Lady writes! It is a relief to look at the like"—and carefully put the stamp away. Ed came in for mail as we talked there. W. wrote Rhys today.

McKay has bound up all the "After All, Not to Create Only"—sheets. Gave me a copy—sent one over for W. to sign for him. W. took and regarded the book with an evident affection. But he laughed about signing it. "I do not think I need to sign it: it does not need signing. There is the name on the title page—then here it is inside again. I do not like to triplicate it—then triplicate the triplicate." He turned it over and over. "It has been a long, long time since I saw it—a long long time." Then he read the Washington Chronicle extract towards the end. "Who wrote it?" I asked, as I read with him over his shoulder. His answer was, "I wonder?"—adding—"It is very good, anyhow," and saying further of the book as a whole—"It is wonderful neat—wonderful! How healthy the print!—the big clean type! Why, yes, it is a revelation to me, also—a new book to me. How many did you say Dave had? Several hundred? It did not sell—did not sell at all. Roberts must have issued about a thousand." And turning to the pictorial cover—"This is my design—I conceived it—it has a good familiar look, after a long absence. The whole book as it is here commends itself to me." I remarked that I suppose Dave got possession of these at auction. This seemed to arouse some latent intention in him, for he instantly addressed me: "I have been thinking, Horace, I should myself like to sell out bag and baggage to Dave—sell him all I have here, copyrights, everything—with permission, at any rate, to publish, ad libitum, to the year 1900. The time has come to me to unload. I shall kick the bucket soon—very soon— then something will have to be done, and what is done might just as well, or better, be done by me here and now." His voice was quite strong, though the tone rather more sad than

I had known it for a long time. "I should like you to get at Dave on the subject: don't push it—try him only, some day—not hurriedly—he will have to be felt at the start. I don't know that he would care to do it—perhaps not—but I think he would. After the preliminaries, if he consents, we may tell him what we have and ask an offer of him. As it is now he is in my power: I could clap down on him in an hour—stop him outright. It is a serious turn for me all around." Gloomily he talked. Whereas heretofore he has fought all notion of making even a 5-year's contract with McKay, now comes this. Unless he urges it again, I shall say nothing to Dave. My personal feeling is strong against a precipitate step, as this would be.

Ed says W. woke up in just such a dubious mood. There have been no visitors nor outward events which could have induced the humor. I asked him if he had been ill. He answered—"Yes and no—not more so than yesterday, but that sick." Was it the digestion? "Yes—that and something more—a great deal more. I am generally ailing—broken up—breaking." Attributes part of it to confinement—yet fears to risk the chilliness out of doors—is so extremely sensitive. Said yesterday to Ed, "We must make a start again." But the start remains unmade. I advised Ed to talk with W. about his departure and he promised he would. When I entered I had found W. struggling with the disadvantages of the dirty chimney of his gas-jet by the aid of a candle, he attempting so to read. It was a suggestive picture, and funny, too. Is disinclined for business affairs. Having matters done about the house, he always solicits others to do them. Repairs on back shed he appealed to Mrs. Davis to attend to. "Don't send them to me," he pleaded.

Tuesday, October 8, 1889

7.45 P.M. W. in his room, reading. Had just been down stairs. While "not of much account anyhow," he "felt better" than the day before. I took him a fine proof of the Morse bust. He was greatly moved by it—contemplated it long—held it at a distance, then took it near, "Well," he exclaimed, "there's something in Sidney after all, something in this nowhere else, in no other picture, to be found. And this is no doubt the best rendering of the bust so far—the best—I like it a great deal." And after a pause—"Here it is, and you, Sidney—in spite of what the fellows say—you have done it!" He turned to me: "We must send the Doctor a copy at once—or as soon as we can. And with it a loose copy of the book if you can get the sheets for me. And I'll tell you what I want—I want the sheets stitched, if you can—and you can?" Returned me the copy of the New England Magazine. To my question, said: "You will find Bucke's book in the statistical, geneological way—as far as that goes—reliable, confirmed: all the first part of his book must hold its own. And then I can verify him and you both when your article is together. Burroughs' book may throw some side lights, too—be useful: I have always found it so." And on the score of illustration—"I will furnish you with whatever you desire."

Some one arranged his room in something like order today. "I am experiencing rather a bad time all through," he said in answer to question as to health—then asked—"Is it too warm here? How is the weather out?" Again said—"Here is something I thought might do for Morris"—picking up from a pile of books a pink-covered pamphlet. "It is a supplement to La Vogue—a French paper"—but here he paused—"On second thought I will not give this to Morris. It would most properly—with most advantage—go to Bucke, who saves all such curios. I have myself sent him numberless such things. He collects them—so the stream may just as well continue that way." W.'s mood altogether more cheerful than last night.

Wednesday, October 9, 1889

7.30 P.M. In his room, reading paper—light on full, and wood in stove burning bright. Very warm with his "Horace— Ah! how do you do?" And his, "Take a seat." Frank Williams in to see me today. Spoke of his desire occasionally to see W., yet hesitation about intruding. But W. said: "Frank should come—he is very considerate—I always like him there. I love him, his wife, his family. They have been very kind to me in ways that provoke sweet memories. Then Frank is a generous, fine fellow, on the right track, too. I don't know about Protection—I suppose he is a Protectionist—all Pennsylvanians are, perforce. What do you learn of it? Is Frank counted the other side for that?"—"But otherwise he was always genuine, hearty." I spoke of Williams' curiosity to see Symonds' note, of which he had heard from Morris. W. thereupon: "He does well to be curious: it is the highest utterance of all—it is the most decisive, defiant trumpet-note of all: not a quaver— not a sign of doubt in it: not a word to detract from, to weaken, it. And we must think who it comes from if we want truly to measure its significance: Symonds, of the literati a distinguished member—among the most distinguished—a man who has made his title clear—labored, succeeded, got a hearing, credited with authority by the London Times, the reviews, big quarterlies, men of distinct literary note: a man of books, about whom it cannot be said, 'he don't know what he's talking about.'"

W. said, "Dave was over today." I asked, "Don't you feel richer than when I was here last night?" And answered with a laugh: "Yes—he paid me a matter of 88 dollars." For how long? "I don't know—the bill is here—" yet he could not find it, so continued—"Never mind—I probably would not understand it better if I had it. I suppose if I set right out to do it— had to do it—it might be made clear. They say, figures can't lie. I would suggest the saying without the 'can't.' That has been my experience." I suggested—"Figures can't lie, but fig-urers can"—and he laughed heartily. "This is better—and they do!"—instancing statisticians; Atkinson and others. Could not get sheets of book today—not yet at Oldach's. Left word for W.'s stitched copy. Nor could I get bust prints; printed, but not sufficiently dry.

Ed has finally decided to go. Has spoken to W. about it. W. is "adverse to a change"—greatly likes Ed—but would not advise him to risk his future, if it was risked, as it seemed to be, by staying. Ed hopes to go on the 20th, but will stay over a few days if we cannot get a new man in time.

I asked W. if he really had any idea Boulanger would enter France, raise his standard there, go to Paris? He answered: "No—I don't think he's going—do you? I know he has got started—has got as far as Jersey—which is on the way—but it will amount to nothing. He is either crazy or a fool or both—probably both. Boulanger is a sort of lay-figure—the essence of all the parties of reaction in France. Yet the wonder is, how small the Monarchists turned up after all at the election—hardly making a respectable minority—President Carnot and his men clearly and easily and assuringly ahead." "Yet," W. continued, "unhappy the country without a party of the op-position—though there are oppositions and oppositions. Even Washington is examined—needs to be examined. I do not mean by a party of the opposition such parties as we have today—but a party!" Then turning the talk: "Herbert was here last night for awhile after you left. He had nothing new to tell—only to speak of his departure, which he has set for February. He pegs away at his picture—his Cleopatra—seems to be in a very complacent mood about it." Here W. broke out in a louder tone—"He does not like the picture—this"—reaching forward toward the chair but not finding what he wished, then explaining—"I mean Morse's picture—the picture of the bust. But I do—I have been looking at it by daylight—it satisfies me greatly—more than I could have supposed. I like it, irrespective of what others may think about it—there's something to it, noble, pure, severe—a beautiful something—who could say what? That last truth—the quality we know in friends, in persons—yet cannot measure in words, or begin to." W. said: "The best biographical material of all—if you wished it for your article—is in Specimen Days: there is no mistake about that—no 'interpretation': what is there is confession."

Thursday, October 10, 1889

7.10 P.M. W. reading. Looked extremely well, and said he had greatly "raised" his "mood." He talked with me for half an hour—tone, eye, emphasis, all marking an improvement over the week past. W. handed me a letter of Bucke's: "It came today. He has quite a spasm there. Doctor gets 'em now and then—gets 'em with me sometimes." I opened it as if to read, he then: "No—take it along—read it as you go. Doctor is there in the Asylum, much harried, I should say, by cares and cares, some of them very petty—hence this impatience."

Remarked that Tom had just been in. On the table a basket of fruit. "That is from my Marlton friend, who was also here today." And still again—"You see, I have been visited. Johnson, from New York, was here also. Johnson was on his way from or to the Knights Templar celebration at Washington—was in high spirits." I asked W. if he had ever been in secret societies? "Oh! no—I should say not—I never believed in them: their damnable nomenclature if nothing else would have been enough to scare me off. As Mrs. Gamp would say, I *despige* secret societies—nomenclature and all—particularly the nomenclature. Sir Knight this, Sir Knight that—imported sounds, with no significance except to excite contempt. Every man you meet is one of them. I have no doubt the fellow who takes away our slops, our ashes—who is dusty at his work sweeping the streets—belongs to a couple such

53

societies, has his dignities, is duly named. The best fellows at this—the best of all—were the niggers in Washington. I remember my old washerwoman—a good woman—who told me about it—had membership in three or four societies—insurance societies, I think—one of them, anyhow, which guaranteed a decent burial—a good send-off. It was quite the thing for the niggers to go into these shows." Then spoke of Johnson again. "He looks very well—very bright. His store, the new store, has been a great success—he has made money out of it. Johnson is never a small potato—is a keen business man—a man who sees enough to send 15 cents after 5 dollars. Don't always get his dollars, but enough times to pay. A typical American. And Johnson is a radical—has great notions of reforming the world—contributes his share towards it—whatever is advised—money or whatnot, and is glad of the chance. I don't know about the reforms but I do know about Johnson."

W. started in another strain by way of acquainting me with the news. "I had a letter from Kennedy today, too. He writes from Belmont still—says he is working away at his Whittier—confesses it is great drudgery—does not seem much inspired by the task. I can see that Whittier should not move him greatly. Kennedy asked me if I had any word, thought, to give him on the subject, I should send it on—it would help boost him up to continue. His letter came in the noon mail—delivered about 2—and I was sitting here—felt particularly in the mood—had a pencil in my hand, a pad near—so wrote him a page, just out of mind." Here W. paused, twisted his chair about—reached towards the round table—taking a sheet therefrom. "This is the paper—a copy of it: I thought I would read it to you—it will take but a minute." Putting on his glasses then and reading as follows:

Whittier's poetry stands for morality (not its *ensemble* or in any true philosophic sense) but as filter'd through a Puritanical and Quaker filter—is very valuable as a genuine utterance and fine one—with

54

many local and yankee and *genre* bits—all hued with zealous anti-slavery coloring. All the *genre* contributions are precious—all help. Whittier is rather a grand figure—but pretty lean and ascetic—no Greek—not composite and universal enough (don't try to be don't wish to be) for ideal Americanism. Ideal Americanism would take the Greek spirit and law for application to the whole, the globe, all history, all ranks, the 19/20th called evil just as well as the 1/20th call'd moral

At the sentence "Ideal Americanism would take" etc. he said: "This may sound very egotistical, but it is not meant so." At its finish I asked, "Will Kennedy print it?" "I am sure I haven't the least idea—that was not in my mind at all—not till you mention it now." I put in—"I thought, if not, I should like to take a copy of this." Whereupon he said: "Take this itself, if you want it. I don't know whether this would be my elaborate opinion, made up of malice prepense for print, but it expresses in some sort of way what I felt this afternoon when Kennedy's letter came. I feel that not Whittier, not Longfellow, not any of them, are to be sounded lightly, in an hour, for all they are. That not only is one great test of power, greatness, in what men stir up in others, but that in order to rightly—largely—measure men, we must consider the whole story—what went before—what adhered to them. That is to say, the great fact is, what a man takes along with him, all that he takes along he is entitled to. It is so with Christianity, with the Bible: they are greatest, not for what they contain of themselves, but for what they imply, what they take along with them, cause. We have had many such books, institutions—perhaps almost as good—now forgotten, buried, utterly obscured. As I often say, we must not consider one limb, one organ, but the whole body, the entire man." "Considered in such a way, it would be hard to say Whittier has been stated yet. I do not see my idea spoken of at all: yet it seems to me the first necessity of judgment."

W. added at another moment: "Kennedy also says in his

letter that Brinton, our Dr. Brinton, writes in the last number of Folk-Lore that he had asked an Indian he had met some question about the actual meaning of word Mannahatta, and that the Indian had told him it was a word used to signify where bows were bought—bows and arrows, you know. But that seems to me improbable: according to the definition I got of it, it meant some center point about which the waters whirl and storm with great vehemence. As I have told you, I feel confident I have the highest authority for that explanation. Judge Forman and the Dutchman, Jeremiah Johnston— were great men in their day in such matters. Oh! how Brinton would have feasted upon their conversation! When I was a young man, these men were interested with others in educating Indians. They reasoned: we will select samples out of the tribes, put them in the schools, colleges,—inform them— use them to our ways—then send them forth among their people, to enlighten, to reform them. And so they persevered—sent out many men in this way—with the usual result: one out of a dozen would come to a little something, the others almost totally relapse." "I am sure, now, of these men—authorities: they came much in contact with chiefs of the Six Nations—there were five of them first, then another asked permission to come in—hence the name, Six Nations. Mannahatta meant to these, a point of land surrounded by rushing, tempestuous, demonic waters: it is so I have used it—and shall continue."

I called his attention to the fact—in re Indian missionaries—that Pepper, of the University, was having much to do with a project to place Hindu young men in factories in Philadelphia to get an idea of our industries, with the end in view of modernizing the industries of India. W. at once said: "That is a fine notion—the very finest—has my entire commendation, it makes for democracy, solidarity—therefore is good— at least, good from our standpoint. I remember the talk with Dudley that time: he said, 'No, I have not got so far that I consider the pauper population of Europe.' But that is not Leaves of Grass: if we have not got that far we have indeed gone a short ways. Leaves of Grass considers the whole earth—not a soul left out, poor, king, any. If I were young I would preach this with a loud voice: but I am not young—yet I can give this to you as a starter."

Spoke of the Morse picture again—how it grew on him. Asked me to send Bucke a copy of the New England Magazine. He was very much disappointed because I had not been able to secure him sheets of the book. Made some amusing comment on "the disinclination of some men—even the printer boys, usually so good—to accommodate." He seemed if anything unwontedly affectionate tonight.

Till I had gone and was on the boat I did not know what Bucke's letter was all about—then read this:

ASYLUM FOR THE INSANE
LONDON
ONTARIO
8 Oct 1889

Yours of 5th enclosing Kennedy's of a year ago came to hand last evening. Was glad to have the latter—in fact am always glad to get anything on that subject. So the presswork on "Dinner Book" is done—that being so Horace ought to have sent me a copy without waiting for the binding—he promised to do that and I am disappointed he did not. Tell him if he has not mailed a copy to please to do so right away. If you or H. have a spare copy of that "New England Monthly" please send it me. Want to see what the magazine looks like. I am real glad to hear that H. will write on you in it he ought to (and I guess will) get up a first-class paper. He ought to know his subject pretty well by this time!

No, I was not much interested in the Pan-American business though it is worth interest—do not see why Canada is not represented—she ought to be. It will all come right in the end only it takes time—good heavens! what a group of nationalities there will be in the Americas some day. Shall you and I see the show, standing together perhaps on Alcyone?

By that time you will be feeling better but I wish you could be a little more comfortable meanwhile I fear you are not having a good time

I am your friend

R M BUCKE

Tell H. to send the book *sure* at once if not sent already R M B

Friday, October 11, 1889

7.45 P.M. W. in his room. Reading Burns. Seemed in a very happy mood, and talked more freely than I had known for a long time, except perhaps last night. I brought him several of Scott's novels from McKay. He had asked for them when Dave was over the other day, and had written a postal afterwards to jog his memory. Three volumes—"Rob Roy"—"Woodstock"—two of them—the third I forget. W. looked at them affectionately—"Yes—Rob Roy—Woodstock"—mentioning also the third—"all welcome—and for all, thanks to Dave, and thanks to you for bringing them." Adding—"Oh! these will ease my days here!" Brought him also a copy of "Gems of Walt Whitman," Miss Gould's book—which he regarded favorably for its appearance. "For looks, it starts out very well," he said, pointing to the cover, "and the title-page—it is good, too, though I never did believe any in the book and don't now." One of the headlines "Gems from Whitman" omitting the "Walt"—I remarked its peculiarity and W. said: "You are right—I like it better 'Walt Whitman' myself: that is one of the points on which I agree with Dr. Bucke—with Dr. Bucke it is always 'Walt' Whitman, never 'Whitman' alone. The 'Walt' has come to seem almost essential." Then laughed a little when I spoke of the Bucke letter he had given me last night. "Yes—Doctor was excited—is apt to get that way at times—it is a part of his nature. Of course I know it is not your fault that the book has been slow to turn up." Explaining: "The letter he speaks of there of Kennedy's was an old one—sometimes in writing little myself I enclose some word from another to make amends."

I spoke of a letter I had this evening in re the fund. W. expressed his liking for B. and described him: "You know our man Sam Grey? Mostly his figure—just such a body—florid—quite gray. He is a man of fine presence—erect—straight—noble. In some respects a man like Arnold—very articulate, warm, enthusiastic—fond of saying his say—not offensively so—the contrary, in fact—but articulate in a sense that offsets extreme reticence, quiet, on the other side, as we see it sometimes." Sheets of book not available yet to-day—W. again disappointed, but laughing it off. I wrote B. last night advising him not to be impatient. Left a copy of October New England Magazine with W. to read. Picture of Wm. T. Harris among others arrested his eye. I said, "That looks a good deal like our Corning here" and he—"It does indeed—*is* him!" Going on after a pause, "So it is meant for Harris? Somehow it don't strike me as much like, yet it is a first rate piece of engraving. I know Harris—have met him—like him. Of course, he's entirely too metaphysical for me—entirely—but as a man he recommends himself. When I was in St. Louis years ago he was very attentive, kind, to me—came to see me—counselled me. I remember he brought me a great stack of metaphysical documents which I made a heroic effort to understand: but it was no go—I could not take the least hold—it was beyond me. Yet I feel the man is very cute, profound, in such things, himself."

W. said at another moment: "Clifford was here today—and the baby, too, and Mrs. Clifford. What a wonderful institution that baby is! and so beautiful!—it was a joy to look at her merely. How the children are great beyond our conception, rules, of power, greatness! baffle us!—shame us! And I notice a difference in children—how great the difference between the parlor children and the children you meet on the streets, in the country, on boats, in the open air anyhow. And they will always resist having their likingnesses forced—will like this person or that, or not, for reasons their own—will not be dictated to, too closely guided." He said of Clifford: "Clifford is quite Greek, isn't he? Even decidedly, markedly, Greek?— what I call gay-hearted, buoyant—especially gay-hearted. I am fond of calling Leaves of Grass gay-hearted—I wonder if it is? Clifford has it in him to be all that—has its complexion, voice, port." He advised me: "Go to work on the article—it is time you were at it: if there's anything at all I can do in connection with it, I stand willing." Remarked the constant odor of the grapes in the room. Said he liked it very much. Had caught a glimpse of the light of the full moon, and asked me— "How does it seem? Oh! to be on the water such a night!" Is having repairs made on the house. Advises Ed to oversee it "just as if it was your own."

Clifford wrote me thus of his visit:

Oct. 11, '89, J.H.C., Mrs. C. and Hilda—three and a half years—paid to W.W. a visit which, for the child's sake chiefly, had been contemplated for a full year. The three arrived at the Mickle Street house just before 12 o'clock, to learn from the housekeeper who cautiously guarded the door that W. had only a moment before "gone upstairs." Learning who the visitors were she consented to take up information of their arrival, and presently returned to say that W. would come down directly. In a minute or two the slow-moving form bent upon the stairs entered the lower room with hearty greetings for all three, and words of special welcome to the child so often reported to him with her "dear old Walt" inspired by love of his various portraits. He spoke of her "wealth of hair" and made some gentle endeavor to remove the shyness with which she, in spite of affectionate prepossession, could not quite help shrinking from the presence which must have seemed to her so massive and mighty. A few minutes talk, then the little group rose to leave, and W. said: "Hearing the little girl had come to see me, I put this big apple in my pocket for her." The great red apple was accepted, and as soon as the child was out of doors its quality was tested with more assurance than that of the giver had been, who nevertheless had declared himself better for the call.

Saturday, October 12, 1889

8 P.M. W. sat in his room, with "Woodstock" turned down on his knee, ruminating. Had rather a fresh, good look. A fire burned in the stove, though it was very mild out of doors. Asked me, "Is it not cooler this evening?" seeming surprised when I said I thought not. He noticed I came empty-handed, so at once exclaimed—"And no sheets tonight again? Well! Well!" I saw design for stamp on cover today. Dave goes away next week, to N.Y. and Boston, but will leave instructions with binder to proceed. W. saw note in today's Critic ("The Lounger")—

Walt Whitman went over in a carriage from Camden to Philadelphia on Tuesday, August 6, and sat to Gutekunst for a photograph. It was a fine day—a perfect day, indeed—and he much enjoyed the sunshine, the exercise, and even the excitement of his three hours' trip. He felt well and looked well, and the natural result was a capital portrait, representing the old poet as he appears, when at his best, in his seventy-first year. Of this I have been so fortunate as to receive a copy. The picture is a large one—nine and a half by twelve and a half inches,—and shows "the good gray" seated in an armchair, his head bared, his left hand thrust into a pocket of his familiar gray coat, and the right loosely grasping a large walking stick. The wide, turned-down linen collar, and the loose cuffs rolled back over the sleeves, are edged with a narrow border of lace. From its framework of thin white hair and flowing beard, the face of the venerable bard peers out, not with the vigorous serenity of his prime, but a look rather of inquiry and expectation.

"It was I sent him the photo," he explained, "I sent him the copy we had here—the one I had written upon. The paper came early—probably a copy sent by the Lounger himself. I probably shall get another. I noticed that he said of my expression—but that does not worry me."

Read him the following from [Harper's] Bazaar this week, written by Higginson:

Foreign nations are sometimes attracted by what is most like themselves, sometimes by what is unlike them. Napoleon and his admirers used to read Ossian; and the Englishmen of today, yearning for some Buffalo Bill at literature, convince themselves that they find it in Whitman.

He laughed: "Oh! how O'Connor used to go for Higginson—go for him with almost a rancor: pierce him, worry him, spear him. Did it several times in the literary way, but often among his friends. Higginson is of the Willie Winter group—belongs with the literary crowd of which Winter, Stoddard, Bayard Taylor, were centers, lights. The good fellows who had an awful belief in respectability—an awful hunger to be gentlemen." Asked: "Did I tell you Weda Cook was in to see me yesterday? She looks very bad—she has lost her lover—mourns for him very much." I asked, "What was his name? W. then: "That is just what I was about to ask you: I thought you knew. He has been here with her." "Gems of Walt Whitman" already on the floor. I trod on it first thing tonight. Mailed Morse a little package of pictures.

W. spoke of the Pan-American delegates: "They go today from Albany—go West, to Niagara—then beyond." As to the comment of some of the English papers that the Congress was in the interest of protection, W. said: "Still I am in favor of it—though it is, I know. But insofar as it means friendship, comity, cooperation, it means free trade, democracy, freedom, too—real free trade. These things transpire so, whether they wish it or no—don't wait to ask if they designed them—" "Not that I weaken on free trade at all. What is valuable but free trade?" Adding: "Protection—high duty—has no justification but on the line marked out by Thiers in France, by us in this country after the war—no justification but in this—that it may give a big immediate revenue, to serve a crisis. And there and here we have had such high duty—they got their big fund, we got ours—we got too much by much— now has the time come to cut if off—to cut it in the direc- tion—to the end—of the most absolute freedom."

Speaking of Morse's bust again, W. said: "I like it and like it: no criticism can shake me. For one thing, see the eye" taking up the card—"open, looking forward—not as I am usu- ally shown, but as I spiritually am. It is exceedingly fine—a revelation of what art can do at its best, when it becomes nature!" Showed me a photo of a ship at sea. "One of the boys brought it in for me. Isn't it wonderful fine? It seems to me astonishing, the vividness of such a portrayal." He put on his glasses. "See the water—the waves—crested—breaking—up and down—I can feel them lift me. Oh! it is a great art, to take hold of the spirit of a scene this way!" Spoke of "the con- stitution and nomenclature" of secret societies as "utterly and damnably feudalistic."

Sunday, October 13, 1889

Did not get to W.'s today. Was out of town most of the day. Saw several persons in the course of the day about a nurse for W.—, two doctors, S. Solis Cohen among these—but as yet unavailingly.

Monday, October 14, 1889

5.45 P.M. W. sat in his room—in the dark—alone. Evi- dently recognized my step, for no sooner than had I opened the door but he exclaimed—"Ah! Horace! Is it you?" And he asked me instantly—"And you have the sheets tonight? That is the most important question of all!" And as I had the sheets and handed them to him—"Here at last! I wished them a great deal for myself, of course, but mainly for the Doctor." I put in, "I have already mailed the Doctor's copy—with it a note, explaining the delay." W., "Good! Good! So the Doctor's is under way? I am glad. I had another note from him today. He is in a devil of a mood—evidently thinks he is neglected, forgotten, passed by. But that is a mistake. I never remarked before that the Doctor was choleric, but there are times when evidence of it is thick. I always knew him to be impatient— all that—but choleric? hardly!" Then added, "I shall read the book myself—never fear." The room was dark. "I shall look at it first thing"—meaning, when the light was up.

"I had a letter from Charles Eldridge today. He is still out there in California in the Internal Revenue service—collecting revenue—managing affairs. He speaks of the brandy they make out there—they seem to make a fine brand of it—and of the difficulty the government has, collecting its revenue— the tendency of people being to evade its payment wherever possible. Indeed, that is one of the arguments for free trade. It seems that in every land, every time, people have thought it little if any harm to smuggle goods—shirk tariff duties. Even I myself—though I have never been in a position to have it tested—even I should probably take the same course should it open to me. We somehow assume at the start there's a wrong in it—in the very imposition of revenue. Our government, in spite of all that is not paid, deserves a great fund from the drinkables." W. said again: "I received today a book from Edward Carpenter—a book discussing the meaning of civilization—a most tremendous and fearful theme! But he handles it well, though gloomily: seems to come to the conclusion that we are in a fair way to go to the dogs anyway. It is singular and interesting, how Edward,—democrat, progressist, reformer,—in this way puts himself on record in almost Carlyle's exact words—coming to his conclusion by other processes. Carlyle—not the democrat—thinking our civilization a bent stick." He added—"But Edward comes to the task equipped: he is a college man, knows history, is intensely sympathetic. I think the book would interest you: I want you to read it. It probably would interest you and some others a great deal more than it would me."

I had a postal today from Mead about the Whitman article. W. said: "I should suggest that you do not make it so much a discussion of Leaves of Grass as anecdotal—making up a sort of narrative—descriptive: making it concrete, every-day—typical, as for instance, of you and me sitting here now, talking." Mead wanted a picture of W.'s "study." W. laughed. "I have no objection to having this room taken, though I should not advise it, and for several reasons. In the first place, it is not characteristic—then, it would be difficult to make—and I think anyhow a written description of it would best meet the case. You must do as you choose." Mead was satisfied with my suggestion of the Gutekunst portrait. Wished also a picture of the house. "I have that," W. said, "somewhere about here—Lord knows where—but it will turn up." Asked me: "Before I forget it, Horace—I want to ask you to make for me a copy of that page I gave you about Whittier. I don't know of any immediate place for it, but I may want to use it, and would like to have it there. A copy will do, and when you can." Referred to printing—hoped book "well in that respect." Then referred to the birthday book: "Ferguson spoiled it for us, without a doubt. I get mad every time I think of it—sometimes furious, even. It had a wanton air, almost: we had prepared the way for one of the best effects and got the worst—the whole business turned wrong and botched." W. said again of Bucke: "He is greatly mistaken—he is never overlooked, neglected. I do not blame you at all. I do not understand his excitement, anyhow. I had no such feeling myself about the book, even at the very first. The Doctor is extremely, unnecessarily vehement." He did not offer to show me B.'s letter. Have not got on track of a nurse yet.

65

Tuesday, October 15, 1889

7.15 P.M. Found W. in his room reading Scott. He made a reference to the books—"though the form in which they are produced is cheap in the extreme, the print is excellent—even superior—and I read it with the greatest ease, enjoyment." Asked me about the news. I said, "You sit here all day and read it, don't you? While we are out making it!" He laughed and said, "Hardly the reading—just these last days there's nothing to read. There are many things up, considered the things of the day, to which I give no attention at all. There is the Cronin trial: I never touch it—avoid, of set purpose: and so with many matters." Had he looked into the much-advertised Ebers novel running in Sunday's Press? "No—I very rarely read continued stories." Talking, though, quite fully, of Ebers. "He is a great Egyptian Nile man—of that sort—isn't he? I remember a book of his I came upon years ago,—grandly illustrated—superbly. I looked into that with a great deal of attention." He spoke of the book sheets I had left with him last evening. "I looked at them carefully. It seemed to me a wonderfully satisfactory piece of work all through—printing, all. I wrote the Doctor about it today." He picked the book up, remarked that "it must have been made up in peculiar forms"—etc, as Dave told me it had been—showing W.'s keen eye. I left with him a copy of the Whittier piece, as he had wished. "Yes—I may make some use of it."

Returned me the New England Magazine for October. Said, "I suppose, however, it is the German magazine which give us the best wood-engraving of the world? That has always been my impression." I had a little volume with me containing Socrates' "Phaedo." W. looked at it with admiration. "It is a book one would have to love"—handled it tenderly—"a heart-book and handy for the pocket—and such printing, too!" I said: "I shall never be set at rest till we have Leaves of

Grass in such little volumes—Song of Myself in one—and so on." He asked, "Won't Miss Gould's book supply such a want?" And on my response, "I don't like it—I don't think it supplies any want," he laughed. "Well—have it your own way. I don't think that book a success myself."

Asked me: "Did you see the news item in the papers, about the desecration of Emerson's tomb? It seems to me inexplicable, mysterious—I do not at all feel I can explain it, even to myself." "They evidently effected nothing—were frightened off." He spoke of the stone at the grave. "No—it is not very rare—but it is beautiful, a pure white—white as alum. Did you ever read that in the old days, sixty years or more ago, Elias Hicks was the rallying-point of such an incident? It was very like, it was in the very week that Hicks died. A party of men—I think artists,—dug him up—took a cast of the face. That was their purpose—not to vandalize but to get such an impression. Hicks was a widely-known man in those days— much argued about—the center of a great fight. A fight not only spiritual but over property. The Quakers were very rich, even then." "Oh! Hicks was famous in those times—I should say, more so than Tennyson, Gladstone, Whittier in our own time. But this cast, taken in such a way, came to nothing. There arose a quarrel among the men, in which the bust suffered entire destruction. I did not write of this in the November Boughs piece, but was always aware of it."

Has been putting a new poem together. Slips, with detached lines, pinned together into quite a bunch on the table. I gave Ed a letter to Gould about a new nurse. Hard to secure! W. said, when I asked him if he intended selling any of the Gutekunst pictures—I having a customer for one: "It never struck me to do it, but now it is mentioned I can respond by saying I will sell you one for your friend and autograph it for $2.50, though not wishing to make a habit of this. I wish most of the pictures myself, to give away."

Wednesday, October 16, 1889

7.49 P.M. W. in his room reading a copy of the Boston Transcript sent him by Kennedy. I remarked his rare good look, and he acknowledged he "felt very well." Then asked, "How is the weather out of doors? Mildened? I supposed so—felt it in my bones. It is too warm here now?" Remarked how the Pan-American Congress had dropped out of sight. "I read the accounts as long as they were to be had. They were some of the things I was sure to read at once and enjoy." He had had a letter from Bucke today. "He said your note was there." B. had "quieted down on the book question"—probably from feeling his book was on the road.

W. described Ed's trip to town. "He was out to see Tom Donaldson. Tom has had quite a serious accident: fell down and broke his arm. He is building a house somewhere—as I understand it, was up on the scaffold—in some way a board broke or slipped under him, and down he went. His arm appears to be paralyzed. This happened in the summer. He seems to have taken quite a fancy for Ed and Ed for him." This led to talk of Ed's going away. W. spoke more on the subject than heretofore: "Ed has not said anything to me about *when* he was going away. So it is so soon as next week, if he can? I wanted him to stay—wanted him badly. I have made no endeavor to persuade him, but have felt he was making a mistake. It would have been a great deal better for him to make up that little matter of the money, the fee—for that appears to have been, to be, the prime stumbling-block. Ed is young—it would pay him—the experience would be inestimable. I have had other ideas, plans, for him, too. It was my idea that he should make this his headquarters—then stretch out some—see more of the States,—before he went back. Stretch to the North—take in New York—and go South to Washington, Baltimore, other places. Oh! it is all of life to a young man to look the world face to face at many points! I

68

have never said anything of this to Ed himself—and now, of course, it is too late—it is overruled." As to a new nurse, W., "We're all hoping it will be the right man." And when I spoke of the virtues of the young negro at Harned's—"Well—I have not the slightest objection in the world to a darky—not the slightest." To my notion that we must not have a reader of books, W. laughed out an "amen!" I had a letter from Brinton today assuring me he would do what was possible, and Ed, I learned, had consulted with Gould,—at first without success, but is to go tomorrow again.

Weston will have in his Ethical lecture course the coming winter Percival Chubb—who he informs me has a lecture on Walt Whitman. He is a young traveling Englishman. W. said—"God help him!" ending with a laugh.

Thursday, October 17, 1889

7.55 P.M. W. in his room, reading Scott. Appeared quite well—talked with some energy. "A letter from Bucke," he said, "but no word about the book. It probably had not come yet, though has now." Fire in the stove—kept stirring it occasionally. On the chair a new poem he had carefully transcribed in ink—"For Remembrance." Said he had "received Poet-Lore. Indefatigable for Browning and Shakespeare" but had not read much in it. We discussed judgment by impression—whether reliable, and W. contended: "It is part of the long search of the soul after adjustment—adjustimenta— not necessarily a conscious search, but a going-towards. We do because we do—believe because we believe—and though not explained by any thought of the moment, something that has gone before does explain it." His own judgment came much in this way and he never attempted to disregard it, because "in the main" it was "justified."

Mills delivered a tariff reform speech in Philadelphia last evening. W. asked where a report of it was to be found. Had passed it in the Press. Then laughed: "Anyhow, the Press is not to be trusted. Has the Record reported it at all? I did not read it—did not see it, in fact." And as to cheers at every mention of Cleveland's name—"Yes—it proves what I have always said—that he is yet afloat." Had also read Cleveland's speech at Sunset Cox's funeral, and liked it. "I noted another fact—or called fact—in the paper this morning—did you see it?—The story that Boulanger has been invited to take up his abode in Canada?"

Renan has delivered himself thus as to Papal temporal power:

(Dated, Paris, Oct. 16)—"He said that he considers that the ultimate departure of the Pope from Rome is inevitable, but that the *status quo* will be maintained as long as possible. The reason he gives for the delay of the abandonment of the Eternal City is that the cardinals are conscious that such a step would be the signal for the breaking up of the hold which the Papacy has upon the Roman Catholic world, and that the certain result would be springing up of schisms in the Church.

"Italy," says M. Renan, "would not indorse the idea of receiving directions from a Pope dwelling abroad, and the fealty of the Italians would soon weaken and die out when the Supreme Pontiff is no longer one of themselves and the old traditions of the Vatican have ceased to be a present fact. The Italian Catholics would, in this predicament, sooner or later elect an Italian Pope, resident in Italy and one of their own people" [quoted here only in part].

W. had "read it with curious and minute attention." "It seems to have some curious meaning. What is the bottom significance of the position—attitude, of the Pope, of Rome, baffles me to say—I could not say. It has a meaning but I cannot get at it. The poor Pope and his nest of cardinals—how they must live in suspense! The horoscope of the future, of the stars, is altogether adverse. I wonder if they realize it? They are men of sense—no fools—must see a thing or two—see that the modern world is all against them."

I left shortly, having to say something to Ed and then go to Phila. Down stairs found Ed talking with Gilchrist. We started mutual questions—in the midst of which there was a ring at the bell. Ed went to the door and ushered in two men—evidently Hibernians: one tall, wearing glasses—the other short and with sandy head. Both strong—the tall man quite voluble, the other markedly reticent. Ed introduced the latter as the man Gould had secured as his successor—the other his friend, a professional nurse. I questioned considerable. Gilchrist went up stairs. My impression not strongly favorable. I advised Ed to take them to Walt and let him question. He did so—Ed and I then going out together, he explaining to me the result of his quest for Gould etc.—leaving me at the Ferry with promise to take the men up to Harned's before they went back to Philadelphia. I find myself very anxious on this point of the nurse. This man may do as a makeshift, Ed insisting on going at once. General Hartranft died today. W. said: "I find it so stated in the evening papers. I never knew much about Hartranft—did you? Tell me for what he is mostly famous." "Knowledge," he said—"that true basic knowledge—comes of long reaches, waitings, not by a push or a tumble." Had not seen the personal paragraph in the Press about Gilchrist, to which I referred.

Friday, October 18, 1889

6 P.M. In his room—twilight—had just finished his dinner. Was in very good humor and voice. "The past 3 or 4 days," he said, "have not been my worst, I have not been in my worst condition: so that I can say I live in a sort of comfort." Had had a letter from Bucke, "but no word anent the book. The mail is subject to capers; we must bide its time!" Said—"Herbert was here last night, after you left. No—nothing new with him." Had he shown him sheets of the book? "No—I did not do so—did not think it worth while." Alys Smith has got over

all right: she was here to see me today: looks well—oh! very well. It was a great joy to have her beam on an old fellow again!"

Showed me a copy of the Transatlantic that had come in the mail today. "I suppose Kennedy sent it. It has a fine look: that is the way it starts out. Not that I noticed anything significant in it—though the typography itself is beautiful, a lesson in itself, a significance in itself—especially after some of our experience." He remarked the picture of Ibsen, which "greatly commended itself." I asked him after a bit what was the result of his talk with the young men last night. He entered into the subject at once, laughing somewhat—raising his voice, talking with great zest, evidently. "We got into a great snarl here together—a great snarl—and the longer they stayed, the worse the snarl. Ed brought them in, not saying what they had come for. I noticed they were Irishmen, strangers, not literary critters: I supposed they were waifs, strays, out of the great sea, come for a look and a word, then to be off again— hardly knowing distinctly themselves what they came for. Instead of that they were the Doctor Gould men. I must have appeared either all gone crazy or a damned fool, or both," he said this several times. "It was ridiculous beyond belief, and stupid of Ed to have brought 'em in that way. After considerable talk, it developed what they had come for. I did not have a chance to talk much with the man himself—his friend kept me busily engaged—but I discovered he was pretty green— had never nursed, in fact. I had it in mind to ask you to make some inquiries about him"—but thought he would not insist upon that—"because I see we can do nothing better than try the man, there is no other way practically to reach his measure. I cannot say I was unfavorably impressed—it was in a rather dim light here, and I don't think I would know him again if I saw him. The proof of a pudding's in the eating. The main thing is, is he square? A good deal of such a man's work here would consist in tact—that nameless something by which to discriminate between visitors—know whom to turn off, who not. Three or four days will tell the tale—I shall soon know my man. He will have to learn the ways—my ways, the ways of the place, people. We'll see, we'll see!" As to the man's capacity to fit the place—"It is hard to predict. Ed fell as naturally into the place as a bird in its nest." I said the subject had caused me a good deal of anxiety. W. responded: "I am sorry for that: I am not in the least anxious. I take the matter coolly—rest in the faith that it will properly adjust itself to the way that is best." "Happily, I am spending one of my good periods now—until the man, any man—he or any other—gets into the necessary points, I may be able to post him, watch him. No—no—boy—we must not let ourselves be greatly concerned." I told him we expected he would speak out the minute he was convinced the new man would not do, and he promised "I shall do so—do not fear—you will know it at once." I told him the young man proposed coming over for a while Sunday. W. said: "That is a good idea—he may in that way get some hints from Ed, while we may get some notions of him—very necessary—both."

Saturday, October 19, 1889

7.55 P.M. W. in his room reading Scott. Fire burning. Rather sweaty. He asked, "How about the weather? It is too warm in here? I thought so myself." He had thrown the door wide open. Looked bright and spoke with considerable cheer. Asked after the news. I had brought him The Magazine of Art—called his attention to a wonderful piece of engraving— Lady Hamilton as Miranda. He regarded it with an affectionate eye. "It appears to be all in the way of power and beauty you could hope for." At another point a picture of Millet—the middle age picture by himself. "That is the best yet—that is the most satisfactory picture I have yet seen—and so quiet and simple the means!—the very antithesis of all that went to make up—was necessary to—a portrait of N. P. Willis, for instance—the other extreme. Willis, you know, was very particular about all his curls, linen, all—what not." As Millet was here "So he was, I know. Oh! this is genuine of genuines!"

I alluded to an enthusiastic notice in The Critic of Salvini's "Samson." He said: "It was not written by Billy Winter, then—that is sure. I suppose Billy has not much of a fling there anyhow." Adding—"However—he has his clientage—probably a pretty good one for size, too—there's no getting away from that: a clientage of the orthodox fellows—the regulation literary men—the men of the Richard Grant White stripe that used to be, as I say." Then he laughed over the literary formalists. Speaking again of Willis: "There is a picture of him in Stedman's book—one of the most approved of them, I suppose." This led to talk of the 11th volume of Stedman's book—W. describing it as "mainly biographical, indexical"—asking me—"Do you think it necessary to sum up what has gone before?" Adding that for his "own part" he would "prefer an interim now before the issue of such a volume—say, two years—or even 10 would be better—though I suppose that is impossible, or unlikely. It will be well as it is, but would be better if not hurried out: hurry is at a great discount in such a thing—at least, is to me."

Called my attention to a postal from The Epoch office reading—"Your attention is called to an item in The Epoch of Oct. 18, '89, in which your name is mentioned." They seemingly had sent no paper. I said I thought they had or would but W.—"No, I don't think so." Asked me to look it up if I "had means to do so." Said also: "I had this letter today—Arnold has written of the visit here to the London Telegraph—someone sends me a copy, and writes a letter along with it. Take both—read them—then we'll send them to Bucke for him to get his look." The letter was as follows:

"THE CHELSEA
"222 WEST 23 STREET
"NEW YORK

"Dear Mr. Whitman.

In case you have not seen it, I send you Sir Edwin Arnold's letter describing his recent visit to you. With it accept the tribute of one who supremely admires your poems' national spirit, and who regards your 'Bravest of All' as the grandest of war-lyrics.

"Very truly yours
"Laura Daintrey."

"England
October 8/89"

This had been mailed in England little stamped, and W. had therefore to pay 10 cents on it. Said—"See what you can make of it, Horace—what, if anything."

Sunday, October 20, 1889

In forenoon, 9.20. W. had just been dressed. Sat in chair opening The Press. His breakfast—egg, bread, potatoes, etc.—on the table before him. Asked me if I had learned any news. He was "just looking to see what was up, if anything." I had gone in, simply by the way, ere going to Germantown, where I was to tarry most of the day. W. spoke of the day— "how beautiful—how auspiciously started!" Inquired if I had yet read the Arnold letter? And on my "no,"—"Well—it is not much—not a positive quality—a sort of after-dinner letter, for reading when a fellow don't feel intense." I read aloud to him this paragraph from The Press about Gilchrist:

"The quiet, artistic-looking man with a quick, swinging walk, dressed in a cape coat and wearing a turban hat, who is frequently seen on Chestnut Street, is Mr. Herbert Gilchrist, of England, whose portrait of Walt Whitman was so highly commended at the London Exhibition.

75

Mr. Gilchrist is a profound admirer of Mr. Whitman and he comes by his admiration honestly, for his mother, Mrs. Anne Gilchrist, was one of the few women who dared to say that she liked the Gray Poet's songs, and, indeed, she once made a pilgrimage from England to visit him."

He exclaimed—"That's Talcott Williams!" Thought he would "make an effort to get out today." I did not continue talk—went down stairs—saw Ed a while—then off to town. W. said he "woke up in very good condition—started the day well."

Referring to the matter of the nurse, W. said laughingly: "It is with that as with the getting a husband or wife: our proper mate no doubt exists some-where, but the grave point with us is to find that place, that person."

Monday, October 21, 1889

8 P.M. W. in his room. Greeted me with an unusual cheer, and admitted: "Yes—I am passing through a period of ease—almost enjoyment. I got out yesterday—out and to the river. It was a rare treat." Spoke of visitors: "They came yesterday—Lincoln Eyre, his brother—Wilson, isn't it?—and a gentleman named Macaulay. What do you know about Macaulay? They were here half an hour. I was pleased with their coming—I like Lincoln—his brother, too. They said they had stopped by the way to find you but you were not home." Then laughed over the fact that the new nurse had not turned up today—made no sign. "He must have thought I was a damned lunatic—very evidently was frightened off by the aspect of things—did not like our democratic ways here." I had today engaged Warren Fritzinger to take Ed's place. They had come into the Bank together to talk about it. Warren had resisted me last week when I proposed it, but had thought better of it. W. "well pleased" and asked me—"It will do, won't it?" expressing his desire that "Warren should take care of me"—etc. "Ed is gone—no doubt is already a good stretch in New

76

York State. He must go that way—by what is called the Lehigh route."

Told him I learned from Dave that Hunter thought of returning to Camden. W. said: "That's good news: I hope he'll come near me—come in often to see me." Dave sold one copy of the big book on his Boston–New York trip last week. Says buyers complain of the cover of the book. W. thereupon: "Let 'em complain! That is my arcanum! If they want to put five dollars or 50 dollars into a cover, let them: the book invites it or helps it. If they kick they must kick: kicking is good exercise!"

He gave me Bucke's letter of the 18th—also read mine of same date, in part. B.'s suggestion as to the book were these:

London, Ont., 18 Oct 1889
I wrote a note this morning and this evening have received yours of 16th enclosing Fanny M. Gr[whole name illegible] quite affecting little letter and Mrs. Spaulding's card. You ask me whether there is anything I desire Ed. to bring me from Camden. I do not know that there is except the pictures wh I mentioned in mine of this morning. I mean the little collection of Photo's and engravings which you are about issuing. I suppose you do not want to send me that 1872 L.of G.? And I do not want you to send it untill you are quite ready—but do not let somebody else carry it off! I suppose you never found that copy of Harrington? I have never been able to get a copy and it seems as if I never should get one. Yes, I think we may flatter ourselves that L. of G. has got a *locus standi* at last. No one now (unless inspired by ignorance as well as stupidity) can hoot at the book as the *unco guid* thought well to do awhile ago. L. of G. has come to stay and *must* be seriously considered by all serious men henceforth whether they like it or whether they don't—what the outcome of the consideration will be (on the whole) I for one have no fear. I asked you this morning whether you had a man engaged in Ed's place—I hope you will tell me this as I am anxious about it
Love to you
R M Bucke—

77

W. said: "That is his notion: another notion is another man's: we all have our notions. We like title pages as we like women: we can't tell why—only that we do!" And as to B.'s idea about giving it general circulation: "I have no doubt it will get about, have its influence: have no doubt it will do us a great good—me, Leaves of Grass, the cause. The book will have to take its fate, whatever that may be." And he added: "I had a paper here—a San Francisco paper—California—in which they said that Wagner, Salvini, Walt Whitman, were the burst-forthers of our time. Did not use that word—burstforther"—W. laughed at it himself—"but words of that import." He said he had not read The Critic notice of Salvini fully—"but I have looked at it—it is very fine—full of suggestion." I spoke in my usual strain of Salvini, and W. listened and questioned as if it were all new to him, evidently enjoying it. "Yes he's our man—I can see him—hear him. The Othello is not the written Othello, but the Othello as the actor makes it. Little Billie Winter, little damned fool, says, 'take Othello to the closet: there he comes most nearly to you,' but that's all he knows." I instanced "the Outlaw" as acted by Salvini as enforcing W.'s argument, and he said—"I can understand"—and when I described S., W. asked—"And on that, that—and on all the great voice? I saw a fine complimentary notice of Salvini in some other paper today."

"I had," he said again—"another paper here to show you." He looked about for some time, finally saying: "It seems to be gone—perhaps I unknowingly sent it away somewhere with other papers. I wanted you to see it. In it was a reprint of Tennyson's new piece 'The Throstle,' and with it a parody— oh! very good! As a rule I would not encourage, enjoy, parodies, but this thoroughly took hold of me—I had a hearty laugh over it before dinner. It seems to me in the poem itself I notice for the first time in Tennyson—the very first time— a trembling, a change, a weakening. I am not certain that this is so—not certain that I believe it so—but sort of suspect it is: which suspicion, or uncertainty, is itself fatal, I suppose. I have heard much, as everyone has the last year about the old man's senility, weakness, going-down-hill-ness, but until this I had no evidence of it in his work." I returned Edwin Arnold's London Telegraph letter with some stricture upon the many absurd inaccuracies, not only of his visit to W. but of Philadelphia matters. W. laughed: "It is so. Dr. Johnson would say even in his time—in his own way—that if you wished really to appreciate the value of history—its reliability—you should carefully watch the reports that go forth of your own friends—what is written—how truth is fallen short of, long, long, even by contemporaries." Clifford had asked me yesterday, anent this report of Arnold's: "Why is it, the people who go to see Walt, in writing about it, seem to try to do their worst—in getting as far from the truth as possible." W. thought "That is so: and why is it so? It is a thing for us to inquire into." He laughed highly over Arnold's description (high-drawn) of their reading passages from L. of G. together. He asked: "Well—what about the Epoch paragraph?" H.L.T.: "I haven't seen the Epoch—but I have had half a dozen people ask me the last two days who the young man is who, according to the Epoch, drives W. out, has taken down every word he spoke, and will lecture on him when he is dead?" W. laughed—"Why—that must be Billy Duckett—who else?" It amused him into great laughter.

I heard Herne, the actor, last evening at St. George's Hall, read Garland's story "Under the Lion's Paw." W., after asking me if it "was worth while" asked further—"What was the drift of the story?" And when I had got along in the explanation to the point, he was quick to see, and exclaimed— "So that was the lion's paw!" Adding thereupon: "I don't know—I should not like to state it for an actual resemblance—but this seems to me much like the case of a man who goes off to a high ledge—to the very brink of a precipice—or to a coping—a housetop somewhere—leans over and over and over till his balance is lost—falls to the earth—then makes a devil of a fuss about the accident. But was not the accident one with the fact that keeps the earth in its place—us on the earth—life in us? Just today I read a paragraph from Bob Ingersoll—it was in the editorial corner of one of the papers—I think a Camden paper—about so much"—measuring about 2 inches on his fingers—"it was on this very point." Adding—"and I think Bob hit the nail on the head." He said of the book to-night: "I feel thoroughly at rest about it now: a day or two more or less with Oldach now will not worry me. The book is a palpable fact—it is printed—we have had it in our hands—our eyes have seen it—pored over it: the evidence is complete! So, let the Doctor worry—we will not!" He speaks of his "poemet" in the next Century. "It is only a few lines—6 or 7—and those of very little importance you will think."

I showed him a crayon of Morse my father had made for me. He regarded it with great and long attention. "What wonderful fine work the fellows do nowadays: it is a skill that baffles explanation with some of us." And he said of Morse—"How handsome he is, anyhow: how chiselled and strong! It is a face to conjure with." Speaking again of what makes players great, W. said: "To Salvini—the great body, the great head you tell me about,—add the voice! the voice!" Then: "I remember a New York experience—a long time ago: an antic that seemed funny at first thought—funny is not just the word, but the only word that comes to me now—it was too profound in its lesson for 'funny.' They would run along the line of the alphabet, pronouncing the letters—nothing else—but doing this so infinitely—in such countless ways—one would now, if never before begin to comprehend the range of human expression." I spoke of Janaushek, in this connection, and he said—"I believe I have heard of her."

Tuesday, October 22, 1889

7.20 P.M. W. in his room, reading—again Scott. Looks well. Does not venture out of doors. Still speaks of Sunday's experience, "so pleasant, so benefiting." Returned me The Magazine of Art, expressing enjoyment of the Millet piece. "That portrait of Millet—the one by him—I took huge pleasure in, looked at long and long, and always with more satisfaction."

"I found the papers I was looking for last night," he said. "The San Francisco paper, with an Arnold interview, and the other, with Tennyson's poem and the parody, which I enjoyed so much. Take them along and after we're done with them, we'll send them to Bucke." He had "read somewhere" that Arnold had written a sonnet about America. "I should like to see it—have not seen it—have you?" Reference hereupon to the Epoch paragraph. W.: "I came across it Sunday, in the Times: and infinitely silly and ridiculous it is, too. If it was a paragraph of importance, it would be stranded, lost—no paper would give heed to it—but being what it is, it is in every newspaper, in everybody's mouth. I am given a chance again to quote my phrase from Dr. Johnson about the credibility of history. I have done so often enough to you—to others. Every newspaper in particular seems nowadays to hire a man whose sole duty it is to get up funny paragraphs—to start out for effect, not truth." And "as a rule these men do what they are bought to do—they get off their paragraphs—innocent—not innocent—mostly, not only not with the shadow of truth, but scarcely with the shadow of a shadow of a shadow!"

Spoke of a letter from Bucke. "I am hearing from him every day now." Had Warren rub him this afternoon as well as last night. I am glad this problem was so happily solved.

"Ed," he remarked, "must be at home by this time—before, even: perhaps this minute is the center of an admiring group—at the Asylum, most likely. The Asylum is about three miles distant from his home." Then he added after a thoughtful pause—"Ed's going seems to me inexplicable, anyhow, I cannot understand why he should have gone at all. I don't think he gave us all his reasons for going. He was not very communicative, not about his own affairs, not about others. He probably never told us the whole story. When you think of Ed's make-up—his years—a young man—popular among the folks,—liked—that this was America—Washington, Baltimore, New York, near—Philadelphia at the door—every freedom to make this his headquarters—the college (veterinary), the great opportunities: finally, his return to that one-horse town—less than that—less than a quarter of a horse town, it is inexplicable—I cannot explain it." I remarked: "When I saw he was positively bent on returning, I did not try to dissuade him." To which W.: "Nor did I. I told him we were glad he was here—would like to have him stay—to that effect—that was all. I suppose, now, Doctor will have a long talk with him—a good talk. I sent by him to the Doctor, a set of the pictures we have been getting out." Spoke of the fact, noted greatly by Bucke, that usually Canadian young men of the stronger class, coming to the States, never returned. W. said: "That answers to my own observation, I have known a number of cases. I have noticed also in certain calibre of Englishmen, the same tendency, having been here once, even though going back, to visit, that America was always the final allurement, that they always—again and again, it may be—make America, our civilization, their cherished object—their worship, we might say. It is a significant, a benign influence, so thrown out—so embracing them."

Wednesday, October 23, 1889

7.30 P.M. Found W. as usual, sitting up and reading. His "currying-brush" as he calls it, lay on the bed. Had been used this afternoon, much—as W. thought—to his benefit. I asked him how he got along with Warren and he responded quickly: "Oh! very well indeed, Warrie and I come to understand each other pretty well—*very* well. I like his touch and he is strong, a font of bodily power." I said: "Yes, he was telling me you told him as he rubbed yesterday, 'I see you are noways weak!'" W. answering, "Yes, I did use such an expression—nor is he. As I was saying, I liked his touch—like to have him around—he has that wonderful indescribable combination—rarely found, precious when found—which, with great manly strength, unites sweet delicacy, soft as a woman's, gentle enough to nurse a child." And so on. This has all relieved me hugely.

Said: "I sent a pocket-edition Leaves of Grass to Harvard College today. A young man there wanted it—sent me the 5 dollars—so I at once dispatched the book. I have sold 3 or 4 copies to students there!" Returned him the papers he had given me last night. I asked, "Which is the more ridiculous—Tennyson's poem or the parody?" He laughed, but grew at once serious again when I asked further—"Did Tennyson really write the poem?"—looking at me scanningly and re-marking—"You mean to hint that you think it is a humbug? a sell? Do you know, I never thought of that and yet I can very well see how that should be an explanation of it. My own explanation was, that somebody or other plagued him for a piece—offered him 50 pounds, guineas, for it—and he said, 'Well, as you insist—as you won't let me alone—take this'—thereon bunching a couple or more discarded verses and pocketing his 50 guineas, pounds, forthwith. Who is Law, the Camden man, who wrote the parody? I never met the name before." Continued, that he was "curious about the origin of that poem—where it was first printed," etc.

We then discussed Arnold's California interview. To my idea, "Arnold is not discriminate' W. returned, "I don't know—I should hardly say it that way: he is demonstrative—demonstrative is the word—perhaps more demonstrative than the average Englishman. He is florid—florid: but then, as meeting this, what may seem, defect, I particularly observed when he was here—it was markedly true of him—that his floridness became him—seemed to belong to him—to be an integer." Here W. laughed merrily: "I was going to give as one reason in excuse of him, that I was the object of some of his demonstrations—his praises; perhaps the fact that I was so addressed tended to excuse him in my eyes. But no—it was more than that. I know we all have spots, if only they can be touched, at which flattery is pleasant, but the story of Edwin Arnold is a bigger story than this. And whatever—he is surely not fearsome—has the courage of what he believes— he talks Walt Whitman from Boston to San Francisco. This is important evidence in point." And he said again: "I see by that piece that he proposes to return to America next year— but who knows? much may happen in a year. I suppose at this very minute Arnold is somewhere off at sea, there on the Pacific. That demonstrativeness is not peculiar alone to him— Lord Houghton was in that much the same sort of a man. I remember he used to say, vehemently, to Americans—(you know he was here in the Centennial Year)—he would say— 'God damn you! What's the use going off to Greece, 3000 miles, or into 20 dead centuries to get what you have right here, within your own doors!' He would say it in almost those same words—blunt—to the point—emphatic. Houghton, as you know, was here to see me—spent 3 or 4 hours with us there on Stevens Street. He was an exceedingly plain, old-school sort of a fellow—his manners altogether simple, unaffected. He expressed some wish while he was with me to see the folks, so I took him down. My brother George was there, and they sat together and had quite a chat. After awhile we broke some wine—I had some Virginia wine"—I smiled and he said at once very defensively—"Oh! and it was very good, too—very genuine in its flavor. It was sent me by Jesse Baker, from Norfolk. I don't know if I have mentioned Jesse in Specimen Days or not—there were 2 brothers of them—Frank and Jesse—both ardent friends of mine, of Leaves of Grass—readers. I had many such espousers in Washington [some] time ago—perhaps have still—these fellows belonged among my friends. Frank studied surgery, pathology, everything else connected with the medical profession—got quite a headway. I don't know what has come of Jesse—I must write to someone—find out: he was always one of the true fellows—plain but firm."

I had entered the room this evening rather silently, and W. said, when he saw me: "Well—you are my ghostly visitor! If I was in the theatrical business and needed a ghost, I would hire you." I asked—"Do I look like one?" to which he said— "No indeed: it's all in the footstep!"

Thursday, October 24, 1889

7.40 P.M. Warren gets excellently into W.'s ways, and W. highly felicitates himself thereon. I left with W. "Yesterdays with Authors," by Fields. W.: "I shall enjoy that, I have no doubt—I do not remember that I ever saw the book before— surely never read it. I have met Fields—his wife particularly was, is, my friend—Anne Fields. I have dined at their house. It was there I met Celia Thaxter, the poetess."

Had laid aside for me The Camden Courier, June 1, 1883, containing 2-column notice of Bucke's Whitman, then just appearing. "It may help you along some with your piece," he said. I did not ask who wrote it, but shall. Speaks of "writing some these days" but always "poemets, slight attempts, moderabilities" etc. But as he is passing through an "unusually good period," his "faculty—old habit,—tempts" him.

On a chair a copy of the new November Lippincott's, which I picked up to scan the table of contents. W. said: "Why should you not take it along? Take it." And when I asked, "But are you done with it?" "Oh yes! I am near enough done with it. Take it along." And then as to Stoddard's essay on Bryant therein: "I read it all through—partly because I knew Stoddard, knew Bryant—partly because it has a certain sort of interest. But it is a pot-boiler—made up—gossipy—a good

85

deal of it the kind of talk that makes up the gossip of neighborhoods. But one thing: it is not venomous—not as peppery as Stoddard's usual style. Oh! not at all like the Poe piece—in that sense a relief—not like that, which was dirty and dirty and dirty—the meanest lowest thing I know among all the biographical, essayical, notices of the time. He deals gently by the good Bryant."

Asked again—"Did I tell you? I have had another scraggly letter from Kennedy—sent it off to Bucke tonight. I find that he really wants to print the paragraph I sent him about Whittier. The question with me is, do I want him to print it? I certainly did not write it for print. What do you think about it?" I questioned—Was that, pertinent though it might be, all he wished to say about Whittier—Would he like it to go out standing thus alone? Between us, who knew all the rest, it was understood, but how with the public? He responded: "And that is a great deal my own feeling—is to be considered—considered carefully. What do you think? Do you think more might be said of Whittier—more in his favor? If I felt thoroughly convinced on the point, I should tell him to use it, but I do not. It presents to me just the aspect you have spoken of. But I suppose I shall let the matter drop—say nothing more about it—let Kennedy pursue his pleasure. As I told you, I liked his letter at the time—paper and pencils were handy—too devilishly handy here—and so the thing was done. My disposition towards it now is, to say—if he uses it, well; if not, well again. And I suppose I can have proof, so that when the matter comes up that way I can suggest changes—in fact, put my foot down on the whole thing, if I choose."

Spoke of Sunday horse cars in Camden as "a slap in the face of the parsons." Asked me about the boats—electric lights on them. "I suppose the steam is turned on by this time? I don't like the electric lights—I am an enemy of the steam also. In the Brooklyn boats they used gas, like this in the room here"—(God help 'em! I thought) "and it was good, too." He did not like the light off at the corner from his house. Several times said so to me, and this evening again.

Friday, October 25, 1889

6 P.M. W. in semi-darkness—had just finished his dinner—fire burning merrily, through the half-open stove-door throwing outward upon the wall its dancing, flickering light. To Warren, who came in and proposed lighting the gas, W. said, "No, Warrie—we will like it this way—to sit in the pleasant twilight—Horace and I." I was there nearly half an hour. He sat part of the time looking out the window—then turned around, stirred the fire, and sat directly facing me. In this position the light of the fire played in his beard and upon his face, with a revelation and an effect very beautiful.

I returned him the Lippincott's Magazine with some frank expression of dislike of Stoddard's paper therein. W. said: "I do not wonder: it is thin gossip and thinner garrulity, and he has the bad taste to lug in more of his personal considerations. There is very little worse writing than that in the magazines." Here his voice assumed a tone of mockery—"And let me tell you, boy—if you don't make *your* paper more interesting than this—more pithy, to the point—it'll fare hard with you!" A letter from Bucke. "He describes some more of their merry-making. He has been off to a place called Delaware, where they always seem to have a good time—went with one or more of his children."

Announced that he had "already read all your book—the Hawthorne part of it"—and "with much interest." Then added: "Fields was a very good fellow anyhow: I knew him. I think a man of means—a man who never wanted for money. He always had to make a fight for health—I think was not strong. He was not an old man, as I knew him—at least, not a man who threw out the sense of age—made you remark it."

To my remark, "I do not think Hawthorne could take Lincoln's measure," W. assented: "No indeed—it is clear he could not. We would be very like to say that, too—Horace. To our fellows—to those insisting upon, so to call them, our standards, Hawthorne's method would never be satisfactory though to the literary craft—to the men who look upon literature as a thing in itself—clear-cut writing—phrasing—mastery of expression an end—Hawthorne would have to be an eminent figure—among the best, consummate. But these are to some of us things of the past. We have had men in our century who have taken the wind out of all theories of literature that confine it, restrict it, belittle it: for literature in its deepest sense defies measurement, rules, standards. Victor Hugo was one of these men—daring with the daring. Oh! who could say, doing how much good!"

I have just been reading Burroughs' essay, "A Malformed Giant," that giant being Hugo—and now said, "John Burroughs would probably not fall in with such an estimate." To which W.: "No—looking at it as John does, it would be impossible for him to do so. He examines it from a single standpoint, that does not wholly display the man. I have no doubt but Hugo is eligible to many strictures—lays himself open to severe criticism—on one score, for his theatricality, his choice of matter, subjects, scenes. But O'Connor, who often enough met this charge against Hugo, was accustomed to complaining, that we judged Hugo as Americans, not as *world*-men, not as Frenchmen. That to rightly know him, we had to enter upon the subject of his times, circumstances,—the French people—what was exacted of him in the nature of things—the arena, in fact, of his life. Then again, as I know, John has the misfortune to come upon Hugo only through—not second or third or fourth or fifth rate translations—but the worst translations ever suffered by a writer. I myself am inclined to believe that Hugo shines most truly himself—is really the most sublime figure—in his poems—the grand, grand, poems, many of them." And so W. went on, referring again as so often before to the French friend who "in the old times translated for me as I sat—sitting with him as I now sit with you—and added to the text, the light of a living eye, the tone of an actual voice—a palpitating expression"—etc. And the consideration of this aroused "other reflections" in him. "In our own life here, see how our writers travel and travel and travel for subjects, go into the great west—into forbidden places—or forbidding—lug in hard cases, crimes, criminals, desperadoes—seek out, as I so often say, the delirium tremens of our national life—display that as the essence of it all—us all—passing by in the act all the natural, unheralded heroisms—the nobility of our every-day life—the romance of the streets, courts, palaces, hovels, by-ways, cities, farms, mines. Not but that our actual life has its hard ends to show— its pimps, panders, thieves, bums, whores,—diseases, dirt, smutch, syphilis—enough to answer for all accusations. Though these to me, in the ensemble, the whole, of our life, are small specks: for we need not go into Greece to know the gods—heroes,—Hercules,—all the great figures: here they are, all of them—the equal of the best—waiting at our doors." I put in—"Could we but open to them." And he—"Yes—a noble thought: could we but open to them, but how often we do *not!*" And he declared: "Bret Harte and John Hay are fond of the Western types, so-called—the delirium tremens type— as I signify them. And the magazines lately have been exploiting various developments of that character. But beyond this—above it, below it, around it—how much more runs on, how much that is different, how much that is disregarded, because it is commonplace, yet is greatest because it is commonplace, too!"

Saturday, October 26, 1889

7.55 P.M. W. in his room, Mrs. Davis with him. She rose at once to go—he resisting her going—but go she did. Has not been quite so well today—yet not ill, either. Looked less easy than for several weeks. Said he and Warrie "are getting adjusted" to each other. I had a couple of pears in my pocket for him, from my sister Agnes. Appeared to be very grateful—smelled them—exclaimed, "The dear girl! so Aggie sent 'em! And how is the good girl nowadays?" I said, "She sent them for breakfast!" "And I shall use them—at least, one of them—for breakfast, to be sure!" Commented on their "pure, fine color"—and handled them affectionately.

Laughed at McKay's monogram. "The object of all monogramists seems to be, to hide away the letters so that no mortal can find them. In that aspect Dave's monogram is a great success." Spoke of a visit from Alice [Alys] Smith today. Had gone downstairs to see her. She did not stay long. "She is going to the college out here—the woman's college. Oh! yes! it is Bryn Mawr. She is here alone—Pearsall, the mother, Mary Costelloe—none of them came on." Reported, "No letter from Bucke and no word about Ed." Had Ed promised to write to him? He did not remember. "Ed was not much of a talker, promiser, anyhow. Rather weak on that point, I think. I have felt he did not come by any natural gifts in the way of description: on a farm, in his veterinary, what-not, he would be an important man, but in the affairs that come to us in the big cities, he avails little."

Spoke of Harned's visit this evening. "He has been over to see 'Der Freischutz'—and seemed to get much enjoyment of it—took Mrs. Harned with him."

I inquired if he had yet written Kennedy about the Whittier paragraph, and he answered: "Not a word—about that or any other matter. As I told you, nothing positive appearing on the subject, I have not delivered myself. It has been a puzzle to me: not knowing whether to say no, not knowing to say yes, I have said nothing at all. But," he asked, with something like vehemence, "isn't it rather cool of the good Kennedy to write me, 'I am going to use it'—never so much as asking me whether I had any desire on the subject, or would rather not? I had no intention of making up a paragraph for print—it came in a moment of vacancy, like the present. It is seriously a question, whether I want that given to the world as my estimate, summing up, of Whittier. But I obey the demon—as Socrates so wisely held of it,—to do or not to do as the demon, the spirit, dictated. And the demon so far, in this, has deterred from any word whatever. I do not know but it may yet put in a question—a positive demurrer—such a question as might settle the whole business at short order, and against printing, even!"

Had been reading a copy of the Boston Pilot. Someone sent him a copy containing matter about Columbus, marked. Calls it, not the Pilot, but, "Boyle O'Reilly's paper."

I had met with reminiscences of actors, in the Press—by Heyward—a reference in one place in high terms to Henry Placide. Asked W. if he had seen it. First said, thought he had—then, "No—I guess it escaped me." Left it with him. Was that his Placide? "Yes. There were two of them—brothers—Harry the great one. Harry, I should say, was one of the greatest actors ever was—not tragic, but in such characters as Sir Peter Teazle he was even elegant—his manner inimitable. He played in 'London Assurance'—Oh! what is the character there? A Sir something Dozzle—what not—nobly done. Harry had the Greek principle closely observed—never overstepped—always considered, to do the thing up to the mark, yet never to overdo it. That was Harry—and so he never offended. A piece called 'One Hundred and Two' was much accepted then, and others of a like tendency." I put in— "Many of them all passed off now," and he—"Yes, all passed off—and their constituency passed off, too. There were fine touches then, wit—flashes of satire—delicate ironies, the vivid effects peculiar to the time, the play, audience—which would not be what it was to the modern play-goers. I doubt if they would appreciate them—though they are very cute, to be sure. But whatever, different tastes, a new generation, fill the stage today." He had been "much interested today in the column and more of the Press" extracting from Joe Jefferson's coming memoirs. "It will take a strong hold on me—does already,"—he admitted. I remarked: "This week I have read in Harper's Weekly an article on Jefferson by William Winter." W. laughed—"He is a Jefferson man, I suppose?" And when I assented—"Yes, but Jefferson can stand it," W. followed— "Oh that is true enough. I think Jefferson one of the greatest." Greater than Booth? "I do not say that—but great—and both are important."

Sunday, October 27, 1889

Did not see W. this day, which I spent in Germantown. But before going was assured all was well with him.

Monday, October 28, 1889

7 P.M. W. reading paper. Room warm, the wood-fire cheerily burning. Received copies of "Camden's Compliment" from binder at last. One for W. who took it—scanned it keenly and was "much pleased." Thought it "looks well—rather formidable—looks like November Boughs, to be sure." Exclaimed—"And there is Dave's monogram, too—confused as ever—achieving the purpose of a monogram, which is to tell a thing nobody can find out!" And Morse's picture struck his eye—"How well it looks here, too!"—seemingly very happy over it.

I gave W. some account of Hilda Clifford's baby description of her visit to W.: that "he came down stairs with his long white beard all on," that she was "afraid of him," that he appeared to her "a bogy," but was still "dear old Walt," for he had given her the most wonderful apple, though she "would not kiss him for it." W. laughed—exclaimed—"How sweet! And what a dear child it is, too! We shall become close friends

92

yet—that is always the end of it with the children. When you see her again, tell her Walt Whitman sends his best love— says that we are going to become the closest friends in the world—tell each other all our secrets!" He had noticed that I came rather early, and said, "Why is it? Where are you going?" I was on my way to the opening meeting of the Unitarian Conference in Philadelphia. I told him Clifford was going to speak. At this his face lighted and he wittily and laughingly remarked: "When you told me you were going to the Conference, I was starting to say, God help you! But now you tell me Clifford is to speak, I see there is no need." Then he added, "Should anything like a report of the speech turn up anywhere in the papers, don't forget to show it to me."

Reported a letter from Bucke today. "But there's not a word in it about Ed—except to say he has not turned up yet—that was on the 26th. But we must wait—it will be all right—probably is by this time. There are reasons and reasons. The only thing is, I sent Doctor a package of the pictures—which of course he has not yet got." He spoke of "obvious things to do" yet "how often those obvious things were the very things we did not do." Spoke about addresses, etc.—on packages. "It is obvious enough we ought to exercise the utmost care—yet, do we?" Spoke of Washington experiences. "I fell in with Adams express men there—I always had a sneaking notion for transportation men, anyhow. They had a building off in Georgetown for the storage of strayed, lost, packages, freight, and it was a sight to behold. Not an ordinary display, not a poor or small building, but space—capaciousness—measure— and such a mass of material there! And yet the men told me nine-tenths of what was there—fully nine-tenths, even barring the necessarily lost goods in the army, would have got to their proper journey's end with a little more particularity in addressing. It was a lesson to me—I have never forgotten it. It taught me my own definiteness of address—what my friends call my superfluity. I thought of the ignorant, the foreigners, the illiterate, the careless, the forgetful, all representatively gathered in that Georgetown building particularly to lesson me—and I did not fail to learn." And he continued: "People have more conscience in such things than is known, believed,—even having in those cases made efforts to find the owners. It was so in the departments, too—the chiefs were very accommodating for instance, in the answering of letters, some of them verging on idiocy—yet all conscientiously consulted, replied to. I have known this not in the case of the clerks alone, but have known heads of departments with whom it was a principle. They made no such arbitrary rule with the letters as I should and do. When I get a letter that seems to have no importance, I reach right over and put it in the box there, or the stove." Warren came in for the mail as we sat there. W. laughingly admonished him— "There are three papers and a letter—yes: now do your best to bring me a letter back!"

Spoke of Fields' book. "I have been reading it—have read it now nearly all through—all the essays. I wrote Dr. Bucke that I was reading it and I said to him that hereafter when I met as I had in the past with those who accused his book of extravagance, I should turn them over to this volume of Fields'. He plasters it on awful thick. Whatever the measure with which Doctor plastered it on, I might say, this is plastereder. It is absolute, overwhelming. The Doctor, extreme as he may be accused of being, at least preserves the attitude, the fact, of giving the other side. Yet I can see for Jim Fields, too, that as he wrote, so it was necessary he *should* write. The best essays in the book are those on Dickens and Hawthorne—Dickens one queer fellow, Hawthorne another, a queerer. They give a good picture of these men—some points not touched upon elsewhere." I interjected something about Fields' modesty—that he did not push his own part forward, whereupon W. again: "No indeed—the book is modest to the last degree. One of the singular felicities—unusual—is the

94

way he reproduces the letters—prints whole letters—don't stop with passages. Today I was reading the piece on Miss Mitford, here are page after page of letters—garrulous—gossippy—yet wonderfully to one's liking. The whole book has that simple pleasing air. And Fields himself was just such a man. I don't know if I have told you, but he has been truly a friend to Walt Whitman. When I was in Boston, working over the new edition of Leaves of Grass, Fields and his wife came up one day—drove up, I think—said they had set out to have me for dinner. If my memory serves me, I went that day. It was before that—money had come to Fields some way—he felt embarrassed, or something, by it—sent some of it to me. At that time he had never met me." Here, after a pause, W. counselled me in a deepened voice: "So you see, we, you, must not forget to bear witness that Fields was one of us— was manly, generous, noble—for, boy, they have not all been so. Oh! many, many not so. Some have been venomous, mean, lying, cowardly, dirty, malignant—Lowell, for one—I count him the most malignant of all." Even than Higginson? "Oh! I take no note of Higginson—he amounts to nothing, anyhow—is a lady's man—there an end!" I happened to mention Higginson's "Buffalo Bill" sentence in Harper's Bazaar, and W., at the name Harper's exclaimed—"That reminds me—did I tell you that I got my piece back from Harper's? Well—I did! They write that it is too much of an improvisation! As if all Leaves of Grass was not improvisation!" Who had written the note? "Alden—H. B. Alden, who is a formalist—a stickler—yet a bright man—even brilliant, after a fashion—at least for his place there, which he must fill to contentment."

Tuesday, October 29, 1889

7.55 P.M. W. sat in his room, handling over quite a formidable roll of newspaper clippings. Some of them looked like proofsheets. I asked, "Are they proofs?" to which: "No—they are one out of the many applications of authors I get. They have just come—Warrie just brought them in—from England. Oh! no one who is not here all the time can know what a center I am of the fancies of young and old—poets, writers, beggars, what-not." He folded up the scraps, looked up and put on them a rubber-band, but just as he was about to put the bundle down on table, a new thought seemed to strike him and he offered it over to me. "Here you take it. I don't know of any better way to dispose of it. The unexpected meal is always the blessed meal. It is not always the thing we crave most, look forward to most, that we most enjoy, but the thing the girl, the housewife, puts on unsuspected—brings in at an unusual moment. So—take this package—see what you can make of it—it may be the blessed meal!" The package of poems, I discovered, was from John Ryley Robinson, evidently of Yorkshire. I have not yet read them.

Referred now to the birthday book: "I like it more and more—it fulfils all expectations. The last few days, as I have gone through it again, the balance of the book impresses me as it had not before—its entire, I might say, singular, balance. I have thought of Herbert's speech there—how well it enters into its place—and of Bonsall's. Bonsall's is a great deal better than I thought it would be—and in fact, all of them. Tom's, too: and they pass on and on—letters, speeches—without interfering, one with the other." As to Morse's bust: "It pleases me more and more—is a constant new revelation—opening singularly to me"—gesturing—"part by part, like the several lays of the telescope." "I wrote Doctor today, that last night you brought me palpable evidence of the book's completion—that I held it in my hand—a bound book—the consummated deed at last!" He commented on the fact that Sanborn had ordered 10 copies from Harned. "The good Frank! And no doubt they'll be profitably distributed—he'll put them into good hands!"

96

Quite a noise on the streets tonight—brass bands, drums, etc. Not knowing for what, I remarked it to him, and he said: "Oh! it is for Grubb—the Republican candidate for Governor—he speaks right up the street tonight"—proving better informed than I of local currents. And he asked: "Do you take no interest whatever in the fight? I notice you seem quiet about it, as if it held none of your stock. Tom astonished me the other night by saying he intended voting for Abbett. I suppose he is disgusted with the family aspect of the management of politics in this county." On the chair a local paper containing a picture of Grubb. I picked it up. Grubb looked badly blurred, and W. made merry over it. "He looks like a Nubian," he said, "we might believe that was intended that way—to get hold of the nigger vote—to show Grubb up as a blackamoor. For my own part, I would not rise out of my chair here to go into the fight—to cast a vote."

He asked me about the Conference. "I read the Ledger account, read Clifford's speech there—thought big of it—of the speech. It seemed to me the report was a very good one." Then after asking, "What is it? A Conference only?" and having my "yes"—he quizzed, "What is it all about? What is it all for?" Following this up with the laughing comment, "It reminds me of a story—you have read it, no doubt—Southey's, a story—poem—used in the readers—at least, used when I was a boy, the Peterkin story. There is an old man—with him a child—a boy, Peterkin: the man is telling of some battle—colors borne high, din, powder, shot, havoc, charges, retreats, wounds, blood flowing like water. And as he goes along enthusiastically in the story, the boy asks—but what was it all about? what was it all about?—the man only replying, no matter, no matter—we had a terrific tussle—and then he goes on with his story—and tells and tells—and again the boy asks him, but what was it for? what was it for? the other still replying, no matter—no matter: we had a big fight—we gained a big victory! But the boy was not satisfied: in the midst of the story—carnage, hell-to-pay—the boy still asked—but what was it for? and the man still replying, I don't know—but we had a devil of a fight and gained a big victory, the poem ending with the boy's question, What it was all for?" W. laughed out his application: "So what is all the Conference for?" Took an absorbed interest in my account of Clifford's noble speech—its unwelcome—its courage. "That," he said, "is the making of Clifford—that *is* Clifford."

I spoke of the general interest in W.'s religious opinions, of the number of people who inquired of me. So markedly was this so, I thought I should like to give at least a paragraph to them in the New England Magazine article. W. laughingly said: "So they want to know if I think the human race is to be damned?" I returned: "No—not that: the people who ask me are themselves mainly not orthodox." He responded: "Well—I do not know, but if something comes to me to say I shall write it down with my pencil here and give to you." But he jocularly turned the matter off by a story. "Did I never tell you the Long Island story? It is a good one—I heard it first when I was a boy." And then went on with a narration, the humor of which as he told it was superb. I lost some of the preliminaries, but from one point on I retained all. "The old lady—the mother—had been converted—taken the Methodist turn, what-not. And her friends were taking good care of her, lest the devil should get her in his clutches again. One night though he came home—it was late—towards midnight, he expected to be received as usual—get bed, eatables, comfort. He knocked at the door—knocked louder. By and bye the old lady's head was thrust out of an upper window. 'Who's there?'

"'It's me—Sam.'

"'Well—what do you want here?'

"'I want to get in: it's late—I'm tired, hungry, sleepy, wet.'

"'Well, go 'way—you can't come in here.'

"'God damn it, I must! Don't act the fool: come down and open the door for me.'

"But the old lady stuck it out. 'No—no—you can't come in here.'" He asks then, 'What's the matter with you, anyhow: what makes you act so foolish?' Then she tells him, she has got religion and he replies—'Well, what does that matter— what's that to do with letting me in?' She informs him, 'A good deal, you don't believe in hell—don't believe men are going to be damned. No man who turns his back on that can come in here!' And he admitted that he didn't quite believe in damnation. Then the story goes on—oh! I must make it short—it is very funny—goes on in this way, the two arguing together, she relenting a little by and bye by asking, 'Well, don't you believe some folks are to be damned?' And he rather inclined to say some deserved to be if they weren't. And she asking again, 'Well—tell me, how many?' 'I don't know—I would be willing to allow, say 200 thousand' which broke the ice—for she said that would do, and admitted him." W. went over this with a thorough laughing spirit—asking me at the end, "I wonder if I am expected to admit the 200,000?" Saying further: "I thought it a happy illustration—that story. I don't think I have repeated it strictly, but that is the marrow of it."

He spoke of the Press article about actors I had left with him the other day, that it was "interesting—and accurate in the main"—saying as to Harry Placide—"he was a great actor—in his way a man whose like I never saw." "People have an idea Jefferson made the stage Rip Van Winkle—but that is a great mistake. The original Rip was Hackett, who was in his prime in my early life—who was a grand man, standing to Jefferson as the old Booth does to our Edwin. A vastly bigger man than Jefferson. The opinion of theatre-goers of those times [of him] was very high, and what I realized myself in Hackett's presence—my emotional, mental, sympathetic self—goes altogether in the way of confirmation—convinces me the public judgment was correct. But I notice in these modern writers a tendency to bring some to the fore who were not thought great at that time and really were not great, and a corresponding tendency to forget others who should be mentioned. I can vividly realize those old stage-settings, characters—the audiences—houses. Harry Placide, Hackett, Mrs. Vernon and a man named Reiner." W. spelled for me, saying, "not Raynor but" etc.—"these were the giants—and giants of real stature." After awhile noticing my interest, he asked: "You find it attractive, do you? I suppose it is: I live graphically in it, sometimes: a touch brings up scenes and scenes." Spoke specifically of all—"the noble, gentle Harry Placide: elegant, yet acting the rough coachman to the letter—with an exquisite skill—the very coarseness of it," and Mrs. Vernon—"English,—a truly gracious gift to our stage." And Hackett "a Long Islander—had a home off near Babylon. I knew his son—met him often." He spoke of Polonius: "It is a great character—a big opportunity—never realized: yet I have known Hackett to realize it—nobly and highly. It was noticeable of Hackett, too, that he did not emphasize the farcical Rip—did not lay stress upon the humor—made rather more account of its seriosity—and here touched bed-rock—was delicately grand." And then: "There were touches in there which would hardly pass current on the stage of this day." Spoke further of "costumes: oh! Mrs. Vernon had what would even now be acknowledged a great wardrobe." Qualifying it however—"but the acting that was the thing—that was what made her great!"

Wednesday, October 30, 1889

7.45 P.M. W. looking over some papers. Had received invitation to Contemporary Club meeting—first of the season—Prof. Fullerton on Hypnotism this evening. But "No letter from Bucke, nor from Ed—not a word, singular as it may seem." Yet—"I can know how the Doctor must want to see Ed—will question him." Adding: "And I am anxious to have Doctor get his books. I hope Tom will send them—has sent them. I am growing into the book. I want to tell Harry Bonsall that I like his speech—indeed, you can tell him for me some day when you meet. I like the book—like it all. It is remarkable in the first place—if for nothing else—as a curio, and then it is meaty—there is a great deal more meat in it than one would be apt to expect. For myself, I can say I am impressed beyond words. Here is the history of Leaves of Grass—here is the whole struggle told—the long years—all. I never expected to live to see this—never. To see such an event, such a book—to see such opinions stated—men deliberately going on record in this way—willing to have the world hear, note. It means vast, vast change of front somewhere." I said I believed Darwin had somewhere said something of similar purport. "Ah! that cuts the line still more deep—makes it shuddering!" Referred then to the picture: "It has a curious fitness, right in its place—tells its own story." He thought: "Even Herbert will come around to it—will see that it does not ruin the book, rather inheres to it. They say of the Devil, that something or other made him of another mind. Herbert will be made of another mind." Alluded then to printing of the book, asking: "What did you say was the name of the foreman up there at Bennerman's?" Saying he thought he remembered the man—"strong, lithe, a pleasant face and manner."

Giving me a copy of the Boston Transcript done up in a rubber, he said, "I don't know why I put this up for you, but I know I did." Handing it to me, "And on the principle that a mouthful out of your neighbor's pudding outweighs the choicest gifts of your own kitchen cook, this may interest you." Thought the book well-printed. "The Bucke life, done there by the Shermans, seems to me with the best. I always placed it with the best samples from abroad."

Harned had been in "looking fat and hearty," but no member of the Conference had been over. "To My Seventy-First Year" he said, "is the name of the Century piece to appear next month. And this," showing me another, in a Curtz slip, "is still a second in their hands, which they have paid for and will print when they choose." Alluded to "the pears you brought me from Aggie. Oh! they were fair as they looked—in that respect unlike some people we know. Tell Aggie I enjoyed them bite by bite—even the memory of them now."

Spoke then of the Theodore Thomas benefit concert Saturday night. "It will no doubt be a true deliverance. I can hear its ring, sitting here, by mere thinking of it. And benefit? I think Thomas deserves all that can be done for him." Asked after routine of the bank work—especially after "its system against fraud." Then adding: "Mr. Odenheimer up the street—now made nearly blind by his financial work—figures, paper, pens—gave me once quite a circumstantial account of the defences put up by the Pennsylvania Railroad. He was with the road many years. He showed, for instance, that, say out of every thousand hands, a third, 333 of them, were practically to check the others. But I understood at one time that it was seriously considered whether it would not pay to do without these hands—run the risk—whether the loss would not be less than the hire. Just as I have been told the Astors do not insure their property in New York, preferring to risk fire. Though I don't believe this, for they are cute men. The point however being that insurance money must in any event be paid, fire money perhaps not." He thinks the business world "an almost infinite bit of machinery" beautifully constructed out of all the past experiences of man.

"I have sent Kennedy no word yet, adopting the principle, when in doubt, do nothing, though this is often argued against as fatuous, which to me it is not." Referring to the Conference again: "What does it all mean? Peterkin still questions; 'What is it all about father?—a great fuss, bloodshed—but what for?' It seems to me, if it means anything, it means evolution—the evolution of Protestantism—the witness of the fact that every 20 years or so some of the fellows step out of bounds and declare, we are not satisfied with the state of

102

things—they do not speak for us, they must move on. Now, if Unitarianism has any mission, it must be this,—to receive any man who has caught the new light—every brave thinker—outcast poet—humanity in all its aspects of the changer, the improver—every seeker—every one who has glimpsed the larger vista. Doing this, it does nothing—is no more than the other sects—is only one more added to the theological clamor. But I know well there are the 20-year's men—there are also the Conservative Unitarians—orthodox—who believe the message is all delivered, signed, sealed, we may say—who protest that you cannot go forward when you have reached the end."

Thursday, October 31, 1889

7.45 P.M. W. reading papers—several on his lap. Not greatly well. "My head has been in a queer chaotic condition—as though in a whirl of phlegm." Said Clifford and DeLong had been in to see him today. "I am afraid I was very stupid—they must have felt it so. I was not in my best condition—this trouble was on me—and so we did not say much." Said Clifford had left a copy of The Germantown Independent containing his speech in full. "I have only so far looked at it—not read it. I have laid it by for a more propitious moment." Afterwards: "DeLong tells me there is a copy of the big book there at Medford, in the library." I exclaimed, "I wonder who put it there?" And he, "I wonder! That would be something worth inquiring about: some daring radical—some outrageous violator of the proprieties." Adding in his laughter: "I have been told that in the Boston Public Library they have a copy of Leaves of Grass, but keep it under lock and key, afraid that it may get out and be read!" But whatever his "dullness with the visitors" he took it "as an honor—as it is: a compliment for the fellows to come over—all this way." I was on the way tonight to the meeting at which Curtis was to speak. W. said: "The best thing I know of him is, that William O'Connor, who was a man not easily satisfied, thought there was something in him—that he stood for something."

Gave me slip copies of the poems "Bravo, Paris Exposition!" and "My 71st Year." with his own written corrections.

"I had another visitor today—a man, Hawley—from Syracuse or Rochester—a doctor, medical doctor. He bought 2 copies L. of G.: one for himself, one for a friend in the city—Kent, was his name, I think. He says he told Kent he was going to devote this afternoon to this visit, and then Kent, who knew nothing about me, gave him money for the book—probably from a curiosity to know how the wild beast looked at close quarters. O yes! Hawley was a medical doctor—a homeopathist. He even started to talk about me—discuss me physically—but I would have none of it—told him I was not open to discussion at that point."

The tree in front of the house has been cut down. W. said: "It was an event—the old dead tree is gone: it seemed to me a public danger. Ed told me at one time he thought he could push it over—so I thought it my duty to get rid of it—remove it." Has been doing considerable repairing about the house, and papering the vestibule. Said a letter had "come at last from Ed to Warrie. Ed has an appointment with Bucke, to go tell him about us. It seems Ed went to work right off on his arrival—that accounts for his delay." W. said again—"There was a slight notice—a paragraph,—of the book in today's Post—but it comes to nothing. Probably Bonsall will follow it up with something more satisfactory." He took from me a list of names I knew Harned had sent books to. "It is to avoid sending duplicates," he explained. And he said later: "I should like one to go to Whittier." As to those to go abroad, I said I thought they should come from me, and he, "Yes—that would be most happy." And he mentioned copies for Rolleston, Carpenter, Symonds, Rhys—"and Tennyson—I should approve of that."

Friday, November 1, 1889

7.30 P.M. W. reading The Century when I came. Referred to it: "Yes—my piece appeared today—and today came the proof of the other piece, too—'Old Age's Ship and Crafty Death's.' I suppose it, too, will now shortly appear—probably not next month, but the month after. I hesitated a great sight over it—whether not to make a change—to make the headline read, Old Age's War or Old Age's Fight—wishing a word of one syllable. But finally I let it go just as it was." I objected to the change, especially towards the new lines mentioned. W. then: "The idea is, these ships—Old Age's, Crafty Death's—stealing upon mine. It is a very definite—some will think a very cheap—idea—as perhaps it is." Said further of The Century: "It has plenty of poetry this month." I asked, "Do you call it poetry?" And he laughed—"Well—butterflies—are poor enough, all, to be sure. But"—lifting the magazine—"see this: this is a picture I have been feasting upon for a long time" opening at the frontispiece—a Head of Aesop, by Velasquez. "Talk about simplicity and breadth!—there it is." It was indeed a striking piece of work, and on my remark that it was the best Century page for a long time, he assented. "Yes, you are right—it surpasses them all—the engraving itself is grand. Who is T. Johnson?" And as we looked further—"How vitalizing! how throbbing with life! Yet it ought to be—it is from Velasquez—the best of them all. Who of us have not seen just such types going about our ways—especially in the great west. I have not for a long time enjoyed an engraving as I have this." Pointed then to the Jefferson article on the first page. "I tried to get interested in that, but it was no go—it is dry as dry. Why! he knows less about them than I do." I said, "Jefferson ought to know!" W. however—"But he don't! It is not in him to know—the living currents have passed him by. What he writes here has no heartbeat whatever." There was W.'s own poem, spread in broad beautiful lines. "Yes, I like it—it looks handsome. The noble breadth of page seems to lend itself to my lines." Further, of the Spanish article by Susan Carter: "It is quite good—and the pictures with it. But as I read I pictured the dilemma of the writer—pictured her as if trying to walk in water this deep"—indicating a line above the knee "and getting there, to be sure but the labor of it wore her out soon."

Again he drifted into another strain. "Ingram was in here today: he went to the Conference meeting last night—heard Curtis, Savage, Hale—liked them all, but thought Savage the best. From what he says I think Savage was the most animated—he gave me that impression." I called Curtis' oratory "Ciceronian, with the Ciceronian penalty of oversustainedness and of being often dull." W., "I can see—that is a true touch." Blake said to me at the meeting last evening, applauding Curtis—"but if only his fancy were imagination," etc. W. taking my repetition of this thus: "I feel it is true. After all, Ingersoll is the man of men—in America, our days, reaching highest, surmounting all the difficulties of speech—the most marked man, yet made so by means of a most astonishing simplicity. He is never passionate in the outward sense, yet every sentence is a thrust in itself—a dagger—a gleam—a fire—a torch, vital and vitalizing—full of pulse, power, magnificent potencies."

I had letters from Mark Twain and Gilder.

Dear Gilder—

I shall not need to answer this letter, I suppose, since I can answer it through you. It seems to be an application for a contribution of from one to five dollars per month. I am quite willing to be put on the list of two-dollar contributors, and I enclose five months contribution in advance herewith.

Yours sincerely,
S L Clemens

Hartford
  Oct 30th '89

55 Clinton Place.
Oct 31, 1889,

My dear Mr Traubel,
   Enclosed please find $10 from me, & $10 from Mark Twain—
(S. L. Clemens) for Walt Whitman.
   I write from my bed. Where's the book?

Sincerely
R. W. Gilder.

W. exclaimed: "The good Clemens! And that reminds me—I
must send him that big book—I have long intended it: now I
must make it a particular point." And: "I am anxious Gilder
should have the books—give Tom a nudge." Also letter from
Weir Mitchell.

S. Weir Mitchell, M.D.
   1524 Walnut Street,
      Philadelphia, Pa.

Dictated.
November 1st 1889

Mr. Horace L. Traubel;—
   Dear Sir;—
   Of course I am interested in the matter. Kindly tell me how
you are arranging the thing, what the expense of a nurse is and how
you are collecting subscriptions. It is needless to say that you may
count on me.

Yours truly,
Weir Mitchell.

"That is like the Doctor—I know him and know of him—his
goodness."
   Said he had a letter from Pearsall Smith today containing
25 dollars. Also letter from Bucke, which he gave to me. "It
tells the tale of Ed. Ed turns up at last—much, I suppose, to
Doctor's relief. I guess they did not have it out this time,
however. Doctor was in a hurry to keep an engagement—Ed

in a hurry to go off—so between the two little was done."
Questioned me if it was raining, and learning it was not: "It is
one of the peculiar fancies of my hearing. I hear what I should
not and do not hear what I should."

Saturday, November 2, 1889

6.45 P.M. W. in his room—light on—reading paper. Said:
"Herbert was over last night—he saw the book—liked it all—
thought it fine, handsome, all except the picture—holding to
his old objection just as firmly as ever." I read him a letter I
had today from Kennedy—this:

>   Belmont
>   Mass
>   Nov 1, '89
>
> Dear Traubel
>   Thank you very much for the beautiful souvenir. I enclose 50 cts.
> It is surely a great honor to appear in such fine company. I yield
> now that it was a good thing to bring out this booklet. I had no idea
> you could elicit so many gems of thought.
>   The "get-up" is capital. I am delighted with the whole thing.
>   I sh'd like to talk over with you the many remarkable confessions.
> Let me personally congratulate *you* on this little ticket to immortal-
> ity you have secured, dear friend.
>   *Please give my regards to Mr. Gilchrist, & ask him to come &
> see me.*
>   Love to all. I feel *ennobled* after reading the "Camden's Compli-
> ment"
>
>   W S Kennedy—

to which W. remarked: "That is exceedingly significant for the
book—a criticism from one who writes from the very head-
center of bookishness, or, rather books. The best proof of a

dinner is in this,—that food is there, that I like it, another likes it, it answers our ends. And so, if the book answers the end, it must be counted a success, whatever some may say of it." Read him also, then, letter from Frank Sanborn:

Concord, Mass Oct. 31
1889

Dear Sir:

I think I subscribed $5 to the publication of the "Camden Compliment," and I enclose my draft for that sum. But it seems too small to pay for ten copies of the beautiful book which I received by express tonight. If there's more to pay, please let me know.

You have made a fine tribute to the dear old man, to whom please give my best wishes

Yours truly
F. B. Sanborn

Mr. Traubel

which struck him forcibly. "The noble Sanborn! true, just as he has been!" Gilder had written me yesterday, "Where is the book?" and W. was anxious I should stir Harned up to sending G.'s copies if not already gone. The American reviews book today. Have not yet seen it. W. thought: "From my point of view, aside entirely from what is said on it, the book is a success from a printerial, artistic point of view—well conceived and as well executed. I do not get over my astonishment, however, that this is for us—that I have lived to see it."

Said he had "another red-ink postal from the Epoch person, directing my attention to The Epoch of Nov. 1st—or 2d. If you are in the way of a paper—look—but go to no trouble about it. This is a way editors have at times of extending their circulation. The average critter will tear mad round the town if he knows his name has been printed in the papers."

Referred to The Century again. "The Velasquez head—Aesop—misled me. On a first look at the magazine, seeing that, I thought—here now is a brilliant number, but I was never more deceived—rarely a number more stupid. As for Jefferson, he knows nothing at all—nothing. The Spanish article—by a woman—a Miss or Mrs. [Susan W. C.] Carter is very good—passable—readable, in a way, though labored enough, too. My own poem looks well: there is a noble breadth given it there—in the mere printerial aspect of it." To The Critic's remark this week on Stoddard's Lippincott Bryant, which "no lover of the foregoing poet should forego reading," W. laughingly remarked, "That must have been another by Dick himself. I don't believe there was a person on the list of its readers who competently thought of it otherwise than as utterly dull and worthless." Spoke of absence of further word from Bucke.

Sunday, November 3, 1889

Did not see W. this day, but he kept well, though not getting out at all. Has been watching for sunshine but the rain today was severe. Sent to Harned for one volume of the Encyclopaedia Brittanica "for a particular purpose."

Also "swopped" with T. one copy of his big book for 12 of "Camden's Compliment." "The only other copy of Camden's Compliment I had I sent to my sister," he said.

Monday, November 4, 1889

8 P.M. W. reading papers, as usual. I had just mailed several books—among them one abroad, to Rhys. W. expressed gladness. Then produced a sheet. "Have you enough to supply these?" he asked. The names were there.

Edward Bertz
   Holzmarkt str   18 Potsdam Prussia
Prof: Dowden
   Winstead   Temple Road Rathmines Dublin Ireland

Gabriel Sarrizin
    10 Rue Troyon   Paris France
T W Rolleston
    Fairview   Delgany Co: Wicklow Ireland
Wm M Rossetti
    5 Endsleigh Gardens   London n w England
Edw'd Carpenter
    Millthorpe near Chesterfield   England
John Addington Symonds
    Davos   Switzerland
Rudolf Schmidt
    Baggesensgade   3 N Copenhagen Denmark

I mention, "And not Tennyson?" and he at once exclaimed—
"Oh! I had forgotten him." So he sent me across the room for
his candle, which he lighted and placed on the middle table,
then opening his note-book, hunting up T.'s address—which
he put on my sheet, he wrote plain "Alfred Tennyson" saying
meanwhile: "I drop the Lord: I understand his wife and children are very punctilious in regard to that—but I don't know.
I am sure, at least, that Alfred himself puts no moment upon
it. It is usually the second and third parties who make much
of the proprieties, decorum. I know it was so at Washington—
in the Armies, departments. When I had anything I wished
particularly to have done, I went to headquarters—up to the
very throne. I remember now, several cases with Stanton.
And I can say this, that I never had anything promised me by
the big guns that was not accomplished to the letter." He
spoke definitely of some of the parties he had thus come in
contact with. "There were many of the old fellows—thoroughly democratic—approachable. There was old Zach Taylor—General Taylor—afterwards the President. In New Orleans—forty years ago—about the close of the Mexican
War—I came to know him there. A plain man—without the
first sign of airishness—yet a man with his entourage of
slaves—a man used to being served—military—a disciplinar-

111

ian, yet a jolly man—fond of a good story—living well—realizing life. As plain as Grant, yet more frank and outspoken." I objected, "But Grant was a man of larger mental parts." W. rejoining: "Taylor was a great man, too—a greater man than is sometimes believed. Grant was far more reserved—more self-contained. He seemed to see the necessity of it—both as General and President. He was grandly non-commital—resolved at all hazards, temptations, not to give himself, his cause, away." Referred also to Randolph of Roanoke: "The anti-slavery men have made too little of the significant democracy of some of the great Virginians—of Jefferson, Washington, others—owners of slaves—slavery men so-called. Think of John Randolph—the poor, horrible physical specimen that he was, yet with a power within that no informed man can doubt. There was a clause in his will freeing his nigger valet. Oh! what a preciousness about these niggers, when once they are loyal—valeting you through life! This one of Randolph's had stuck to him from boyhood. Now was Randolph's time to prove himself—and he did. When he was on his deathbed—several gathered around him—a group—lawyers—others: fearing the clause in his will with regard to this nigger would be lightly carried out, he said: 'Gentlemen, I charge you to bear witness that I put this clause into its place with all solemnity—and I charge you further to see personally that this man'—putting his hand on the nigger's head—'is duly given his freedom.'—That is authentic, I know all about it—had the means of knowing—and though little is made of it in the histories, to me it has a profound significance." This led to some mention of Conway's recent piece on Edmund Randolph, W. saying: "Yes—that is Conway's forte—getting into curios of investigation—discovering mare's nests—that there is no devil, for instance. A surprising discovery this, to be sure or, rather, more of a dicovery to discover there was one. I remember once with me, he sat full an hour, arguing

about the existence of the Presidency—that it had survived
its right and its usefulness."

Tuesday, November 5, 1889

7.40 P.M. W. sitting up—reading—looking ruddier than
usual. "I have been out of my chair today—had a delicious
trip—the day fine beyond words. It is a great day to move
about in. I went up to Tom's—knocked at the office door with
my cane—but evidently nobody was in." Alex. Cattell had
spoken of the portrait in the book as "a daub" but W. insisted,
"Many men—many minds—we must not forget. Jim Scovel
was over today. He didn't like the picture either. But no matter—we do—and that for us conclusive." Referred to Gosse's
high estimate of Tennyson's "Throstle" with a shake of the
head. "I sent the paper to Bucke, knowing it would interest
him."

Laughingly said: "I can't picture Tom in a dress coat. His
stovepipe hat seemed to me the steepest descent possible for
him to make, but this would beat the steepest steep!" Directed my attention to a French paper in the chair. "It comes
from Bartlett's son, now in France. See the postmark there—
isn't that Millet's place?" It was marked Barbizon. "The paper
contains a translation of my 'Bravo Exposition' piece, whether
good or bad I do not know. And this"—picking up a square
canary envelope—"is from a Frenchman who writes me a
poem—a long poem—in numbered verses—all in French—
which, however good, is not good enough for me to understand—is all Greek to me!" Speaking of a certain qualifying
book review W. said: "Some men find it impossible to give a
straightforward compliment, an 'if' or a 'but' is always planted
in the way."

W. said: "While out in the chair I remembered it was elec-

113

tion day—still did not vote. Did you? I always refrain—yet advise everybody else not to forget."

Wednesday, November 6, 1889

7.45 P.M. Seemingly ruminating. Mrs. Davis had admitted me down stairs, the dog giving forth his usual dismal howl. W. now inquired, "Was it you the dog was howling at that way?" Adding after my nod of assent, "Well, if there's anyone in the world he ought to know by this time—would know, if he had any sense at all, as he has not—it is you. He is the nastiest, noisiest, silliest, stupidest, horriblest dog that was ever born—a pest, a continual sore in my side!" Adding still again, "Any useful dog—any manly dog—gets to know his friends, betters—but this dog, never!"

W. inquired which of the books I had sent off: as proved, all but Bertz's and Schmidt's. Read him a letter I had from Garland.

My Dear Traubel:

You have done yourself and all others credit in your editorial work on the Memorial of the Banquet. I shall try to sell a number of the volumes because I think they will sell other of Whitman's volumes. I am always aiding in the spread of the Great poets fame. I am still too poor to do anything in money. I hope soon to send you a little something. A genuine lover of W. W. is Kenneth Cranford painter and teacher in the Cowles Art School. I also made a partial convert in one [of] the Conservatory faculty—I saw some excellent poems from your pen in *the New Ideal*. You should write more. You have the right ring in your words. Did you go to hear my good friend Herne read while he was in Philadelphia. He is my convert to the Single Tax. By the way does W. W. indicate interest in it still?

Give him my love. And as for yourself—put your shoulder to the Single Tax chariot when ever you can. We have their big meeting projected for November and December.

Fraternally
Hamlin Garland

114

He laughed over the single tax. "Interested in it still? I do not know what it is! I asked Garland himself, and either because of my stupidity, which is very likely, or of his way of telling it, or of the intrinsic difficulties of the case itself—for one of these reasons—probably the first, I was left entirely in the dark. The good Garland! But however the single tax, there's all the rest!"

Edelheim in today—gave me 20 dollars for the fund. I remarked it to W. as from a man he had never seen, and he said, "And noble it is too! Who is he?" And when I explained, he—"A noble baker, to be sure! A noble baker!" Adding: "I think I must right soon get up a little poemet, about so long"—indicating two inches on his hand—"'To My Unknown Friends'—aiming to take in these men you have with you in this undertaking." I took up with the suggestion at once, "Yes,—and give me copies to send to each one of them." W. then: "That would be my idea: to get them in such a way that I could sign them and have each person have a personal copy."

W. "stirred to rejoicing" as he said, by the result of the elections towards Democracy: "It shows a turn in the tide—the Harrisonian Republican on the downflow." Talked of protection. "I can see how it appeals to some people—how it must appeal to them. I can even see how protection protects. As they say in the story—whiskey makes a man strong: put a glass, or two glasses, of whiskey, in him, and he is a giant—he can do tremendous things—lift great weights, heave, draw, energize—the transformation is marvellous." "But how about tomorrow?" I put in. And W. at once: "That's it! How about tomorrow! It is the tomorrow people don't see: protection protects—today!—but tomorrow, whose ox is gored? I never knew the time when I could be led to the slaughter that way; in my earliest years—even as a boy—I saw the tomorrow of this humbug—the day of reckoning. I was never deceived—and experience does no more than confirm me.

115

But it is in this—in politics—just as it is in religion—some people get an idea of the necessity of believing certain things, not so much from weight of evidence, out or in,—but from mere mental and emotional set-ness: they intend believing—and that all there is about it!"

A copy of Trübner's periodical on a chair. I picked it up, W. remarking: "I have not examined it myself yet. It came today among a lot of other things. I have a friend there—Josiah Childs, who sends it along, issue after issue, faithfully. Did I ever tell you about the Trübners? You know, there was an old man—the original Trübner, who is dead now. The present Trübner is a young man—at least, in the sense of being the first Trübner's son. The old man was quite a friend of Leaves of Grass—sold it for me—and Specimen Days, at a time when every book sold was an important event to me. At that time sent me over several hundred dollars. But this son, ascending the throne, beheaded me at short notice—quickly concluded that Leaves of Grass was not the book for him to handle. Josiah Child—sort of confidential man there—himself very friendly towards me, was not satisfied to have the book driven out in that style, so looked about and secured agents for it there and several of them. And as he is of a financial turn, kept the accounts strictly straight for me—made remittances from time to time. The last one—the closing one—just the last year—in this room—since my sickness. I never saw Childs—nor Trübner either. This, you see, is part of the history of Leaves of Grass—I have been driven from post to pillar, yet by virtue of these things, a man gets the pick of his friends, to be sure—they come near and near—are indissoluble."

I spoke of somebody who remarked the "religiousness" of "My 71st Year"—W. smilingly replying: "I suppose they must have had in mind that last line. The general view of what constitutes religion is very cheap—not only confusing theology with it, but making of religion—Methodism to the Methodist,—what-not, and that only. As if religion had not its wide readings—readings wide as worlds to a grand world-wide man." There was Adler in New York—"serving the people—and for what? His devotion superb—yet in what but this is devotion—religious faith—faith that counts—embodied? All but this can be spared." I mentioned Abou Ben Adhem and W., "Oh! the noble little poem! What is there to surpass it? It is in place today—the standard—at the forefront—nobly stating all that indicates moral advance. This the world knows—or will know—must know in time."

Had made up my bundle of portraits, endorsed as follows:

> Portraits of Walt Whitman
> from life at different ages
> *Horace L Traubel*
> from his friend W. W.
> Nov: 6 1889

Had sent French paper to Dr. Bucke but the manuscript poem still here. Did he wish Morris to translate it? I suggested letting M. see it. So, if worth while, to translate and print translation. W. was willing—would "hunt it up"—already buried in a heap of things.

Picture of Symonds on mantel—cabinet. W. said: "I think Mary unearthed it, cleaning here. I did not know I had it. Every now and then something turns up that way. I don't think this picture anyway near as good as the big one."

Thursday, November 7, 1889

7.40 P.M. In his room, as usual. Looked pretty well, though tired. Said: "I have been spending one of my usual unrelieved monotonous days—feeling very well, except for this strange, palling weight in my head, which wears down, a constant pressure upon me." And there was "nothing new. A letter from Doctor, sans news, and something from the society of

Old Brooklynites"—this with a laugh. We laughed at Bucke's vehement ridicule of the title-page of the book, I saying—"His opinion is relieved of much of its pith by his violence in uttering it." W. laughing: "Yes—no doubt. I remember, however, that that is what John Burroughs would say, has said, of O'Connor, though"—shaking his head, an dropping into a serious tone—"I don't think that is true of O'Connor."

Elections still attracted him. "I see as the returns come in, it looks more and more a likely result for the Democrats. Harrisonism is on the move—is getting found out. And among the most comical things is the struggle of the Republican papers to account for it. Why—it is accounted for in the very nature of things! What more is necessary?"

I received from Frank R. Stockton a note today about the fund, etc., thus:

> Convent Station
> New Jersey
> Nov. 4: 1889
>
> Mr Horace L. Traubel,
> Dear Sir,
> I am in receipt of your well-put and considerate note; and, in answer, will say that I will join you in your good work in regard to Walt. Whitman thusfar: I will give ten dollars for a plain copy of "Leaves of Grass" with the author's autograph in it. This much I can do, and it may be there are others who would do the same.
> I do not know that Walt. Whitman ever heard of me, or that he would care to hear, but he has my sympathy, and best wishes for a happy remainder of life.
>
> Very sincerely
> Frank R. Stockton

Dictated:

W. exclaimed—"Indeed I do care—all those things are touching—go straight to my heart. Tell him so—tell him so." Promised to send book tomorrow without fail—$2.00 edition. The rest of the money I will put in with the fund.

W. much interested in American notice of book—this:

Mr. Horace L. Traubel has edited, and David McKay, (Philadelphia; 23 S. 9th St.), has published in good style, with the title "Camden's Compliment to Walt Whitman," the record of the testimonial meeting and dinner at Camden, N.J., May 31, last, in honor of the seventieth birthday of the poet. Mr. Traubel's work is so well done, and the material for the volume is so substantial, that he has made an appreciable addition to the Whitman literature. This results from the character of the addresses on the occasion, the letters of response and compliment, and the excellent historical and descriptive sketch which the editor prefixes. All of this, with rare exceptions, has more than a temporary or perfunctory character, and much of it, by suggestiveness, by critical judgment or by other quality, helps to an appreciation and an estimate of Whitman's work. There are letters, for example, from Wm. M. Rossetti, Edward Dowden, John Burroughs, Stedman, F. B. Sanborn, and John Addington Symonds, and there are briefer ones which are notable, also. We congratulate the Camden friends of the poet on their spirit in devising and conducting the testimonial, and on having it so worthily put on record.

American. Phila. Nov. 2, '89.

Exclaiming as he finished reading: "Well—that fellow has read the book, anyhow!—which is a point gained with a critic anyway—so few of 'em do—or appear to!"

Gilchrist came in as we sat there talking. Did not stay long—we going finally off together. Gilchrist spoke of seeing Mansfield's Richard the 3d—W. thereupon curiously full of questions. "What is he trying to do with it?" and others. "The last forty years, all the actors have taken to experimenting with it—half doing, half undoing, its legitimate powers, beauties, wonders. It gives play of itself, naturally, without interpretation so-called, to grandest, most vital forces, passions, emotionalities. It is always the actor's opportunity." Then voiced talk of Gilchrist's goings-about—of his departure in February. Talking of American art in the wider sense, the question arose, had we yet produced in music a great composer? No—not indeed! W. however interposed: "Our best work so far seems to be in the direction of nigger songs, some of these are superb—'Old Folks at Home'—'Old Black Joe' and such. Exquisite specimens, some of them, out of the heart of nature—hitting off nigger life South there with wonderful expression."

Also reference to the Kendals, now in town. G. having seen them—W.'s first question was: "Is the woman the best?"

Gilchrist having asked if W. had seen any other London Telegraph letters from Edwin Arnold, W. exclaimed, among other things: "Oh! we have captured him—there's no doubt! America has captured him!"

Friday, November 8, 1889

7.45 P.M. W. in his room, reading Scott—laying the volume face down, on my entrance. Conversed then for full half an hour together, he seeming to be much freer in feeling than last night. In going over the news of the day he said: "Things are always very quiet here, I depend on you generally to bring the outside world in. I got a wholly unimportant letter from Dr. Bucke today, and I wrote Mrs. O'Connor—addressing her still in Massachusetts. But I have sent Frank Stockton his book—his autographed book. I found I still had a copy of the Osgood autographed edition, which I sent him."

I said I had been rather surprised last night by Herbert's remark that he liked my introduction in the book very much. W., amid his raillery of me, exclaimed—"That was praise from St. Hubert indeed—from veriest St. Hubert!" Adding then: "The book is the book, whatever the boys may say of it: and it is not only a force as it stands, but a greater force in the sense that the acorn is a force, or Hercules a force—for their potentialities—their high promise—future. I remember O'Connor's great touch—the baby Hercules in the cradle—strangling." W. ending in this strange way—assuming I knew the rest, and saying: "O'Connor rarely indulged in a figure [of speech] but when he did so, he did it with a trip-hammer effectiveness." I quoted Emerson's description of Carlyle: "A trip-hammer with an Aeolian attachment." W. saying: "Yes—it is very great—very Emersonian: I would have recognized it." Going on reflectively: "In the big metal works, with their trip-hammers—I have spent many a long, fascinated, inform-ing hour!—many!"

Writing to Sanborn last week acknowledging his letter about the book, I had asked what he knew of the Whitman footnote in Edward Emerson's book. To this today the follow-ing reply came:

Seventeenth National Conference
of
Charities and Correction
Concord Nov 6, 1889

Dear Sir:

I had forgotten the allusion to Whitman in Dr. Emerson's life of his father until someone in your book cited it. Doubtless it ex-presses *one* view taken by Emerson of the poetic *form* in which Whitman chose to write. Emerson took views of his subject, what-ever it might be, from more than one point; and that which he expressed to Whitman himself in 1855 was his more constant way of looking at Whitman's genius. He thought less highly of Whit-man's War verses than I did or than he did of Leaves of Grass, which he told me in 1855 was "a combination of the Bhagavat Ghita and the New York Herald." His son never took much interest in Whit-man, and was perhaps not unwilling to cite an utterance which seemed to agree with his own opinion. The whole note is too much in the *de haut en bas* style, and does not represent the real feeling of Emerson towards Whitman, as I have heard him express it often. He was, in fact, greatly annoyed by W's printing his letter of com-mendation, and he disliked the too frequent mention of the organs

121

of generation. But he had a much higher estimate of Whitman than of a "healthy and vigorous young mechanic" and he would never have used that tone in mentioning him.

I do not suppose you will need to show this letter to Whitman, but you may communicate its substance freely to him as something you have learned from me, but *not to be published anywhere*. There are good reasons why I should not appear as the critic of Edward Emerson, however much I may differ with him.

Yours truly
F. B. Sanborn

I read this to W., knowing no better way to give him its "substance." He listened with great attention—had me re-read certain passages. I said: "That is a valuable letter, for me carefully to hold." W.: "Yes indeed—like the cards held in reserve by the great Emperors, Kings, premiers: a power unknown, but great. I think Edward Emerson is constitutionally my enemy. Power strangely goes by alternations—now great strength, now great weakness: first Oliver Cromwell, then Richard—an ass! First Emerson *père*, then Edward and Ellen. It only goes to say again what I said to you more fully a couple of weeks ago. Now do you still persist in your notion of writing to Edward Emerson?" And to my yes, "What?" And to my explanation what, "Let me predict, then, that it will be of no avail. Edward Emerson is a determined liar—determined. Those children—Edward, Ellen—are a bad lot—bad. Two successive generations of a family are rarely alike—of equal power, nobility. He will not satisfy you." I confessed, probably not, but he would answer—and be forced to give extracts from his father's journal if there were any. W., "He will invent them." I objected—"I do not think he would do it." W. then: "No—not deliberately. But invention is as much in the air of an utterance as it is in its words. Take the very paragraph there in the book—as dirty and lying a paragraph as ever was written." I remarked, "Clifford will be gratified with this letter." And W.: "Yes—he will and ought. I may be a little mad in talking of this thing, Horace, but I know, as no one of my friends know—not one—the bitterness of attack— the virus of these past years—the story of Leaves of Grass." He spoke of Sanborn's "temperate statement—a native cau- tion in him which holds him slow to confess himself and mod- erate in his tone." I said: "Well—we'll speak of him in this way then, to the critical world: 'Look you now, we admit we are extremists—Whitmaniacs—but here is a man—poised, deliberate, sane: what have you got to say of his opinion?'" W. laughed. "That is well put." And when I added—"It is as natu- ral for Sanborn to be that as for others to be radical, and he is just as firm in that as others in their Radicalism." He ex- claimed—"That hits the nail on the head! I feel that to be true!" Likewise, when I held—"This letter of Sanborn's is just for Emerson's sake rather than yours" he at first looked in- credulous—then said: "Yes—I see: it never occurred to me to look at it that way before, but now you point the way, I allow it to the full. But then," he added—"for my sake too—for all our sakes!"

Saturday, November 9, 1889

7.55 P.M. W. had a book in his hands as I came in (bedroom, as usual)—laying it down and remarking: "I am at Fields' book again, you see." I said: "I thought you were done with it?" And he then: "Well—I pick it up again and again. I have been reading about Hawthorne tonight. What a devil of a Copper- head he was! I always more or less despise the Copperheads, irrespective of who they are, their fame—what-not: but aside from that, all my tendencies about Hawthorne are towards him—even affectionate, I may say—for his work, what he represented. I never saw him—no. My impression of Julian as I met him here at the dinner was a good one—very good." Had never read Lathrop's "Study of Hawthorne"—though "might like to." I quoted a paragraph about Williamson's Hawthorne collection from the "Lounger" in The Critic this week. "That's the way the fellows do—get their kink—work it. I know a lawyer in New York, MacKee is his name—who is after relics of John Howard Payne—has been collecting and collecting for about 30 years. So, you see, one man has this, one the other, notion—person—to attend to—attends to it—and the matter is done." "I have enjoyed the book immensely—have repeatedly gone back to it. I like the way in which Fields put it together—the letters, for instance—put in there entire—just as I would have desired." And when I spoke of Fields' modesty: "Yes, that too. There's no doubt Fields is one of the scarce good and true men—Emerson, Frank Sanborn, Jim Fields—these, anyway—and others I cannot remember now—a sterling and modest man."

Had he had new thoughts of the Sanborn letter today? "No new thoughts—but some thoughts. I wrote of it in my letter to Doctor—that you had such a letter—that it was not to be publicated, at least now—that you would undoubtedly talk with him about it some of these days."

Apropos of Williamson's Hawthorne collection I said: "He would much like some Whitman manuscript—wrote me once that he would pay a good price for it." W. thereupon: "Well—why should we not give him a bundle—a good bundle,—without pay? I would be willing—in fact, would be anxious—to give it him—give it anybody who had staked on us—stood up for us especially when putting up the actual cash, as he has done."

I received today a letter from Mrs. O'Connor. I read it to W.

South Weymouth, Mass.
Nov. 8, 1889.

Care Mrs. E. T. Joy.
My dear Mr. Traubel,

Your kind letter of a month ago, Oct. 6, came duly, & I have only waited to answer it till I should know what to say in regard to the stopping to see Walt on my return. I was on the point of asking you if on the whole it would be more a pain or a pleasure to him in case I could arrange it, when yours came. Of course it involved my staying over night some where, as I could not return from Camden & get back so as to reach Washington before night, & I could *not* return to the lonely & shut up house alone at night. The staying over involved a Hotel bill unless I could stay with a friend, & I think now that I have been able to arrange it. It is humiliating to have to confess that the question of a few dollars could stand between one & a dear friend. I think sometimes that it is a disgrace & crime to be poor! I am very sure that William never foresaw where his lavish generosity would land me, & in his last years, after he was himself disabled he could hardly refuse any one in need. I also feel sure that he also felt that my home would be with my dear sister Mrs. Channing, now of Cal. where William spent some six months; but they are now in such pecuniary trouble that I could not add to their burdens.

As I said, however, I think I have arranged it. My plan is to leave here on Monday next, the 11th & go by Fall River, & stop over in Phila with a friend.

From there I will send you a line;—or is it not necessary;—to say when I will go Camden. I wish you would send me a line *as soon as you get this*, & tell me what cars to take, & how to reach Walt's house. I am wholly deficient in locality, & always go the wrong way unless I have plain directions. My dear Jeannie used to say that when I should be an old lady she should never let me go out alone.

I don't know who will be my guardian now!

I have not been very well, my head, which seems to be the great trouble, giving out at all times, in the most unexpected fashion. I have lingered long, & must own that some cowardice has mingled in my feeling; the dread of returning to that lonely house, that has been shut up since I left. I have not heard from Mr. Kimball, he was to send if he had any good news in the way of getting a position for me.

Give my dear love to Walt, & be sure that I am ever truly and cordially yours—

Ellen M. O'Connor

W.: "Then I am to see her probably in a very few days! Good! Yes—I think it may have—is likely to have—the good effect both ways—to her, to me." I wrote to her at once this evening instructing her how to get to W.'s.

W. said: "The worst piece of news in the papers today to get over is the defeat of the Tilden will.

[Samuel Jones Tilden, a distinguished American statesman, died in New York in 1886. The bulk of his fortune, which consisted of several million dollars, was bequeathed to trustees to be used for establishing a great public library in New York City, but his will was contested successfully. An heir relinquished her share of the estate and this was the nucleus of the Tilden Foundation of the New York Public Library.]

"It comes of the damned pettifogging of lawyers. What we need is something of the definiteness of Baconian principles. It was Bacon who, as the story goes, sitting in a contested case, cried out"—W.'s whole manner vigorous—head thrown back—finger raised admonitorially—voice strong—"cried out to the big wigs, who were fighting like fury over unimportant technicalities, statutes—'Gentlemen, Gentlemen: we are not here, that this statute or that statute should be proven true, but that justice may be done!' Our lawyers never seem to think that—do not seek the manifest integrity of a case, but the trifling lapses—the weak points—the little indefinite-nesses here and there that are bound to occur, whatever the caution: for no more is a law perfect than lawyers—than any being, fact, that ever existed: Socrates, Aristides—the best land, nation, age, person, theory—nothing but what ever le-gitimately has weak and failing purposes—much more failing purposes if pecked at—turned over—inspected for such! The great lawyer is the sun—shining to illuminate, not to distract. I sometimes think that this is the dark and damned spot of our national character: pettiness, prettiness, quibbling, fin-ery. We have everything—we are big, heroic, grand, smart—

oh! as for smartness, *damned* smart! too damned smart: but
after our heroism, *this*. And what will come of it? that is the
question." I called it "Agnes-Repplierism," and he: "Yes! a
good word! It often occurs to me, escaping all other dangers,
will not this finally engulf us? We seem afraid of the natural
forces. John Burroughs puts it well, says, if the American is
only dry, he is not content to take a drink of pure cold water,
but must put sugar into it, or a flavor. To me, these things—
the things of which these are the type—are the prominent
dangers in the future of our America. The Greek character
was not without them—without smartness, for one thing but
then the Greeks had something more—something beyond
that—which was its master, a sublime surpassing idealism—
its saving quality—possessing the whole race— giving it its
immortality." He discussed this in the most earnest way.
"Even in the French," he continued, "with its finesse, dress,
ribbons, delicacy, persiflage, is, at the spine, strong, pure,
whole-serious: indeed, I do not know but it can be said of all
the European nations, that they possess this final reserve
force, fund, on which to draw. Our America has her many
serious problems." And he said again: "If anything were wanting to make Bacon's immortality sure, I think his definiteness,
rare justice, would be that straw. Our big-wigs seem never to
wake up to the truth that the law should render justice—justice always—justice alone. What case under heaven but in
the hands of a cute lawyer may not evidence white black and
black white. But that is not justice—not America—cannot secure our future. The damnedest, pettiest technicality outweighs the most palpable facts. In this case, there's not a man
in America who does not know what Tilden wished done with
his money—not one: yet here are the big-wigs—the medieval
quibblers—who do their utmost to confuse the issue—defeat
the noble purpose—out of the lowest instincts of their craft.
I could not tell from the papers this morning if this ends the
matter, but it is lamentable for us all." And once more: "After

America's grandeur, promise, breadth—then this drop of poison."

I asked him if he had yet prepared me the religious statement for my New England Magazine paper. "No—but I will: I will put together a budget of opinions: then you can quote what you elect from 'em! In the meantime whack away—scrawl notes on all the odd bits of paper you come across—they'll all find a place when the time for construction arrives."

Alluding to the "Tilden pettifoggers" again: "They are like our romancers—you remember what I said the other night about Bret Harte—men of that stamp: how they take up a single phase of our life—lay such stress on it that it would be supposed all was concentrated there—there was no other life—when in reality this is but a drop in the sea."

Sunday, November 10, 1889

Did not see W. today. Out of town. But he got his trip out of doors—the day exceedingly beautiful and mild.

Monday, November 11, 1889

5.15 P.M. W. sitting in twilight. Had just finished dinner. Greeted me with his wonted cordiality. I said: "Having a quiet time all by yourself?" And he responding: "Yes—I always do. There is no other way about it. What a glum sort of a day, too! I have been sitting here looking at the clouded, misty, sky for a long time." Talked then very freely of various matters till nearly 6. I alluded to the sermon from Clifford last evening on the Sunday question and C.'s quotation of Taine's satirical picture of a London Sunday. W. affirmed: "I can see it—see it all. I was out in my chair yesterday—Warrie took me and we went up towards the city hall. Generally, on weekdays, there are boys playing base ball—a fine air of activity, life, but yesterday everything was glum—neither boy nor ball

to be seen. I thought then—told Warrie, too—how much better it would be for the boys to be in the place—how much
better the play, the open air, the beautiful sky, the active
movement, than restriction, Sabbathism." As to his own trip:
"I enjoyed the fine day beyond the measure of telling—oh!
far! It did me a great good."

I had met Dr. Reeder, who broached W. W.—I thereupon
explaining to him W.'s philosophy of the body, Reeder instinc-
tively declaring: "Every doctor will affirm that—every one."
W. said: "It is so, too: the real doctor, the genuine scientist—
he is my man—he every time. He will say to all of Leaves of
Grass 'Aye'—and then 'Aye' again. But the followers of the
colleges, the churches, the schools, the tradition—these will
never know." And to the general position of science now—
Huxley's 'working hypothesis' for instance—"It is the super-
best issue out of time: I know no higher gospel." As to
Reeder's finding even his Hicksite Quakerism bigoted,
squeezing him practically out of meeting, etc. W. said: "The
invariable, inevitable tendency—however liberal the organization, finally restrictions, limitation, revolution." Of L. of G.
again: "Leaves of Grass is *evolution*—evolution in its most
varied, freest, largest sense." Referred here once more to
Bucke: "He has the best combination—physio-spiritual combination—I know, using institutions as he finds them today,
yet ready for anything that may turn up."

A copy of The Boston Herald had come to me in his care,
containing a notice of the birthday book, evidently written by
Baxter. W. said: "We have some of our best friends in Boston—friends of thorough-going reliability—Baxter, Kennedy,
Garland. And by the way, I came across a poem of Garland's
today—extracted from the Youth's Companion—very pretty,
nice—I enjoyed it—I want you to read it." Kept The Herald
to read.

W. had a letter from Mrs. O'Connor today. "She goes over
mostly the same ground as in your letter. Says she fears to go

into the lonely house alone, at night, with all its cluster of sweet memories—sad. She promises to send me word of her coming—will probably be here in a day or two."

The cashier of the bank brought me a catalogue of rare books today—one book L. of G., edition 1871, marked at $8.50. W. said: "I can see how it occurs—most of that edition went abroad—two-thirds of it anyhow. I would get them 100 at a time. Dillingham at that time sold for me in New York and I want to say for him that he was the only one of the publishers there who did not gouge me. All his actions towards me were of a manly character, he was straightforward, honest, made genuine returns. I have always respected him. At that time, 20 years ago nearly, he was still a young man." "But," continued W., "except as curios, these old editions are by no means as good as the new. The '71 edition was nice, I know, but the Boston book is so full of changes, so liberally interspersed with additions, it should not be given up for any old one. I consider this pocket edition—with 'A Backward Glance' and 'Sands at Seventy,' the cream of all—if I may be allowed to use that word." Then he told me of a new project— of "a new edition of Leaves of Grass—much like the pocket edition, yet without the flap, and bound plainly in cloth." He is still "a little mad at Ferguson," he said laughingly, so is not certain if he will not have Sherman print for him. "Still I am not mad at him only, but fond of him too—and my sneaking notion is, to go there again." Until he decided, I should do nothing in the matter. I asked if he thought a popular edition of L. of G. would go. "I do not know. I feel sure, however, that if a hustler got hold of Leaves of Grass the book would make the fur fly in many places it don't touch at all. And Dave is not a hustler—I know that well enough." But "I am fully determined upon getting out a small edition—say of two hundred; no, 3—3 is better—for my own use." As to the pocket edition: "I stick to my liking. I had it in my earliest years—that to put a book in your pocket and off to the seashore or the forest—that is an ideal pleasure. I was on the point of getting out a pocket edition of Leaves of Grass many years ago. A woman—and a very cute one, too—objected. There's not one in ten—one in a hundred—wants it so. People as a rule like to open books on center tables, in parlors, and so on and so on. I took entirely too much notice of it at the time—let the matter slide then—now return to it."

Asked me if I could tell him anything about George Chainey—"Where is he now? what doing?" Adding descriptively—what I well knew: "Chainey proved a good friend of Leaves of Grass. He was there in Boston for awhile: ran the gauntlet of the faiths—all of 'em—was orthodox—Ingersollian—everything by turns. At the last I heard was a howling spiritualist. I have been wondering if he has taken the full leap back yet? I expect to hear of him back in orthodoxy. He was a wonderfully fluent man—had something of William O'Connor's fluency—something of his very figure, too. I have met him—was favorably impressed indeed."

Remarked: "I have just sent up to Tom some scraps, debris, quite a bundle for his Philadelphia lawyer-friend"—and noticing my look of not knowing: "Oh! you don't know about it. Tom was here yesterday, with Mrs. Harned—a glad visit, to me, it was, too! He asked about it then—just after Mr. Corning and his daughter came in." I spoke of C.'s "soft-soap"—and W. then laughingly: "I see what you mean. And Warrie who has quite a curious nature at taking instant instinctive likes and dislikes—he takes our view—and Ed's too, for that matter. But we must not be too sure—not too sure. I remember a case in the army. Unconsciously—altogether—I too was affected by the opinion of one of the army corps that a certain member of the staff, who was truly a dandy, delicate, dressy, shirty, tie-y—all that—was *only* a dandy. But never was there a greater mistake, for we found afterwards that he was the bravest man on the staff. I know there is no rule for that—perhaps not for anything. I don't in fact think nature after all

131

works by rule—at least, by any rule we know." Alluded to Kennedy as "a good fellow to brisk us up in that Emerson matter: he is cute, instinctive, in the Boston swim, yet not of it—knowing men, means, everything related."

Tuesday, November 12, 1889

7.15 P.M. W. reading the paper. Laid it down—then talked readily. Said at once that he had been out today. "And we had a breakdown—one of the springs of the chair gave way. We had to stop in the blacksmith shop and have it fixed. The fellow hammered and fussed a great while and we had to wait. I sat down—enjoyed it. We seemed to be an object of curiosity." This led to reference to trades generally. "I sat there—learned a few new words—words of trades and they are poems to me—a word is a poem of poems! In my early years I had a great fondness for names in trade—names among carpenters, bricklayers, transportation men—always learned, always retained them. If I knew one and forgot it, I would be much worried. But as time wore on, while my curiosity remained, its direction changed somewhat. Instead of minor names—names of objects—I now hungered for names of trades themselves, occupations: so much so that Dr. Bucke now vaunts that he knows no trade or occupation that is not in some way mentioned in Leaves of Grass—though I do—many of them. But Bucke declares he has tried to detect one, but never found it." Of course, it was this which had led to what so many of W.'s critics called his cataloguing. "But I am not in the least disturbed by that. Do you know, of all the charges that have been laid at my door, this has affected me least—has not affected me at all, in fact. I have gone right on—my bent has remained my bent,—everything remained as it would have remained otherwise. In Doctor Bucke, all this—this peculiarity of mine—falls like seed on good ground— he has caught the significance of it. Bucke is a Doctor himself, a scientist, free, exuberant—and he has happily comprehended (and this is essential, the crowning requisite) the *physiological* Leaves of Grass—the Leaves of Grass nursed in these native occurrences, facts—the occupations, habits, habitats, of men." "For instance, Doctor would never stumble over the word diarrhoea, to which the Saturday Review so objected. Doctor would see it naturally falls into its place, a part of the sequence of affairs—would see it as a necessary factor—while the Review came to the word as a word—came from traditions, stock rules, and contended that poetic it could not be, was not, and no man but at his peril would dare to stake it as poetry." Talked on thus interestingly of his own practice.

On the table was a brown-grey sheet pencilled with notes of Aaron Burr. I asked: "So you have found the lost Burr piece?" But he shook his head: "No—I have not—that is new to me. I have for a couple of days been trying to get my hand down to the work of jotting my impressions—my childish impressions—of some of the men I met in our early New York— of Burr and Lafayette, at least. I don't know what will come of it—how well the memories will revive and my pencil stay them. But the work is begun, as you see. What will come of it is altogether in the air—is like next year's weather." I put in laughingly: "But we know there will be weather next year!" W. responding: "That's so! And perhaps the article—but what *of* the article, who can tell?"

At this instant Warrie came in, saying: "There was no mail for you at the Post Office, Mr. Whitman!" W. asking him merrily: "Oh! and are you certain you did not bring me bad luck?" Warrie retiring with a laugh and W. explaining to me: "That was a touch you did not understand—Warrie did. Last night I had him here telling me sailor-stories—stories of the big steamers. He has served on 'em—on the Adriatic, the Etruria. He was describing to me the manner of diversion—what the passengers occupied themselves with—gambling among other matters. There was a game going on one day, the sailors, working about, could see it through a window—some of them gathered there, interested—gazed through. There was a man inside losing bravely—getting rapidly mad: suddenly he spies the boys up at the window, seizes a bottle of wine, hands it up this way"—indicating—"and says, 'Here you fellows—you give me bad luck: take this—away with you—drink to my good fortune!' That was in substance what Warrie told me—only told it better than that—and that is why he laughed at my question."

Asked me to be sure to send a copy of the dinner book to Stedman. Said he had sent one to his brother Jeff. "On my trip out today, I stopped and left a copy of the leather book for Sam Grey. I wanted to give him one." And here I reminded him: "Would it not be a happy thing to give a book of some sort to Harrison Morris?" W. then: "Yes indeed—I intended to—you are right—I consider that in the translation he did us quite a decided friendship. Which shall it be—the leather book, the big book?" Would endorse one for me to deliver. "It seems sometimes as if the spirit of professions led to noble developments—the doing of positive generosities—like this in Morris." Had a letter from Bucke. "Not significant."

Thinks he still weighs his 200 lbs.: "My 200 lbs. helped break down the vehicle today—and the jolting together." Said too: "If any friends at the club tonight enquire after me, tell them I am not yet utterly broken down, though our chair was. Like the chair, a bit mended—but for how long?" I received a letter from Weir Mitchell sending 25 dollars for the fund. W. in handing me some string said: "It is genuine flax and I have trouble in getting it—Ed always had a siege. The world is bent on shoddy, in string and [everything] else!"

Wednesday, November 13, 1889

7.30 P.M. W. reading papers. Mrs. O'Connor had been over today. Mrs. Justice told me at the club last evening that Mrs.

O'C. had come on. Was staying with the Lewises, and wished to see me there. W. spoke variously of her. "William O'Connor and Nellie O'Connor occupy a large place in my memory—not in my *memory* alone, but in that larger life—my emotional, sympathetic, poetic, life—which has most importantly commanded me. And now that William is no more—now that William is gone—gone forever, from physical sight—the great, surpassing William!—all my feeling, once divided, seems to flow out to Ellen alone. I am quite surprised at it myself—at its extent. I did not suppose I could be so summoned, so moved, so appealed to. But there it is—revealed to me today if never before. She was here a long time—paid me quite a long visit—even now is not long gone. I was surprised to see how well she looked. I supposed the long trial—the wear and tear of watching, waiting would have bedraggled her—but it appears not—time has clawed her but little. That worst dragger-down of people—mental worry—she has survived. Oh! we had a long fine talk! She told me many things about the funeral—about William's death—the last days—which it was only possible to get from her, and from her lips, at that—not from notes (always insufficient, thin). It has been, I guess, 15 years since I saw her. I went back to Washington after the paralysis—stayed with them—stayed several months there. How much I owe them!—not alone for scriptural hospitality—for Oriental food and raiment—but for that other force, accretion, gift, effulgence—*soul*-force, let us call it, for want of a better word: the making of my poetic self, such as it is! Brave woman!—and cheery! She told me about Kimball's promise to get her what is called a position at Washington. He talks something about having to wait a year or two to get it! That's a hell of a note, ain't it?" And then he asked: "You are going over to see her?" W. had noted her address for me, not knowing I knew the Lewises well. When I spoke of them he inquired: "Radical, abolition, anti-theological, all that?—and Friends, besides? I love to hear it. I have always felt, what my mother often said to me, that these old folk of the grand type were made for me or I for them. I have always had a craving to be near them—to affiliate—draw of their treasures!"

Said again: "I am quite decided about the book—to have the new edition of Leaves of Grass printed. And I am decided, too, in the notion to give Ferguson another chance." W. told Warren, who happened in, to be up promptly at nine to give him his rubbing. Corning, who came in while we sat there, inquired after W.'s health—asked him if he did not feel better than a year ago—W. only responding: "I have a good nurse, good friends—I am under what they call a sort of massage treatment—Warrie rubs me every day—or twice a day—pummels me—and here I am! Perhaps I'm like the New York fellow they used to tell about, who was very sick and was told he must die. He did not take to the notion at all—exclaimed"—here W. put up his right fist and set his eyes to a mock fire, laughter almost preventing him telling the rest of the story—"exclaimed—'God damn it! I'm not going to die—I don't want to die and here now, you,' to the doctor—'You—I want you to save me—you *must* save me—you are paid for it and must do it!'" The manner in which he told this was convulsing, but he added more seriously: "Of course that's a story—will do to go along with other stories. For after all, the best attitude for man to be in is, of willingness to die—to be resigned to it." Corning subsequently asked him if he was doing much writing: "No—very little nowadays."

Hypnotism had been discussed at the Contemporary Club last night. W. read accounts in the papers—thought "special sort of agents required in hypnotic subjects"—asked curiously after the subjects last night. When I said Dr. Hammel, the tractable patient, was a minister, he exclaimed quickly—"I see: that explains it." He was not "disposed to ridicule investigation of the sort," but for his own part he was "staggered by facts rather more impressive than these." He doubted if *any* one can be hypnotized—there is a quality in some that would invite it."

Thursday, November 14, 1889

7.40 P.M. W. reading as usual. Said at once that he had been out in the chair today. "Left a card at Harned's." The dog made a terrific howl as I entered—never learns to know me. I said to W. jokingly: "I'll shoot him some night, if he don't get over that." W. at once responding: "And I'll not complain of the deed in the least! He howls a hundred times a day, at all hours. In the night too, generally about one o'clock when the rest of the world wants to keep quiet."

I had spent a part of last evening with Mrs. O'Connor at the Lewis'. Now it was her turn to say she was surprised to see W. look so well! I laughed to W. over their mutual fears that the other was a wreck—and he laughed too—saying however: "Externals cannot always be trusted. I looked wonderful well, no doubt, as she said: but you know how it is with one who meets the friend he has long desired to see—he is exhilarated—his heart hastens—his blood flows increasingly—and this explains me as she saw me. As they say in the story, man was but a lump of clay—God breathed the breath of life in him at once he was a living, palpitating, aspiring throbbing soul. And so I was breathed upon by her presence, what the sight of her recalled—the grand days—William." Out of the envelope of pictures W. gave Mrs. O'C. Mrs. Lewis had been attracted to four—the butterfly, Lear, Gutekunst phototype and the Sarony hatted picture. Could I get them for her? I inquired of W. who said he would gladly give them. Then, in speaking of the Lewises: "Of course, anything I think or say of them would be in the nature of a guess, yet I conceive of them as hospitable, but more than hospitable—a soul-hospitality." I described Mr. Lewis as a man who never rushed in with his opinion, yet came in later on, and was always given

137

weight etc. Subsequently—when I had given W. a little message received for him by letter from Mrs. Fairchild today—W., picturing her—said: "She is what you say of Mr. Lewis—rather reserved than otherwise—never obtrusive, demonstrative. I know some such persons—wonderful cute—who wait, as it were, till all the evidence is in before speaking—then speak with great effect. I know there is a danger in this—danger of having no opinions at all, or of feeling as if opinion was not worth having—certain enough. Here in my own case I go even to the extreme of hesitation, so to call it but I suppose I am saved by a native vigor, pulse, animality, that will never be betrayed. Mrs. Fairchild is, as you say, vigorous, direct but she is a little woman. Handsome, too—oh! very handsome!—not, perhaps, what you would picture her, however. Have you read Mrs. Siddons' book about actors, plays? In it she speaks of Lady Macbeth—the Lady of the plays—insists that she was not what the world conceives her—not the large, masculine, powerful woman, but probably a delicate creature, refined, beautiful, subtle. I have read that with some interest though it does not convince me at all."

I said to W.: "Nine people out of ten dislike the Morse head." But he responded: "Never mind, they'll come round to it after awhile." As to copies of the book I had sent away: "It is bread cast upon the waters—and good bread, too—and that it will have its good result I do not doubt." I read him a piece by [Henry] George in this week's Standard denouncing the Copyright League for its compromising spirit in favoring a bill giving copyright to foreign authors who had their printing and binding done in this country. W. listened with the greatest interest to the vigorous paragraphs—then said: "I felt as I heard you read along that there was something that gibed perfectly with my own conviction—that I could say amen to it all—not only to its substance, but to the way of saying it. I suppose the retort would be, that is as much as we can get now, so let's take this step! It is not an answer, but I can see how it comes up that way to others, and leads to the result it does. The average man—even the authors, for that matter,—look at it entirely from the standpoint of the pocket—America's pocket: whereas I should say, if pockets at all are to be considered, let it be the world's pocket, not America's alone, for America now should stand for the world—should bear witness not only to her own success, but human solidarity, universal union, the largest possible circle of comradeship." And then: "But whatever the current view, it is a great fact to have a man stand as George does, unhesitatingly, uncompromisingly, for simple justice—simple freedom."

The Contemporary Club card he signed the other night for Anne Montgomerie was his first espousal of anybody for entrance to the meetings.

Friday, November 15, 1889

7.38 P.M. W. talking with Warren as I entered. Gave him injunction to come back sharply at 9. As to his mail (Warren had just been to the Post Office): "This whole week my mail has been small, and what has been has been of an unsatisfactory nature. *Autograph* letters in plenty—and these of no value except in the return stamp, which I confiscate." They have added a delivery to the mail routes in Camden, and W. is disturbed: "I suppose I will get adjusted to it, but now the mail seems to come all hours of the day." He ridiculed the idea of its necessity—especially someone's suggestion that it was done for Camden's business men. "Where are Camden's business men? Where is Camden's business?"

Has been writing some today—a new verse, and some few paragraphs about the New York Exposition of 1853. He said: "It has been a long and draggy day." At which I asked: "Haven't you been well?" "Oh yes! As well as usual,—all days are draggy, monotonous, to one penned up, confined—some

139

more so, some less—but all dreary. I envy you fellows who can go about, who have something to do—who cross the river, work, see the sunsets—free, unhemmed-in, untrammelled." I suggested his age—that he had had his own long period of activity ere this confinement of recent years. "That is true—that is to be considered—I *do* consider it. But then one's life is not always the thing it is supposed to be—has its periods and periods—dark, light, dark again—spots, errors, damned foolishnesses. Looking back over my own time—looking into the period starting with '61—'62—I have nothing to regret, nothing to wish reversed. But then, it might be asked—why is it, just when a man gets his height, his purpose, begins to live, comes the thwarting signs, the hedging-ins, the breakups, the ending? Why is it?" I mentioned that as a question that occurred to Samuel Johnson and was one of his drifts to immortality. "Yes, I can see—and Johnson was right." And there was Johnson's own work, left undone. W.— saying thereto: "Yes—wanting the crown—pursuing his game— almost upon it—light in his eyes—then the sudden dissipation! It is a vivid touch out of life—I see it as if physical phenomena, this moment before my eyes. And not of this life alone—all lives!" In all of this not complainingly—his tone one of seriousness, only.

On another line, spoke thus: "I have had a picture sent over by George Childs—a Gutekunst picture. It was for Mrs. Kendal, the actor. He said she was anxious to have a copy— wished me to sign it—which I did." She had been reported present at the Ethical meeting last Sunday. "She must be radical," I said, telling this to W. "Yes—and I was about to ask what you know about her—I have a great curiosity to have somebody tell me. Sometimes the conviction is quite strong that the women on the stage are after all way above the men. I say this of malice prepense: I have seen a good deal of both. There was Macready among the men—a great figure in his day—famous—I could never enter into the enthusiasm over

140

him—never. He never seemed to address himself to me. And so with many of the men. But I have seen Ristori in her prime—on her first coming—and then in Washington, again, and always with the same admiration. And Ellen Terry—from all I can hear far exceeds Irving. Irving himself I do not think would appeal to me. He is polished, intellectual—yet could never arouse me. I demand that my whole emotional nature be powerfully stirred. I can believe Salvini to be the greatest of all. There is a testimony to that effect which carries conviction along. I have seen Janauschek and liked her—saw her in Maria Stuart—she took the part of Mary—but the other woman, who was the Elizabeth, pleased me quite as well. I always felt myself attracted to Mary Wainwright—she didn't stir me like the devil, but she stirred me." And he drifted along in his desultory reminiscence and criticism. "How could the little critics say more than they do of Salvini? When an unusual power appears, they are baffled utterly." The great Kean? "On no! I never saw him—but in my early years, in Brooklyn, when I loafed a good part of my spare time on the ferryboats, I learned about him. It was in a peculiar way. The companies hired a sort of major-domo to take charge of the cabins—the ladies' cabin, chiefly. The fellow I have in mind was odd, fanciful, fat, took violent likes and dislikes—gossippy—would sit down by the hour and chat, narrate. I was luckily among his likes. A Dickensey character—told me many interesting things. It appears he had once been head-dresser for Kean. One of Kean's fancies—he was a man of fancies—was his fancy for this man. The man told me he got in the habit, after Kean was dressed, of leaving the room in charge of his assistant and slipping into the pit, to see and hear—how this became almost necessary to him. He thought Kean the greatest actor that ever was—a man of tremendous flashes." W. remarked again: "It is singular, in connection with Forrest—actor as he was—that he has waited till future generations to be know for what he was." And "What could Willie

Winter know of the real big fellows?—he, the most miserable little whelp of all!" And yet—"Winter has his place—take his company, and he fits to it." But as to *power*—"I never heard it mentioned in the same breath with him."

I referred to Sam Johnson's respect for Grant to the end—Morse's letters to me describing it—how Johnson had regarded Grant as possessed of certain solid qualities—reserve power etc.—not common in America. W. thereupon: "And Johnson was cute enough to see it, naturally. I know Grant—you remember in your book, in John Burroughs' letter—where John speaks of the prime defect of the American character—that it lacks *inertia?* He uses the word *inertia*. It is very good as so used. Now that you speak of Grant—telling me of Johnson, I realize that there was Grant's power—he had this inertia—had it in marked degree." The world often attributed Grant's successes to pertinacity rather than mental force. But W.: "That is a mistake—Grant had all the more power from his care not to show it. He had inertia, with all that it implies. I don't know if Lincoln had it, but Grant, certainly." I said: "And John seems to think you are the only man in our literature that exemplifies him." W.—"It is a high word: one would wish he were the man even if he were not!"

Saturday, November 16, 1889

8 P.M. W. in his room, reading. Spoke of Alice [Alys] Smith as having been over, and Mrs. O'Connor again. Flowers from both on the table. "Nellie is evidently having a good time in Philadelphia. Goes home Monday morning." Left with W. November Scribner's. Article therein on Goethe's home at Weimar. W. "sure it will greatly interest" him. He held the magazine stretched before him. "How fine it looks!—and the type inside, too!" Had he ever sent anything to them? "No." Would he not? "Who knows?" And then he inquired: "Can you tell me the editor's name?" And as I could not, "Well,

find it out for me" adding: "Some little piece some day may tempt me their way." Mrs. O'Connor had not said anything today about William's stories, but he was "in favor of having them put into book form." He had not given Mrs. O'C. Mrs. Lewis' pictures because she said I knew better what were wanted. Hunted and found all but the Gutekunst portraits while I was there. Gave me a copy of the Lear for Aggie, who projected having a big charcoal copy made by my father. "I might send her a number." W. said, "but she would no doubt select this one anyhow."

Little heard so far from those to whom books were sent, but W. said: "They will yet come straying in, one after another." And he remarked about the book, when I said Clifford thought a good deal of Forman's letter: "It is remarkable how men's views differ. Out of the dozen and more who have spoken to me critically of the book, no two have the same preferences. A number have spoken to me of Tom's speech—Tom himself thinks Clifford's speech the best—but the Symonds and Sarrazin letters—undoubtedly and far ahead the best things in the book—go without mention: no one appears to discover them." I remarked that the world at large knew little of Symonds himself—that in order to realize his letter, its background needed to be known. "Yes, that is true—that is an answer—I don't know but a final one. But the diction of Symonds' letter itself—isn't it superb—simple, direct, like the elementary laws?" And further: "But the grand feature of the book is its power to grow—its ever better and better aspect—and its remarkable continuity—no one man stepping in another's bailiwick."

When he learned Howells had sent me some money in Whitman fund: "The good fellow! the good fellow!" Alluded to Hilda Clifford's description of him. "The opinions are very interesting—tell her that back of their mere words is a profound metaphysical something. We will become acquainted yet. When we were out the other day in our chair up at Lee's, the stationers, near the Post Office, was a little girl. It has been years now since I saw her. In the old times I held her, dandled her. Now I said: 'Come here little girl, and kiss me' but she ran at that into the store shocked, evidently. She little knew that her shock was her shame—that here, in this, was worked out the prudery of a false society—its influence in the growing child—the kiss, the public, what-not, feared,—its natural impulse lost." As he tied up a bundle: "There's a talent in knots. Warrie has been giving me lessons: I thought I knew some—but I had no idea how many there were—the mystery of 'em: every true sailor has his deft control of the secret."

Wondered "if this is a good latitude for people to live in? such violent changes," etc. Boston, however, "is damp, raw—and the Bostonee by no means takes commensurate care of himself. The great features of the typical Bostonee are intellectuality, consumption, dyspepsia." I laughed: "Shall I quote that in the New England Magazine?" He laughed, too, saying, however, neither yes nor no. But asked, "What has become of the magazine? Have you seen its last number? A new one is out." This brought up a matter which had evidently moved him: "Over in town the other day, evening, Kennan spoke: and after he was done, a man in the audience, a preacher, got up and proposed that our government be called on to present a protest to Russia. But no—no—no. My advice would be in the words of Punch in its picture—the little word of four letters, printed as big, said as loud, as could be—d-o-n'-t! And had I been there, I should have in the moment spelled the word and so advised. We have enough ills of our own to rectify: let us stick to them. There are two sides to all these matters. I glory in Kennan's pluck, grit, brains, indeed, if occasion should ever offer, I want you to say so for me—but these things are not properly for government interference. I applaud all he has done—I say with the moral plowman: God damn it! let this earth be ploughed up and up—let it be turned—let it be given to the light of day—let us see what it has hidden—what comes, atrocities, blessings, the worst, the best—let nothing escape! But all this can best be done apart from the state. It seems to me the part of noble enterprise for a great magazine like The Century to set apart 15 or 20 thousand dollars and to say, this—whatever else—is left to be devoted to the investigation of Siberia. I know no better deed."

W. greatly attracted by reports (vague still) of revolution in Brazil, Dom Pedro's abdication, the declaration of a Republic. "Losing Dom Pedro, they're lucky if they do as well with a Republic." To Howells as to all other friends W. counselled me to say, "Walt Whitman's not yet sunk—still has his head above water." As to Percival Chubb's lecture on Walt Whitman (Chubb expected in Philadelphia in Dec.): "If you get a look at the essay you can without a doubt set him right where he is wrong about us—knowing more," etc.

W. said then: "I got the Transcript from Kennedy again today. In it there was a great display line—head line 'Daniel Dougherty's Eloquent Bosh'"—in relation to speech at opening of Catholic University—W. adding—"I was certain of the 'bosh' but about the eloquence, not so certain." Advised me to tell Howells if I wrote—"Walt Whitman is still on this earth, head-up, sorto'"—and he laughingly spelled "sorto" saying—"It is a word I often use—one of my words—a trace of dialect."

Sunday, November 17, 1889

Did not see W. today. Weather bleak, and he did not get out. But maintains good physical cheer.

Monday, November 18, 1889

7.15 P.M. Greeted me as "a stranger"—for having been absent yesterday altogether. Had laid out a copy of Leaves of Grass for Morris—pocket edition. I dipped his pen in the ink and looked over his shoulder as he transcribed it to M. "from his friend the author"—he saying—"Morris is good—he has been kind to us—and kindness is a thing we must not forget, whatever else must go." Had also laid aside pictures for Mrs. Lewis—transcribing these, also—but regretting he could not write her down "Mary or What-not"—Lewis instead of "Mrs. Enoch Lewis"—not knowing her first name, nor do I.

Warren came in and reported "no letters"—had been to the Post Office. W. expressed as usual his childlike regret. Warren putting in then—"Well, it's all right—you got a lot this morning." W. then, with a laugh: "Don't say it's 'all right' Warrie—though I admit it is well to remember the morning." But after Warren had gone out W. said to me: "While I got a good many letters, the mail was of little weight except the note from Buxton Forman. I had a note in the mail—and he sends a poem—a manuscript poem—which I have not read yet—have laid aside. You shall have it." Morris' piece on the Sarrazin Whitman in this week's American. M. brought me papers—2 for Whitman. W. said he would send these to Sarrazin and Bucke. Did not read while I waited.

He "wondered" if Mrs. O'Connor had gone home. Asked me, too, if I had seen her last evening, and learning I had, inquired and commented. Mrs. O'Connor had given me an expression of W.'s to her the other day: "You and Dr. Bucke strengthen my faith in immortality." I asked W. about it and he talked quite freely on the subject. "I don't know—it is a tinge of the leaf—a season we are going through: perhaps the truth is, we are not so sure we are sure—not any of us—it is our age, in which the tendency of belief is, not to be so damned certain we are certain." Mrs. O'C. had remarked that Burroughs' faith in immortality was by no means strong, if existing at all. W. to this: "John's temperament to that extent is the scientific: he is not so sure he is sure and as long as this is the case, he will not say he is sure. There are many men of that mind in our day—perhaps the best men. There is a name

146

by which to signify it—oh! I have forgotten it. John is naturally—or by philosophy—a heretic, though that is hardly the
word. This spirit—the not-too-damned sure spirit—is the
glory of our age—I do not know but it's also [?], but with all
its drawbacks a wonderful growth out of time—the most wonderful, I sometimes think, so far given the nature of man—a
modesty, humanity beyond hint or word." I remarked, whatever science taught of personal immortality, its revelation of
life—the whole universe (not man alone) vivified and throbbing—was great and inspiring. "It is indeed," he said, "I know
nothing that better satisfies my own feeling, conviction."

Spoke about his work in the Attorney General's office at
Washington. "I was the Attorney General's clerk there," he
said, "and did a good deal of writing. He seemed to like my
opinions, judgment. So a good part of my work was to spare
him work—to go over the correspondence,—give him the
juice, substance of affairs—avoiding all else. Stanberry was
the man—and a real noble fellow he was, too—Western—not
graceful in carriage, but with fine face—a Lincolnish sort of
man, though not Lincoln by any manner of means. He had
much to do in the Johnson trial, and the big wigs valued his
counsel highly. A quiet, unobtrusive, but ready, man—good
at rebuttal—re-rebuttal—almost loggish in some of his ways."
And digressing somewhat: "Johnson was not a foul man—I
knew all about him and I knew that. All hands now see that
the trial was a mistake—that he had done nothing impeach-
able—had done his best, according to his integrity: a real integrity, too, of his own order—an inherent integrity." And he
added: "You know, Horace, the tendency was then—and it is
a tendency that is still strengthening—towards the aggran-
dizement of Congress—of both houses—of the Senate particularly, the giving of higher and higher powers—and to curb
that, Johnson's victory was a happy lift." I had remarked that
probably some day, his department books would be curiously
examined. He only laughed.

147

Said of the "Compliment": "It is like the flower—ever unfolding and unfolding out its new beauties. A significant revelation to me as well as to others." The report of revolution in Brazil confirmed. W. asked: "What will Castelar say to it? I see he was recepted in Paris just yesterday."

Tuesday, November 19, 1889

5.40 P.M. W. in his room—which was utterly dark. Having finished his dinner, "siestaed," as he said. Asked me, "Can you see anything at all here?—my figure?" And when knowing I could, rested satisfied, and so we talked without striking a light.

Knew I was going over to the Thomas concert. "I can almost say I envy you," he remarked, "but then, I have no place for envy." Still had not read Forman's poem. "It lay quite untouched there all day." But had read Morris' article. "It interested me very much. Morris seems to aim above all to set forth Sarrazin,—to relegate Morris. And he has well done *that*—and well done the other matters, too—the paragraphs, connecting the extracts. I think I see in Morris that he is getting quite a glib pen. The time seems to come with the writer when expression is easy, flows on without break—and then he can attend to his thought and let the language take care of itself, as it will. Morris gives signs of having reached—being near—that stage." Asked me if I had delivered the book to Morris. Morris was "profoundly appreciative."

Touched upon slang. W. laughed over the word "gentleman"—said—"America knocked spots out of 'gentleman' and out of other words, too." The subject had been started by my use of the word "dive"—an oyster "dive." "I like the word," he said, "like it a great deal. How much better it is than parlor, or saloon—of all, saloon is the worst. The word saloon came into use first to my knowledge in this country fifty years or so ago through a novel, by some one celebrated in that day—probably now forgotten—a novel treating of the Salons of Paris. It was a novel of the gentleman class—the Disraeli stamp. Some critic or other said of one of Disraeli's novels, that there was not a character in it with an income of less than five thousand pounds a year. This novel was the like."

And then: "I have been making a supper of stewed oysters, stewed peaches, a mug of coffee. I like the oysters simple—simple—a delicious dish it is, under all *simple* circumstances." Gets a letter from Doctor "nearly every day, these days": "Doctor very industriously keeps me lettered—though he is not writing marvels."

I received a cordial letter from Brinton about the book today. Gave substance to W., who said: "It warms me up, to sit here and know that such men think such thoughts." Often his hand is cold when I feel it. I remarked today's warmth. He thought it was from the warm room "keeping things at a high temperature here."

Wednesday, November 20, 1889

7.15 P.M. When I entered, W.—head leaning on hands—dozing—the sight fine—the light of the gas illuminating the hair and face—I stood for several minutes, unheard then by some instinct he raised his head "Oh! it is Horace! How did you come here?—I did not hear you enter. How long have you been here?" I asked if he had slept and he answered: "No only dozed"—waving his hand along above his head—"floated along in the mist—just floated along in the mist." Tone fine—and he adding explanatorily: "You remember the expression? Have you read 'Dombey and Son'? it is there—I don't know whether with Paul or his mother. It is the death of one—Dickens, with his inexpressibly fine touch, pictures the soul—its departure—its floating off in the mist—oh! beautiful! A trick, perhaps, yet how fine!" And then: "Dickens is full of that—a delicate, sweet flavor."

149

I read him Dr. Brinton's letter, of which yesterday I only gave him the substance.

> 2041 Chestnut Street,
> Philadelphia.
> Nov. 19, 1889.

My dear Mr. Traubel:

I have received and read over with admiration the book about Walt Whitman which you have so felicitously edited. It will stand to, who can say how many generations? as a testimony to the "honor, love, respect," in which the poet was held by the men and women of his own generations; and as a refutation of those prejudiced charges against the spirit of his writings which have been levelled against them by those who could not or would not understand their deeper meaning, nor recognize their subtler beauties

Repeating my thanks and congratulations. I remain

Very cordially yours

D. G. Brinton.

He exclaimed: "How penetrating and sweet! Certainly that is so far the best, simplest, most significant word you have received. And the best point about it is, that we can feel it is representative—that the Doctor speaks for others as well as for himself." As to the little book: "I put it down as a success. First of all a writer likes to know—to carry with him the consciousness that he has pleased himself—has in a measure accomplished what he started out to do. After [being] assured on that point, then the understanding of his friends is welcome—oh! how welcome!".

He had a great bundle of mail to send off by Warren—papers to go right and left. "I make that a practice. I know no better way to help along the smaller hours of life. Some of the folks way off that way are wonderfully cute—more cute than city people. I send papers to friends and friends of my friends—often to people I have never met. I had one experience, however, which shocked me—halted me for awhile—

though" with a laugh—"I survived and recovered from it." Detailed the incident: "It was my old Alabama admirer, who came up here several years ago—was talked of in the papers. I thought after he had gone back—back into remote parts—I could do him no better kindness than by sending papers from time to time, which I did—bundle after bundle. But by and bye I got a protest from him, in substance—don't send any more papers—I don't want your papers. Just as if he shook his fist at me—or the papers—and declared: 'God damn it! I don't want your damned papers! Please hold off in the future till I signal you!'" W. laughed and added: "That staggered me for awhile. I wondered if I had not made a mistake sending any papers anywhere. But finally I realized that this was a case in which the exception proved the rule and so have continued my habit. My old friend did not cease his admiration, so far as I know. I still hear from him—sometimes in quite long letters."

Had saved me a copy of The Boston Transcript containing notice of the banquet volume. Referring to use of words, W. remarked: "In my abolition days, some of my friends were furious at my allusions to the *blacks*: as if *colored people* were nearly so definite—*colored*, which might mean red or green as well as black. It is a violence we do the use of words."

Thursday, November 21, 1889

8 P.M. W. reading papers. Was very cordial. "Tom Donaldson has just left," he said, "Tom was here for quite a while— we had a good talk. Tom is a better fellow than you think for. I consider him one of my true friends. He looked well and fat—his arm nearly recovered. Tom is *himself*: like all of us— and that is the worst you can say of him. He brought me over the money six weeks ago." "I had a note from Mrs. O'Connor today. She is in Washington again so I suppose I shall turn the stream of papers that way, as I have in the past. I know she

appreciates them—thinks they have a place with her." And he added: "I have sent both the Americans off—one to Bucke, the other to Sarrazin."

Suddenly he looked at me and laughed: "I got my poem back from Harper's Weekly," he remarked. I asked, "What poem? I knew of none." "Oh! I thought I had told you. 'The welcome to Brazil.' They returned it with a letter—very vague." I asked humorously—"It did not worry you to get it back?" "No indeed—I am used to having pieces rejected—it is no new sensation. Then besides, a man at my years and condition must not worry about anything." But what of the poem? "It was only a glimpse—a hint—a sort of handshake and hug, to show them we were here, met them in the democratic spirit, warmed to something more than mere formality. It is a trifle, put together in that sense—no other. The editor of the Weekly is John Ford." And then he added: "Tom Donaldson thinks the priests are at the bottom of the matter—that after Dom Pedro, in the order of succession, comes a daughter—unpopular—absolutely in the hands of the priest gang: that it was to avoid this daughter, this gang, that the people got rid of the whole family." And in this connection he added: "Sarrazin has the prophet-eye, he says, it is not here that the ideals of democracy will be tried, but in America, in the Australias"—though W. shook his head somewhat—"True—true: but a civilization that can produce a man like Sarrazin has not all gone out by any means."

Returned me Scribner's. "I not only read the Goethe article—read the whole magazine through. It is wonderful interesting—the print itself an enticement." Was much amused by a note brought in by Warren—written by Foster Coates, from New York—asking W. two questions (as he asked other prominent men). 1st—What was the happiest moment of his life? 2d—In what he thought happiness consisted? W. read the note aloud to me, laughing very heartily. "Poor fellow—out on such a search! I suppose he'll have to wait a long time before I tell him to find out what happiness is."

Finally got up instructions for a new edition [of]—Leaves of Grass. Intends to insert the autobiographic page out of my book—also a new advertising page, which he wrote today. Otherwise there will be no changes or additions. We will probably have the work done at Ferguson's—at least the composition. Left that in my hands. Gilchrist in for a time this evening after I left, but told me afterwards he did not stay but 5 minutes or so, W. looking so wearied. Harned's lawyer-friend, for whom W. left the "debris" as he called it, was Hampton L. Carson, of Philadelphia. W. could not remember his name, Harned informing me.

Friday, November 22, 1889

7.45 P.M. W. gave me his customary cordial greeting. Sat in his room, reading a paper. "I have had Horace Howard Furness here with me today. He had his trumpet,—we got along very well. His own speech is to me just the thing—his voice just the right pitch for my ears." And he added: "Horace is a noble fellow—a right royal man, truly among the rare characters in literature."

He handed me a postal enclosed by Kennedy in a letter received today. Sanborn had written K. on another matter, and at the foot of the postal added—"What a good volume that about Whitman!" W. thought: "That outweighs all that can be said to the detriment of the book." And as to notes of dissatisfaction heard locally: "I do not see what they are for. The book is full, noble. I don't see what more could have been said. There were speeches enough."

Gilchrist said at Harned's last evening, upon hearing that Mr. Coates had retired from the fund—that there may have been some connection between that and the poem "To the Year 1889" which had in some quarters excited criticism. W. said now, upon my questioning if there could have been the least idea there of resenting the aid of his friends: "I am not conscious that I thought at all on the matter—every man must give his own interpretation. If anybody is determined to think that, he will think it no matter what may be said to the contrary." I said my explanation of it as only of general meaning—having rather to do with the abstract view of his condition and the needs it aroused had easily been accepted by Morris long ago. W. then: "I think Morris' basic quality, soil, measure, is human kindness, generosity, sympathy. He is open to statement, open to candor and he is eligible to see right, to grow, build up—at least in on the way."

I left with him the current North American Review. He "wished to read Ingersoll and Burroughs"—articles from both therein—Ingersoll on Divorce, Burroughs on "The Corroboration of Prof. Huxley." "I see there is a new fortnightly—The Arena. Its appearance would seem to signify that the public is in for heavier matter—wants it. This"—tapping the Review, on his lap—"then The Forum—now The Arena. They have had many reviews—this or that—in England, abroad. In the early part of this century they were much for literary explication, examination." And as to Keats' sacrifice under criticism: "That is what is said of it, though it is vehemently denied too. But I have no doubt that had *some*thing to do with it. Keats' whole being seemed absorbed in what is called beauty—the sense of the beautiful—perfection of form—polish—aesthetic beauty. It was on him, on this, the criticism fell. It was vitriol. On Keats, Bryon, Kirke White, others, this scurrility, abuse, contempt, was bestowed. Byron prospered under it—indeed, I don't know but that was the greatest factor in his development. He published his first book at 19 or 20 or 21, thereabouts—Hours of Idleness—and very good ones, some, too. But it was left for the later experience to make him what he is now known to have been." I asked W. if the old reviewers had ever been more bitter in discussion than their followers in what was said of L. of G.? And he at once said: "No—I think our treatment was almost beyond precedent. No one can know it as I know it—not my nearest friends of the old days—not even William O'Connor, not even John Burroughs."

He spoke of the Mrs. Kendal interview, over which, as Harned puts it: "Walt came up to my house and drank with me a glass of champagne." "The interviewer seemed to get hold of her just as she was leaving—putting her coat on—and she was very free to confess. I have always seemed to have a good clientage among the actors—clientele—women, men—irrespectively. That abroad is at least as emphatic as that at home, the fact is one I deeply respond to."

He "wondered" at the accuracy of the mails. "I have a young man friend down in Mexico—a place called Jesus Maria—something of that ridiculous sort. I sent him a package of these photos awhile ago—sent them doubtingly: and yet here today a letter comes from him—an effusive, gushing letter—saying the pictures had arrived, intact—not a break—not a damage. Think of the distance—the facility—the integrity with which the mails are handled: even on the way to Jesus Maria—to Mexico—to the land of priests, theology!"

Saturday, November 23, 1889

7.15 P.M. W. said quickly, after our greeting (he in his room as usual reading): "I was out today, for a while—enjoyed it very much. It did not seem to me cold, but Warrie seemed to be afraid it was, and hurried me back. We went as far as the bank—went about a little—then home. I did not get out of my chair." Said he had had letters "but nothing significant"—even Dr. Bucke's letter "only cheery, not newsy."

Had read Burroughs' article in the Review. "Much to my surprise, I became interested in it—greatly interested. I think it the best thing John has lately done—the best thing of that sort he has ever done. He cuts way below the crust of the Christmas pie—cuts way into the Christian pudding down deep and deep—to the very vitals, with a penetrating blade. If it is true—if John is right, then it's all up with Christianity—then Christianity had better emigrate." Had also read the divorce articles: "Read all of them—the Cardinal's" [Gibbons']—"the Bishop's" [Potter's]—"and Ingersoll's. But it struck me none of them—not even Ingersoll—got near the heart of the matter. Divorce is not to be argued of as a thing in itself—unrelated—a flower of today. It is like the French Revolution, a result of results—the growth of soil on soil on soil on soil—layer after layer: and looking at it as that, we find it is counter to restraint—that it is the rebound against restriction—that the human critter seizes this with other modes of escape from false entanglements. We know that marriage as it is today justifies itself for today—but for the future—who shall say?" And as to Prof. Adler's proposed discussion of it in Philadelphia tomorrow: "I doubt if even he will have anything to contribute in the matter. Marriage is an affair having ways of its own—coming, going, growing—defying prophecy or statement."

Asked quizzically: "You did not bring me proof?" But I had—this reminding me. I gave the sheet to him out of my pocket. The printer had not followed his instructions, as I knew, and his laughing condemnation amused me. "Why, he has in no sense followed me out. Has he eyes? Can he read? He could not have done worse if he had set out to do everything the opposite of my instructions. Damn him! I'd say it to his face if he was here!" And where the word "enveloped" appeared as I have it rather than with W.'s "'d", and we looked it up and found W. had inadvertently placed it so on the copy, W. laughed again. "Yes—I'll be bound! If there's a mistake you make, that goes in—but the rest, they suit their own pleasure with!" Adding then: "The printers are determined to have their way whatever abides." And laying the proof aside: "I'll look over it tomorrow—perhaps accommodate myself to their ideas, as they won't to mine!"

Referred to a letter from Alys Smith at Bryn Mawr. "She is 19 or 20 or so—is not studying with reference to anything in particular—neither medicine nor anything else—simply going to school." And then of her merriness and buoyancy—continuing: "She is most Greek, I believe, of any girl in America—Greek from top to toe. That is what Sam Longfellow said of Leaves of Grass a long time ago— that it was Greek from top to toe." I wondered if Longfellow still adhered to that view—W. simply quietly repeating—"I wonder," but arguing upon my comment on Longfellow's conservative temper, "That seems to run in the blood—is hereditary. Henry was extremely cautious—as he lived along he dipped more and more in European literature—German, Italian, Scandinavian"—I put in with a laugh—"Especially Scandinavian"—W. echoing me with his own laugh and words—"Yes, especially Scandinavian!" Was H. W. Longfellow ever known to give an opinion of Leaves of Grass? "The only authentic utterance—and that about a specific piece—was about the little song, 'A Child Went Forth.' I learn from several quarters that he put a generous estimate on that—quoted it sometimes." He had told me this before, only as referring to Whittier. This I told him. "Did I? I did not mean it for him, to be sure. It was Longfellow—I know all about it." "Sometimes that piece is much talked up: I do not understand it: it is the most innocent thing I ever did. Yet while some take the Longfellow view, there are as many—in fact, many more—who take the opposite view—deny. There was one critic who quoted from Wordsworth to prove that my picture was not only not new, but was deficient—was neither rich nor strong. He brought forth certain lines of Wordworth's—conventional lines, I was going to say, but I hold that back—the subject could hardly be treated conventionally." I referred to Clifford's reading it from his pulpit—not mentioning W.'s name— and his amusement over the surprise of some people when they learned who had written it. W. then: "I think Clifford has a fine vein of irony, among his other strong qualities. That seems to be characteristic of the true-born Yankee, anyhow. It was in Emerson though I don't know but a better word might be found—ought not be found. Ingersoll has the quality, too—only in him it is extraordinary in its power—deeper—subtler—more penetrating."

Sunday, November 24, 1889

W. spent a quiet day. Went out in his chair a little after the noon hour. Enjoyed the trip—but regrets that the cold season threatens to keep him at home altogether. I did not see him today.

W. left proof of advertising page at the house for me—himself in chair.

Monday, November 25, 1889

8 P.M. W. in his room, reading. I could not get him his fresh proof of advertisement, but he did not seem disappointed.

Had a letter there from Bucke today (written Saturday) on which he had written "send to Morris." Called my attention to a passage within—this: "The article in 'American' by H. S. Morris on Sarrazin's 'Walt Whitman' was of course especially welcome. Morris seems to be a genuine reader and understander of L. of G., and has made a capital exposition of Sarrazin in a short space." W. said to me: "I like to do as I am done by—so I send this to Morris, even though it amounts to little." Notice of banquet volume in the Ledger this morning. Non-committal as to W., who remarked: "I consider Thomas McKean, who has charge of the Ledger—as not only not my friend, but one of the strongest foes of Leaves of Grass—of me. And it is through McKean the whole paper is colored." Has been writing up some poetic lines—"The Unexpress'd," but "all work is slow—this, for instance, has been a horribly dull day all through—damp, cold."

Remarked the dullness of the papers—then: "I see that Dr. Talmage is abroad—that he has been orating, sermoning, on Mars Hill"—laughing heartily. I happened to say at one moment: "It is not always the musician who catches the heart of the symphony" and he responded: "That is a fine way to say it. I can see how a man with the musicianly nature—the real inward receptivity, response—should easily measure the symphony where the technical musician, perfect in his art, should be completely foiled." A letter came from Ed Wilkins today—the first W. had received. He says he wishes to forward it to Mrs. Mapes, who is now in Kansas. Described its contents. Spoke of the world at large—its doings, etc. "I suppose nothing startling is going on—yet the countless rills run on, the rivers, the seas flow and flow—incessantly the stir, incessantly the growth, developments!" Said of Sarrazin again, apropos of Morris' paper: "He will stand a good deal of explication: he needs to be taken in large measure—there is no other way."

I read him a letter from Mrs. Charlotte E. Stevens, North Andover, Mass., cousin of Oliver Stevens—written to Clifford on receipt from him of a copy of the birthday book. Was much taken—thinks good women "anyhow, very often likely to penetrate the heart of Leaves of Grass." Rather amused to learn that Ed Lindell had taken a fancy for Clifford's speech in the book. Lindell a ferryman—not a reader of books, though a thinking man. "I should not have expected that: Clifford is right there, to be sure—but he is transcendental of the transcendental." Talking of literature W. quoted Margaret Fuller: "She says somewhere—and it is a deep, deep cut— that a country may be full of newspapers, books, and yet not have a literature. Oh! that is a deep, deep cut!—not the less deep for being to all appearance innocent and yet how true— how irrefragably buttressed!"

Tuesday, November 26, 1889

7.40 P.M. W. said to me as I entered his bedroom (he extending his hand): "I have been reading again, Coquelin's piece here on Molière and Shakespere. It is wonderful full and deep." I had brought him proof sheets, revised. He wished to hold them over till tomorrow. Handed me a copy of the London Spectator. "There is an article in there about Emma Lazarus—nearly a page—interesting. I thought there was some one of you who took a great interest in her—Mrs. Baldwin or some other."

I had received a letter from Dowden, dated the 16th. Read to W., who commented at some length. "Yes, I have no doubt all of them, especially Rudolph Schmidt, Symonds and Rolleston—will stick to it—turn it over—turn it over again—view it in all lights. It will be to them a revelation of the critter—a revelation from those who knew him in flesh and blood—the walking, talking, acting, man—as a man who drinks wine, takes a good dinner, shakes hands, among men is a man. Heretofore I have been known to them as the author of Leaves of Grass—the man himself unknown, untold of." I said it was in this line I projected my magazine article. He assented: "That is a very good determination—adhere to it—there could be no better way, no better course; give them the concrete narrative—the rest will take care of itself." I put in: "Yes—my purpose is, to start off with Symonds' passage, elevating L. of G. above any single book so far known—then to go on—here is the man, so thought of, long in our midst—what do I, as one of his intimates, make of him?" And I added: "Such matter must be put down as it is seen if at all." W. then: "That is so—that is Dr. Bucke's principle—that is the principle of all men who aim to get at life itself—yet, though the critics will admit it, they start out invariably to do the other things—to make up their estimates from an opposite—a formal, an artificial, basis. The little book will do more than anything else to bring us together—writer, friend, all, face to face." As to Dowden's letter itself: "That is Dowden—conservative—you might almost say, non-committal. In many respects Dowden may be called a duplicate of Sanborn: though the fires inside burn like the devil, like a volcano, they en-

WARREN FRITZINGER, SHOWN HERE WITH WHITMAN, WAS THE POET'S
MALE NURSE FROM OCTOBER 1889 UNTIL WHITMAN'S DEATH IN MARCH
1892. "WARRIE" WAS DEVOTED TO HIM AND WAS IN TURN THE FAVORITE
AMONG HIS NURSES.

MICKLE STREET, CAMDEN, IN 1890, SHOWING WHITMAN'S HOME AT 328—THE TWO-STORY HOUSE ON THE RIGHT. WHITMAN PURCHASED THE HOUSE IN MARCH 1884 AND DIED THERE IN MARCH 1892.

"LAST WORDS," SHOWN HERE IN WHITMAN'S HAND, IS IN A SECTION OF UNPUBLISHED POEMS IN WHITMAN'S *Leaves of Grass*, COMPREHENSIVE READER'S EDITION, EDITED BY HAROLD W. BLODGETT AND SCULLEY BRADLEY (NEW YORK: NEW YORK UNIVERSITY PRESS, 1965), P. 684. WRITTEN AT VARIOUS TIMES IN 1889, IT NEVER ACHIEVED THE FORM THE POET WANTED, SO HE NEVER PRINTED IT.

Francis Howard Williams (1844–1922), Quaker poet and drama-
tist, in whose Philadelphia home Whitman stayed as early as
1883. He wrote a number of articles on Whitman and is referred
to more than forty times in *With Walt Whitman in Camden* in the
most friendly way. He was a speaker at Whitman's seventy-
first birthday party, in Philadelphia, May 31, 1890.

deavor to keep the exterior, the facade, cool, calm, contained. They are, in a sense, personal Vesuviuses. It is the Spartan story over again—the youth who stole the fox, of which, though it gnawed at his vitals, he gave no sign." Entered into details of the story: "It was a principle with the Spartans that there was, for instance, no particular harm in stealing—in theft—though it argued inherent vice to get caught in such theft—and so, suffer anything and give no sign. Some cute critic has instituted a comparison between this and the Athenian ideal—the ideal of candor, of expression—if to weep, weep; if to laugh, laugh—men, women—and has said, here they are—you are at liberty to choose as you choose—but if you wish a frank opinion, which commends itself to me,—the principle of suppression, the principle of candor, certainly the Athenian is everyway ahead and that is Greece in a nutshell— Greek art, Greek literature, Greek philosophy—better than these, Greek life, the highest of all: if you are base, act basely,—if noble, nobly stand forth for what you are." But he added with a laugh: "Sanborn and Dowden can't fool *us*—*we* know them."

W. said then: "What a grand idea, that of your father's—the last bard! He was in—showed me a photograph of his picture—today. I am going to stop in some time to see it." Expressed his pleasure to learn Hunter was back in Camden.

And W. said further: "The key to the Greek character is this—freedom, expression, candor, passion, weeping, laughing—yet all these reined in, reason prevailing over all, reason, understanding, the last, the preserving, the balancing, the governing, quality."

Wednesday, November 27, 1889

7.55 P.M. Went down with Morris Lychenheim. W. in bathroom. We sat waiting for him and chatted. Finally heard him coming: I sprang to the doorway—and dim as the light was, he recognized me from the distance. On his arm his coat. "I will ask you to take it," he said. "I know the way well—I can get along—and then the railing here is very strong," he added. Once in the room, he thought he would put on his coat, which I held for him. I remarked his size and weight. "I am noted for neither," I said, "I could not even get on the police force." He took laughing exception: "Never mind that—I remember the doctors at Washington—and the Generals—especially the Generals—telling me that the greatest heroism, the best marching, the most enduringness, was among men who were under-size—not only under-size, but underweight. The doctors made that report to me in the hospitals: how they liked best, the fellows who would yell, indescribably growl out, moan, fuss, over their wounds—to these there seemed more hope. The quiet men—these the doctors feared for. I remember one man—he was a small man—for whom one of the doctors had serious doubt. The doctor confided to me that the man was a marvel of quiet—was too quiet—had settled into a sort of sweet resignation—though suffering undoubtedly the greatest agony, never made a sign of it—evidently facing the worst undismayed. I can sort of feel how this justifies itself—this growling, howling, yelling—this giving vent to the sensation of the moment: like the opposite of constipation, a sort of clearance, at least for the time being. Yet this is not all—we cannot set out rules: there is one man—there is a second man—a third—so on—all to go by their own impulses, unconstrained."

This led to discussion of oratory—"great public speaking," as W. called it. I thought Ingersoll's speeches undoubtedly prepared. W. said: "I do not know—I heard him several times—once in full, and his great force then seemed to be in his spontaneity—in his marvellous, indescribable bubbling up. After other men, a refreshment of the first order. There seems to come a time with the speaker when he reasons, that what he is to say the public will print, retain—so instead of

162

waiting for the impulse of the moment, he sets down before-hand and primes himself—marks his whole path out with de-liberation. But then he is done for. I remember Beecher said—said to me—that he fell into such a danger himself—realized it, however and henceforth trusted to the moment, his hearing, his own impulse to carry him through—only us-ing a few notes on a slip of paper."

On the floor was an advertisement circular which I picked up—the Magazine of Truth. I laughingly asked W.: "Are they not all magazines of truth?" W. then: "The better question would be, is there *one* of them that is? or newspaper, either?" Remarked: "The world seems agog over Tom Aldrich's new poem—'Wyndham Towers'—what have you seen of it?" I said it seemed to me an "elegant poem" from what I had read. And he: "Yes—that is just the word, 'elegant'—an elegant poem: that is Tom!" And to my remark that Aldrich however was much more likable than Stoddard, except for some of S.'s early poems, W. said: "Stoddard at the start, read Hood—modelled himself on Hood—unconsciously, perhaps, but did it—showed the influence."

I touched upon a point in one of Bucke's recent letters, that he was reading Sydney Luska[?], and with interest. W. said laughingly: "That's not the whole of it, either—he has been taking to Rider Haggard—reading him—liking"—, but W. added: "Doctor is like the lover—who sees charms in his mis-tress because he is eligible to see them—not so much *because* they are in her as because they are in him." I remarked—"I used to say sometimes, half of Shakespeare's greatness is in his reader, which startled people." W. then: "That is the same idea." Returned me the North American Review—remarking: "John's article is fine—the best he has ever written in that direction. John has that great quality shared now by the great-est men—the faculty that is the mark of the their greatness—not to be too damned sure about anything." I spoke of some I had met who questioned me about W.'s spiritual condition—

what did he believe about immortality—were not satisfied with anything less than cock-sureness. W. laughed. "Yes—I know the critter—I have met him—he is plenty; they want a categorical explanation."

W.'s phrase, "The Last Bard," describing my father's picture—had attracted me. "It is a great subject," said W., "would make a great poem—your father's little piece itself is fine—I liked it a good deal." Then discussion of the word "bard"—I saying I had noted a recent tendency to confer that word on him, as including poet, but covering more, something else. W.: "Yes, I have noticed it, too: though it hardly forced my attention. But I can see we ought to look into it—see to its subtler meanings. I suppose, even if it had not that broader meaning, it might be justified in having it at the hands of those who use it. We should look into the Century dictionary—see what is said of it there." I spoke of a man in the city—a scholar—who told me he thought the dictionary a failure. W. said: "I do not think so"—quoted Dr. Bucke's enthusiasm—yet finally said:—"I wish, however, you would inquire of your man in what way it fails. It would be well to know—we ought to know!" And then: "I sent my own word in to Whitney: not to him direct, because I do not know him—but to Dick Gilder, enclosing it on a card and asking that it be forwarded. I don't know that it'll go in, but if Whitney knows himself, it will. Presidentiad! There is no word like it in our language and it has all the authority of its root—is rooted in the soil—has parentage. To describe for instance the term in which Jefferson, Adams, Monroe, was President—what other word is there?" I asked if there were not other such words in Leaves of Grass, and he admitted there were, only this appealed to his fondness. "This not only has its origin—but is native, too, autochthonous—smacks of the soil—belongs to America." Lychenheim spoke of the word Sesame, and W.: "We have no equivalent—yet are adopting *that*. We come in all this under the protecting consideration that the

English anyhow is a composite tongue—is made up of world-contributions—the Century dictionary having 200,000 words. In this last hour or so in which we three have been talking together, I suppose 9 out of every 10 of the words we used are derived—and this applies especially with respect to America, for America may well be—must be—in her language what she is in her physiological composition—a complex of agencies from all quarters of the globe—a mosaic—the most remarkable natural combination of time."

In leaving with him a copy of Current Literature I tried to point out an extract from Ingersoll, but could not find it. W. said: "Never mind—I shall not miss it: I always keep my eyes open for Bob." Talking of persistence of the functions W. said his "sense for fragrance has lasted almost if not quite unimpaired." I told him that Foxy, a deckhand, had sent him good wishes for Thanksgiving. He exclaimed: "What! Foxy, that fat deck-hand? The good fellow!"

Said among other things about immortality that "only the tyros" were "certain" either way. Alluded to "that damnable combination that is sold in the saloons as whiskey." Gilchrist walked in the front door just as we were leaving. I had a few words with him.

Thursday, November 28, 1889

10.45 A.M. W. reading papers. Had just finished breakfast. Looked well, and said that, for him, he was well. Referred to prognostications from the weather department. "I see we are to have a blizzard or something of the sort—at least, that the weather men announce it. It makes me think of the fellow in the play: he says to some other—'I can invoke spirits from the deep'—to which the other says, 'True enough, you can invoke them—but will they come?'—and so with the blizzard: will it come?" I did not stay long. He spoke of his mail as having been "scarce."

Agnes designs a big charcoal reproduction of the Gutekunst picture by my father. W. likes the idea, and proposes to send her a picture from which my father can work.

The day cool. "I doubt if I will get out—not for the coolness alone, but because all the folks are going away—even Warrie." On the floor were several boxes of fruit—one pasteboard—one wood—the latter from New York. Wished me to partake, but I did not. Later in the day he sent proof up to my home. Added to it his Rossetti letter.

Friday, November 29, 1889

7.30 P.M. W. in his room. The night cold. He kept his fire burning at a great rate. The Current Literature he said he had read. "I found Bob. How wonderful fine it is, too! How grandly he can do that!" Adding—"I notice by the paper that he has received what is thought a great honor—has been invited to deliver the annual address before the American Bar Association on 'The Imperfections of the Modern Law' or what not."

I spoke of Chubb—and questioned: "After all, are you not best understood abroad? or accepted more widely?" To which W.: "I wonder? And if I am I am—I must stand it! Often, the rule in our offices—not the rule so much of the editors as the publishers—is delicateness—delicateness—everything sacrificed for that—everything." He had noticed the snarling of the dog on my entrance down stairs, and remarked: "There are good dogs and bad dogs, like there are good Irishmen and bad. A good Irishman is a tip-top fellow—you want no better: but a bad?—Oh! there's hell to pay!" He laughed. As to influence of whiskey in the Irish character, W. thought: "I feel the philosophy which says—whiskey—drink—whatever, is the *truth*: that what inheres to a man mainly, the drink will bring forth—reveal. This might not be a general rule, but it is a rule."

I laughed with him over the Current Literature personal (already much met with in papers) that a young man of 12 who drives him out, likes and will lecture on him after he is dead, having taken notes of all he has said. A blundering passage, probably originating in Billy Duckett. W. said: "Billy was here to see me the other day, but they would not let him in—the people downstairs." Expressed no regret that it was so. "The personal has most of all, *lie* in big, big type—flaring, flaming then underneath, in the smallest possible compass, the most diminutive proportions—the type of truth—almost not to be seen at all!"

Referring to the proof I said—"I suppose there will be no change in the autobiographic note?" He asked: "Is there anything in it which you think ought to be changed?—I should like to hear. I have a sort of remembrance that at the time it first went into type, you felt so. I don't know that there's any point at which it can be attacked, except perhaps this—about the New Orleans trip—passing over Lake Huron"—he quoted the line. "Strictly speaking, that is not true—I see now that I did not at that time cross Huron—at least, I do not think I did. Now, what is your opinion? Should I change it?"—I said—"I suppose the man after origins, would insist upon the change." W. then: "That's so—I can understand"— and with a laugh—"That's Dr. Bucke—he gets as mad as the devil over the least doubt. I very vividly recall one of his catechisms: he would ask vehemently—'You were not there? That's enough! Out with it then!' and so, out it went. I might in that way do something for him which I might not do for other reasons. Tom will come in—want an autograph, a scrap of manuscript,—*debris*—what-not—perhaps for a lawyer-friend. I may not care a damn for the man—may not know him,—yet I would do anything for Tom—do this." "Then," he added, laughing again, "I always have the printers in mind— in heart—I have been a printer myself—I know what it means to make such a correction."

167

Some one writes McKay that he has come in possession of the manuscript of "Carol Harvest." What idea could McKay give of its value? W. laughed: "How could Dave tell him—*any*-one tell him? That's a merely as-it-may-happen price, anyhow—up or down. There is a story about that manuscript. Do you remember The Galaxy? There were two brothers had it. One of them, passing through Washington after the war, asked me to write such a carol, which I did. They took it and paid me for it—paid me well—I think 50 or 60 dollars, 60 probably. Before they printed it, they entered into some arrangement with a London publisher—sold the poem to him—for more than he paid me. It was schemed to have it appear contemporaneously there and here. At a conference some of us held at that time, the question was brought up— the moral question involved. I thoroughly felt—O'Connor was very clear—that the Galaxy men were honor bound to me for a least half that sale price—but they did not think so, evidently. I was at first disposed to make a point of it, but thought differently—decided not—in the end. They wrote me very complimentarily about the piece—and they were rather nice men. It must be that manuscript which has fallen into these new hands—caught up out of the remains of the Galaxy possessions."

I had with me the Parker manuscript from the hands of Samuel Johnson. W. looked at it curiously—thought it "fine manuscript"—suggesting: "When you print it, call it 'Theodore Parker'—that alone—don't give it more. I suppose it is in the line of my piece on Hicks?" Then dwelt upon the "little currency of Parker and Hicks"—adding: "Hicks was a Carlylean man—a forceful personality. Carlyle cared nothing for theories, principles, abstractions—sent them all to hell—but a forceful personality—a flesh-and-blood personality—appealed to him—like his Frederick. To me Frederick appears only half-good: he was half bad if not more—but he was forceful—had certain powerful and impressive characteristics."

And after further inspecting the manuscript—remarking Johnson's "fullness and care"—he exclaimed: "Oh! those notes—materials!—they pile up on a man—pile him under! How much of a relief it is to come upon a work which gives out the air of unpreparedness!"

W. had laid aside for me a letter from Rolleston (written at Wiesbaden) enclosing an extract from Piccadilly emphatically and favorably reviewing the German edition of L. of G. Also put with it a letter from Caroline Sherman (Chicago) containing a printed article of hers on Edward Carpenter. She spoke of the latter as having "a great deal of interest."

Saturday, November 30, 1889

7.30 P.M. W. in room—light down—not reading. Called my attention to the Century. "Morris has a poemet there," he said. Mrs. Coates represented there, too—and he spoke of her "readiness." Then: "The Lincoln piece this month is extremely taking—at least for me: not as much in what it may say in the way of summing up, but for its documentary evidence. This is not *the* picture of the time—the teller of that story has not come yet—could not in the nature of things have come: the theme is too tremendous: we cannot measure it at so short a distance. This book itself, like other books— all, so far—Southern, Northern—is but material, soil, out of which to make up the history. The historian will come. *When,*—who knows? Not in our day, certainly."

Speaks of his "phlegm" as his "saving quality." Referred to his Brazil poem, manuscript of which was on the table—saying he had not sent it to any other publisher after the Harpers refused it. But "perhaps would."

W. looked with interest at the list of Chubb's lectures sent me by Weston. Two of these, under the general head—"Two American Literary Influences in England"—are about Thoreau and Whitman. Instead of speaking at Toynbee Hall Monday night the 18th, as proposed, I shall suggest that he give these two lectures—bring them together, if possible. W. thought my suggestion a good one.

Sunday, December 1, 1889

9.30 A.M. Stopped in for an instant only, to leave with him the Sherman and Rolleston letters. Just up and Warren gone to get him hot water for washing. Said he woke "feeling very well"—and that his "days nowadays" were of "a better cast." Promised to send proof up to the house later in the day by Warren.

I saw Adler later on (he spoke in Philadelphia today) and he asked if W. would give him a word of introduction to John Burroughs. Weather rather cold, and W. "somewhat afraid to venture out in the chair."

Monday, December 2, 1889

Detained in city—could not get to W.'s, even with proof I had secured from Ferguson.

Tuesday, December 3, 1889

7.40 P.M. W. accosted me as "the stranger," but reached forward his hand and cordially pressed mine. I had left proof for him this morning, though not seeing him. This he had looked over and enveloped for me. Had decided to issue a circular first, advertisement on one side, autobiographical note on the other—both subsequently to go in L. of G. "I had half a notion to send it over to you, but a day or two really makes no difference." And added, "I had the greatest difficulty in getting it just as I wanted it—you knowing disappointment at first. The printers all have their own ideas, too. I think some men are marked out from all eternity to be printers. That would have been Fourier's idea, and wonderful good it is, too—justified, in a sense, by all that we know of human nature, and so, the printer is born"—saying this with a laugh—"to contradict us—to have his own way—at least, sometimes. One man is born to be a printer, one a book-binder, and so on and so on. I never felt this so much as with nurses—how some have the nurse's gift. I knew one man, a Tennesseean—it was wonderful, his power to uplift, to spread cheer, light. It was good merely to be near him—yet no one could tell why. I myself, felt the contagion—the inspiration—and what of the poor sick boys, then, do you think?"

Called my attention to a copy of The Illustrated London News sent by Pearsall Smith. "See," he said, "that is the way we are done up again." I exclaiming at once, disappointed in the portrait, "Yes, *done up!*" W. thereupon laughing and say-ing: "Dr. Bucke has seen it and damns it as a failure—in which opinion I can fairly say I concur. Is it necessary for the engraver to see the critter in order to reach an effect? Yet I suppose, not." And he "wondered" if, sending the Gutekunst pictures to Paris or Berlin, "it would turn out well—adhering to the truthfulness of the original"—for the original, people said was good. "And of course," he said merrily, "I consider them wise in that." And then further: "The Lounger [in The Critic] thinks he sees something in the eye that arrests him—a peering, inquisitive, inquiring look. And I don't know but there is a point that will bear looking into." He pointed to the Symonds picture against the wall: "That, for instance—how beyond measure that seems. Doctor's there" on the mantel "I always liked extremely, but when I turn to this other, Doc-tor's must take a second place."

He said the Hall life of Lincoln "did not appeal" to him. "It has parts of which I have my doubts. There are places, occa-sions, when a man's postwar bitterness might show to advan-tage, be as it should be—asserted, made known. But I do not think that is the place. When Tom Donaldson was over last, he spoke of Herndon's Lincoln. Do you know anything about it? Tom seemed to think it contained credible stories, interesting, throwing many happy side lights. We do not seem to realize, even at this late day, how many loyal men there were at the South—were too of the most tenacious patriotism. And there was New York *halved*, too—the very rich and the very poor allied strangely together in Southern sympathies."

I saw Salvini in The Gladiator last evening. W. speaking of S.: "It is the objection of Billy Winter—and of him alone—that Salvini lacks intellectuality. But what does that signify? I suppose that nature lacks intellectuality, too, for that matter."

Developed some talk of adulteration, W. saying: "If there's anything that will destroy our American people, our States, it will be fraud—the element of fraud. It is the poison, the danger, of our civilization." Instanced the buildings going up "in Philadelphia—in Camden—rows of shells—not a genuine house among them. Mr. Smith and his wife come along—see a house—it has a neat, dainty facade—all is fair without. Here then is what we want—and they take it. But a year passes—now they see their bargain. It gapes, yawns, strains—not a joint secure. That is one side of our life—a side that makes American boasts farcical. Yet I don't know but we are now paying the penalty, that at last we will safely issue." Adding: "Kirkbride, water engineer in Brooklyn, many a time told me of it. He went abroad—reported the old Roman masonry, aqueducts, as sound, apparently, as when new. My brother George knows the fraud. He was a pipe inspector there in New York. The henchmen thought his place, salary, belonged to democratical purses, so he was removed. But finally they had to re-engage him. Everything for politics—for the principles nothing."

W. called my attention to a curious circular issued by his painter, Curtz. "Patronize him," he urged, "if you have any little jobs, take them there. I do, I have given him many. He is old, poor, sometimes ridiculed."

Wednesday, December 4, 1889

6.55 P.M. I went down with Agnes, staying about 15 minutes myself, and leaving her with him when I left. I went upstairs first and told him she was there, at which he instantly said: "Why certainly, let her come up!" So I went downstairs and had her follow me up, W. crying without waiting for her entrance, "Come right in, Aggie, you are very welcome!" And as she came near, took her hand and kissed her. Had been out today, but the weather was too cool, so they soon repaired homeward.

I was on the way to Othello. "I almost envy you," he said, "but the next best thing to going yourself, is to have a good next fellow tell you. So I rely upon a good account from you to make up for my loss." And then to Agnes—"Are you going too?" And learning not, he said, "Well—Othello is a man's piece, anyhow." Agnes demurring, but W. insisting—"It *is* a man's piece, nevertheless." Then, as if this reminded him of something: "The best thing I have heard about Herbert's picture there" pointing to the table where a photograph of it stood "is a little story Herbert brings me from London. You know about Lord Elgin—his treasures. Among them is a piece representing a horse rising out of the sea, shaking his mane, as if to throw off the water—so"—indicating—his hair flying wildly as he did so. "And someone told Herbert that he never looked at that picture, or that old, old piece of art, but that one reminded him of the other! It is a capital story. I was almost saying the story was better than the picture." And then he added to my remonstrance that the picture did not satisfy me—"I am not always sure but you fellows do Herbert injustice—at least, fail to do him justice. Certainly the London fellows like the picture. The opinions of it from England, he tells me, are high in their praise. The opinion of the man who has not seen the actual critter—seen him as you see me here—is to be considered, too. I was myself too much in-

173

clined—am yet inclined—your way. Which is perhaps the reason I am putting up this defense now. It is true Herbert was and is a good deal more conventional than we like—than we could be—than consists with an entire rapport: gave me, for instance, the Romeo curls, while certainly knowing I did not have them. Yet he and the drawing-rooms no doubt, thought I *should* have 'em if I haven't, and that was enough." I put in: "Look out! I am not always sure that you fellows do justice to Herbert!"—and he laughed heartily, then going on: "I was about to say, we ought not to be so certain of our own notions, seeing how they are crossed at their most sacred junctures. Horace Howard Furness was here the other day— he won't hear either to the Eakins picture or the bust. Yet to me it seems almost incredible that anybody can look at either and fail to see their immense power, vitality, vivification." "But then, with Herbert's as with another's work, we must apply Heine's method faithfully: What did he start out to do?—has he done *that*? If he has done *that*, then it's a bee— whatever our feeling that the aim was wrong." Then, however: "And yet my friend Arnold would say to all this: You would not talk so if you were a reader of Leaves of Grass as I am!" W. saw my sister's inquiring look and knew what it meant. "No, not Edwin Arnold, another Arnold, a friend whom I knew well."

"I have been reading 'The Merry Chanter,'" he said, before I went. "Frank Stockton's story here in The Century. It is very interesting. I very rarely read these things."

Thursday, December 5, 1889

7.45 P.M. W. at his usual spot—but not alone—Mrs. Davis sitting there conversing with him. She rose to go when I entered, but W. said: "No, sit still Mary, there are other chairs here, and that is what the chairs are for anyhow." But she withdrew. Had been reading Current Literature, now on his lap. I saw Brown today about circular. Asking me about it, W.

said: "After having delayed things as much as I could myself, now I am impatient about the least delay in others. That's human-like!"

Asked me about Othello. "I read the piece in the Press. It was in the main favorable—very favorable—but it had a bone to pick, the amount of it being, this Othello is *brutal.*" I followed with, "Yes, as an average reader would think Children of Adam brutal—naked, bare, natural, but brutal. Or think anything brutal, that impresses them direct out of nature." W. thereupon: "Yes, I could read as much between the lines. I know the signs of it well. It is the Willie Winter criticism, a thousandth time, a millionth, repeated." There were lines in the play last night in which Salvini's magnificent voice and passion forced a close resemblance to O'Connor. W. listened to my detail of this with apparently intense interest. Of the play itself he questioned me closely. "What was the Iago like?" and so on. "I have seen many Othellos—Forrest's for one. Then there was an actor named Adams [Gus—or Edwin?]—about forty years ago—who was very fine, strong. The greatest Iago of all was the elder Booth. After him nobody can play that part." Mrs. Bowers had been in yesterday's cast. W., who had known her in old theatrical days, asked me questions as to her vigor, port, voice—how all had lasted. "I saw her Emilia long ago. Emilia is not a great part. I think anyhow, if Shakespeare had any weakness, it was in his women. All his women are fashioned so: in King John, in Richard—everywhere—the product of feudalism—daintily, delicately fashioned. Yet I suppose all right, occupying a fit position—in themselves a reflex of their times, though to us, to our eyes, open to criticism."

He said afterwards: "It has been a dull day," but attaching to that a qualification in the shape of an exceedingly comical account of one of the day's incidents. "I have had a visitor from Harleigh Cemetery. We had quite a talk. He wishes to give me a lot in the Cemetery, I to write a poem on it." I called it "a curious bargain" and W. assented merrily. "I know it is, but I promised to consider it favorably. So you folks had better be prepared now for the worst!" I inquired, "Haven't you a lot at West Laurel Hill?" "Very likely. I am very careless of my possessions. I have a farm somewhere which I have never seen—and lots, the Lord knows where. A more possessing man, you see, than you thought I was!"

I read him a letter from Blake, received today, acknowledging the birthday book, and going on in this strain about an old promise and his remorse.

21 Laflin St.
Chicago, Ill.
Dec. 3 1889.

My dear Traubel,

I must thank you warmly and gratefully though rather tardily, for your book, the Whitman testimonial. It is very good. Your work in it is excellent collecting and editing and warm earnest writing. I am displeased with myself for not having my name in that company as you kindly gave me ample opportunity to do. The fact is the subject was so august to my mind that I never got courage or time to sit down to it. If I had supposed I could lift myself into that company by such a shabby little note as some of them sent, I would have done much better than many of them I assure you.

Now about my obligation on November Boughs, I despair of doing what I wish to do. But an idea has occurred to me. I like once a year, when I can, to give my people a good thorough dose of some noble works. Last year I took the Kalwala [Kalewala?] and gave three lectures in one week, 2 hours long each. Now I have bethought me of doing so this year with Whitman, studying him slowly all winter and then in May giving three or four long critical sympathetic lectures. I get 100 people to listen. Now if shortly I send you the money—$6.00, I believe—for Whitman's entire works and then give those lectures, will you not call it square on November Boughs?

Heartily yours,
J. V. Blake.

Grateful remembrance and homage to Whitman.

W. was considerably taken with the note and thought it "a good exchange—one we ought to rejoice in." Adding that he "could well see" that Blake's work would again be, as it had been, "solid and colorful—we might say authoritative."

As to someone's taunt that in a poetical compendium W. W.'s portrait had been conspicuously omitted he only said: "It's not the first time, Horace, I have been left out—nor likely to be the last! Leaves of Grass and I have had a great many leavings-out in our day."

Friday, December 6, 1889

W. went to Harned's to tea. The first such outing since June '88. I had to hurry to Philadelphia—to Salvini—so did not see him. Professor Cope there at Harned's—Cope lecturing later in the evening at Unity Church on evolution. Got W. some few sheets of circular.

Saturday, December 7, 1889

7.45 P.M. W. in his room reading a volume of Stedman's cyclopedia which he laid down. I had in my hands a package of his circulars, from Ferguson. "What's that?" he asked. And on my rendering over, said: "It looks well—and on good paper, too!"—so was quite satisfied.

"I was out to supper last night—evening—" he said, "up to Tom's. Tom had there Mr. Corning and his daughter, Professor Cope, Frank and me—and of course Mrs. Harned. After the meal was over, all the rest of them went off together to discuss the gay and festive subject of the descent of man—of which I doubt if anybody knows anything at all: but not any of that for *me*, you can be sure. I was in New York some years ago, attended a meeting of the Liberal Club there. It was at the time of the blue glass craze and they were discussing blue glass. Some of them wished to hear from me on the subject

177

and I refused by saying that I did not wish to add to the misinformation on the subject." In today's papers were notes of McCosh's debate with Griggs on Presbyterian doctrines. W. referred to it heartily: "I hope they become mutually informed"—and adding, "There was a conference of which some word [was] in the papers the other day, adopting a resolution in connection with the damnation of little babies in their little-babyhood. How rich all that!—making nuts for Bob to crack—and he'll crack 'em!"

"Professor Cope appears to be a lively, interesting man," W. said further. "Do you know much about William Kingdon Clifford, the English scientist? He is said to have been a man brimming over with human kindliness—would go to parties, dance, joke, prove himself a generous, expansive man. But that consumption! He tried to fight it off—went to Italy—but it was of no avail. It was an hereditary case." Referred again to his enjoyment of last evening. "And coming home, the fine transparent moon! I stopped a while to look at it—and the whole air so sweet and mild. I doubt if the Mediterranean—the north shore—the south—can show a better. And how is it tonight?—just as mild? All last night—all today—we seem possessed of a spirit of peace—of purity." And then he told me he had been out today. "I went along, in a carriage, to Harleigh Cemetery. Mr. Wood, the superintendant, stopped here for me, then we went up to Tom's—took Tom and Mrs. Harned with us—all went out together, were gone about an hour and a half. I gained some quite new views of the country. Tom and Mrs. Harned and I sat inside—the rest out. They said nothing to me about a lot, nor did I broach the subject."

"I see the papers are full of the death of Jefferson Davis"—which expression [his] led to some discussion. I set up a mild defense of Davis, W. then: "I don't know—I don't see it that way. I noticed in one of the papers this morning an expression of admiration for the old man's inflexibility, which I suppose has a sort of nobility—admirability—in itself. But Davis was absolutely without lubricity. Was like a general, having made a mistake, with time for retrieval—but was too proud to unbend, to acknowledge his mistake. If you grant that, then goodby science—to the devil with progress! The top-most glory of science, our science, today—is its spirit of tolerance—its broad human spirit of acceptance—its admission equally of every view—making dogma of none. Davis was of a damned bad type—of the type which, liking cabbage (to give a homely instance) or onions, would damn anybody who does not. But that is not modern—that is not up to us—we have reached beyond and beyond. The South has had some of the best samples and some of the meanest. I have seen Davis often—we measured him long ago. It would not be well to have an America of such men. He was a venerable looking man—a little like our carpenter over here at the corner, do you know him? Slender and tall. I saw in the papers that he was *tall and straight*. He was tall—but *straight* I doubt—was rather round-shouldered as I knew him."

Adler had asked me last Sunday for a note from W. introducing him to Burroughs. W. said: "I will gladly give you such a letter for the Professor. Tell him so." I had word from Chubb this morning that *he* had a letter to W. from Edward Carpenter. W. remarked, "It was not necessary." We talked over Salvini's Gladiator, which I saw last night. I detailed the story to W., who then went over the sketch of Bird's Gladiator, saying at the end: "The plot turns on such points, small points, as I think them." And then—"Salvini must have given you a glorious performance last night."

Turning again to Jefferson Davis—"No, he is not our man. There was Carlyle: there was something genuine in Carlyle— we always feel that he stood for something—if not our something, still something." I left with him a copy of the New Ideal in which there was a review of the banquet book. He returned me Current Literature—"which I have taken up again and again." Gave me also a copy of the Photographic Journal

179

containing a piece on the Gutekunst portrait—a picture of bathers there reproduced had "struck" him "favorably."

Warren got off a good thing tonight. He does not much like Corning—therefore said: "It's all very nice in them Unitarians—but their Unitarity ends with the church: outside the church they're anything you choose!"

Sunday, December 8, 1889

Not in Camden today. But learned from W. that he did not get out, the day being slightly inclement. Read his Press, "the books, what-not—took things easily and dully, as usual such days." Getting out or not, he seems much impressed with murky atmospheric influences.

Monday, December 9, 1889

7.15 P.M. W. reading Stedman's big cyclopedia. After he had shaken hands with me, he said: "The McClure syndicate has taken my Brazil piece—may use it as a little Christmas bit." He had finally decided to send it there, overcoming his inclination to make no use of it at all. He spoke of it as "the Harper rejected poem." Asked me of the night. "And is it true the stars are out? I could not have believed the shift possible. I have spent a dull day. No—not sick—but sluggish, dull." Said he had sent off nearly all the circulars I had brought Saturday. Was not able to get the rest today. Shall tomorrow.

Gave me back the copy of The New Ideal: advised sending it to Bucke. "Oh yes! I have read *your* piece—every word of it—you may be sure of that. Doctor would be interested: he has a big net—puts forth his net into many seas. He reads copiously—has a maw—oh! what a maw! Gets into all roads and by-roads."

Reference in this morning's Press to the popular and artistic disappointment at Millet's "Angelus," now on exhibition in

New York. W. said: "I am not surprised." And then spoke of Col. Shaw's collection, as he often had done before. He said of Shaw himself: "He has a home full of treasures: Japanese ware—laces—decorations—the most incredible mass—the finest, rarest. Shaw is a good specimen combination of the Bostonee and the travelled man. I don't know that he has any deep artistic, aesthetic appreciation of the things he has collected there—doubt very much if he has. The Angelus was like the Sower—there were several versions of it. Col. Shaw has what is called the first version of the Sower: I liked it profoundly—was much more deeply moved by it than by the later versions. There was in it what, for the want of a better word, I should call a *wild fury*. That was a great day for me at Shaw's: I went with quite a party—encouraged the others away, so that I might be alone—and *was* alone there, gazing, gazing, thinking, for an hour—for several hours."

Morris informed me today that he had been written to by someone from Canada who had seen his article in The American, asking for advice as to the translation of the Sarrazin book entire. W. said: "Let him do it—it is a big mouthful to chew. To ask a man to translate such a book is to say to him what was said to the man in the Roman excavation who had unearthed—and broken in unearthing—an antique statue: 'Having broken it, I shall expect you to restore it as good as new.' That is a big statue to restore, after all the breaks, tumbles, of translation! But of course it is public property—he must do as he chooses with it." As to such a translation making the publication of ours unnecessary—"Not necessarily—we may feel that there are reasons and reasons!" Robert Louis Stevenson said in his sketch "The Lantern Bearers"— "—or he would not be average. It was Whitman who stamped a kind of Birmingham sacredness upon the latter phrase; but Whitman knew very well, and showed very nobly, that the average man was full of joys, and full of a poetry of his own." I quoted this to W. (having first read it today)—whereupon

181

he said: "Stevenson commenced by being, as I understand it, overwhelmed by Leaves of Grass. Oh! there was no word for it, it was so great! Then a year passed—then another year— then another—and now he got the suspicion that he had better be more cautious, had better not commit himself too far in that direction—had better, in fact, recall some of his gush—and this he did—writing a vile and silly essay—which was published in the book, you know. Then again time passed—and with passing time passing views—and this time a return to the original applause. He questioned himself if after all he was not right in his first instincts. But he did not withdraw the piece—evidently feeling,—well, that was what I felt at the time I wrote it, so let it go as part of the record. There was a book published some years ago called 'The Night Side of Nature'—I have often thought, if there was not a night side of human character, too—of literature—of personality— a sort of phantasmagoric *delirium tremens*." I had used the word night-marey as describing "The Lantern Bearers" and W. exclaimed—"Good! it is an apt word!" Again when I spoke of Stevenson as "of Hawthornesque tendencies, without Hawthorne's body," he assented: "That is profoundly true. In Stevenson it is opium—I know the sign of it well—the opium nature." And then back after a pause: "Mrs. Stevenson has been here to see me—I like her much." He thought despite "the morbid delirium of his nature"—"Stevenson has his audience—I don't know but a large one. Scribner's gives him a great welcome—an abounding welcome, and he is paid well, without a doubt." He desired that I read the Whitman essay spoken of (I had not so far). "I have the book here—within hands-reach, no doubt—and I'll find it, lay it aside, for you."

I picked up from the floor a Mss. in pencil of an early draft of the Exposition (Paris) poem. He said I should "put it in my pocket" if it was of interest— "though how can it be?" Had further to say: "Today I found the Forman [?] poem at last— it turned up out of the mass and ruin of things here"—and advised me to "see what could be made of it."

Tuesday, December 10, 1889

7.40 P.M. W. reading again in Stedman's book—"a perpetual resource" he calls it. Room very warm and he noted it. I had scarcely entered and been greeted (passing over to him the bundle of advertising circulars, now all here from Ferguson's) before he said: "Here," offering me a cup from the table—"Here is some cider. I want you to drink it with me— it tastes very genuine—is very much apple-y." And on my protestation of having just come from supper—"Oh! this will do you good even if you have!"—and then passing me a plate of cakes, insisting that these would "help the cider down." This led to talk of odors, in general. He instanced Schiller and his penchant for rotten apples. "That story," he said, "has a long—a very long—tale." Then of "the wonder—almost the majesty, of odor." His own sensibility to odor had always been great.

The personal quality in literature discussed. I alluded to Mrs. [Annie Adams?] Fields' Scribner paper on Leigh Hunt, and he expressed a desire to read it. "The freshness, attractiveness, of biography is perennial." I said: "That confirms to me Leaves of Grass"—and he then—"It is good doctrine— and yet dangerous, too: though I do not know that I should say that, having myself exampled it in the freest way. But there is Lockhart's Scott—it has an endless charm—I come back to it again and again. Scott was a great talker—almost garrulous—yet a talker in the sense with which talk delights most the man who hears." I referred to poems in magazines: "I doubt," I said, "if a flaw can be pointed out in them—in rhythm, rhyme, syntax, everything, they are absolutely correct in all modes of art—" W. finished for me—"And yet they do not move you? That is what you were going to say?" And when I added—"Tom Paine—never elegant or correct according to the schools, today is throbbing and life-giving." W. then: "True to the bone! And what better illustrates the case than letters? Subject to all the defects, yet full of heart and movement. Warrie sometimes brings me his letters—letters from sailors—stumbling, tumbling: yet full to the full of expression and force."

Had been out today. "I spent a fine hour and a half about in the chair." He gave me a copy of Book News: notice of the dinner book therein. Called my attention to some of the illustrations. "They are exceedingly fine," he said, "they reveal great progress"—adding his faith in newspaper illustration "ultimately"—instancing— "The Sunday Times had the best samples of that I have so far seen."

Expressed pleasure to have Hunter come to see him— "spend several hours here—take a meal—his ease." Also so spoke of Brinton. He is working up his new poem: "The Endless Catalogue Divine"—about 30 lines or so as standing now. I read him Mrs. Baldwin's letter containing an extract from The Boston Advertiser (received today). He much pleased with her comments thereon and amused at the exception to the "oblong" shape of Miss Gould's book. "Of course—they could not let it go without *some* dissent!"

Wednesday, December 11, 1889

7.45 P.M. W. again reading the Stedman book. I left with him the Scribner's containing Stevenson's "The Lantern-Bearers." As to Stevenson's "Birmingham Sacredness," W. was "not sure" that he "at first look" touched near its meaning. Asked me about the Contemporary Club meeting last night. "Were you informed on that Eastern question?" And when I said—"No, I gained very little indeed"—he went on—"I thought not—I read what was in the Press there this morning, and it seemed entirely empty. I have long wished to come upon somebody who could enlighten me—give me a good general idea of affairs there. But so far I have had to go ignorant." Had been out today—briefly but enjoyably.

Gilchrist said to several who were in a group discussing Eakins' Agnew picture in the Haseltine Art Gallery last evening—the Contemporary Club meeting being held in the next room—that while it was true a certain thing in it was natural, was as it appeared no doubt in nature, still the putting it there was an artistic defect—some way should have been taken to overcome it. W. said, having listened all ears, as I could see: "That is very significant—I don't know but there—open there, lies the whole question—the question of art. To us it seems very obviously not true as Herbert put it. Yet there is an interest to that view not easily ignored. I should like much to get at a full statement of reasons on the other side—for that side obtains, without a doubt—is dominant, in fact." But his own "love, affection, penchant," was for the "simply, grandly natural—not a line readjusted in the interest merely of art."

Asked me: "What of the evening? Is it clear—beautiful—moonlighty—out of doors? I suppose the world moves on equably. Are the waters stirred? Is the world at peace? The Bible has it, the spirit of God moving upon the waters." I said: "The spirit of God surely has moved upon the waters this evening." And proceeded to tell him of the river as I came across tonight: the cold and early moon—the full-sailed sloop—the cutter swinging in the tide—the tug puffing its way up the river—multiplied beauties that much impressed me. W. further as I paused: "It is almost incredible what a little stretch of nature will do to arouse a fellow—convert him, so to speak. I cannot think of a rarer experience than one I met on the river Saguenay, up there in Canada. The river's water is an inky black—a curious study, I believe, to this day to the scientific men: take it up in a bucket, and it is still unmistakably black—the color of the stream. Oh! that great day! Down the stream a boat—sails open—wing-a-wing—one one side, one the other—patched, stained, heavy—but oh! how beautiful! It was a curious revelation out of little means. Wing-a-wing is rarely fine anyhow—I have not known it much in pictures—but few artists can accomplish it. See then, the large result of what may seem a small impulse. Why should we go hunt beauty then—I should rather ask—where can you go to get away from it?"

He thought "ministers and professors" anyhow the last men to impart really vitalizing truth. "I once told Collyer, years ago, in New York, in a company of people—they had been talking with a great flourish of the mediatorial office of preachers—to me a ridiculous pretense. I said then, that I could not allow an importance to that view. To me the time propounded other questions—indeed, I wondered if the time had not arrived for the entire abolition of ministers and churches; I said I could conceive how five centuries ago or so the pulpit could have had a function—but today, all and more than the pulpit did then, is better done by other forces. There were several of my friends present there—vehement friends— and they thought I had made a great mistake to talk so—and perhaps it was uncalled for—I am not prepared to say *not*— but it is a long-held notion with me. It seems to me that in these days ministers exist as in the nature of things, obstructions. I should ask of them, why cumbereth ye the ground?" And while most men might disagree [?] to this—"yet in the realm of thinking, nine-tenths of men amount to nothing, anyhow."

"Even the Unitarians have an orthodox respectability," he said again, and as to a newspaper that seemed statedly to avoid mentioning Walt Whitman—"I can understand the newspaper index expurgatorious: so much the worse for them if they can't stand me." And he laughingly narrated an experience. "There was one of the department heads at Washington who conceived a great dislike for the word *virile*—gave out orders that it should not be used in any of the documents issuing from that department. I was very curious about it, and asked him once how his antipathy (and it was a *virile* antipa-

186

thy!) arose. He said that he hated the word—that it called up in him images of everything filthy, nasty, vile. It was very amusing. I remarked to him: 'Did it never occur to you that the fault is in you and not in the word? *I* use the word—like it—am never once brought by it into touch with the images you speak of.' But he was obdurate—remarking only: 'Well—whatever: I won't have it! I hate the word!' And yet he was a man of force, filled his place well, in all the usual ways was sound and sensible."

Referring to the current N[orth] A[merican] Review which I had with me W. said: "To me the important thing is, to know what the fellows are talking about rather than to read in detail all that is said." Called my attention to a letter from McKay. "He enclosed me payment for the three books. One of his questions was about the Carol of Harvest—now printed as 'The Return of the Heroes'—I answered that question at once. But then further along he writes that some one has left with him a poem for me—which he did not include—why I don't know. He suggests that you stop in for it." This I promised to do.

Then—as I was about to go: "And that reminds me—now the point is on: I am going to do something again that you did well for me last year. I want you to go to the mint—bring me along 5 three-dollar gold-pieces: you got me three last year." And as he took out his pocket-book and from it a 10 and a 5-dollar gold-piece: "There's a history connected with that ten. When Horace Howard Furness was here a few days ago, he told me of a man off in Australia—a devoted friend of Leaves of Grass—who, writing to him, the said Furness, sent along ten dollars, as testimony, and all that." I remarked: "Your friends are at the ends of the earth." And he: "I am not surprised to have friends in Australia—I am a sort of Pacific, Oceanic, Californian critter, anyway." And to my remark: "Australia is more American than English, anyway—" he said: "Yes, it is so: see how well Sarrazin confirms you in that."

Thursday, December 12, 1889

7.55 P.M. Went to W.'s with Morris Lychenheim. Stayed full 45 minutes. W. quite willing to talk. Said: "I have had a visitor—a young Mitchell—not Weir, nor the Doctor-son who has been here to see me, but another—a younger. I sent a copy of the leather book through him to his father." At this I alluded to the 25 dollars recently sent me by Weir, this being a considerable recognition. "I liked the boy," W. said, "it was his first visit—he seemed bright, intelligent." I said then: "I have another of my contributors who has given me 80 dollars so far" &c.—meaning Edelheim. W. at this suggesting: "We ought to give him a book, too—it is the least we can do"—and questioned me, whether this should be a complete Whitman or a leather volume. I finally advised him to make it what he thought best. He ruminated—then: "Probably the morocco book is more appropriate than the other: for what it starts out to be, it is complete—though not *all*, as the other is." He laughed that Tom had called the cover of the Complete Works "damned shabby," and interposed—"Others—who have handled old books—old-book-men—would say, it is well—most well—just as it is."

I had brought him the 3-dollar gold pieces. Also the poem from McKay, elegantly done-up, type-written—Dave not wishing to risk it in the mail. W. did not read it while we were there—only remarked: "It is finely type-written, if not other-written, anyway." Returned me the Scribner's. Had not read the Stevenson piece entire. "I read what applies to me. The piece seems forced—as if he set out 3 or 4 big sheets before him and declared—these will I fill." As to the "Birmingham" reference—"I hardly know what to make of it except to say what you do yourself. I have been much criticised for my use of the term—'divine average.'" I reminded him of the man who had said of Cleveland—"We love him for the enemies he has made"—so of L. of G. Then further, me: "I always tell the

188

new reader of L. of G., who comes to me: you will be shocked and staggered at two points at the outset—you will stagger at W.'s disregard for literary form and tradition—you will stagger at his spiritual attitude towards the body: but if you can stand up after these, you are all right—you will know L. of G." W. exclaimed: "That is very fine—inclusive: I know no better." As to Morris' exclamation to me in a discussion today—"If you were to see those Corots you would see an art that is better than nature"—W. said: "All I can say is, if a man starts out for an instant to get something better than nature, then I say, God help him!" Lychenheim quoted from Ruskin about the impossibility that young people could be critics—but W. said: "That is easy to say, but hard to justify. Criticism has no rules—you cannot predict it. As a rule it is a humbug anyhow: it means only this—that Jones' digestion is good or is not, or, if the critic is a woman, that perhaps she has not been invited out to the party at Mrs. Johnson's. The most minute, the most personal, factors color the criticism. I had a friend who had always to ask—well, how shall I write, adversely or to applaud? And the young? Oh! the young hold the stage after all. There are things in young lives, young critics—imaginative quality, elasticity, vehemence, power, which years cannot supply—only dim. These are treasures after a high kind. As some one told me once, in a comfortable old age—'yet for all I have there is one great gap—one avenue closed. What now can make me happy as in those days when I was content with my dinner-pail—the bread, pork, sip of coffee out of a pot— and digestion was good, and mid-day brought me rest.' *That* is past, irretrievably!"

Said he had not been out today—"I suppose for the main reason, that Mary was out—leaving Warren and me to keep house." And then of his meals: "I don't know—for a good, strong, healthy man three meals a day are none too many, but to an old, broken-down, badly digesting [one]—the digestive apparatus very shaky indeed—two meals will do. I get my

dinner about 4 or 5—and my appetite keeps up amazingly—
I don't flunk one meal out of 20: I have a very ready appetite
even for breakfast." And he asked then: "Don't you see how
fat I keep?"

On the table an old German paper (1883) in which were 4
portraits, Whitman's with Lindau's, Heyse's and one other. Of
its kind the portrait really very good. W. said: "I recovered
that from the debris here for Dr. Bucke. You are right—that
is altogether satisfactory—a good picture. The Germans anyhow excel in that line. I have hoped our fellows would cap-
ture the burin as well as other instruments—but so far they
have not." And he pointed out Lindau's head to me: "It is
fine—strong and fine: I have had a long look at it today."

Gave me a copy of the big Gutekunst portrait for Agnes,
who means to have it reproduced large, in charcoal, by my
father.

Friday, December 13, 1889

7.30 P.M. W. in his room, but not reading. Hands folded—
meditative. Said: "We had a good outing today—two hours,
fully—went up and into the ship-yard. Oh! the incredible inspiration of it to me!" He was positive he had much benefited
by the trip. I left with him a copy of the N. A. Review, the
contents of which he at once proceeded to look over.

Immediately on my entrance, almost, he spoke of a volume
he took up in his hands—Roden Noel's "Essays on Poetry and
Poets." "I laid it out for you—it probably will interest you—
maybe more than it does me, though I don't know that I
should say that, for I find myself going back to it, from time
to time, which is one test, and a good one." I spoke of the
letter I had addressed to Noel, anent the celebration—that
was returned to me (though addressed care of The London
Times, with request to "forward")—with inscription—"person
unknown," or to that effect. W. much enjoyed my story, ex-

claiming: "That's John Bull—that's the bull of him—supercilious, disdainful—thinks his character is in danger of being misunderstood if that is not made very patent. This trait will hang on to him yet for a long while. Of course they know who Roden Noel is: but then, it would not become their reputation to admit it. I usually take all risks in a case like that—send with a simple town address, perhaps in care of the P. O.—and as a general thing they go right: though it goes against my grain to send off a letter or what not with an insufficient or doubtful address."

He read today a poem sent to him through McKay. "It is quite good," he remarked, "I am very much done up that way of late." There was a New Yorker, W. J. O'Reardon, who sent him a "greeting" about the time of his birthday, which still remains intact.

Again he spoke: "And so Browning is dead! Who now, except Tennyson and Whittier, is to be talked of? Although some would object, I think Whittier distinctive, typical of something, striking a pure note that lifts him up and up, I think very high—with the great. Some would say, Holmes, too—but I should not say Holmes." And although there were manifest ways in which Whittier obviously lacked world-mind, "yet after that is said, more remains to be said—the best yet, to be said in his favor." But as to Browning: "He died suddenly—has created much—yet I know little about him, in reality. I ought in fact to take him up—weigh him—make sure of myself—but I doubt if I should in any way tie to him. 'The Ring and the Book' I have read pretty thoroughly, but that is all."

The morning papers announced by cabled dispatch, Tennyson's new volume. W. had seen the notice and it excited his interest. "I should not wonder but the New York Herald or some other paper would have the whole book or a part of it, cabled tomorrow. If it does, I am going to ask you to get me a copy. It would be a feast! If men only knew that they were to become great—as they never do—how well they might prepare for it! Start in youth, fill the table drawers with poems, stories, whatever: then, when fame is on, and the editors will take most of anything a man writes, bring 'em out!"

Some one had brought him in some fruits—bananas, dates—and cakes: and another, flowers. He spoke affectionately of the visitors who so remembered him. I brought him back the Sarrazin book with a little letter enclosed from Morris.

Saturday, December 14, 1889

7.35 P.M. W. lying on the bed—the first time in weeks I have found him so. But getting up and slowly making his way to the chair he explained: "I laid down, rather because I had nothing else to do than because I wanted to sleep." Returned me the N. A. Review. Had "looked through" most of the articles, though "Gladstone's on divorce, was one I skipped altogether—did not read at all."

While we sat there talking, Hicks came in. W. asked the question at one moment: "What did Jesus mean when he said a rich man could no more enter Heaven than a camel go through the eye of a needle?" Hicks volunteered to give his view, viz.—that Jesus meant that riches could only be accumulated on the misery of our fellow-men, W. then saying: "Yes, that is one explanation, but that does not satisfy me—it seems to me necessary to say more if you say that much." But he did not follow the question up. W. not especially talkative, though cordial. Referred to St. Gaudens, whom "Watson Gilder and some other bulked high up"—but who to W. was "not a man of greatest calibre, though Morse thinks something of him, and Sidney's judgment in sculpt work was always very cute—very much to be relied upon."

Commenting upon The Critic's applause for Dr. Brinton's pamphlet on a world-language, W. said: "I doubt the world-language very much—yet if it must be, the English will be that language. Oh! I thought that was all settled! There are profound reasons for it: the English is more naturally the world-language because of its composite character—its absorption—gathering from all quarters, elements that give it strength, variety, vitality" etc.

Sunday, December 15, 1889

I met Clifford and Chubb at Broad Street Station at 3:15, and we went to Camden together, reaching W.'s house at about 4 or a little after. Learning from Mrs. Davis that W.'s dinner had just gone up, I put the visitors in the parlor and went and talked with W. a few minutes in his room. Urged him not to hurry. We would wait, etc. and he then: "Well—do so then: and I will come down when I am ready—and shall not hurry—shall quietly finish my meal here."

So we sat downstairs and talked some 20 minutes, after which I up again and W. now willing to repair to the parlor, as he did, laboriously, sitting there by the window. And we then talking with him fully an hour, his power unmistakable and unusually positive for these days. Indeed, he said to us at the close,—"I don't know what has started me to chatter so." He had hardly got seated and put his cane in the corner before remarking towards Chubb (who had greeted him with ready words)—"I always used to flatter myself that I could always and easily tell an Englishman in his talk—but lately one or two instances have come up which completely stagger my faith"—meaning Chubb, for one, who, for his own part, remarked the resemblance in the speech of New and Old Englander, W. however insisting—"The New Englander I can detect with the greatest ease. The typical *Bostonee*, the travelled man—the travelled Southerner, the Englishman,—are remarkably alike; but the average New England man is not hard to point out."—"Even Emerson had it, though in Emerson later on it was all flattened out" etc.

Chubb gave W. a card he had had from Edward Carpenter, and then W. inquired curiously after Carpenter's recent days. Impelled by questioning on Chubb's part, W. talked with considerable vehemence, and at length, about American literature and life. What was the prime defect? He responded: "Its gentility—the disposition everywhere to be genteel—to have houses, goods, ten thousand what-not a year, all that." And this, he said, "affected our poetry, as well as the general life of America." "Our people want their cake—their sugared cake—with all the delicate traceries of the confectioner's art." He asked if we had ever seen "the delicate pipes" with which this work was done—Clifford interpolating that in the factory they were not the pipes of Pan. "The old Biblical fellows did not make the cake," W. declared—Clifford wittily suggesting, "but they take the cake," and W. after laughingly saying— "Yes, but they did not make it"—and he spoke of their "aboriginal force, so to speak"—over men "pursuing elegance as the first quality"—Longfellow instanced as typical "yet a man who must be read—may be read long and long, perhaps for all time"—"the truth being, the confectioners supply what will sell—the writers what the current public want." But he did not despair of America: "There were years in my life— years there in New York—when I wondered if all was not going to the bad with America—the tendency downwards— but the war saved me: what I saw in the war set up my hope for all time—the days in the hospitals." And these convincing "rather by what they revealed of the common people than by other agents"—and "these not chiefly the facts of battles, marches, what-not—but the social being-ness of the soldiers—the revelation of an exquisite courtesy—man to man—rubbing up there together: I could say in the highest sense, *propriety—propriety*, as in the doing of necessary unnamable things, always done with exquisite delicacy. And in the hospitals, illustrated in extreme considerate-ness, gener-osity—as in this case: one man will have a dozen oranges sent him; he will not hoard them—he will keep one—give eleven to eleven others."

When Chubb inquired of the big cities—whether they did not militate against America, W. responded: "I think I can say without hesitating about that—*no*: I accept all the cities—all that America so is—then ask for more," that America were "less going wrong in what she has than what she has not."—"Sometimes I fear that the mass of the people may become venerated, honeycombed—then something grand occurs to reassure me—to make the issue clear." He did not think the years since the war had known a decadence of the heroic vir-tues—"for in the war itself, it was not the war that was great, but the deportment of the actors," and that had lasted. I joked with him that he liked cake and candy too and he admitted—"Yes, I have quite a sweet tooth, but I look upon this as a cultivated, not the bottom taste—for after all the cake is only incidental, while for my daily food I must have bread and butter and coffee and mutton broth, and what-not, to sustain life and keep it pure."

He alluded to Browning. "You asked me upstairs about Browning, Horace, and in today's Press there is an editorial much better than common, about Browning: written, I should say, by Talcott Williams." And then of Browning: "I don't know whether he is for me—I really know very little about him. He is a man who needs to be studied out, and that I can't do, even if I were inclined to. And yet the best readers seem in our time to take most delight in just such writing." Clifford asked, why "the *best* readers?" And W. added: "Per-haps that is not an admirable—the best—word: I might put it, those who seem the weightiest readers. And I do not know that it is a drawback or a lapse to be as Browning is—I do not know that he ever set up to be anything himself—the world has been left to its own conclusions—and the future may make much of him—much. He is not a man to be read as you go along, but what of that? Is a strip of sky to be seen or penetrated as you go along, or the river, or a boat, or the men on the street?" And on this bent he passed into rapid review—with poetic expressiveness—his voice at its sweetest—(to the comment of both the visitors when we left)—"For what after all do we know of nature—of a tree,—of anything? There are a thousand convolutions—a thousand circles—one upon another—on and on—and what we see—what we grasp—is about the quarter of one circle." His expression that he had "no doubt America would evolute" to higher things: "America individuated, leading all by representing all, rather than by a system of exclusion." When speaking of Browning's obscurity, Clifford had asked W. if *he* had been taxed for meanings, and he admitted with a laugh—"Oh yes! often!" Then added with a funny gesture: "There is something irritating in the question."

Chubb speaking of some who questioned Darwinism—rather, evolution—*but*—and W. said: "It sounds funny to hear that said: it seems like questioning the tides." But he was greatly interested in Chubb's statement. It was in such vigor he seemed. Inquired of Clifford after his family: assured Chubb that a call any later time before the return to Europe would be welcome. A message brought from Stedman coming in connection with facts pointing to S.'s own nervous prostration, greatly touched W. In return he wished his affection particularly sent to Sanborn (who also had sent a message by Chubb) and Stedman. Reference having been made to Cleveland's Boston speech, W. inquired of it—"Is it good? Worth my while to look up?"—and assenting with a "do—be sure to do it then" when I suggested bringing my own paper down.

Monday, December 16, 1889

8.35 P.M. Detained late in town. When I entered W.'s room, he was resting his feet in a basin of water, saying to me about it: "This is one respect in which I follow the Biblical counsels—I do not always do that, but here is one case."

Asked me about the night. "Do the stars shine?" And "how is the air?" I supposed "it was his bed-time, nearly," but he responded: "No—I have no bed-time: I go when I get tired, irrespective of the hour." Harned, he said, had just left the house. Had I not met him? "He brought me down a dozen copies of your book. It seems Judge Garrison is to take them, and wants my signature. Oh yes! I shall sign them—sign them for Tom and for the Judge, both—for their sakes." Referred to Tennyson's book again. "I see it is called 'Demeter'"—spelling it—"and from what the papers say, these poems—most of them *little* poems—are as good as ever. I read something to that effect in The Transcript." Adding—"I have several papers here on the table for you—the Press, The Transcript, another"—handing them to me—I at the same time handing him yesterday's New York Times.

Said he: "I have been laying the timbers of a new piece. I have called it this: 'Old Poets,' then, dash, and in parenthesis 'and other things.' I am not quite sure about the title—it may be defective, misleading—I have not absolutely adopted it yet. A literalist would object to it and say 'Poets and other things'—how could *that* be,—poets are not *things*—but after all that would be a narrow construction to tie to." I laughed slightly and said I had no fear of his head-lines, under any circumstance, and W. to that: "Which would be all the more reason for us to look out now that we keep up our standard—though the pitcher was taken to the well a thousand times unharmed, now last comes the hour of ruin! There was 'Leaves of Grass': what a fight I had for that name"—and to my interposed idea that time had settled in its favor,—"Well—for 15 or 20 years, everybody objected to it—even my friends." Even O'Connor? "No—not William—but about all the rest. I remember one ardent friend I had—Theodore something or other—a poet, a man of parts. He asked, 'Who

197

ever knew of a *Leaf* of Grass? There were *spears* of grass—but leaves?—Oh! no!' There was one night the question came up: a very erudite—a scientific man—a botanist, in fact,—having stood it as long as he could—spoke out—set me quite up—said that, whatever was the case in literature, in science *leaves* of grass there were and doubtless would be." And he added: "My critic gave all the intellectual reasons in the calendar, but of the emotional, the sympathetic, he could say nothing—nothing!" And further—"A headline should be large—capacious—expansive—should cover its subject, explicitly—then something more."

I had Roden Noel's book with me, under my arm—and he asking me "How do you get along with it?" I responded, "It does not fascinate me." W. laughing: "It does not gripe you, eh? I should rather say, *grip* you—nor does it me. That is sad news indeed," he said, of that which had been brought from Stedman, "but now that I have had time to think over it, I can see that it is just Stedman—men of his nervous make-up—whom such a thing would attack. . . . A good deal of it all, I reckon, comes of the damnability of possessions—of houses, carpets, 2 or 3 thousand a year—these to be kept up, whatever goes—even if health goes. Poor Ed! A noble, affectionate fellow, too!"

Tuesday, December 17, 1889

7.30 P.M. Not at W.'s more than ten minutes. He was taking his evening bath—I loafing in the bed-room meanwhile. Left with him Herbert Aldrich's book on Alaska, copy of Scribner's with Mrs. Fields' article, Cleveland's Boston speech. He took all—"a feast for tomorrow"—thought—"this book will interest me: it starts well—the print itself is a temptation." I had a note from Morse this evening, but no time to stop and read it. W. smiled—"It will do tomorrow!" Has been reading Oliver Twist. Day inclement—no outing.

Giving me a copy of The Transcript for the 14th, he said: "Something further about Browning—and it may appeal to you—as it did to me." Adding—"But the marks are Kennedy's—not mine." Afterwards I found why he was particular to say the last—that Kennedy had noted an item headed "A wife-beater thrashed by the Justice instead of being sent to prison"—exclaiming with red pencil inserts by—"Good! Ha! Ha!"

Wednesday, December 18, 1889

7.05 P.M. W. in his room, the light down—ruminating. He raised his head, ensplendored in light at the tips of the fine grey hair. "Oh! Horace—is it you?" The night stormy—the day such as had kept him at home. "You look as if you had come in out of the mists," he said—as I had—the fog strong—my coat collar up—moistened on moustache and hair.

Called my attention to Herbert Aldrich's book, turned—open—face down—on a pile of papers. "I am nearly half through it," he remarked. "It is singularly non-literary—very non-literary, indeed—I was going to say, *happily* non-literary—and why not? And yet, as is apt to be the case, it is—at least to me—wonderfully attractive, fascinating. I wonder if we are ever to get emancipated from the literary tyrannies—to get out to freedom, nature. We certainly are not emancipated now—are bound hand and foot—sugared, prettied!"

Read him Morse's letter, in which he was deeply interested. Then in turn discussed his letter received from Burroughs today. The street address W. "gave up" laughingly. Burroughs now in Poughkeepsie. W. promised again to write a letter of introduction for Adler to Burroughs. "I had completely forgotten it." Questioned me, what had Chubb said of his meeting with Sanborn. Sanborn had assured Chubb much as he had me in the recent letter, in perhaps even more emphatic language—in the Emerson matter. W. said: "That is very significant—I don't know but the most significant." But as to my proposed letter quizzing Edward Emerson he was still doubtful. "I predict that you will get nothing from him— or getting something, will find that something itself a mystery, ambiguous. In the courts they have a sort of witness who baffles all prediction—passes all off with an air of uncertainty—an I-do-not-know or am-not-sure attitude: and I think you will find Edward Emerson such a witness."

Thursday, December 19, 1889

7 P.M. W. sitting in his room, but not reading. Very cordial and spoke of my birthday, this day. "Thirty-one! You would pass for twenty-one, you are so quick, so spry—so alive!" He spoke of his watch—asking me the time. "I have a good deal of trouble with this piece, now-a-times—it don't go by method any longer." And when Warren came in shortly, he commissioned him to get off to a watch-maker with it.

I had a copy of The Standard in my pocket. Read him from it an editorial on Browning, in which the writer went off at a great rate about the poetic "artifices" of our time, W. laughing and assenting with considerable vehemence—at the end asking, "And who is it is saying all that?"—remarking that somehow the agents of truth arrive and have voice—"here and there—and often in the most unexpected place." At this calling my attention to a copy of Poet Lore, "Do you see it?" Adding: "What a host of papers, magazines, seem to exist now for no other purpose than to expound, exploit, poets—Shakespeare, Browning, Shelley. I can see they may have an importance, too, of their kind—recondite, curioish"—W. laughing over the "exercise" of "some of the fellows" in Poet Lore (Morris, Williams and others) in imitations of early English balladry. A letter therein, too, from Donnelly, in applause of O'Connor. "My first impulse was, to have you read it, then pass it on to Dr. Bucke; but on second thought, I saw that

Nellie O'Connor has the first right to anything that concerns William—so I shall send it to Washington."

The other evening I picked a copy of the Boston Transcript from the floor—found in it Emerson's letter to [?] Wheeler, recently in print for the first time. W. now referred to it: "I have read it. It is interesting, as all Emerson's letters are, but not what would be called notable." Going on then to Sanborn's letter in a later Transcript (17th): "It aims to set somebody right who says Thoreau did not go to Staten Island tutoring. I know that Frank was right in what he says, because it was in one of those periods Thoreau called on me. I think that Sanborn has Thoreau on the brain: I mean that in a high sense, of course. It is not a matter of our affection for Frank, or again no-affection—but a matter only of judicial opinion— how far he is right, wrong. The great vice in Thoreau's composition was his disdain of the universe—his disdain of cities, companions, civilization. I have very little room for the man who disdains the universe. One of my first questions is always that—not always spoken—not methodically *thought*, even— but in a way taking its measure: do you, or you, *accept* the universe and all that is in it? It is an important question." I laughingly queried at this point: "Can't you leave it with the universe to settle with the man who disdains the universe?" W. responded seriously: "O yes! that is to be said, too—indeed, I think if Frank was here with us now, and I should say to him what I have been saying to you, he would warmly take it up and remind me that the universe contains and sustains the man who disdains it as well as the man who accepts. But yet I think there is a damnable disposition sometimes to deny, to affront, the substance, the spirit, the life, the joy, of things." And he continued with amusing vigor, referring to "the women across the street—eight of them—who will come out instantly after a storm with their stinking buckets, to drive all the neighborhood crazy, to wipe out all vestige of the storm—as if nature had been about a bad business." This was rather occult to me, the point of the reference—though he followed with saying: "That is typically damnable. I know it is severe to take such ground with Thoreau, nor do I, only measurably—but Thoreau does not at every point show the marks of the greatest nature." He appreciated "Frank's loyalty," "say what I have to say qualifyingly of Thoreau nevertheless." Gave me The Transcript that I might read Sanborn's letter therein.

Friday, December 20, 1889

7.35 P.M. W.'s room. Asked after his health. He pleasantly shook his head. "Pretty good—for me!" and proceeded after a little silence: "I must always put it, for me—qualify it. In these days I must be thankful for negative blessings—be thankful I have what I have. There was an oriental tale—I always thought it a profound one—about a man who had no shoes to wear—was too damned poor for anything—and so for a long time had to stay at home. Till one day, somehow, shoes came and he was a free man again. So out he goes, and the first person he meets is a man who has no feet. It seems to me"—with a laugh—"the moral of that is sufficiently obvious!" W. had got out, to be sure—"to Vine Street and back again."

The papers today speak of Whittier rather doubtingly. W. now: "Yes—he is 82, and quite feeble at that, too. It is quite wonderful how some of those weak fellows live on and on, into many years. Lord Brougham there in England, was a good sample." I called Brougham "an important man in his time," and W.: "I can believe that is in a way so—yet not wholly so: he was rather penetrating than imaginative—of the intellectual type." And anyhow—"the highest type personalities—I do not look for, do not find, in the literary class. Emerson shines as a superb example—exception. As I have been more and more confirmed in believing, Emerson, by his striking personality, suffices to redeem the whole literary class. This is his greatest fruit—his best result—showing after all, the infinite literary possibilities—certainly a rare gift— rare for any age." I said, when it is asked what America has done for literature and art and so on—I point to Emerson, Lincoln and Whitman, and ask what could be more propitiating?—a trinity of giants, etc. W. said: "I should make a better reply: I should say, the glory of America is in its possession of 40 million high average persons, the brightest, cutest, healthiest, most moral, hitherto." I explained: "But in what I say of the particular persons, I imply all that. America produces them—they come of her soil. As if we spoke of a tree—of its grandeur and exceptional beauty—keeping constant remembrance of the air and the rain and the soil out of which and through which it came. In these men America is vocal." W. thereupon: "I see—and that's the point, exactly—a point to insist upon. America is not so great in what she has done as in what she is doing, as great, as I am fond of saying, because of her intestinal ebullitions—her cleansingness, so to speak— or tendency thereto." And as to the three men being what I thought them: "I see, you are right in your logic: I hope they are what you think they are."

He had finished Herbert Aldrich's book—"Arctic Alaska and Siberia." When I asked about his interest—"I was not desperately, vehemently, so. Yet it is a book of the sort not to be denied, dismissed." Discussing German "tendential" novels: "I think Bulwer's 'What Will He Do With It?' must have been written on that method." And as to the wordiness and *ornateness* of Bulwer: "I always realize that those for whose critical judgment in general I have the most respect, would say what you have just said. Yet, after all, with Bulwer as with others, I come back to the question how it strikes *me*! which has an importance—a first importance—to me. I have never yet fully made up my mind whether I should most like to have that fine balance of critical judgment—dispassion—or not: it seems enviable to me: Emerson had it—had it to the full."

Saturday, December 21, 1889

8 P.M. W.'s bed-room. Said he had been out today. "We stopped at Tom's office on the way, but he was not there." Enjoyed it much. Alluded to "the forthcoming number of Lippincott's." "It contains a piece by Stoddard on N. P. Willis. Strange to say, this is marked by the entire absence of Stoddard's usual sourness, asperity. I don't know how close he came to Willis. Willis was evidently kindly-disposed—indeed was anyhow the best of men that way—a polite man, a proper man, in a sense I have never known in any other, and to an extent, almost brusque, entirely free of soft-soaping, yet never giving out the impression of offense. This piece of Stoddard's amounts to nothing at all—I could write more myself, though my knowledge of Willis was not ever intimate."

Another matter: "The Press this morning printed quite a liberal culling from Tennyson's book. Oh yes! it was good—yet not remarkable, either—very soft, sweet, very Tennysonian. Demeter is another name for Ceres, and Tennyson gave that story over again—a story often done, and well done, by men of the past—this may be called the Tennysonian version." I quoted Harper's Weekly, that Browning "alone in his generation has contested the palm with Tennyson," and W. said: "I suppose that Time must settle all this about Browning—Time, which may be said to settle all things. Browning may be the man for 200 years hence: that remains to be developed. I do not think all this investigation of our time goes for nothing." But when I said, "contemporary fame is chance," he assented—"Yes, nothing more so"—but Browning "seemed to have a quality which defied his envious contemporaries, too—and this it might be which by and bye would most largely persevere."

Spoke hereupon of Mrs. Fields' Scribner article on Leigh Hunt, returning the magazine to me: "Fields had his possessions in plenty—I saw them, in a way—books, pictures, china, bric-a-brac—I don't know what all. Yet in his models he was the most orthodox of men—afraid of individuality— planting himself on the old forms, literary traditions"—but a man "of first-class quality of its kind." He was "not surprised" that Stevenson should not understand Scott. "How could he? the antipodes of Scott in all things! Scott was too simple, too natural, for him. Scott had a great love for the medieval— persons, equipage, what-not—a real love, running in him deep: yet was as free as a child—loved to get out in the air, breathe, grow, commune with nature—a splendid, healthy personality,"—Stevenson "morbidly of another type."

Speaking of his health he said: "There is an old man comes to see Mrs. Davis, and when she asks him how he is, he re- plies curiously—'still doing my old business—still making baskets.'" And W. then laughing: "I am still at my own busi- ness—still making baskets and baskets." He thought "we have a good friend in Judge Garrison here in Camden: I think he must have distributed as many as 30 copies of your book—I should say he has had almost that number from Tom." Of the London Illustrated News picture he said: "If you don't mind, let me give it to Herbert: I wish particularly for him to have it." I suggesting, "He is welcome—I have no desire to keep it"—W. then: "Nor do I: I do not want it about," but thought "there are particular reasons why Herbert should have it."

While sitting there we heard the play of the whistling buoy down the river at one of the ship-yards at the foot of Camden. It has a rising inflection—sings on for a minute or so, then dies by gradation away. W. put up his hand—we were silent— "Did you hear it?" he asked. Then: "Sometimes when I sit here and the wind is south, it is extreme in its power, music. It has a large and liberal—an expansive—tone." Then of steam-whistle-tones in general: "Some are incredibly fine— as in the case of boats, often. I never realized a demonstration of the sort that was as striking as on the Saguenay river, up in Canada. I heard it—it was distant—a sound, as I thought, of

a band—insisted that it was a band—though they tried to persuade me not. Yet it was a boat leaving off steam—that was
the whole mystery. I had a hard job to believe it."

Sunday, December 22, 1889

Did not see W. The day clouded in the forenoon—clear in
the afternoon. W. did not get out, the clouds not passing off
till it was too late for him to venture—the evenings growing
so chill. I had written to Mead asking another month for my
Whitman article, and he proves content, to that or even
more. Can more satisfactorily work if not under pressure.

Monday, December 23, 1889

7.40 P.M. W. reading a little red book, which I found to
be "The Awful Disclosures of Maria Monk"—property of
Warren.

Left with him a copy of The American containing Browning
Symposium—Morris, Williams, Wayland, Thompson, Appleton, Miss Bennett and others concerned. "I was going to use
rather a harsh word—to say, we can learn almost as much
from promiscuous babblings about a man as from the sympathetic careful statements of critics—but that is hardly just. I
have no doubt of Morris and Frank Williams at any time—
they are both in the right drift—particularly Morris—Morris
is *going there* without question. Mrs. Gilchrist's favorite saying about humanity was, "I don't know *where* we are going—
what port bound for—but that we are going *somewhere* I no
more doubt than that we exist at all.' And Morris is going
somewhere—it is in him to go—and Frank too: Frank's trend
is superb. We must give them all room and time to grow,
expand."

Alluded to his outing today. "We took quite a trip. In a
shop-window up town there were a couple of pictures of
Goethe and Schiller—fine—they possessed me—evidently

by your father—lithographs." He was no doubt right in this. Spoke of enjoyment, the release of these days—we now passing through a season of propitious weather.

The Critic this week—in The Lounger—discusses W. briefly—W. asking me: "Who is the Lounger? I wish you would try to find out definitely who the Lounger is—I never really knew. Sometimes I have thought it Joe Gilder—sometimes De Kay—then again—as now—neither—some other. The notions would come and vanish." Perhaps it was no "intended secret" and I could inquire. He would rather not personally. As to The Critic: "It is never vehemently interesting—yet a paper we all feel rather as if we could not go on without." Gave me Lippincott's, advising me to read Stoddard's paper on Willis. "I know it has no weight, yet we seem to need to know what clever fellows have to say." This paper had some unwonted virtues, considering it had "none of Stoddard's usual sourness," etc.

I read him a letter which I had received today from Stuttgart, from our friend Bush, now wandered far off.

Blumenstrasse 27[1]
    Stuttgart, Germany, Dec. 8th 89
Horace L. Traubel, Esq.
    Camden, New Jersey *U.S.A.*
Dear Mr. Traubel:
    I had already decided to write you to day, for, during the past week, I have been making a list of letters that *must* be written, and this morning I rec'd yours of the 18th ult. again enforcing my obligation.
    I remember that I hoped to get to Philadelphia and to see you, but I could not do so.
    I have been working very hard in the past year and, in addition to my work in Lachine, have had 2 patents (in which I am only part inventor) on my mind, with much writing and drawing to do in all my spare moments. I had much to see to in Springfield & New York before leaving, and left with some things undone and without going to Philadelphia, as I had hoped to do

We sailed Sept. 25th. on the Germanic of the White Star Line. If you are not rich, and ever come over, this and her sister ships have some inside cabins, forward, which are perfectly ventilated, and, unless it is so calm that port holes can be opened, just as pleasant as outer and as cheap as accommodations on much inferior lines.

We had a rather rough passage, but with favorable winds, and the quickest one this ship ever made coming this way. We saw only a little of Liverpool and then went direct to Glasgow where a friend showed me steel-works &c, and where we saw the Cathedral—not well known, but having the finest crypt in Gt. Britain. We could give only 2 days to romantic Edinboro town and 1 of these I gave to the Forth bridge, most stupendous and hideously ugly of bridges, having 2 spans each of 1600 ft (same as Brooklyn) and many smaller spans and probably costing nearly $50.000.000. We were fortified by the Century articles on Cathedrals and saw Durham of Norman and York of Gothic architecture. At London we also saw the old Norman church—St Bartholomew's the Great. We spent 8 days in London and then went to Paris—arriving as we had planned before the close of the Exposition. As a fellow Eng'r. I had been able to show a little courtesy to M. Eiffel's son, lately in U.S.A. and Canada and the card he gave me to his father was enough for the latter to take us to the top of "La Tour Eiffel," not only to his private room—above the highest point tourists reach, but also up the small tube until we stood just under the electric light, which, every night flashes the tri-color over the surrounding country. The Exposition grounds and buildings are beautiful. The show itself is like all others very wearisome. The wonderful exhibition of French art interested us much, for we had not seen much of it before.

Coming on to Stuttgart, we came to live in this house where we found a young Canadian musician to whom we had letters. He had just had a hemorrhage, but every one thought he would soon be up. However after 5 weeks (since we came) he has died and is buried to-day. This, as much as any one thing, is why my time has been broken into and why I have not written sooner.

I am studying German daily and wish I could stay long enough to master it. Mrs. Bush is studying harmony and musical composition with a Prof. Goetschius from Paterson N.J. He has been here 15 years, written two books and done such remarkable work as to

earn the king's apppointment as "professor." This title means something here and can not be *assumed* by any 3d. rate musician as in
America. In fact our own government might learn much here. The
German gov't is working not only for this generation but the next,
and the land and the forests and all the natural resources are sa-
credly guarded. Mrs. Bush (I see I have digressed) is studying
piano with a very talented woman here, Frau Hauptmann Hoerner.
She is a friend of Rubinstein and Leschetizky and was of Liszt and
Kullak. She takes only those pupils who give her pleasure and she
says Mrs. Bush does. However, though Mrs. Bush has so much
talent, she had not the best instruction early enough to make her a
great public player, and she has little taste for much of such a life.

Yes, I remembered that my payments were only up to Nov. 1st
(through Oct.) and as I had expected to start for home before this I
thought I should not be much behind-hand, and so made no provision for same. However, as I shall not now start, until after New
Years I will ask a friend in New York to send you the am't for 2 or 3
months and shall then be able to attend to it myself.

I am sorry I have delayed writing you so long—but I have been
having such a good rest, you will, I know, forgive me. We both send
a great deal of affection and Christmas greetings and best wishes for
the New Year to Mr. Whitman and yourself.

Please keep the little book for me.

Sincerely yrs.

H. D. Bush

You did not answer about the Leaves of Grass. Shall hope to get
them of you.

He was extremely interested: "His resume is extremely
taking—it sounds as if given intimately—as if from one chum
to another—stating the most definite particulars. After all,
our men—men of men—are the scientific men—men having
a basis in sublime common sense—an exalting common
sense. I know of nothing developed in history to exceed the
value of this." And he wished me to "message" his love to Mr.
and Mrs. Bush "at the first writing."

Today had brought me likewise from Rudolf Schmidt—5
pp. notice of the banquet book from the periodical (Copen-

hagen) "Literatur og Kritic.." Much to W.'s curiosity (as mine, since neither of us could read it). "We are always curious to know what is being said of us—particularly by the man who views us from the outside. Even if we realize that he don't grasp us, we see an importance in his statement. We must certainly get some translation of this."

Tuesday, December 24, 1889

7.35 P.M. Stopped in but briefly. W. reading. Was in bright, cheery humor—color good. Had been out. "I went to the Cemetery with Mr. Moore—selected a lot there." And as to removal of his mother and father to that spot—"That all depends—I do not know yet whether that can be."

Asked me: "There is a question I wished to put to you—this: did I ever tell you that Schmidt—Rudolf Schmidt—got his book? I feel that I did—yet I am not certain." I thought it probable—I had an indistinct remembrance of a postal of acknowledgement. "That is probably the case, then. I have marked in my note book 'rec'd'"—spelling it out—"and no doubt for good reason." Adding then: "Symonds has his copy of the big book, too—safely arrived, written about. Here is a letter from him today—a marvellous letter—which I have laid aside for you to read"—taking it up and handing to me. "It perhaps surpasses all he has so far said about us." Reflecting then as to the mails: "How wonderful the delivery of our packages—the great distance no obstacle at all! It all draws in the direction of solidarity—that is its best lesson, its best hope. I have told you about my Chihuahua experience. The wonder is, that they go at all—particularly that book—a big, lumbersome, clumsy book—only going through at all by a stretch of conditions—because its more than 4 pounds is in one volume instead of more."

Asked me if I thought Morris knew that his Sarrazin piece in The American was partly quoted in The Critic. Returned

210

me The American. Several Christmas presents have been sent in to him. He keeps them there and refers to them appreciatively.

Wednesday, December 25, 1889

Christmas

11.30 A.M. W. in his room, making up a package of portraits—ribboning it—autographing—etc. On the chair a sprig of holly, which he called my attention to. The little things—so-understood—which make up man's life!

Left with him The London Illustrated News containing the portrait. As I returned to him Symonds' letter, I called it "a great letter." And W.: "You think it is? I should not wonder." Saying further after a pause: "Coming from Great Britain—from a man of books, a world of books, it has a quality highly significant." I remarked: "But it is a letter *you* never could have written, however much your love or reverence for another." W.: "You think so? That it will not do for democratic America? It is gushing?" I responded: "I don't like that word—but it is not a letter you would have written Emerson, or Emerson you: it is too much in the spirit of discipleship." At this his face lighted up. "Oh! I see! and that's very penetrating, too—very good—I don't know but the final truth." "And now," I put in, "what becomes of Kennedy's saying last year that Symonds was too timid to avow himself?" W. argued: "I remember—but that was written from another base, coming of Symonds' letter at the time of Swinburne's—shall I call it?—diatribe of me in the English magazine. But after the letter in your book—and now this confirmation—this clinch to that—I think no more need be said on the other ground." He afterwards asked me: "After all, do you not think this letter better than the one you printed in your book? It is more intimate, more personal, more throbbing. I have been speculating what to do with the letter—whether to send it on one of my combination trips—to Burroughs, through him to Kennedy, through Kennedy to Bucke. At any rate I want to read it again, and carefully, myself." As to the missing line or poem spoken of by Symonds, W. declared: "I am not clear about that line—are you? If it was dropped, it must have been for some good reason—for I have my reasons—to me the best of reasons—for such changes as I make. Yet I do not in the least remember the line, though it was no doubt there and may come back to me when I start to look it up, as I shall." And then he asked me about Symonds' Greek books—advised me to read. "Take my books! Long ago I first came across them—cherished them: they have been part of my household for many years—a lasting refreshment."

Went further into experiences. "Did I tell you I went out to the Cemetery yesterday? I selected a beautiful lot—to me the most beautiful in the place—the land slopes down to Cooper's Creek. I think there must be fifty or more buried there already." I asked: "Do you intend it for a burial lot—do you wish to be buried there?" He at once assented: "Yes! that is the intention. I know about the lot in Laurel Hill—Pearsall Smith's—but this I deliberately select, with a serious end in view." And as to the man who wished to know "if W.W. was content to be buried in such a damned place as Camden"—he said: "What comes then is not to be worried over. I wish you would go out to see this lot sometime—go tell Mr. Moore you want to—I should like to know what you think of it."

Gilchrist was in last evening after I left.

Thursday, December 26, 1889

8 P.M. W. reading Stedman's big book. Commented on it to me. "I think that some of the best features of this book is in the pictures—some of them, not all; for on the other hand there are execrable samples. Look at this"—turning the pages over and showing me the Channing page. "What do you think of that? I have no doubt it is a caricature—a caricature of the

worst kind. I don't think Channing ever developed such an appearance." And at this, laughing—I having picked up from the table the Illustrated London News version [of W. W.]— "And that! What a libel *that* is! Tom Donaldson—he was here last night—said he had seen it: What! that a picture of *me*? Psha! why that's *foxy*—foxy! It's no picture of me—not the slightest! I have no doubt the London artists of the lower orders, and the engravers, are a damned supercilious class, without the sense to know what is owing to fidelity, truth, nature. Artists there or anywhere are some of them eligible to be what they say the Parisian is—the typical Parisian— Paris to him is the center of the world, his coterie the heart of Paris! Resolved, that the elect shall put their stamp on the world—Resolved, that we are the elect! Something in that spirit."

My father has been making a large copy of the Gutekunst picture and W. said: "I shall probably stop in to see it tomorrow if I get out. I passed the house the other day." I laughed—"And there are no Romeo Italian curls on it!" He then—"I hope not! I hope not!" Adding, "I was out yesterday—out today—for brief stretches. Yesterday I had a Christmas dinner, ate it home here—ate of it too heartily, I'm afraid—I am not over it yet." But Christmas had brought him friends. "See here"—lifting up one foot and showing me a new slipper—the other in a box near by—"this was one of them—nor anything more fit! And Tom Donaldson paid me quite a visit—brought along this bottle of whisky"—taking it up and reading the label to me. "He cracked it up high— according to that propensity in men which makes for the individual *his* minister, *his* doctor, *his* lawyer, *his* champagne— *his* what-not—the center of all world-importance. That is one of the great charges foreigners bring against America— against typical Americans—but I doubt very much if it is especially marked here—if it cannot well be found in other countries."

I asked him if he had not found a rather sad strain in Symonds' letter, and he responded: "You mean a pensiveness? I don't know. That hardly struck me. The thing that most impressed me was its almost passionate utterance—an almost abandon of passion—a marked, a remarkable, effusion of color—power—glow."

When I came in he had asked me, "And have you news?" And on my negative merrily exclaiming, "Nor have I bite!"— explaining afterwards: "Two fishermen are together, and one asks the other, have you bite? and the response is, Nor have I bite! Tonight, bite is not yours, not mine!" Referring to Henry Grady, the brilliant young Southerner now dead: "I don't know as much about him as I should—but he is a man— or was—of distinct parts—as I imagined, a sort of John Boyle O'Reilly of the South."

"I have had quite a curiosity," he said once more, "to fall on the track of my Brazilian poemetta—I looked for it to appear yesterday, but there is no sign of it." Referred to the Philadelphia Press as "specially well printed—even the illustrations—not remarkable in themselves—showing to advantage."

"Did I tll you," he asked, "that I had an order today from a lady—for the pocket-book edition?—And there was the big book I sent off the other day to Sag Harbor—also to a woman."

Promised to write me out a check for Billstein.

Friday, December 27, 1889

5.40 P.M. W. had finished his meal—sat there in the twilight, looking out to the north-west. He knew my step—and of course knew my voice. "Shall I strike a light?" he asked— and when I objected that I could see enough—"I suppose— but it is unlighted here, and a light *may* be had." However, no light *was* had, and I stayed till 6.30. He was in excellent mood. "I stopped in at your house today—saw your father—

your mother—the picture. And this picture I should take to be quite a work—I don't know but the most effective extant of me. Who knows but that 20 years from now Aggie may find herself possessed of a valuable curio. How broadly your father has treated it!—making of it an almost perfect piece of art. And you say he loves it, eh? perhaps that explains a good deal—to be *con amore* with your work—your duty—signifies a world of advantage to start with. This picture struck me because it impresses without calling in any adventitious aids—no color, no tricks—a pure specimen of black and white work. One thing"—laughing heartily—"Tom Donaldson, if he saw it, would not feel called upon to dub it foxy. That London News man's!—why, damn 'im!—that's no portrait at all: that's a bite, a wart, an excrescence." It was true he could imagine the News man's environment—"put myself in his place—in some measure realize his position—see his work as he does: a skilled man, after the world's approved manner—up in his art—maybe even in the good grace of the crown—with art ideals, tyrannies, of his to uphold, see to." Back to my father's picture: "When you go home, take another look at the eyes for me—see if they are not a bit dark—if they do not in some measure convey the impression of black eyes. I don't know that this is absolutely so—I know that with artists some emphasis of this sort is required and allowable. But the question is, if, 20 years from now, anyone seeing that picture would not think I had dark eyes—which you know is not the case. I had no other suggestions to make—even this I was inclined to brush away at first—but it has followed me home here—stayed—so I concluded to speak to you about it. How different this portrait from London!—in which I am dressed up as a tailor would dress a puppet—not as fits me, but as seems the mode to him. Tom Donaldson said someone who knew he was quite friendly towards me had brought him that picture—he looked at it a long time. It was then his 'foxy' came into his mind as the only word that would apply—and that is very good—very. Tom is very happy, often—misses sometimes, but is curiously apt in the main. Your father seems to possess particular faculty in this line, and this picture, I think, is his *chef d'oeuvre*. Noble works of art—fastened, clinched, held close to nature—are rare, rare, rare. In portraits anyhow I think I see curiously stereotyped forms. In what is averagely done in England, on the continent, among the painters, they make a man barbered, combed, after an emperorish fashion—a rule we must all conform to" etc.

Afterward we were turned upon another theme. "I had a letter from Doctor today—he ran to speculating—said he had been weary, overworked—would he ever get relief from this pressure? If the meter brought him lots of money, would peace *then* come? or would that simply augment his trouble? or all this failing, then would the life to come, our immortality, supply the defect of this—diffuse joy and *rest*—or would that life, too, be but the round of labor, duty, this one is. I turned the letter over in my mind a good deal today, and this evening, as I ate my dinner, the light dying in the west, the letter before me, arresting me again, I thought to myself—'Ah! Doctor—what boots this inquiry after the *uses* of immortality: better be certain first of the immortality itself!' Doctor is a very busy man—has many cares, many irons in the fire—not the least of them this worrisome, if not wearisome meter—and he is sensitive to the high performance of anything in the way of duty—I know him well on that side!" I alluded to the Doctor's remark to me that physically he could no longer work with impunity and stand unweariedly what was a light task of old—insensibly a change had come. W. at this: "Ah! yes! I know it well!" and then: "The English, men abroad generally, have unerring circumspection in some respects—they take care of themselves—often, rather, are taken care of—have wives, sisters, mothers—veritable and abiding providences. Incomparable, however, the valets on the continent." He well remembered Brougham, Gladstone, Disraeli, Palmerston—"What a wealth of performance even in their old age made possible" by the "watchful valet—an almost sacred instinct his." "In America we have no such person—no girl, no valet, no wife—expecting it—to do it—fortunately, few needing to be so taken care of. I remember a little incident with Herbert [Gilchrist] when he was here several summers ago—Morse was here at the same time. Sidney was one day blacking his shoes—an Irish woman was here—working, at the time, assisting Mrs. Davis. Herbert remarked to Sidney, that he should have let this woman attend to the shoes. I put in, that if we dared do such a thing the woman would probably up and curse us and leave the house. And yet Herbert explained, that what he touched upon would not have appeared strange in England—that in fact, the girl they had would feel hurt if not allowed to shine his boots. I could only say in reply to that, that this was democratic America—another state of society—in respects, another age." etc. I spoke of my preference, rather for the independent instinct of the Irish woman. W. then: "Yes—so do I: I abate nothing of my democratic sympathies. The self-reliantness of America, brightness, cuteness, remain to me what they have been, the top of the heap." But the valet service I said was consistent with democracy—might be cooperative, and W. then: "Yes, entirely consistent—the doing of all I have spoken of consists entirely with the most profound democracy." But our living was false, too often—not gauged by circumstances—"as the Arab, in his spare sand—living on a crust—no stomach, belly—yet adapted to his place—defying all our wonder how he can subsist on such means. You catch what I am driving at?—I seem sometimes to speak in enigmas."

Advised me to go out to Harleigh Cemetery. "Doctor has written me for fuller particulars. Do you go out there sometime soon—ask for Mr. Moore—the superintendent—tell him I sent you. I think it promises to be a fine place by and bye. It is a mere walk—you can easily go it—why, two or three years ago I should not myself have thought it much of a walk."

I left with him the Bazaar in which was a Rembrandt— "Rembrandt as officer." "He is one of my prime favorites—the earliest of all." Would send with me a banana for my mother— handed me one—hesitated—then brought forth another from the bag. "One looks mean," he said.

Saturday, December 28, 1889

7.55 P.M. W. in his room. Welcomed me and said: "I am reading a story here of Amelia Barr's—in the November Century." Adding—"And it is quite interesting, too." It was "one thing" to "while away the time." Had he been out today? "No," he said—"I was not permitted today. Warrie, boy, there, has been quite sick—he lies in the next room there now. Yes, I suppose it is the grippe—" now rampant in Philadelphia. Asked me therefore curiously about the weather. Said he had not yet sent the Symonds letter to Dr. Bucke— "though I have told him I had it"—wishing to read it still himself.

"And now," he said, "the year draws to a close—again and again, draws, draws." I asked, "And 1890—is it to have a greeting from you?" He "hardly" thought so. I said: "The last year's, to some, was savage."—And he: "I don't know but it was sort of that way—it must have been if it affected so good a friend as Mr. Coates—which is Herbert's version, isn't it?" His Brazilian poem has not yet turned up. "Have you come across it anywhere in your travels?" he inquired. Returned me the Bazaar—remarking of "Rembrandt as an officer"— "That picture is wonderful fine—yet not so good, I should say, as his Burgomaster—the best I know from him. Not the least part of that is the engraving, which is superb." W. had seen a reference in The Critic—"The final chapter on 'Toward the Subjective' reminds me of Walt Whitman's prose, without the brilliant flashes of genius found in the writer across the Delaware." This in treating of a book of John Darby's: W. thinking it "generous and kindly" though dubious about that word "brilliant" and the "flash," which "hardly apply."

I read to W. the letter from Stockley [the proposed translator of Sarrazin recently spoke of]—of which extracts are given below—written to [Harrison] Morris and left by M. with me today.

It is very kind of you to say you would like to see my translation and that Walt Whitman himself would or might. Your advice I should only be too glad of. If it is not accepting too roughly your generous offer of advice, may I ask if I could in writing to M. Sarrazin be in any way introduced? He would naturally be more disposed to listen to his would-be translator. . . . You kindly said you thought you could get M. Sarrazin's address. Might I have it? [etc.] . . . Do you know of any publisher in whose special line such a translation would be?

W. listened and remarked: "If he is but about to translate, then I wish him good luck—if he wishes Sarrazin's address, that we can give him; if he asks advice about a publisher—no, no name occurs to me—I have nothing to say on that point; if he means to hint for an introduction from me, *there* emphatically no—emphatically no. He will have to go his own risks, letting come what may upon the event. Much will depend upon his own work." The Sarrazin book "is public property: let him get his book out—abide the result."

Alluded to Symonds' "exquisitely fine nature." I called his passage very strong in which, as I said, "After questioning about the missing poem, he pulls himself up suddenly by saying in substance—but here now, this is not Leaves of Grass—this is detail and L. of G. demands the mass." —W. exclaiming—"Good! good! So you think that's the way it sounded?"

I told him the Haydn story (I think Haydn)—the Künfurst[?] or Duke or somebody, patron of his band, who for economy's sake was to dispense with the band finally—how Haydn composed a farewell piece, for a performance, in which one instrument after another could be dispensed with, each man putting his instrument away etc., and passing off as it was done. W. exclaimed: "That is a poem—exquisite—grand and fine—high among the best I know!"

Sunday, December 29, 1889

9.45 A.M. W. in his room—had just finished breakfast—reading The Press. I took him down the new issue of Current Literature, which last night he said he would like to read. "I shall get feasts of feasts out of it," he said, "it is an organ of and for many tastes." He had "woke well"—and "eaten a hearty breakfast," and now was "comfortable and serene, as you see."

Referring to the Illustrated London News picture, which lay on the table before him: "It is not worth talking about: it departs so from all that is true and fine, I have no patience with it."

His "Christmas Greeting" not yet published. Did not know if he would feel moved the next few days to "address the year 1890" or not. "I had better not, I guess, if there is to be any such result as last year's"—referring to the surprise and sensitiveness of some of his friends. Curious about the weather, but as Warren is still sick, "I hardly expect to get out today."

Monday, December 30, 1889

7.15 P.M. W. sitting in room reading in Current Literature. "I am looking into Waldorf Astor's story," he said—a chapter there from "Sforza"—and he added, "You see, I keep on reading this magazine as long as it is here." Was quite well—"comfortable, in *my* sense." Had looked carefully in all the papers for his "syndicate" poem, but so far it had not "showed up."

I told him the Charles T. Brook story of "the great I am and the great I ain't"—and he was much amused, laughing a long while, and saying—"It is the best thing I have heard in a long while—entirely new to me"—"with a pith and point quite obvious." We talked very freely for full half an hour, W.'s voice and whole manner easy, however deliberate. When I left, knowing I would not visit him tomorrow evening (work at the bank to be urgent and detaining me) I kissed him my New Year's wish—he holding my hand and exclaiming—"Good boy! good boy! And we will hope together for best things—the very best."

I read Clifford Symonds' letter yesterday. Clifford had said: "It is good he is 3000 miles off: it saves him the disappointment of putting his questions to Walt and having them avoided."—And then he inimitably mimicked what would be W.'s manner of avoiding the dangerous ground. W. asked—"So Clifford has heard I dislike to be asked questions?" Not *heard* of, I said, but has observed it himself. W. thereupon: "Ah! and that is the truth, too! Some years ago there was a young Englishman came here—he was introduced by Mrs. Gilchrist—I liked him well. He told me that Mrs. Gilchrist had warned him before he came that if he wished to be at his best with Walt Whitman, he had beyond all things to avoid asking questions—that she had met many men in her time but no man more markedly set against the inquiries of the curious. And he wished to make a good impression. "Walt Whitman and I," she said, "have been the profoundest of friends, but even between us my inevitable questions have badly cracked the rope." Hicks had told me he always found W. so "reticent" when he came, and I suggested—"Perhaps you ask him too many questions?" But he was "not aware" of any marked reticence, say of Mr. Hicks—"I shouldn't wonder but that *was* the case! William O'Connor was probably the prince of conversationalists—in the high sense brilliant—not tawdrily so, as brilliancy is apt to be—but brilliant nobly, profoundly. He needed to be free, to have the right person with him—then all went well—probably just as he was that time you saw him." Then: "I laid Symonds' book out for you" but

221

he could not find it in the "debris" as he calls the litter. "It has been to me a great resource—a great reservoir—time and time again, for years and years, it has afforded me wonders of release."

Observing my interest in a copy of The Critic I picked up, he remarked: "It don't amount to much: once in a while there is a piece, a paragraph, of some interest—but as a rule, it don't amount to much—puffs, scissorings, pot-boilers, to little effect—weak, often, puerile—a review now and then by somebody who knows what he is talking about. There are several fellows connected with it, probably, of the Joe Gilder stripe. At the start Jennie Gilder had much to do with it, and she was the life of the paper—but she probably finds now that it don't pay her well enough, and she has withdrawn mainly to other quarters. Mind you, I don't tell this to you as a thing I know—it is only my guess." Had he thought there was a change of feeling towards him? Was the applause not fainter than of old? "Yes, I can say I have, but of that I do not absolutely know, and certainly do not care."

Why did Emerson leave W. W. out of "Parnassus"? "I never knew why. All we can say to such a case is, if the fellows can afford not to do it, we can afford not to have it done. Bryant issued such a book, too—in the first edition omitting Leaves of Grass—but it seems—so I have been told—that in editions since Bryant's death—I have been represented." I quoted against this my own edition (1876)—which W. had not seen—in which W. appeared. At this he said: "Well—that accuses me—that makes me see it may have been rectified by Bryant himself. [C. A.] Dana, in his 'Household Book of Poetry' quotes me rather copiously." [Not in Eleventh edition of 1868.] Mention of R. H. Dana's "The Buccaneer"—which I had never read—I asking W. —"Do you think it would be worth my while to hunt it up?"—"I certainly do—if you have not read it, it would certainly repay your search highly. It is a really noble poem in its class—has more the ring of Scott than any poem I know in English. Scott's is so free, so high—

has itself so grandly the ring of balladry—is perennial. I did not know that side [of] Dana's at all." But he had read "Two Years Before the Mast." "This Dana was a young man of consumptive tendencies—seems to have concluded that the thing for him to do to save himself was to go to sea—to ship before the mast—which he did, with the result that that book was written."

I spoke of reading Noel's "Byron." W. then inquired: "Have you ever had occasion to read Macaulay's essay on Byron? I always liked that very much. And there, too, is Arnold's essay on Heine, on the same order—to me the best thing Arnold has written—the only thing among the essays having for me a deep and lasting influence, interest. It is here somewhere and I have looked into it more times than I could give account of."

Tuesday, December 31, 1889

Did not see W. today, as I had told him would be the case. At the bank till 12.15.—Weather cooler and good.

Wednesday, January 1, 1890

1.30 P.M. W. in his room reading The Ledger. Said there was no sign of his poem yet. "Have *you* caught it?" he asked. He had read the Gladstone–Blaine controversy in The North American Review about the tariff. "Gladstone does not appear to great advantage as a controversialist. I can see that Blaine might knock him out on that line. Yet the arguments for protection are mainly special pleading. I see some one wants a duty put on bananas: that seems laughable, but I see in it the gist of the whole matter." Then referred to Gladstone's age—"Eighty! Oh! a great age! And Whittier 82—and Tennyson 80!"

Spoke of the New Year's noises. "That's the average nigger's, average man's, boy's, idea of amusement, to make a big howl—and they succeed in doing it, generally." Asked about the appearance of the Philadelphia streets, and was much amused with what I saw of the midnight orgies, so to speak, on Chestnut Street.

I asked him for Sarrazin's exact number for Stockley. W. thereupon, as he took up his memorandum book and looked for it: "Did you know that Troyon was the name of an artist?—a famous artist?—as famous as any? They have a way there in France"—evidently having Millet in mind—"of ignoring their men till they are dead—then making a devil of a noise about them." I asked: "But do they not do this everywhere?" "Oh yes! and being done is well done, too: it is a consuming force—gets rid of the fellow who puts his foot in it!"

Today he had received his copy of The Century. "Who is Bryce?" he asked, as I looked at the frontispiece—and on my saying what he was, fully—"Oh yes! I remember: I had forgotten all about the name—how it was connected. I have never read the book: an Englishman and writing as such—I see!" And of Henry James' article on Daumier, the caricaturist, W. said he liked the illustrations "very much." The Camden Post yesterday contained a poem by James Law (of Camden) on W. W. W. had secured a number of copies. Written in Scotch dialect—W. had "no opinion to deliver" on it. In giving me Johnston's address (N. Y.) which I had asked for: "The best typical American of the business class I know—a man of ventures, losing in some, but in the main coming out profitably—a man warm for good causes—cute, alert—not afraid to send 5 dollars after what another man might call a chimera."

I stayed but briefly, having to get a train. W. looked well and said he felt well. Weather drizzly—would not, of course, get out—nor had he been yesterday. Asked after my work last night—seemed and said he was "pleased that you got out so well."

Thursday, January 2, 1890

Detained in Philadelphia in the Bank—with a meeting to attend late in the evening—therefore could not see W.

Friday, January 3, 1890

7.30 P.M. W. in his room reading a book which proved to be Hedge's "Prose Writers of Germany." When we commenced talking he laid it down, but by and bye took hold of it again and said to me: "Do you know anything about this book? It seems to me a great, a teeming book. I have had it about me for a full thirty years, and from time to time gone through it again." And he asked me about Hedge himself—"Alive still?" as he is—calling my attention to some of the portraits—particularly Schiller's—saying of this—"What a beautiful man he must have been!"—and being very curious about Jean Paul. "There is no mention of Heine, but I wish there was." His copy is an edition of 1848. "I guess I have had it nearly from that date." I read and translated for him the German text on the title page, signifying the profundity of the German nature rather than its delicacy etc.—and he thought that "a profound reflection itself."

"I have a letter from Doctor today. Yes indeed, he speaks of your note—seems to be in great glee about it—about me. Says you give him glowing good accounts." I laughed at the glow, but told W. what had been the substance of my letter: then asking him: "Don't you really feel yourself more comfortable than last winter?"—"Yes indeed"—adding—"I was out today—enjoyed myself to the full—it seemed a little cold—did it to you? but it was fresh and fine." And he acknowledged that these were "the saving of" him.

"Tom was here last night," he said, "and he brought along a big bottle of whisky—the best you ever saw." Then adding,

225

after some reflection: "I think I shall mix a pitcher of toddy tomorrow." Asking me then amusedly: "Are you fully and irrevocably determined against it?"—adding—"Well—if you are, then I won't save you any." I put in—"No—keep mine for your own profit." And he laughed—"Profit? No—I shall drink very little myself—it would not do—only enough to taste—to be satisfied it is right—that my cunning has not left me." This day's papers much given to accounts of the death of George H. Boker yesterday. W. said: "Boker seems to have been a genuine man, a good liver,—genial,—eating, drinking. He is Elizabethan, I should say—one with the men of the Elizabethan time—with Shakespeare, with Marlowe, with Johnson: brilliant, versatile, alert." He admitted "Francesca da Rimini" was "much of a play"—adding—"I knew Boker—met him: he had the look of a man with the best to drink; the best to eat; warm, florid, almost effusive in his ways." And—"He seems to have suffered a good deal toward the last. Poor fellow—poor fellow!"

Said he had not yet sent Symonds' letter to Bucke. Gave me a check to settle up with Billstein. I had a letter from Brinton in which he gave me the names of several Danish scholars. W. said: "To a man understanding us, our ways— taking an interest in us—such a reading and translation, pencil in hand, would be an hour's pleasant diversion."

That Mrs. Fairchild signed herself "Elizabeth Fairchild" in the letter I received today seemed to awaken a curious line of reasoning in him. "Is it some sudden new development of woman's-rights-ism?" he asked—some [?] of independence?"

Saturday, January 4, 1890

7.50 P.M. In his room. Was out and at the shipyards today. I asked on entrance (he sitting there reading one of his old Customs diaries)—"And did you have your trip out of doors today?"—he replying, amused: "And here he enters with a

226

question, knowing that of all abominations, that is the worst to me." And asking after a slight pause—"And how is the weather now?" I saying—"Another question"—and he—"To give one question for another! I have heard of a man who said, I *take* treats but never give them. I did not know the man, but have heard of him."

After all, he had "not inclined to make the whisky toddy today." Called my attention to the book in his hand. "This is one of my countless memorandum books—I have had hundreds of them—this is a Washington one—now 20 or 25 years old. I do not know by what combination of circumstances it has been preserved—but here it is, turned up after many days— old, grimed. Every name, every date in it, recalls a thousand scenes, multifold memories—persons, events—army incidents—those fruitful years. The written record but a drop in the bucket—I may say, a drop in the sea—to the whole story." And even the glimpses in "Specimen Days" were "but the most fugitive—the most slight—most brief." Bucke made some suggestions as to head-line for my Whitman essay thus:

I hope great things from your Whitman paper. Yes, make it personal by all means, and put it in as simple a narrative form as possible. Yes, nothing could be better (as an illustration) than the last Aug. photo. (which looks across the room at me as I write). A photo of the "den" too (if it could be well done) wd. be most interesting (wonderfully so to those who have been in it more or less often). "Walt Whitman at date" would do:
how would you like:
"W. W. as I know him"
But (after some hundreds of them) I am a little tired of papers, paragraphs, sonnets, &c. &c. &c. called "Walt Whitman" in any shape. How would something like one of the following titles do? (of course I have no pretention to *name* a paper I have not even seen):
    "The Poet of the Modern"
    "The First American Poet"
    "The Avatar of Democracy"
    "The Bard of the Dawning Era"

I read to W. who exclaimed: "No! no! I can say without hesitation, that, as far as *I* am concerned these would all be promptly rejected." I explained that they would not fall in line with the personal flavor of my paper. I had initial paragraphs of this with me, and read them to W.—who said when I had done: "Yes—that is good: but too eulogistic—too eulogistic! I should suggest—make it very concrete—even statistical—and then a close. But I ought to add of this, as I would of my own writing—you are the man who is writing it, or I am, as the case may be, and it is for you or for me, therefore, to follow our own bent, please oneselves, whatever the other fellow may believe."

"And so poor George Boker is buried!" W. said at another juncture. "Come—gone—a true high man. And the years— oh! how they go and go! I am amazed: this little book here— this bunch of memorandums—already a quarter of a century old! It is hard to realize lapse after lapse the slipping away of time."

"The papers appear to be full of society news, gossip, controversy—just now, the solid things all ignored, unheralded." I referred to the Thoreau-ish Herbert, gone out on Long Island from professional life in New York, to live as a recluse and farm an acre or two—having already written a book about it. —W. explaining the topographical and other character of Long Island—its "very jagged coasts at some points" and its "salt-marshiness," especially towards the east. "I know the whole shore well and well—have wandered it, I can almost say afoot."

Sunday morning, January 5, 1890

9.45. W. in his room reading The Press. "The papers are full of stuff, and yet one keeps on asking, what is there? What *is* there? *Nothing*, that I see."

He has a great way of asking, if you have a bundle in your

hands—"What have you there?" This time it was [J. Vila] Blake's essays. "That is good—the paper label—not but that the label itself could be better, but the label because a label is a good idea—is not amiss. I remember a farce, when I was a young man, theatre-going—'The Captain's not a-Miss'—not a bad pun, as puns go, on the word—seized from some point in the play. Yes, it is quite dead now, I suppose. At that time it was the custom to close an evening—even a tragedy evening—with a one-act farce. There were always two sets of theatre-goers—one that came late, one that came early: by the insertion of the farce, both ends were pleased." And then he went back to the book. "So this book is by the preacher-man. It is well printed—goes back to the old style—not that the old style is good or bad, but that it is old, is the significance."

I asked W. about the Booth pictures in Jefferson's Century article. "They are quite good—have merit. I don't think anyone who ever saw the elder Booth in his prime—at his best—could believe our present man to hold a candle to him. In fact, to one who has seen [James Henry] Hackett's Rip Van Winkle, Jefferson seems very much smaller and narrower. Hackett did not play it often. Jefferson's is modelled a good deal on the formal theatrical rules—he makes too much of the farcicality of the play—like Byron, who was said to like the rum that cut his throat as it went down. Not but that it was good and I have enjoyed it, for I have. I have seen him many times—liked him best in the plays he plays least, or now not at all—did play in his early days—as Noggs, for instance, in the little piece from Dickens."—And then he commented directly on Jefferson's article. "These fellows do not seem to know as much as is supposed—if I had it in mind to write an article about the acting of those early days, I should certainly get nearer the heart of the matter than Jefferson does—of the marrow, what-not, he knows little or nothing." I told him I was glad to see a picture there of Harry Placide, of whom I had heard so much. "The picture is pretty good but not very good. Placide was not what would be called facially a handsome man—he was a man of the old style—by that I do not mean that the old style is to be preferred to the new—only, that the man of the old style—say, Zachary Taylor—with whom I one time rode north from New Orleans—or Henry Clay—or Abraham Lincoln—men who on the Greek principle would be considered ugly—had yet a positive magnetism, attractiveness not to be gainsaid. Placide had this power, if not the gift of beauty." Jefferson lacked the highest touch by being "to inclined not to reserve anything." W. knew Salvini was intense—"but to Italians, the Spanish, the French,—to Oriental natures—this is the necessary and fit thing."

Monday, January 6, 1890

6.20 P.M. W. in his room, just lighting up. Gave me a cordial welcome. I picked a cracker up from a full plate on the table. He laughed. "Hungry? Take more—take half a dozen— and take some cheese with it—there is cheese there. If I did not know it was useless I should ask you to take some toddy. All the ingredients are about me,"—pointing to stove and table. I was just on my way home from work. He added: "I can easily make a good plain meal out of bread and crackers— have often done so."

"The world," he afterward said, "appears to be going on its own pace, nothing in the daily records to move us greatly." He hardly ever knew "a more placid" era "so to speak." Had not yet read Blake's book. "It is one of the good things to come."

I was reading today the Hay "Lincoln"—now at the point of L.'s assassination. I referred to it as "a lost opportunity." W. thereupon: "Yes—it is absolutely without the vivid touches that belong to the event. One is hardly excused for writing of it at all if not better than that. Beside, as you say, it lacks entirely in perspective—is partisan—full of blackguardism, so to speak." I had put it: "The writers seem utterly unable to protect themselves—to get in other hearts but their own. They cannot get over the idea that Booth was a scoundrel— any other notion seems impossible to them." At which W.— "You hit the nail on the head there. They are not in the least Greek, Homeric. Old Homer, as long ago as that, had the good sense to make Hector a great man—to fill him out— make him expansive—indeed, so markedly so, as to incline some to demur. But it was a true instinct, necessary as well at this time as that. I think I see all through this life of Lincoln a tendency to blackguard the South—the Southern men— this is a spirit that ought to be altogether gone."

He had "heard somewhere that Stedman has come into a fortune"—adding—"What do you know about it? Somebody was here—told me: I was going to say it was Tom Donaldson, but it was not—it was some New Yorker, I am sure. How good that would be for Stedman! I hope it may all be true! How it comes—of all that—I know nothing."

Said Boyle, the sculptor, had been over today. I knew him slightly, and knew *of* him from various quarters. W. inquired very specifically. "I was wonderfully taken with him—he was so plain, so hearty. He came about the cemetery lot. When Donaldson was here he spoke very enthusiastically of Boyle— said he was just the man I wanted. I was very favorably disposed to hearing him. But I don't know—all is in the nebulous condition—I have no *ideas* on the subject at all." Speaking of Boyle's work—"I should think the danger of his work— as of the work of all sculptors (and others, too, for the matter of that) is in the temptation to make their work genteel—to bow before the gentility of the world—and you know there's no one in the world more despises all that. I am a confirmed enemy to gentility, respectability—yet, as I often say, more respectful to both than their own advocates—finding a place in the scheme undoubtedly belonging to them—insisting, in-

231

deed, they shall have it. How much the artists, writers, sur-render to gentility! It is astonishing—the extent of the sacri-fice." —"I am so opposed to respectability, they think I'm not respectable!"

Referred to my father's big charcoal Whitman. "I hope he has not touched it since I saw him—it seemed to me on the whole there was nothing more to be done. The devil in artists is to keep pegging away at a thing after it really is all done—pegging away at it *done*, till it is *undone*." I happened to say Tom Harned did not like that version of W. "That surprises me some, because that is so obviously to me among the best if not the very best." —I objected—"Of all but mine on the wall there at home!" W. then—"Well—I know: Tom Eakins always would say to me—'that is the chef-d'oeuvre—that has the indescribable something called magnetism in highest de-gree.' And I know O'Connor liked it immensely."—I put in—"And saw resemblance to Hugo (or Hugo to it) in it." "Yes—so I believe. And I can see why you fellows like it—its power, its mid-age immensity"—"as all pictures of an able-bodied in his prime ought to be."

I picked up a large blue envelope laying loosely with other matters on the floor, and asked him whose it was. He put on his glasses. "Ah! Bertz! I think you will find it worth while to take that along with you." It was a letter of last July, contain-ing an extended account of B.'s American experiences and how he came to know Leaves of Grass.

Tuesday, January 7, 1890

7.45 P.M. W. very well, though the damp weather keeps him indoors. He has not been affected by "La Grippe," the prevalence of which is great. Warm days still prevailing, he expressing his regret. Wonderfully frank about his graveyard preparations. Is considering whether or not to put his mother and father there in the lot. The question raised by some of his friends that he should spend his last years in other cities—Washington, New York, Brooklyn—he has quietly settled by this act. "It is all nebulously conditioned," he says, "but we shall know, in time." And as to the poem he was to write in consideration, he laughed—"Oh that!"—and that was, "if anything," more "dubious than the rest."

Said he had been reading Amelia Barr's Century story today. "It is called 'O'Hara' and is very well done, too—brilliantly, but well." And "I have been reading, also, Tennyson's little poem—I found it here in The Critic—'Across [Crossing?] the Bar'—and ever so good, too." He handed me a little volume—12mo—gilt stamping—rough edge—"See this—there is a new poet risen—this came today."—A Putnam volume—written by Wm. T. Washburn, of whom neither of us had ever heard. W. said: "He makes a big dash there—several hundreds of pages." The book had been sent without an inscription, and W. had cut none of the pages except a half-dozen at the end. But the typographical setting[?] of the book, and its cover, had "struck" him—and this he dwelt upon. I went about a good deal. "When do you get time to read and write?" I answered, "On cars, boats, &c." W. then—"I don't know but that's best of all. People think it distracting, but it is not: there's everything in getting used to it."

Seeing something that glistened under the stove, I leaned over—found it was his mammoth pen-holder. He laughed. "Ah! the long-missing pen! My pens are very elusive, like my handkerchiefs—I have uncountable dozens of them somewhere about the house—but when I want one, it is not to be found." Gave me Contemporary Club tickets for Clifford and Mrs. Baldwin.

Wednesday, January 8, 1890

7.20 P.M. W. reading—in his room. Growing much colder this evening. Had been out today, in South Camden, but only briefly. He admits: "Out-of-doors is my savior this winter." Sets it off contrastingly against the entire confinement last winter. I met Donaldson—big, stalwart, ruddy—on the steps of the Custom House today. He commented on W.'s condition—his selection of the cemetery lot—calm disposal of affairs for the end.

Left with him Harper's Weekly containing Winter's article "Shakespeare in New York"—and joked with W. about his "friend the enemy," as the journalists put it. He would only say in his laughter: "Never mind—we must welcome Winter and a thousand others. Besides, it is well, as I say, to read it, to be satisfied that you know what you talked about when you predicted it was empty." And turning the pages of the Weekly—"This is my despair—all this sumptuousness, elegance. I remember in Washington, when I was in the Treasury Department—and some great dinner was preparing at the White House—some powwow of the chiefs—there was a fellow would come for me—take me up there. I was greatly impressed—thought to myself—it's a vast muchness to have seen all this, if without a bite, or even an assurance there's anything to eat—the decorations, plate, everything, elaborate past imagination." He had never been himself a partaker of these dinners—"they were for the big guns exclusively. And these papers, magazines—Harper's, the Century—impress me, though there be no fruit in them all—no meat, no nothing to satisfy an appetite. Certainly the world of our time achieves richness, magnificence, if no more."

There was a picture of Boker in Harper's. I asked how it struck him. "Yes—I knew Boker,—this is reasonably good— you would know it. I met Boker a number of times—dined with him two or three times. He was good company—a man you might want to be with—a good man for neighbor, to stop in to see you once in a while—good brain, good heart, good many things—yet I would not say without irritability, though the irritable side of him I never saw." Clifford had wondered

how much of B.'s life was wasted?—given up to easy living
&c. W. insisted: "I should hardly say his life was wasted—his
life will bear deeper looking into than that. He was Elizabethan—polished to the core—like the Elizabethans, seeing to
it to have a thing handsomely done, a piece of art, irreproach-
able from that standpoint." Boker had once written some sort
of pasquinade—"Yes, I have heard of a volume of that import.
Boker had that too in common with the Elizabethans—lug-
ging his personal quarrels into even his poetry, his art. Shakespeare had it—putting his enemies into verse—into a play,
what-not. They tell a story of Michael Angelo—that he had
an enemy—that he was painting some sort of an apostolic picture and gave to his Judas the face of this man. But that afterward it came forcibly to him, this was not wise, not large—
this was a weakness—and that finally he erased the portrait—
put in some other face. It has been many years since I learned
that—read it—but I have given you its substance. I doubt if
the greatest, biggest, fellows ever gave way to such temptation. Boker was a fine sample of the physiological man; a good
diner—and yet more than that, too, just as we know that
often-times the biggest body is consistent with the biggest
other things—soul—spirit. Boker at bottom—the base of
him—as was true of Burns, too—was hypochondriac—not
that he was altogether that, without higher, other moods."

He spoke rather curiously on another matter—laughing the
while: "I got a letter today from a man in New York named
File—the envelope was marked Editorial Rooms New York
Sun: he asked for a piece—enclosed me a check for 10 dollars—but what it was all for, Lord only knows—the letter itself gives no sign of a purpose, except the general one that he
wants something for print." Hunted the letter up—it had already got badly confused with the rest of things in that corner. Finally, however, he fished it out. "Here it is—judge for
yourself—read it." Letter extracted was a short communication from the Tribune from someone who parallels recent re-

sembling verses from Whittier and Tennyson. File wished from W. 5 or 6 hundred words on the subject. W. asked, "How do you interpret that—is it verse he wants or prose?" It was easily prose, for he suggested to W. "it might be happy to quote in your matter some extract from your own poems." "Ah!" said W. "Then you think that concludes it? I guess it does—I proceeded on that basis." Then—on my asking what he had clipped from the Tribune extract (I noticed it was cut): "There were two verses quoted—one from Tennyson's poem 'Across [Crossing?] the Bar' and the other from Whittier's 'Burning Driftwood'—I thought the last a fine touch." I asked: "So you acted upon the man's proposition at once?" "Yes. Wrote the matter—sent it off forthwith. How it will hit *him* is another thing. Do you know anything about File? Never heard of him? Neither did I." Then he inquired: "What do you take to be the meaning of the word *verse*? O'Connor used to insist that one line was a verse; but that is not the general understanding, however generically correct." And he supposed there was no longer any way back to O'Connor's meaning, when the whole world had set upon another.

Thursday, January 9, 1890

7.30 P.M. W. in his room, reading the Boston Transcript. Asked me if I had heard "the good news about Kennedy." That K. had "got a place on the Transcript—is proof-reading there." Advised me to write K.—"You ought to write often— he would enjoy the notes."—"If you must, write short notes—little touches—Kennedy himself does—then lets 'em go." He started out today—"but we stayed only a few minutes—I am very sensitive to the cold: but Warry thought we ought to go, if it was only round the block."

I received today the following note from Adler, which I now read to W.

The Society for Ethical Culture
Address
1025 Park Avenue   New York,   Jan. 8'th, 1890.
Dear Mr. Traubel:
      Thanks for your lines. If there is any reluctance on Whitman's part, or if he has any scruples, no matter what they may be, please do not urge him in the least.

Yours sincerely,
Felix Adler

W. said: "No—no—that is wrong—I have no such scruple. On the contrary I want to give it to him." So, as if to prove it, he took up a writing pad and pencil and on his knee wrote the following:

Mickle St Camden
Jan: 9 '90

Dear J B
      This will be given you by my friend Felix Adler & I hope you will have a good talk & good time anyhow. Nothing very new or different with me—all is going on the same, & fairly—— Write, & when you do tell me your P. address & any proposed movements

Walt Whitman

"Send that to him," he said when it was done, "let him have that—and welcome, too."

Returned me Harper's Weekly. Had read Winter's piece— "but it did not impress me—is absolutely wanting in *content*, as they say. There are very pretty pictures going along with it. But there is Mansfield—I am more and more certain that Mansfield amounts to little—is in no way our man. Indeed, when I look around—think of the men that have been on our stage—Booth the elder, Forrest, others—I am in a sort of despair—for we have no men to keep up the high standard of their work. There are some who believe, that among other qualifications to be one day assured, America has a dramatic future—a glorious play-future. "But"—shaking his head—"I

237

don't know—I doubt it seriously. I have a young friend—oh! I forget his name now—an actor, a New Yorker—and a handsome man, too—who is quite eloquent to that effect—quite. But I can't share his enthusiasm—I see nothing just now to warrant it."—"Yet the little flies like Willie Winter go buzzing about that it is already accomplished—is already here."

I showed W. a card the President of the Bank had given me today. He had passed 25 dollars each to the bookkeepers, and when one started to thank him drew this forth and said: "No, don't say anything about it: I believe this."

THINK OF THIS

"I expect to pass through this world but once. Any good thing, therefore, that I can do, or any kindness that I can show, to any fellow being, let me do it NOW. Let me not defer it or neglect it, for I SHALL NOT PASS THIS WAY AGAIN."

Upon hearing it W. remarked: "There's a spice of humor in it—I'll bet it's Dutch in origin—and it has a kernel."

Prof. Richey, writing to Dr. Thackeray about his book on the land question, said among other things: "I have to congratulate you on the accuracy with which it is printed, a thing not ordinarily met with in American books." W. insisted: "This is not wisely said: there may be said to be certain inevitable errors of typography, but these may be expected, and found, in other as well as American books. Now if he had said something about the *printing* of our books, he would have had more point."

As I left he insisted on giving me three doughnuts to take along. "One for Tillie, one for your mother, one for Aggie— one for each. Mary Davis has been making them today—and they take my time—and we like to share a good thing when we have it." I did not go directly home—gave Aggie her doughnut in the city, at a meeting, when refreshment time came—she slicing it into 15 pieces and passing it around as W. W.'s doughnut—a muncher thereupon saying, "Here goes to Walt Whitman—may he live long" etc.

Friday, January 10, 1890

6.40 P.M. Though not severely cold, it was too raw and moist for W.'s getting out today. When I came into the room, he had a lap full of papers etc. "I am reading the Spectator," he remarked, "some thoughtful person keeps on sending it to me." And nearby was the Pall Mall Gazette—full of Browning—with a curious portrait—of which W. declared: "That is a study in engraving—strangely lined, outside of the usual—but on the whole very effectively done."

I told him the episode of the doughnut. "Oh! that was interesting—and how good of 'em!—Thanks—thanks!" And after a pause: "I say 'thanks' for the want of a word more expressive." I put in—"Bucke says you do not say 'thank you,' except rarely." W. hereupon—"Oh! but I guess I do—plenty often enough, for all practical purposes—or other!"

He never was able to decipher Burroughs' Poughkeepsie address as given in the last note. In sending the introductory note on to Adler I had to advise him of our ignornance. W.: "Correspondents have the strangest and most persistent idiosyncrasies—a sort of hate of being explicit. They are very fond of beating the devil around the stump. You will not credit it, but I once sent some money to someone who was in need of it—but there came no acknowledgment. I had letters, but never a word about this—not a word. I wrote a second, a third, would you believe, a *fourth* time—in no way the word I wished!" Even at the last, when an answer *was* given to my question, it was still so indefinite I could not make it out—do not know to this day if my 8 dollars were actually received. I don't suppose I have a big correspondence at all, but I suppose one-sixth of the letters I receive are of the worrisome kind—letters for autographs, letters begging for money (they have heard I am a kindly old man!)—letters for literary advice—not the fewest, these—letters without number from men—famous men, as the world goes, who write bad hands. Just today I got a letter from Mrs.

Mapes, who, as you know, has gone west. She has a poor old aunt or somebody out there, and I sent a little money for her. I think the letter must be very interesting, but it is written in the palest of pale ink—ink all watered out. I wrestled with it some 15 minutes, then gave it up—handed it over to Mary."

The papers this morning extensively announced the death of Judge W. D. Kelly. I asked W. if he knew the Judge? "Oh yes! I knew the Judge quite well—had many a talk with him—not a bad fellow; but a man from head to toe—from the crown of the crown of his head, to the sole of the sole of his feet, the henchman of the protection interests—a man who is like a preacher: he preaches his creed so often, so long, he believes it must be true. Our man Dudley here is much the same kind of a man. They believe America could not be, could not last, but for this particular dogma. Yet Kelly was not all of this sort—in most things (I don't know about religion)—he was radical: a plain man in his ways, much of a democrat."

I happened to say tonight in one of our discussions: "The most important lessons of history are of avoidance—avoidance rather than guidance, except as avoidance *is* guidance." W. exclaiming, "Why how profound, how fine, this is! I have often struggled to say that, in my own way, but a less way."

Saturday, January 11, 1890

7.45 P.M. W. sits sometimes, as a shepherd with his crook—his cane in his lap—ruminating—not reading: often, with the stove door open, the embers therein flashing warmth into his face—playing with his great head and hair. So it was tonight, the eye unwontedly calm, the whole attitude, very wakeful but very soul-dwelling. When I came in I stood a moment—he did not see me: then seemed to wake to my presence with a start, shook hands cordially and heightened the gas somewhat. He asked me, as he usually does—"Well, what news? What do you hear?"—and when I said I had no news for one who so industriously read the papers as he did, he laughed, and retorted—"Well, no news is good news, they used to say, and I don't know but they hit the nail squarely on the head in saying so."

He was very curious and querying about a phrase I used— "The average miscellaneous unsuspected reader of L. of G." "Who are they? Do you actually think there is such an audience? Who knows, to be sure?"—adding that "It is true all sorts of good greetings—unexpected greetings, endorsements, what-not—turn up from time to time."

He spoke of Gilchrist's dislike for the London News picture. "He would not accept it at all—he thoroughly embraced Tom Donaldson's criticism—that it was foxy—foxy. Tom is a keen, good fellow—has the faults of the politician—yet is more than the poliician at the last. I consider him a true friend of mine. Five years ago or so, in the nick of time— when I needed, as perhaps no one knew, could have known, I needed—he was the fellow, with Talcott Williams, who came in at the pinch, engineered the escape. Tom of course, is a fellow who cares too much for the stamp on the coin— thinks less of the silver—the quality of the silver—than of the stamp that is put upon it; not that he don't think of the metal, too—but the fact that the United States has consented to put its face upon the coin weighs heavily with him."

I asked him if he yet had the book for Edelheim? He said— "No—but I can get it any time for you—tomorrow–tonight— anytime."—Hereupon leaning forward, picked up a copy of "Two Rivulets" (1876)—"Why not take this to him? Wouldn't this do?" At my assent, writing therein. I described Edelheim to W.: the bustling business man, active, talkative—but open-handed, to be depended upon for all promises, etc.—W. exclaiming: "I know the class—I have met them—Johnson is one of them: sometimes I think them the justification of America—of that part of America which we are so fond of decrying—the explication of the mystery—the assurance of our future!" Adding: "Well—somehow I warm to your man: he has been generous to us, and we must show him we are not wanting in the power to reciprocate—or the wish."

Sunday, January 12, 1890

10 A.M. In but a few minutes. W. reading the Press—the Record on his knee. The day beautiful—and he "calculated on getting out" by and bye. The temperature high, almost to a spring figure.

He had found me volume 1 of Symonds' "Greek Poets"— "though volume 2 is yet somewhere in the haystack, unseen." The volume endorsed "From the Author." by Symonds himself, with W. W.'s Stevens Street label pasted therein, and W.'s inscription.

Sent me by Symonds himself—must have been 1881. For years—1882–'89—I dip and drink from the two volumes. They and Walter Scott's Border Minstrelsy are feasts never exhausted.
W W

and pointing this out to me, he said: "I still stand by this— Walter Scott first, for many early years—the initial predilection—O! the joy and wonder! and what it has done for me! Then this book of Symonds'—then both—both, as now: they have been a constant, unvarying resource."

I delivered Edelheim his book today—much to his surprise and gratification at the gift.

Monday, January 13, 1890

5.30 P.M. Stopped in at W.'s on my way home—stayed till six: twilight: he sitting by the fire, the door of the stove open an inch or two, letting out a flaring, flickering light, darting up into his face, from which he fended himself from time to time by intercepting his hand. "It is not colder? There seems

242

to be a high wind blowing?" I talked of the great sunset, and he was all ears: "I think I see—yes, I *do* see it—the river there—the boats—the open-way to all that is pictorially grand." He had not been out today: the moist cloudiness had persisted.

I referred to the curious Bible metaphor "as the waters cover the sea" and W. said of it, as if it had been a subject of his thought: "Yes—it is used several times—I think in both the Old and New Testaments: it can be said for the translation, that it is perhaps the best they can do: though I feel persuaded that the original explicates itself—that there all would be found rightly adjusted—the word right-valued—in its place. I can remember a figure O'Connor liked to use—I think it must have been Elizabethan: 'it fits like a cup'—'it fits your head like a cup'—very suggestive—powerful—Baconian." And then, in discussing O'Connor's gift of speech: "It was a rare bestowal—those of us who knew him well, knew how rare. He was in the highest sense what is called a born orator. I never heard him in a public meeting, but have had vivid accounts from those who did; and it appears he was in that situation just what he was in any other—grand, high, impassioned. Impassioned, truly: a sort of Greek passion—the driver of a dozen steeds, all mad for freedom, but all easily reined by his circumspection, judgment, certainty. That would typify him. Did you ever read William's piece on John Burroughs' book, printed at that day, in the New York Times? It was thoroughly strong—characteristic. No, I do not think O'Connor ever did much such work. Raymond was exceedingly warm towards him—invited him to come over—to take a position as editor on the Times staff. But O'Connor was doubtful about it, afraid, feared he could not get along, and so decided against—and wisely, for he could *not* have got along—would have fallen out at short order. He was the last man in the world to submit to emendation—would not hear to the displacement of a comma."

Brinton speaks tomorrow evening on Bruno at the Contemporary Club. W. "taken," as he said, with the prospect, though he could not hear the address himself. "Someone has sent me a piece on Bruno which may turn out to have some pertinency. I will look it up tomorrow. Bruno was the salt of the earth. All the men who are worth tying to—whose good judgment we respect—place Bruno high—with the highest. To me that is very significant—though in the way of details I really know very little about Bruno." He thought "Symonds probably the best man in all Europe to report on Bruno"—and it was for [from?] such judgments he "imbibed the highest respect" and for Bruno "they are many."

We discussed a question—involving religious orthodoxy—how far orthodoxy limited great men. W.: "I suppose there is a way in which that can be, should be, said"—that greatest men necessarily fail the orthodox standards, or exceed them, rather—"but then again we may point out, there is another orthodoxy—an orthodoxy deeper, more generous than the current orthodoxy—a sort of Hegelian orthodoxy—in which true big men put their hooks—to which they tie: the orthodoxy of Jesus, the orthodoxy of Mohammed, of Confucius, of Socrates—Socrates probably the greatest of them all—Socrates made much of it. Of course, the orthodoxy we see about us—the ministers, professors, churches, class-leaders, all that—and the creeds—of course they are all gammon—*all*—must disappear. I am not sure after all but the most needed man is Ingersoll—that Ingersoll is in advance of us all." He doubted "if a first-rate man—a real first-rater"—ever accepted "the limited in preference to the broader readings of faith."

Gave me Bucke's letter of the 10th, in which much account was made of the prevalence of La Grippe at London. W. spoke of the disorder—inquiringly—and noted that he seemed not to have been in the least touched by it.

Tuesday, January 14, 1890

7.15 P.M. W. in his room, but not reading, though the light was full on. Not out today—it was too cold.

I have been reading Roden Noel's Whitman. I said of it, for one thing, this evening: "However friendly and admiring, he still takes scarce measure of Leaves of Grass." W. thereupon: "Well—our utmost anyhow would be to say: it is very friendly. I have always felt that the book was amateurish—the work of a young man. That copy I have I suppose Noel sent"—but there was no name in it. I resented also the notes of Noel—stating Buchanan and Whitman in too-close terms. W. laughed at my warmth: "Do you know much about Buchanan?" Adding, when I asked him about B.'s "genius." "I don't know. Buchanan has a great idea of making money—has written plays, novels. He lost a wife of whom he was very fond: it was a great change for him. She left him a niece—a fine young girl, Harriet Gay, who afterwards went on the stage. It is for her Browning writes plays—makes a part for her—to fit her. She has been here a couple of times—has grown up a handsome, bright girl. Although decidedly girlish, crude, youthful, now—she is of the Byron kind: I should not be surprised any morning to wake up and find her famous. Yes—I have seen Buchanan, too—twice, if I remember right—he has been here. He is a typical John Bull—short, thick, ruddy, assertive, brusque—thick-necked. He came once—I think I have told you—we sat down-stairs—in the sitting-room—the room underneath this. It was a cold day—I found it difficult to get comfortable even with a fire—was hustling up the fire. Buchanan came in a carriage—jumped out and came indoors. After he had been in some time—a half hour at least, he said something about the carriage and some one he had left in it—and when I inquired *who* he told me Harriet Gay, the wife's niece. I asked, 'What, and you have left her there and in the cold all this time? Go out this instant and bring her in: she must be frozen to death.' And he did so—I not keeping her in the parlor but sending her back in the kitchen, where it was warmer and where Mrs. Davis gave her a cup of tea to thaw her out." He told this story with great vehemence and then said, "But of course Buchanan is more than that—has a comradeship side to him," though "these human derelictions a man don't altogether get over."

I was on my way to the Contemporary Club meeting, Brinton to speak on Bruno. W. wondered if we "could get up a discussion about Bruno"—for "an opponent of Bruno seems hard to conceive—especially in America."—Adding then emphatically: "There is but one side, and that is Bruno. Bruno is the genesis of the modern—Bruno is democracy—is science (that greatest democracy, science!)—the other side has not a peg to hang its hat on. Surely Tom Davidson—no one—will come there to hatchel Bruno; in this age, our land, it seems impossible—utterly so. After what you said to me last night of Brinton and Bruno, I can see that Bruno is our man—is America—*that we cannot escape the logic he in his own person is.* If you see Brinton, give him my love—tell him he has my prayers—though I suppose he cares nothing for prayers, mine or another's."

In a letter from Kennedy today he says: "Tell Walt that I am going to send $5.00 to pay for that beautiful edition of L. of G. he sent me." W. exclaimed when I read this to him— "Money? I won't have the money! If you write to him tell him I don't want his money—tell him the book was sent as a sort of New Year's present—something for him to have, not to buy." And then he asked, "What does he mean by jealousy?" And again—"The *foxy* Scotchman? That manuscript encounters a bad fate."

Kennedy's letter:

246

Belmont Mass
Jan'y 12 '90.

Dear Traubel:—

Thank you for yr very kind and fraternal letter. It is good to feel that the mean jealousy one hits against so much is absent from the hearts of a few tried & warm-hearted friends.

I enjoy very much at the Transcript office talks & chins with the good dreamy cigar-scented & smoke-encircled fellows—Hurd, Chamberlain (who, by the way, has just left for the Youths Companion office, but will continue the *Listener* chat), Hazewell, Clement, Edwards *et al.*

Who is Chubb?

My brain gets exhausted by working under pressure so much so good bye.

Tell Walt that I am going to send $5.00 to pay for that beautiful ed. of L. of G. he sent me. The foxy Scotchman doesn't return my W. W. *ms.* yet. I can't make him out. Just talked with a young stock-fancy-farmer-neighbor-colt-tamer. He treasures L. of Grass, & has read the Ox-Tamer.—Miss [?] Bates still alive! reported dead!

Kennedy.

Wednesday, January 15, 1890

Did not see W.—was at Germantown, with Clifford, Mrs. Baldwin and Anne, editing the Johnson Ms. about Parker.

Thursday, January 16, 1890

5.45 P.M. W. was just arranging to light up the room, preliminarily closing blinds, etc. I did not offer to assist—rarely do, for I know he would rather do this for himself. The weather all through the late afternoon had grown colder, a high wind prevailing. W. said: "We tried to go out today, but found it too cold, had soon to retreat."

I had secured from Brinton the other night the manuscript of his address on Bruno, which now I gave to W.—who ques-

247

tioned me about its purport and about the ground on which McConnell had opposed it. "I know I shall look through it—read it all—with the greatest satisfaction. You don't know if it is to be printed anywhere? I should like to have a copy for Symonds, who takes a special interest in that direction—none more so, probably no one in all Europe."

Afterwards he reported: "I had an English admirer here today—a young man, a member of Wilson Barrett's company, now in Philadelphia. Yes, somehow the actor-boys—and girls, too, for that—have a soft side for me, as I certainly have for them." "I have received," he offered again, "a letter from the man we sent the book to—what is his name? O yes! Edelheim! He appears to be strangely grateful—which shows that our remembrance was a happy inspiration."

As to Bucke's question about the Symonds letter: "The truth is, I have not sent it yet—it is on the table there now. It has been suggested to me—self-suggested—that I print it—in some way put it in type; and for that reason I have for the present put it aside there—retained it. Doctor will see it, or a copy of it, in due time."

I told him I had met Boyle at the Club—B. talking of W.'s project of the vault, saying he would possibly like to enlist Wilson Eyre, as being both an architect and a lover of Walt Whitman. W. said to me: "I don't think I ought to start out with saying I don't want this and that and the other. But I have a very clear notion that I do *not* want anything elaborate, anything artistic, elegant, delicate, refined: [should] look on the contrary, for something of a natural, native, rugged character, suggesting strength and first sources rather than anything sculptural or architectural. I should like to say this to both Eyre if he is enlisted, and Boyle. For Emerson they found nothing but a simple stone—all they would get him to consent to was that. I should not second him—imitate—only his example is suggestive—beautiful. I like Boyle—my first impression was a very good one. I can sense he will finally hit upon something I want." W.'s limit of price was "about a thousand dollars." Boyle has been to the Cemetery and admired W.'s choice greatly.

W. had a letter from Dana Estes, Boston—asking W. for his presence or some word for use at the memorial meeting for Browning, Jan. 28. He gave me the letter. Had he sent his word? "No—I did not send anything: Browning was not a man who had taken any hold on me—did not seem to me our man. I do not feel as if I had anything at all to say."

Said Melville Phillips had been over to see him today. "He came on a special mission—is editor or something on Munyon's Illustrated World—wished to know if I could not be counted on to give them a little *something* every month—a contribution. O yes! I consented. I have been wondering if George Childs did not back up the paper. Of course I don't *know* he does. Some two or three years ago or more a Munyon himself was over to see me and I wrote him one little piece." He said he had been "rather impressed with Phillips, who is young, looks the clerical college man to the end. I had a notion before he came that he was quite another person—a notion I had met him years ago somewhere—2 or 3 years—I think in the Press office itself—and not liked him and snubbed him. But the instant I saw him today I knew he was not the man. I had a way in the old times—as I have not now—of saying something very snubbing to a fellow I thought impudent—and it was to this I treated the man there in the Press—probably some temporary upstart." He remembered Phillips' review of November Boughs but not the fine notice of Cabot's Emerson.

I told him I had advised Boyle—"Make the vault *elemental*—keep it strictly to elements: it more fits W.'s character and tastes than anything else"—and W. now said: "That was a good thing to say—just what I should have said or wished said—and we must keep them to it."

Hearing the nature of some of the arguments against Brinton the other evening, W. said: "Yes—there is something in urging Christianity as against that scientific tendency, but"—and he added—"It is an argument, and I don't know but a good one, in its degree."

Friday, January 17, 1890

7.15 P.M. Found W. reading "The Deerslayer"—in which he admitted he "found" his "old interest." Thought Cooper one of our "native fine souls—flavored of the soil." I had the Magazine of Art containing Swinburne's new poem—"Loch Torridon." W. asked, "What is that?" in his boy-curiosity—and when I told him and proposed to leave it—"I am not a Swinburne devotee—yet I read him—he has his points." And as to the appearance of the poem—"This print strikes me with envy—I never see anything so good but I am persuaded out of my skin."

Asked me about my father's portrait, whose now complete state I described to him. "I liked it greatly as it was: now—if he has succeeded in taking from it the suggestion of dark eyes, I don't know but it may be considered, as far as art will permit, perfect—yes, perfect. Have you seen it? And you are satisfied with it? That goes a long way towards satisfying *me*: for you ought to know—and I know you never go off into useless enthusiasms." Given the opinion I avowed, with what he knew of it—"it ought to be one of the very best pictures extant. There is a damnable tendency in artists to over-refine—as a rule a copy is worse than an original, a second copy than a copy and so on: you can stake yourself for this. But in the case of your father, this picture, then, comes as an exception."

Said he had written to Kennedy. "Only a postal. It came into my mind I had not written to him for a fortnight, so today I sent off a short message, but a very important thing I forgot entirely—the only thing in fact that really needed being said.

I mean about the book, the pay—the gift-book, New Year's. Do you expect to write within a few days? If you do, tell him for me what we have been talking about—tell him on no account to send the money." Said Gilchrist had come over last evening. "I was about to go to bed—he was here a short time. As luck will have it, or circumstance, he always comes about that time—late—too late. I suppose he works up to the last glints of light—then is not satisfied till he has gone out—breathed the fresh air—stretched body, soul—all!"

Sometimes in jest we use Symonds' expression—"Whitman's Bible." I said this evening I had an impulse to write to Symonds myself—I did not know to what effect, but *something*—W. advising me: "Yes, do so: every such impulse is to be obeyed: I should like you to write and I have no doubt he would like to hear from you—that you could tell him things no one else could—things he would like to hear."

W. had read Brinton's lecture. "It is very fine: I have not for a long time read anything that so possessed me. I sat down last night after you had gone and read it through—every word of it—which, for me, in these days, is remarkable—is a tribute (rather, a *respect*) in itself. I wish you would thank Brinton for me—tell him he could not have had a more rapt auditor and that I weighed every word—with this advantage: that I was here, read it at my leisure, could pause, go back, re-read, chew on it—weigh passages which an actual listener had to pass at an equal pace: and some of the extracts from Bruno demand such attention. I hope Brinton will have it published—I should like at least one copy of it—one for Symonds—and perhaps others. It has a splendid, simple, high, force—momentum. Brinton evidently starts out to be judicial—*is*—his whole paper is Greek—poised. There is one thing about it I particularly delighted in—a theory of which Taine makes the most of any man I know. The part enacted by environment, surroundings, circumstances,—the man's age, land—all that went before, generations—is today. I know this

251

is not new—only, I do not know of its having been elsewhere put into such a prominent place. It was so with Hegel's principles—they had been hinted of, spoken of, by others—but nobody had so brought them to the fore—insisted they belonged there."

Saturday, January 18, 1890

6 P.M. W. out today, but again only in a brief sort of way. Speaks repeatedly of his sensitiveness even to slight experiences of cold. Said he had written Bucke telling him of B.'s error in regard to the Symonds letter. Thought he would have to come up and see my father's picture.

Left with him Harper's Weekly. In it a picture of the new World office, N.Y.—a great, marvellous structure—striking us both with wonder. W. said: "They'd better hurry up and get it under way. Things are not at all certain in this world. If we don't get them done at the first flush, there's a doubt in all the future,"—and pointing to a stove-pipe-hatted, comfortable looking, coated man in the foreground—and laughing lightly—"That's New York! New York to the bone!"—and to a fruit-stand—"and that, too!"—and then variously—"and all else, too!"—and if I would leave the paper he would "enjoy looking it over at more leisure."

Gave me back the Magazine of Art. Had he read Swinburne's poem? "I must own I have not: I read some lines of it, but it did not get any grip on me. So I did not attempt it all through. But the magazine itself interested me—the pictures: indicating what the boys are doing, right and left." And then quite vigorously: "There are Holy Families again—and some every month in the Century"—adding, when I said there was a Tadema picture in the Bazaar which I wished to show him—that it was a Roman subject—"I am almost against it from the start—yet should see what it amounts to. To some things in art—Holy Families, Roman chariot races, lords, ladies, all that—I stand a witness against. *We* ought attest our opposition to them, unalterably—not opposition to their past, which was legitimate enough, but to their importance for the present. Of course they have had their place—their world—but that time is gone—all gone. The saddest part about it is, that they still have a following, a constituency. Not that the Century publishes them so much, but that it is very certain they would not publish them if there was not a demand—the preciousness [?] therefore in the demand." And he did "not know if nature anywhere in Europe had its real votaries—even in France or Germany—or (though I would not dare say it if Herbert were here) in England—where art is in a very dubious quantity anyhow."

"What is dry-point?" he asked, and we discussed dry-point somewhat. Some doughnuts there on a plate. Would have it I should take some home. "If you are going direct home I want to send one to your mother, one to Tillie, one to Aggie and one to the father—to the father particularly this time."

Sunday, January 19, 1890

Did not see W. W. today. Fine and clear—still strangely mild, weather much softened even upon [?] yesterday. Astonishing (if anything in nature is that) tenderness of season. W. out during the day, though for no length of time. Was up to see my father and the picture, with which now he expressed himself perfectly satisfied, the visual objection no more to be urged.

Monday, January 20, 1890

7.55 P.M. W. reading the paper. As the day had been a rainy one, he had not been out. But spoke of his outing yesterday and visit at my father's. "The picture seems a great triumph," he said, "now that the eyes are set right, it takes almost a perfect color to me. Your father certainly shows remarkable power in such work. One of the fine points of the picture is, that though he uses no color whatever, I can see color everywhere—a most subtle illusion—rather, actuality." And as to the copy for Mrs. Fels, to be really in color and to represent W. in his own chair, not the upholstered one,—"I confess I look forward to it with considerable trepidation. It would be a miracle if he did as well a second time as this first." And then he laughing warned me: "Tell him when you go home to let the picture be absolutely as it is—touch it in no way further." And then swinging his chair about and looking among things on the floor—"That reminds me, there is a book here I want to send to your father—you can take it along now—a book with Gray's poems—or containing Gray's poems—one of them on 'The Bard,' of which I spoke to your father." Finally, after much search, found it. It is a book I have had about me for a long time—read it off and on—particularly in war-times, when I had little baggage—3 or 4 books in all, probably in a handbag. Here was Milton—the best of Milton, I think—of the two Paradises. And there was Collins and even Young, who is well worth looking into, in a way—in spite of George Eliot's singeing"—and here with a laugh he turned to a note he had written in the fore part of the book:

"I used to read this Vol: to pass away long 'waits' &c. at Washington, at the Army Hospitals, or waiting for the boats bringing loads of wounded, &c.—dipped it into [means 'into it'] those years 1862, '3, '4 & '5 there & since in Camden N J 1874 to 1888—

"have had it with me over thirty years—scribbled this in Mickle Street Sept: 20 '88 Camden New Jersey

"have dwelt a good deal on Gray—read George Eliot's roasting of Dr. Young as poet and person (in one of her essays)"—

The last in the little book he had for me [for H. T.'s father]. On the title page he had written

Walt Whitman
Dec 1863

in blue pencil, and at a later date underscored it with a pencil of another color—purple. At the life of Milton therein he marginally wrote: "(who is the author of the biography?)" He had pencilled dates of birth and death at each one of the biographies, and pinned in at one place (dating it 1888) an extract —"The Poet Gray's Unhappy Life"—from Arthur Benson, Macmillan's. The volume was one of Grigg and Elliot's, Philadelphia 1841, and contained Milton, Young, Gray, Beattie and Collins. We discussed some of the minor poets—Herrick, Motherwell, Lovelace—of late years revived. "This book has been a companion of the first order: there were times when I could not be found without it."

Still consumed to know if the "good news" about Stedman has been confirmed. Said his mail had been "pretty thin," but "there was a letter from Logan Smith which was cheery, anyhow." And added—"Alys Smith was over yesterday. She was *en route* for Millville—has a bosom friend, a girl, there." Returned me Harper's Weekly. I left the Bazaar there—he wishing to look at the Tadema picture.

Tuesday, January 21, 1890

7.10 P.M. Sat in his room, with a package of the Curtz slips containing "Old Age's Ship & Crafty Death's"—making minor corrections. Said he had been out, but, as before, "it was too cold for persisting: we made but a few minutes of it."

Returned me the Bazaar, remarking of it: "My wonder more and more is, over the pictures—how much of this comes into the world's way for 10 cents—not indifferent good work, but absolute good work. It seems to me another thing in the march, the trend, of our democracy—of opportunity, freedom, gift, to the average—the average man." Gave me a copy of Stead's Review of Reviews. "It is a new thing—this just came today—I am not impressed with it. There was a letter came along with it from Stead asking for a contribution—but I do not know, I do not know!" Then—"Take it along. I have seen all I want to see of it—when you bring it back I'll send it up to Doctor." Called my attention to some new doughnuts on the table. "They're a new batch Mary made up this forenoon—the best ever was." And he gave me two—"One for Tillie—one for Aggie—we must not forget the girls!"

Again expressed his curiosity—who was "The Lounger" in The Critic? "I asked Melville Phillips when he was here the other day, but he did not appear to know, saying that he thought it was Jennie Gilder—but thinking is one thing and knowing another—though he says he will be going to New York shortly and will make it a point to find out." Hicks was over to see him today. W. called him "My young English socialist friend" and thought—"There is a mystery about him—he does not appear to be cockney, yet"—and abruptly switched off—"He is a socialist I know. It is a great point, how America is more and more the goal for these fellows—the young, socialist, anarchist"—I suggesting—"and curious, too, as the goal and end of the Pope as well." W. then: "Yes, that is grand—very grand—and on the principle that even the Pope has a right to exist, this is naturally a good way for him to look at it."

He touched upon [J. Vila] Blake's book. "I have been looking at it the past few days: it is very strongly—directly—moral. More so even than Emerson— it is [?], extreme [?]. I mean to go on, at least a little more, with it." Touched upon Bacon's compactures. "How he must have filed away at every line, every word—laid, long and long over every sentence."

Talking of Brinton's lecture before the Ethical Society on Sunday, which he would have me explain—W. said: "I suppose he will have all these things out eventually in a volume?"

I said—"I don't suppose you would care to read B.'s book 'The Origin of the Religious Sentiment'?" He hesitated a minute—(I knew he would say *no*) then—"I hardly think I do—I do not dare get into abstract arguments these late days."

Wednesday, January 22, 1890

Did not see W.—went to Germantown—not home to tea. W. did not get out today—weather too severe.

Thursday, January 23, 1890

5.35 P.M. Went down to W.'s with Harrison Morris, who was to speak this evening (and now has spoken) before the Young Peoples' Section of the Ethical Society on Browning.

W. instantly asked us about the weather, "Isn't it getting colder and colder?"—Twilight—a cheerful fire burning in the stove, the door of which was partly open. Said he had not been out "of course—though I was out—let me see—on yesterday? No—I guess not—but certainly the day before." As to his good health—"Well—here I am—I can still answer to my name." I returned him the Review of Reviews. Morris made some comment on W.'s interest in the magazine—W. assenting—"I like to read reviews and *resumes* of books, even if I find nothing in them—to find there is nothing is something!"

Morris engaged him talking of Tennyson's new book. Had brought W. English papers from Gilchrist. Did W. think Tennyson could keep up or add to his former work? "I doubt whether the old fellow can: with my taste, appetite, gusto, I do not come away entirely satisfied. I doubt if Tennyson can add anything to the already-delivered message. The main thing is, is he able to keep it up—keep it up indefinitely." And yet—"I hardly anticipate anything more—that 'Crossing the Bar' was very pretty, pensive, pessimistic. It has a virtue,

a characteristicality, its own—a decided character of its own."
And he called it again "a pessimistic poem," adding to Morris'
question—"Yes, I think it markedly so." But should he call
Tennyson a pessimist? To this he was averse. "I should not
call him that—not apply the word—but pessimism is an element, a strong element. I think he's the poet (though he's in
a sense manly, strong, sane,)—that on the whole he stands for
that which signifies *ennui*, decadence." And yet this was no
merely Tennysonian flavor—"rather, it inheres to the age—
the time. I think almost all of the fellows—literary fellows
(poets, writers)—except Emerson—are led off, astray, into
the field of despair—led off by a tendency of the moment.
Emerson is exceptional—I think Emerson inevitably begets
a healthy don't-care-a-damn-ness—the feeling of a man who
goes out in the snow, buffets weather, storms—don't care a
damn! Longfellow—even Bryant—are a part of the same tendency—there are few if any of the moderns who are not. If I
have any council to give you young fellows, it would be, don't
start out in that vein—don't dissipate life, waste it, in such a
venture—the venture of morbidity, despair, sickly sweetness!" And again—later on when Morris led back to the question—asking if Tennyson was "artificial"—"I should not apply
that word—I should not myself start out with a crying-in-the-
wilderness impulse. Only, there is no doubt a great many
even of the young men are set that way—the poets so-
called—set the way of darkness, introspection, disquietude."
And the women—what of them? "Perhaps they are, perhaps
they are—I should rather say of them, let them go on: but for
the men—the poets—oh! I would have them be careful.
There is an ominous tendency against us—in fact, we all have
a side that way—the vessel is filled nearly to the top: in fact,
literature, the literary profession, rather begets it. It's like a
taste for certain kinds of relishes—you soon get it, grow into
it, are *of* it. But in America—we in America—with all the
future before us—our outlook, what we are, expect—we

should be the last to deliver to that tendency." And when Morris asked him direct as to Tennyson's pessimism, W. responded: "Yes, I think there is some of it—much of it—in Tennyson." Then of Whittier's "Burning Driftwood" said almost contemptuously: "Whittier has a tendency to pad out: there are portions of the poem of the utmost beauty—wonderfully fine—but Whittier makes a great mistake—seems to think a poem is good in proportion to its length. About one-quarter of 'Burning Driftwood' is very fine—nearly three-quarters padded. If I were the absolute master of the proof, I should have hacked out one-half at least—probably two-thirds." And again: "The wonder about Whittier is, that he still holds out at the great age of 82—that he can work at all. Whittier is very abstemious—has always been: like Carlyle, who was always unwell—but lived beyond all the rest." At this a touch at Quakerism—W. saying: "The Quaker nativity seems to tell, somehow—the absence of too great artificiality—a certain sort of almost impossibility to make-believe. I think the Quaker—the typical Quaker—is a certain sort of materialist—they like the world, and all that: but a certain spirituality remains—a purity, aspiration. After all that is said and done—a Quaker can hardly be without *some* of this—whatever the form of belief: and his materiality is itself his own—like bathing, keeping clean and all that. To see Quakerism—its practical, living side—you must see it on Long Island, as I did, those first years." Spoke of "the center of Long Island—Jericho"—the two opposed meeting houses in one enclave—an impossibility in Pennsylvania—where "they not only split off but quarrel like the devil—won't have anything to do with each other"—and so on—finally: "I don't know if any sect has such a democratic feeling—one fence elsewhere rarely includes two bands of worshippers!"

At first we sat in the dark. By and bye, noting I drew near the fire to wind my watch, he turned his chair about—got up and fixed the window. "I'll strike a light"—and refusing Morris' offer of help—"I act just the same when my friends are here as when they are not—I always reason that they like it best so."

As we rose to go, he protested somewhat, but on learning that Morris had a Browning essay to read at the meeting in town tonight, he said: "Then I won't urge you to stay, of course"—adding however—"But you, Harrison—you would drink a toddy if I mixed it for you?" Morris assented and W. thereupon swinging about in his chair to the center table said: "I take pride in my toddies: I am vain enough to think no one knows how to make them better." Before he started however, he suddenly snatched a red rose up from the table and held it out. "See what a fellow I have here—that's from the Odenheimer girl: ain't it grand?"—then setting to work, mixing M. a strong dose which was with us the joke of the rest of the evening. As to himself partaking: "No—I shall not drink—I have been eating a very full supper. This is some of Tom Harned's whiskey—he brought it." When Morris called the dose *strong*, W., ironical and smiling, said: "Perhaps it would taste better if I put a little whiskey in it!" But M. did flinch in the ordeal. W. also gave us doughnuts, explaining to Morris that they were Mrs. Davis' make, but remarking when he learned we were on our way to take tea in Philadelphia: "Then I won't urge you to take more—to fill up on them."

Friday, January 24, 1890

7.20 P.M. W. in his own room, reading. Despite severity of weather, W. went out in his chair today—making a trip (downtown) of about 25 minutes and coming back quite blue from the cold. He thinks, however, he is "greatly [braced]" by the fresh air so gained.

Asked me about Morris' lecture last evening. I gave him "Demeter," brought in to me by Morris today. At first he did not see M.'s inscription to him, "with veneration and love," saying "Oh! so this is the book! I shall take good care of it, give it back to him before long"—but when he did, exclaimed—"How kind! I have ardently wished to see the old man's last, and here it is! It will be of great interest to me"— looking through it—"Oh! how they've 'drawn it out,' as the printers say! made the most of it—leaded it, double-leaded, yes, triple-leaded!" And examined it closely, commenting on headlines as he went along—admiring the printing—noting it was foreign (Macmillan publishing).

He is still reading "The Deerslayer"—now about half through. Referring to the recent Old English imitations done by some of our young poets: "What the devil are the boys up to now?"

Saturday, January 25, 1890

8 P.M. Jake Lychenheim along with me when I went to W.'s. Found W. in his room, the Boston Transcript on his knees, and in his hands "The Deerslayer," now all but some 50 pages read. He cordially greeted us—not looking as well as mostly of late days. Had not been out. Spoke of "the long, dull hours" and asked that I bring him Cooper's "Red Rover"—"which will help me to while away the time." Jake's furnace at Swedeland *chilled*, entailing a loss of 10 or 15 thousand dollars. W. curiously inquired of it.

I asked about "Demeter," and he answered: "It is gone already—Tom was in today and took it along—took it at my request. It is well worth looking into. But the greatest wonder is not the book itself but the fact that the old man, now above 80, pen in hand, paper, with his own arm, accomplished it, effected it."

He had been reading today the debate over Presbyterian revision. The "lugging-in of Bob"—[Ingersoll] had "tickled" him, as he said. "But the points that took my time, mainly, were in debates on infant damnation, heathen damnation: it

261

is a great fight for strong men—a great fight!"—his laugh ironical. "I suppose the time has not come for the caricaturists to
get hold of this—at least, the time for them to *dare* to—for I
suppose no paper in America would venture to make much—
if anything—even allow—caricature in that direction, much
as it is needed—much as it seems in nature called for." I
showed him the Tribute parody, written by W. J. Peterson.
He read a stanza—laughed—and said: "That is a step in one's
famosity, to be parodied: so they say."

Morris had given me a rather amusing account of the
memorial meeting held by the Browning Society in Philadelphia. W., to whom I detailed somewhat, said: "They are to
have quite a big pow-wow in Boston, before long—the
28th—: let me see, this is the 26th: 27th, 28th: yes, Tuesday
is the day. Tonight is Burns night in New York, I believe—
and at this very moment I guess General Sherman is 'preparing to pucker,' or is puckering—and there's lots of hot Scotch
flowing (to me the abomination of abominations). But these
fellows, here at these dinners—what do they know about
Burns? The average critic bases all he knows, says, thinks, of
Burns, on two or three or four poems—on 'The Cotter's Saturday Night,' 'Tam O'Shanter,' 'The Twa Dogs,' 'The Twa
Brigs'—some of which will answer the tests, standards, they
bring to measure them. The real Burns was the Burns of out-
of-doors, frolicking, drinking, farming, ploughing the fields—
of women—of poverty—of struggle: the Burns we see in the
letters, for instance—those incomparable, heart-given letters—and of all this these fellows make little account, if they
even know. The fact is, as William O'Connor would say, that
Burns has become established—it is safe to enthuse over him,
to endorse him—and the world does it. And besides, it is a
Scotch enthusiasm—a patriotism. Somehow—naturally,
somehow—all Scotchmen are subject to the Burns enthusiasm. Even Dave McKay, I should claim, would resent an im-

peachment of Burns—Dave, the coolest of mortals, who don't seem to have any fire at all in him—and our friend Hunter, too, who came the nearest in this to warmth of anything I know—having the greatest *penchant* for Burns." And this warm espousal, he further declared, "is much more marked toward Burns than toward Scott." And explanatorily after awhile he said: "The fact is, there is a tremendous element of pathos in Burns' life—in these drinkings, strugglings, laborings I have talked about—and it is these that take hold of the human critter. The mass of men—all of us, I suppose, are impressed by the tragic, the serious, the pathetic—it appeals to us—takes our sympathy by storm—we do not attempt to resist: all is well so given—we at least feel it well, do not reason it out—better not! We can almost be said to flourish in the tendency in us—reading Burns by the light of his idiocracies, idiosyncracies—all men so. Death, murder, pain, assassination—how much they put into history! Think of Abraham Lincoln, profoundly constituted throughout as he was—of deep political, moral, spiritual subtlety, reachings—open to varied influences—everywhere a big man, type, in himself—and simple—simple as a child in his power—of world-capaciousness—one of the greatest, sweetest souls everyway—think of him—think how much even Lincoln owes to his taking off, assassination! Immensely much, without a doubt." I instanced Amy Robsart in "Kenilworth"—and W. then: "Yes, that, too—Amy owes her persistence to that fact—to the fact that a trap was laid for her, and she fell into it—and so through all history—there's no end to illustration, instance, along the same line." This mention of Scott aroused his Scott-enthusiasm again, and he spoke variously, urging me to "read Scott, read Scott—you can get none better"—and saying again: "Yes, Kenilworth is one of the best—and have you read 'Quentin Durward'? Get it—get it in some 25 cent edition—paper—soft." And he added further: "There's

'The Pirate' too"—and laughing heartily—"get that, too—it is not one of Scott's best, but is one you cannot afford to miss—tasting the whole feast, that will be 25-cents more! There is a great satisfaction getting a cheap book—a soft book you can mush in your hands, so"—indicating—"a book you are not afraid to injure. 'The Pirate' is hardly a sea book—hardly to be rated with Cooper—Cooper's 'Pilot.' There are several shiftings-about at sea—but the story as a whole is a land story. But you will like it—it is the sort of thing I think belongs to you—to your tastes."

W. quite facetious over the Rembrandt in the Bazaar this week—"The Wife of Christian Paul Van Bereskeyn"—saying, as to her neckgear: "It looks like a Dutch cheese: is most hideous—a Dutch cheese with a hole for the head to poke through"—and yet—"Our modern dress is about as bad—male and female: almost past idiocy."

Sunday, January 26, 1890

10 A.M. W. just finished breakfast. Stopped in to leave "The Red Rover" with him. He spoke of "the good illustrations" of his "first-rate remembrance" of Long Tom Coffin. Gave me for reading, Carpenter's red-covered volume—"Civilization—its cause and cure." "No," he said to my question, "I have not read it all—it is solid reading"—his tone implying "too solid."

I had my much-marked pocket copy of Leaves of Grass with me. He took it and looked it over curiously. "This appears to be a good copy—one of the best—for printing: most of them are damnably poor—so poor a fellow is ashamed to think of them." As to the poor binding of Carpenter's book: "I understand that certain of the English books are bound with reference to being bound again." I am betting this is one of them.

"The day looks heavy," he remarked, and he was dubious about getting out. But he sounded better than last night.

Monday, January 27, 1890

7.40 P.M. W. in his room on the 2nd. floor, reading "The Water Witch." Though he had been out for a brief stretch, Mrs. Davis told me W. had not been "nearly so well" today. Advising me to take my summer trip to Canada and Dr. Bucke—W. said: "Yes, go—you will be most welcome: Doctor will put it so, the favor will be on your side, not on his: that is his way—no one knows it better than I do."

Again: "Frank Williams was over today—came about 3. Frank seems to come as a duty—thinks he ought to come."— I put in—"But is *glad* to come, too"—W. thereupon: "Yes, I hope it is a pleasure, too—think it *is* a pleasure to him: but there's the sense, the call, the appeal, of *duty*, as well. I can't get away from that impression." And further: "Frank is one of the fellows left who is invitiated [?]—he is under certain of the worldly influences—gives them their due—yet is under his own influence, too—his own organic influence." And to what I said in warm tones of Frank's modesty—"I believe I can endorse every word you say in that line." The plan, suggested in the fall, to have a reception for W. in Philadelphia has fallen through evidently. W. said to me—"Better so, too. Better fallen through than happening."

Another of his expressions about Bruno: "How can there be two sides to the question? Bruno is the modern, science, democracy, America. Are there two sides to the modern, science, democracy, America?" Speaking of Tennyson—his "almost parloriness of style at times" and "always elegance,"— W. added: "From what Herbert tells me, Tennyson as a man is quite different from this—elemental, aboriginal—a man who will go into the mud-ditch, gutter, blood, for illustrations—a rough, rugged, sane, healthy, nature—very Socratian at the last—unmistakably gifted in unspoiled power."

At my entrance W. asked, "What news do you bring?" I said: "I come to get the news—from you fellows who make it." But he responded after his laugh: "There is little news made here, in this room—in this cane chair: silence, mainly, or nothing." Commenting on a picture of Zola in the Transatlantic: "It is a strong head: he certainly has done enough to be a man of intellect—as he is, without a doubt." Again: "Did I tell you I had a note from Melville Phillips? It came Saturday or yesterday—only a few words—in effect these: Don't forget the little poem or poems you promised me. So today I set to work—pieced a poem—'Osceola'—the Indian chief across there"—pointing to the old lithograph tacked on the wall opposite—"he was in our early history, you know—taken prisoner—died in prison from confinement."

Said he had received 6 dollars from Blake (J. Vila, Chicago) for complete W. W.—"which I have sent off—which he ought to get tomorrow—or next day at farthest." Again: "Frank Williams said there was something in yesterday's Times about us—about so much"—measuring 4 or 5 inches—"and I judge from his description that it is all spurious—an invention. It seems that among other things I am said to have been surprised at Boker's death—putting it as though it had been a set-back to me—when the fact is, although I had always had the kindliest thought of Boker, he was never a great element in my life." And, after something further anent newspaper lying: "They handle us freely—did Grant, Lincoln: do so now: and safely, too, for they are all gone—and General Taylor, and Scott: having known them all, I know how they were harried—their memories harried—by lies."

Tuesday, January 28, 1890

7.15 P.M. W. writing on my entrance. Did not appear well, nor was he. Had been out, however, in spite of the severe weather. Invited me almost on start to take a doughnut. "Mary does it well—I know no better hand—and these last are her best!" Commented on the announcement that Tennyson had consented to sign an edition of 100 copies of his poems. "I suppose they will have a tremendous market-value—be produced in unexampled elegance."

Gave me a copy of the Open Court—a marked article therein by Cope, but W. had not read it: "I find little to interest me." Gave me also his Contemporary Club tickets. Expected "Old Age's Ship and Crafty Death's" in the next Century. "I can give you a slip of it now—I have them here—but perhaps I had better wait a day or two. I am quite punctilious on that point as a usual thing. I get the slips printed as a measure of protection. I have been so annoyed at different times, having commas left out when they should be in, and inserted when I did not command it, that I thought a printed copy the only final safety. The devil gets into printers, and then all's hell!" This led to mention of proof-readers. "Very few people know—very few readers of books—literary people—what we owe to proof-readers—the indefatigable proof-reader. I knew one, Henry Clark, a man not of extraordinary appearance—plain—but a man who seemed the deeper, more expansive, the more a fellow looked. He was a Boston man—the reader of the final proofs of the Boston edition of Leaves of Grass." And then: "I have long intended making some note of this—to make an article of it—not speculative, disquisitional, but in the main reminiscence. And in such a work, what it is to have a bright boy—copyholder! I think I must not forget to include the boy in my story."

"I had a note—a curious note today—a postal—all the way from Nice. It was written by John Swinton. He writes to tell me he had seen my Brazilian poem in a Parisian paper—says he likes it—congratulates me that I am strong enough, with ability still to write so." But how the poem had got to France—"and we had never a glimpse of it here"—W. "could not account for it." "I am mystified. I supposed maybe Mc-Clure had altogether decided against using it. Evidently it has appeared *some*where, and escaped our vigilance." But try his best, he could not find the postal to show me—it having "undoubtedly slipped on the floor in the mess somehow."

Project of dinner in Philadelphia revived. I was in to see Lincoln Eyre about it and have spoken to Harrison Morris. Date, April 14th.—at the Art Club. May assent if Morris and others of his standing go in, but shall not if the boys now talking it over are left to manage it. Talked to this effect to W., who said: "That is right: that is the right view: learn what you can: I leave it in your hands: when we know what they want of us we can make our answer." Met Brinton in Philadelphia today, who sent his greetings to W., who was much pleased, as is always the case. Brinton very eulogistic of W. Said on general matters when I told him W.'s attitude towards science and the orthodox church: "In that he agrees with the main body of modern scientific workers, who feel that the orthodox church is an obstacle in the way of progress."

I asked W. if he had ever heard Theodore Parker? "Yes—I think I have—I am sure I have—but the impression is mainly gone. My impression of Father Taylor is very vivid because I heard him repeatedly. One's memory rusts a great deal—things coming up in the reminiscence way are confused, often utterly unless as matters of authentic record." Later, as I left, he said: "I ought to tell you I got 5 dollars today from Kennedy for that book: he sent it in spite of our protests. And only the other day I expressly told him not to. Well—well."

Wednesday, January 29, 1890

7.15 P.M. W. reading Cooper. Spoke at once of the Brazilian poem. "Here's Swinton's card—turned up today," he said. But he could no better now than yesterday clear up the uncertainty of its issue abroad. "Why was it?—how?" W. asked. And I questioned: "Why was it not printed in this country?" W. then: "I don't know. There is a line in it which reads and that may have deterred the orthodox journalists." But would it deter his friends? "No—they would not fear it as my friends but as journalists. You've no idea how the fellows stickle at such things—the timidity has no limit. The line is apparently innocent, yet I made it the expression of a deep-rooted idea—an idea I much affect—I should not wonder but the idea of the poem—Swinton calls it 'noble.'" W. spoke with regret of Swinton's complaint of "nervous prostration"—describing: "He's of a temperament intensely inclined towards nervosity. Mrs. Scovel once told me of an old play she had heard of or seen—a play in which much hangs upon the saying of one of the characters—*beware of being the creature of one idea*. I'm afraid John has been a man of one idea—and here is the effect of it." He said further,—"I sent the poem to the Post, which prints it." And he hunted me up slips—gave me two—one of them with changed headline (from "A Christmas Greeting from a Northern Star-Group to a Southern"—to another dropping the word Christmas, as it was declined in the meantime, though written in 1889)—and another the 4th line changed from

"Ours, ours the present throe, the democratic aim" etc. to dropping "present throe, the"—.

Referred to Castelar: "Our folks here seem afraid to say anything about the new republic—a disposition just the opposite of that of the European fellows—especially in France—which is one of hearty welcome. We seem in a state of fearing expectancy. "And as to a report that Ingersoll had said something to the same effect,—"I should be thoroughly inclined to *Amen* Bob!" And again: "Castelar, a man there in the peninsula, writing of democracy, does it with reference to a thousand things we can have slight or no idea of here."

Received proof of "Osceola" today from Phillips and was amused to find the printer had alternated the lines, indenting every second one. Of course he instantly wrote to set it right.

"On the artistic side," W. said, "and the side of simple nature—there are lines on which Goldsmith is far more marked than Burns." And yet "Burns on the whole was the bigger man."

Thursday, January 30, 1890

5.20 P.M. W. in his room—had just concluded dinner. Warren came in while I sat there and took the tray off. W. had asked several times about it, so today I secured the Times of Sunday, now giving it to him, and he remarking: "I have not read a word of that—yet I would be willing to make a wager, there's not a word of it authentic." To the statement that he had said the death of Boker "rattled" him—: "That sounds just like me, don't it? Rather, it sounds more like Reddy!" And when I looked mystified by the reference, he laughingly particularized: "Did I never tell you about Reddy—the fellow who invented me on the cremation issue? He was called Reddy—had red hair—and a scamp he was, too! He is dead now. The way that came about was this: he had the impudence to write me—it was several days [later]—and explain that he had a chance to make 3 or 5 dollars by collecting opinions on cremation—had collected some but had not time to come over to see me. And there I was, in the most conspicuous place of the three-quarter column. It was a fair sample of what we call American journalist cheek. And this—the one in the Times—is probably another. I should not wonder at all but Jim Scovel wrote it, anyhow!"

He spoke with great warmth, and more fully than yesterday, of Castelar's speech. "I have read it through now—every word. It is thoroughly frank, thoroughly characteristic. There are not a few things in which we need to learn much of the Spaniards, Italians, French—and this is one of them. Castelar's speech is impassionate egotism—yet an egotism of a high and noble nature, which we presume eminently fits and becomes him. It is a confession—the song, utterance, of personality—in substance this: that Don Pedro is not the man he is credited with being—is not the broad King of the reports: is Emperor: that in the old times, 20 years or more [ago] in Castelar's need in Spain, the Emperor insulted him—and so on, suggesting in every way the happy right Castelar has to his feeling. None of our men would dare allow themselves such a personal statement—they are in every way afraid to let themselves out—all of them—litterateurs—all. Except only Emerson, whose every word somehow seemed an eternal fitness in itself—needed no explication. But Emerson stood alone." And further: "What has Arnold contributed for us? Of course I speak of him a good deal with reference to what he said of America—of us—of Emerson. What did he know of us? What value had his divining rod? Sweetness and light? Damn sweetness and light! We have already too much of it! I like the north-west winds—the fearless tides: to brace these—to take these naturally, heroically—as in themselves matters of course! It would seem as if our civilization was doing all it could to get away from all that signified of inherent nativities—of what at best belongs to us all!" He knew that John Burroughs had some notion that "Arnold was the man for England"—but—"It's a great pity John did not use that logic in his consideration of Victor Hugo—he has been a bitter antagonist of Hugo without and within. The world is surfeited of the Arnoldisms. All the fellows are bent on being correct, elegant. I hate the man"—this with a laugh which took all the edge off of "hate"—"who comes to me and speaks to me of his perfect English. Perfect English and perfect sense don't always go together!"

He remarked again: "This, now, is Thursday. I suppose I have received more than a dozen letters this week—nearer 2 dozen—and out of these a full three-quarters are applications for autographs—some of them very insinuating. I wonder if the disease don't sometimes take a stronger turn than at others?"

Friday, January 31, 1890

Did not see W.—was detained too long at the Bank. But received a letter from Bucke broaching the hospital matter again, aroused thereto by a sentence in one of W.'s recent letters.

PRIVATE   [London, Ont.,] 29 Jan [18]90
My dear Horace

You know that for a long time I have thought (and I believe you have thought the same) that Walt Whitman should have more comfortable surroundings and to this end I have from time to time urged him to live in some good hospital where he would be regularly seen by good Drs and waited on and provided for suitably. I could never get from W. any consent to this scheme and for a long time I have ceased to urge it—have not mentioned it for months—. I was surprised therefore when I got the other day a letter (written 22d. inst.) containing the following passage: "If I had a good hospital well conducted—some good nurse—to retreat to for good I sometimes think it would be best for me—I shall probably get worse & may linger along yet some time—of course I know that death has struck me and it is only a matter of time—but may be quite a time yet." Upon receipt of this letter I wrote to W. saying how glad I was that he had taken that notion and how much better off in many ways he would be in a good hospital. At the same time I wrote to Osler of Johns Hopkins asking him whether W. could be received there as a pay patient—what the rate would be &c. I have just received Osler's answer this afternoon saying that there wd. be no difficulty about W.'s reception and that the pay for every thing would be about $25. a week. This letter of Osler's I have sent to W. Osler is to write me again more in detail *at once*—this letter also no doubt I shall send to W. I should be sorry to have W. out of daily reach of you & Harned but in all other respects the difference between his present life and life at Johs Hopkins would be like the difference between a laborer's life and that of Vanderbilt—the difference would be far more than that because at Johns Hopkins he would get (besides all other good provisions & attendance) the constant, daily, services of the best physicians in America—in the world. perhaps, and this would be of immense importance to him in his present state—I have little doubt that at Johns Hopkins his life would be made greatly more bearable—even comfortable. You see of course why I write to you—I want you (as I know you can) to forget yourself—your own feelings—and help me to move W. to this step. Should it be once settled that W. will go I propose to at once visit Johns Hopkins, see just what accommodation he would have—arrange all details and come on to Camden to take W. on to Baltimore—and I should hope that you and perhaps others would go too. About the payment of $25. a week or even more—surely there could be no difficulty (?) W. would perhaps like to pay some part of the rate himself (?) or if not surely you could run the subsidy up to this amount—I would willingly make my $3. a month $5. others would no doubt do the same or new names could be got? the payment of twice the amount ought not to be any difficulty. Should I go to B. to look into the sort of provision they would make for W. at J. H. perhaps you or Harned would meet me there and look into the matter along with me so that you would be quite satisfied with the step before it was made (?)

Have a talk with Walt on this subject (get him to open it if possible) and tell me how he feels about it and very fully what you and Harned think of it.

Willy Gurd has been here all January but has been sick ("La Grippe") all the time. At one time (3 weeks ago) I feared he would die. He is now slowly recovering—the gas meter is made—we may establish a Co. to manufacture here under the Canadian patents to prove the thing practically—we have done nothing yet as Gurd got sick almost immediatley after his arrival here and is so still—I have good faith in both the gas and water meter

Your friend
R M Bucke

Saturday, February 1, 1890

7.50 P.M. W. reading the Century—and after cordially extending his own and grasping my hand—spoke freely of the magazine. "It is in some ways an interesting number. There's

273

a fine picture of Forrest—one of the best I know—I suppose it would be called a success. On the other hand the Emerson picture—much spoken of—is a failure—at least, that would be my opinion. It is full figure—and the figure not bad—the body. I saw him many, many times, at all stages of life from very young years—when he was not famous at all—really only *debuting*—and I judge the body, as we have it here, not unfortunate. But the face—oh! the face is badly amiss. I don't know but it has that same quality we would not admit of in the London News picture of me—a sort of foxiness—sourness—sick-at-the stomachness—at no time belonging to Emerson. But the article, giving the boy's recollections (Woodbury's) of Emerson, has a quality which will attract you, as it attracts me. What is there about Emerson which we would *not* read?"

I had not yet seen the Century. Had his poem appeared? "Yes—it has its place. And I don't know but I have a slip here to give you"—hunting in a package held between two pieces of pasteboard—handing me the slip finally. "I think that is the last." And further: "You must take it anyhow, even though it appears the last. There are so many of these 'last copies' of this thing or that turning up here every day that I often wish they really *had* been the last."

Asked me after news: "We have no news here—we are retired from all that."—And again—"What about the city—Philadelphia: is it busy, varied, gay, businessy? Warren was over today, and came back describing the streets—everybody in a hurry—the cars—noises—cries—children." Again, of domestic matters: "Harry Fritzinger opened his grocery store today—or perhaps you knew of it?" And W. laughing with great heartiness: "It seems the great demand today was for clothes-line—numbers of people coming in and asking for clothes-line! What a mystery the human mind has come to be—the critter—or always was!" How about the Times interview? "It was a surprising patchwork—Jim Scovel's without a doubt: it sounds like Jim—it don't sound in the least like me." Scovel has admitted its authorship and spuriousness to Harned—said even that there was much more that the Times people had cut out.

W. questioned: "Who will be the laureate after Tennyson is gone? Has William Morris the right quality?"—but there was Morris' radicalism—"I suppose that is enough bar: he could hardly be stomached." He regretted Tennyson's absence from Browning's funeral. "He should have been there—should have gone—if he had to be carried: I do not like his absence."

The debate in Congress (House of R.) over Reed's ruling to count all members present towards a quorum, even if they did not vote—had arrested W.'s attention. "My first impression was that the Republican position was right—but since I have seen various signs of arbitrariness which I do not like—which raised doubts. All these fellows are petty—are today's men—work *for* as *in* today. I remember Gurowski, how, in giving us points on Russian affairs, would indicate certain special men and say—these men are working not only for today but with reference to the next thousand years. The wise Count—after he was done his swearing! But our fellows never show so big an eye—they see only today—sometimes only the small part of today—as these fellows now. I used to think Colfax was a great 'muff'—until one day in Washington a little affair came along which set him up in our estimation. The question was over some member clapped in jail for contempt of Congress. Colfax had letters belonging to this man in his possession—and a member of the Committee in charge asked him a question: would you not deliver up—open—these letters? And he negatived the question. What! not even at *command*? And at this the old man fired up—I never knew *how*—never supposed there burned that much in him—fired up and exclaimed—though not quite so profanely—'No—

no—I'd see us all in hell first!' To some of us—O'Connor—me—Colfax was that night famous. It gave me much hope of a latent substance even in the old cods from whom so little usually is to be expected. But all in all Colfax was a little man—was ascendent by something else than native power."

I did not tell W. I had heard from Bucke, but asked him if he had—and this led him to speak of Bucke's hospital proposition. "He made a good deal of that some months ago, then dropped it. Now the fault seems to be mine—to have come from some little reference in a letter I recently wrote him and of which Doctor makes the most. I am not inclined to change from my old position. Doctor makes too much of one side of the prospect—there are a hundred other influences of which he can know nothing at all—perhaps no one can know but me. It is the attitude of the neck-tie man, to whom all civilization, prosperity, advance, what-not, hangs upon the ups and downs of the neck-tie trade—high power or low—big orders or little. And yet the world includes just about a million other worlds about as big as his own." I urged: "But he sees certain material benefits in such a change for you and thinks they would compensate, and more, for all you lose." But W. shook his head: "The hospital move does not impress me—I see things Doctor cannot see. I do not tumble to the idea at all!" And again—"Don't worry that I will go off without letting you know!"

One of his expressions: "We all make our plans for living out-of-doors—but never live there (I am as bad as the rest!)" Spoke of days in Washington "when some of the fellows would come down from New York, Boston—Otis was one of them—and bring copies of the big dailies—one for me—one for O'Connor—perhaps for others. They were great treats!"

The fact that I heard Brinton lecture on the peoples of Africa Friday caused W. to urge me to ask B., to what extent if any, the Moors were related to the negro. "I have always had a suspicion they were not related, but my suspicion never rose to a certainty."

When I started up, W. asked: "Where are you going when you leave here?" And learning to Harned's, he pulled open the table drawer and gave me his whiskey-bottle to get filled. "Harned has the best viand under the sun," he said. Then he made up a couple of doughnuts into a package, "one for Mrs. Harned—one for Tom"—which he insisted I should take, as I did.

Sunday, February 2, 1890

9.45 A.M. W. just finishing breakfast. Looked fresh and well. I gave him his bottle of whiskey, secured from Harned last evening. It was not the bottle he had sent, but a better one, which he remarked, adding comically—"and I guess it holds just as much, too—which is important!" Asked then: "How are they all at Harned's? And the baby? Oh! the dear baby!" At this point, looking out of the window, I saw a bright, beautiful baby playing inside the window opposite—remarking it. W. thereupon: "Yes—and we are great friends, too," —at this starting to look for something in the confusion of the table. My inquiries developed that he was looking for a cork to stop a little bottle on the table. "I was going to send you over to lift the window and give the baby a little bit of cologne, but somehow the cork is gone—utterly gone—at least for the present, and I'll have to postpone my good intentions—or their enactment!" And still he looked and looked, finally, however, giving up the search. "The scoundrelly cork is here somewhere—but not here to my asking. I think I inherit from my father a disinclination to throw anything away—I keep every odd and end that falls to me."

The little snow that had fallen in the night was now fast melting—the day of the dreariest character. W.'s description of the snow: "It don't seem to have a manly character—it seemed rather to sneak in—now to sneak out again!" I picked up from under his rocker a striking portrait of Johnston. "It came yesterday," he said, "and surprisingly good it is!" And after fruitlessly looking for something else—"There came along in the same mail, from the men up in New York who have invented the Walt Whitman cigar, a label—but it, too, is lost, just now, here in the general mess. There is a portrait—and all comes with a letter. I intended you should have it."

He suggested to me: "Go to see the Alexander picture at the Academy—see what you can make of it—I want to hear. And tell Aggie to go, too—tell her to look at it—take what measure she can of it. The papers are making some to-do about it, but then I put no value whatever in the newspaper criticisms—the snap judgments of editors." "But," I said, "here is Harned, he has met Boyle, who says it is of high merit." At this W. added: "Well—I should not so airily reject that—that has considerable pith, coming from such a man. But anyhow, you go see it yourself—tell me what are your own feelings." And he reminded me again—"Have Aggie go—with you if she can—*but go*." On the score of Boyle's severe criticism of Gilchrist's Whitman, W. protested—"That is putting it extremely, I guess, but"—and he said no more—the "but" standing for a certain mild participation, as I knew, in Boyle's repulsion.

A thought he frequently has on his lips, he repeated this morning: "The children should be taught to draw—among the first things. How were Brinton's charts Friday night? So much comes easily to a man if he has some knowledge of drawing; especially to the speaker. See what power you say Morse wields by being able to make his statements, justify himself, armed with a piece of chalk!"

I found on the floor, under the wood-pile (which I accidentally disturbed) a broken picture (unmounted) of W. W. It was

278

cut in half—a picture rarely used—a hand supporting the head—a Bryantesque look throughout—less the vigor, more the polish, than in nature. W. said as he gave it to me: "I did intend to destroy it, but if you must you must! I put no value upon it."

Clipping from a local paper (unidentified), dated Feb. 2, 1890 re the 60th—Annual Exhibition—Penna. Academy of the Fine Arts

WALT WHITMAN'S PORTRAIT AND THE REST

Mr. J. W. Alexander's portrait of Walt Whitman, which was fortunately painted before his recent illness, easily leads the portraiture of the Exhibition in one direction just as Miss Cecilia Baux's beautiful pastel [of Miss Burnham] does in another. Mr. Alexander has chosen to minimize the vigorous physical personality of his subject, and he has left the robust poet sitting on something very like a bicycle saddle. The head is, besides, a bit vague in the treatment of hair. But the work, as a whole, is noble, effective, and elevated. It has about it a dignity and poetic feeling to rejoice over, and gives with great fidelity a high and tender side of a great man and a noble figure in letters and life.

Monday, February 3, 1890

7.35 P.M. W. said on my entrance: "Someone has been sending me a copy of The Scottish-American in which there is an account of the Burns celebrations. I find that the drift now is towards musical celebrations—no longer banquets, speeches, hot-Scotch. It is a sign of the times."

W. had been frequently making lunches and sending them to the sick girl next door. As to the Philadelphia dinner: "Do what you think best. No doubt in some way—if it is quiet, unpretentious—I will connive at it some way. I accept the spirit in which such things come; could not, consistently myself, disregard them." But—"as I have said, simplicity, simplicity—informality—no brass bands!" Said he was "thoroughly sensitive, responsive, to the enjoyabilities of such a compliment." Added: "You know, I love the good things—am awake to personality, contact, sympathy, emotionality, at all times, anywhere."

I read Woodbury's Emerson sketch in the Century today, and now said to W.—"The reference made to you there was somewhat mystifying." He then: "So I thought." Woodbury reports Emerson as saying: "'Leaves of Grass,' by Walt Whitman, is a book you must certainly read. It is wonderful. I had great hopes of Whitman until he became Bohemian. He contrasts with Poe, who had an uncommon facility for rhyme"—&c. W. continued: "That sounds Edwardish, as if Edward Emerson had a hand in it. Some of the fellows had—still have—the idea of me, that I'm a big, blustering, swearing creature—going about with a red shirt on—sleeves rolled up—quid of tobacco in my cheek—saying 'lubber' and 'damn' and achieving a general toughiness. This article is collated—put together from various occasions. I can see Emerson in parts of it—but it lacks sap—is no doubt a good deal, even if unconsciously, made up. For no matter what a man hears, if it is not in him to do so, he will not report faithfully—like an artist who cannot paint out of his good intentions alone, but must have a bottom to him somewhere." As to the portrait of Emerson in the same magazine: "It finds its way into you anyhow." I told him of tbe humorous insistence of Shillaber that Emerson's was an *idiotic* smile. "No matter for the smile: a man is made not by his smile but by the measure of his personality."

Said the appearance of his little piece in yesterday's Press was "the first notion" he had that "it was bought by a syndicate"—"This tells us who File is." We had an intensely interesting talk over what W. himself denominated his "whether-or-no-ness"—whether he felt "self-justified" in his later work—the work of recent years. Morris came in the bank today in high pleasure over the Century poem, which he called "of the highest." W. said: "I am glad to hear that from Morris—from a fellow trained in the art-side of life. There are times when the verdict of a craftsman counts for something." And then: "I set this off as a distinct thing, for instance, from Bucke's comment. I feel that Bucke is apt to take it for granted that everything is all right. There are times when we prefer the questioner. I for my part have never been deeply convicted on the point of the late poems—never absolutely certain of myself—of results. To be sure I am convinced all has forged forward from a poetic background—out of appropriate, deepest poetic seeing, emotionality—uttered in a setting of genuine sympathy: but whether here at last comes morbidity, introspection—forbidden, forbidding appearances—in that is the rub." W. said further: "I have put the bucket deep in me—brought water from the deepest deeps—questioned—and though inclined to be convicted, am not." But I argued—why necessarily weakening because changing field? Death, pain, age, are only disease when the observer makes them so. W. thereupon: "So it seems to me: and I think it is in such a conviction I shall abide. I never forget Mrs. Gilchrist's solicitude—and she was one of the cutest women ever born, and signal among my friends—; her solicitude in fear—dread—that I would go off into pensivity. She would say, What has Walt Whitman to do with sunsets: I cannot conceive of him having anything to do with disease, old age, pain, invalidism, sunsets, sitting in an old cane chair—or housed in any way—or the like. That was Mrs. Gilchrist."

Tuesday, February 4, 1890

7.30 P.M. W. reading—gathered close to the light. In his room as usual. Had been out today. But Warren was of the idea "It did him more harm than good." Still, W. insisted on going. Day altogether damp. Rained hard in the forenoon. Reads The Long Islander (regularly sent him) weekly. Thought he was not so well today. When I said: "I shall tell the fellows at the Club you are in first-rate condition." He said: "I don't have any objection to your telling them so, but I'm not." And—"I am not having a great time these days—not at all."

I questioned him again on the hospital matter, but he said—"I have heard nothing from Bucke since that letter." Then: "I had a letter from Ed Wilkins today. He reminded me that I had promised him a dinner book, so I sent him one. I suppose I must have made him such a promise." "Ed," he said again, "sticks to his tasks there, I should guess."

Called my attention to a paragraph from Labouchère, quoted in this morning's Press, discounting the poet fraternity. Amused W., who said: "There are the choice people of our time—there are many of them—who always fidget for something pungent, sharp, cute, telling, witty: are not satisfied with plain, native foods, but crave for spice, viand, whatnot. Labouchère answers to such a call." Adding again: "Our Agnes Repplier shines by such a light: I guess nobody could safely question but she is very bright; but she is the dog up the alley, waiting to pounce out and seize the first good leg that comes along. Yes, she is smart—has the smartness of vitriol, of salt." As to the Goethean critics W.: "There are persons of the small pietistic turn—of extreme notions in that order— who do pause at Goethe's peccadilloes, amours,—get no further,—know nothing of the *ensemble*—of the man as a whole."

Though he had had proofs, had not yet seen the Illustrated World piece. Said again: "I met with a very happy phrase from Stedman today: what he calls, 'the stained-glass' school of poetry. It seemed a very happy thought: and there was another expression as fine—let me see—no, I cannot hit upon it now. The 'stained-glass' applies more or less to Dante Rossetti—'The Blessed Damozel' and such."

To my further declaration that I distrusted Woodbury's use of the word *Bohemian* in the Emerson report, on the ground that Emerson was surer than that in his characterization, W. said: "You are right: Emerson was wonderfully apt—wonderfully discerning—seemed to read a man through and through—through and back again!"

Wednesday, February 5, 1890

7.30 P.M. W. has improved over condition of yesterday. Less depressed. "Out today? Oh, yes! We took quite a long jaunt." And again: "I had a letter from Bucke to cheer me: it was a jolly one. He does not refer to the hospital matter again." One of his curious statements: "The fellows who wrote up Socrates—Plato, whoever—had many axes to grind—so they ground them and put Socrates' name on the result." The Emerson writer in The Century "dialogued—reported—Emerson efficiently, after a sense." But was the dialogue dull? He thought so, "therein certainly losing position when contrasted with the reports of the Socratean conversations."

He spoke of the Nicolay–Hay Lincoln. I called it "a lost opportunity"—the death of Lincoln opening up much which they had not availed themselves of. W. then: "You think so? They stole a part of that from me—not in this number but in the last—in the account of the assassination—not successive passages—here and there I could get glimpses—not of me alone but of others." I spoke of W.'s own vividness and pulse—and then of Brinton's speech the other night—"So simple, they thought nothing was in it: yet it was crowded with matter." W. then: "That is good—that is noble—that is the whole story—so simple they thought there was nothing in it! That is the whole story—the inevitability of the result, out of the simplest means." Questioning me of Lumholz—I promised sometime in my leisure to give him an account of curious bits of information imparted. When he sees me now with a copy

283

of L. of G., he jokingly asks—"Whitman's Bible eh? God help you!"

This is one of the ways he illustrates narrow reasoning: "Like the man who gets sick and blames all his trouble on boiled oysters: he had been just on the point of sickness— anything would have turned the scale—the whole body was eligible to disturbance: then he takes the oysters and the deed is done! A thousand other things would have caused the same trouble—the oysters only brought matters to a head— yet the oysters alone are rebuked."—"It is a good sample of average reasoning, where men don't look for the cause *of* the cause of things."

He spoke of "how one's egotism carries him a great way towards endurance. It is so with me—I have stuck and stuck—through a something within me which my enemies would think hopeless conceit." And so, of "the rounded Leaves of Grass" as turning up in the recent poems about old age as in previous poems of the then contemporaneous—"You are quite right there—I am fully convinced on that point— my egotism, if nothing more, holds me fast there."

Referred to Stedman's "stained glass" epithet again and then proceeded to talk of stained glass itself. "I was in such a stained glass establishment some years ago in New York. What wonderful work they do! I looked at things long and long and long. Going at the old rate, what must they not be able to do now." We had some talk about the proposed dinner. I explained that it was the opinion of Morris and Frank Williams that W. should not embrace the tender—that the young men were more concerned to advertise their journal (Society) than for anything else &c. W. said: "I put myself in your hands. You say Morris and Frank are quite agreed? Then let me give the declination courteous!" And even of the proposed celebration of his birthday, which we have long had in mind,—"Don't force anything: if anything suggests itself—

arises spontaneously—proceed—not otherwise. Don't get into anything extreme: as I told you, no brass bands!"

Thursday, February 6, 1890

7.35 P.M. Went down to W.'s with Hugo Hund. W. was very cordial with him—questioned about his name till it was spelled for him. "I am always curious to know the make of names—to know the meaning of names, if there is a meaning. That was one of my pleasures in George Kennan's articles in the Century: when he struck a bad [hard?] Russian name, he would indicate how it was spelled. That seemed especially made for my benefit!—which is to put it pretentiously: for there's in fact no one thing on which an old fellow prides himself especially but is found the possession, gratification, so some other, many others."

W. said again as to the dinner: "The journal—paper—there: Society, is it?—had better look out how it takes me up, thinking to boost themselves by doing so. Is there not a gun that reacts? Don't our best guns sometimes fire back as well (or worse) than front—more fatally. It might prove so to these fellows. I had some visitors today—Rees Welsh and one other, coming with him. And, by the way, they brought me some whiskey—which they mostly drank up themselves, till they were quite conversational. Welsh especially was affected by it—and told me about Morrow, the Methodist minister in Philadelphia—who took it into his head several years ago to espouse me—sent a letter to the papers—was prominently known in some such way at the time. It appears—so Welsh put it—that Morrow had an engagement to lecture a few days after—down here at Pleasantville: they had heard of his boldness—greeted him with quite a storm—a great noise—would not have him lecture: unless he said he was sorry for what he had done, would not hear a word from him. It was a new story to me and I was curious to know if he had retracted, for in that was the significance of the story—but Welsh did not tell me—and I did not ask."—"These fellows—any of you—may get into just such a mess—if you aren't cautious!"

He took a photograph—marked 'J. Johnston—England"—which I picked up from the chair and questioned about. "That is the picture of one of a group there in England—a cluster—not a considerable number—but enough, many would say, considering their object!—which is the study, expounding of Walt Whitman!" And yet, he said: "We must make the best of the good words of our friends—even the few friends, if so be it our friends are few—as they have been all along, true enough! And the opposition, which is plenty piled on plenty—that"—throwing his hand gesturingly, and laughing sweetly—"That we will brush aside, not notice, as of no avail to deter us, despair us, hold us back, give us reserves."

Discussing the question what was truth, what was lie, W. said, at different points: "The question would appear to be relative—the fact, rather. I remember my Washington experience: here were lives just wavering in the balance—life on that side, death on that"—giving his raised hand a swaying motion—"and the physicians would say, this man you ask about, he is just on the verge, may go over, may retreat. Oh! to those I would lie like the devil: the object of objects, to bring them about." And—"Yet there are some moralists who will contend, a lie is a lie, under whatever conditions (as no doubt it is)—a lie is never justified. But in certain critical cases, as in those I knew in the hospitals—in the case you tell from Helen Taylor"—I had just recited the *pursued-man* illustration: would you term the unjust pursuer *wrong*?—"a man's emotional nature would settle the case without elaborate preparation, self-debate: he would say the word, do the deed." Of course this was "debatable ground"—and "much is to be said on the other side." Yet we were to note "the great story-tellers—the writers—say Walter Scott, whose genius for taking us on the borderline of questions was great, superb, beyond precedent—are not eager to use situations of obvious results, decisions, but those that can excite divergence of judgment."

Had Melville Phillips been in today? "No—but I had a note from the proprietor, Munyon—telling me the first picture experiment had been a failure and saying he would be over—send over—to take another. And tonight the men came—three of them: and here, with their flash-light (which nearly blinded me) they made their new trial. I sitting here just as you see me now. The fellows were wonderfully takable—I fell to them at once. Can you explain why it is I find such an attraction about transportation men, actors, men like these?—especially the actors, in which I flatter myself—tickle my egotism—by assuming I have quite a clientage?"

Referred to "The Canadian preacher who set out to make me define—was bound to make me define my attitude towards Ingersoll—to condemn him, show our disagreements—which I would not do. The fellow finally made me mad. I said to him substantially: 'I think it a great thing to have a man who will tell the truth, irrespective of where it leads him—of what it leads him to deny or affirm: to me the recompense of everything or anything that had to be lost in the process.'"

Friday, February 7, 1890

7.50 P.M. Weather was inclement today, W. consequently confined in-doors. Reading the Boston Transcript. Gave me a letter from Bucke in which was some message to me. "I laid it out for you yesterday, but it slipped my mind when you were here." McKay's Shakespeare at his feet. He had been reading today "The Merchant of Venice."

Spoke again of his declination of the dinner, and added: "I can see more and more why I should not get involved with such arrangements." Repeated that he "looked favorably" on our birthday project, but would "say nothing till you tell me what you want of me."

Treating of disease W. said: "The stomach seems to be the seat of all—all headaches—everything (to put it a little extravagantly) hangs upon good digestion. Indeed, I doubt if a good doctor, hearing whatever of a patient, ever prescribes except for the stomach, however he may not appear to." Harned has been ill—probably "La Grippe"—W. concerned, speaking of having missed him.

Saturday, February 8, 1890

7.25 P.M. W. in his room as usual, reading the paper. Did not look comfortable and said he did not feel so. Day badly inclement. No outing.

Complained somewhat: "I haven't heard from Phillips— Melville Phillips. I hope he will send me proofs. It is provoking to be left without proofs." And as to any "contract" with M. P. (I heard a contract reported in Philadelphia among the literary fellows)—"I am not conscious of a contract—indeed, should like to know *what for*—what it *could* be for—"&c. The photograph he had not heard of. "The result is dubious. Once in many, many trials something turns up unexpectedly good—but in the great mass of trials the outcome is a damned farrago—a libel of libels—past all one's patience."—"They have the metal, the light, the room, me—yet have none!— that is, they have them really only when they have them in a certain way—in their harmonies."

Referred to Carlyle's latter-day sorrow over "the toil and moil" of the world—wrong in its coach-and-four—right then trudging afoot. "I do not think any trace of such a thing is to be found in me—in my book—in Leaves of Grass: I know it has never animated me—put me by a straw's measure to right, to left: altered my career, life, work, in any way—not affected it in the slightest. I would no more question it—the

288

existence of such facts—nor that they mean the best, either, than question the law of gravitation. If John Smith leans too far over the housetop—falls over—it is sorrowful for him, but good for the universe: if the universe spared *him* the law— what then? Facts are divine—they are so and so. The toil and moil side must not get too strong—or at any rate a dark— hold on us. I feel that I am exempt—that Leaves of Grass is exempt—from the faintest tinge of a tinge of a question!"

Book sale chronicled in the Critic has a 1st. edition of L. of G. selling for 15 dollars. W. said it "amused" him—and added: "If I had some of 'em now, I might have 'em set me up!" Then, poking the fire and laughing: "They say—some of them—that the first edition sold—sold through the good Emerson's let- ter—but that's not true: nobody would have 'em, for gift or price: nobody: some even returned their copies:—editors— others. You can rely upon Dr. Bucke's book on all those mat- ters: it is all verified—there is no mystery there to clear up: that is all thorough, authentic—substantially from my own hands."

Thought Garland's enthusiastic greeting of Howells in the current Standard as *the* American novelist, *par excellence*— the man most typically hitting off American life—"probably with some justification"—yet—"I am not a reader of stories— would not dare say a word in that direction myself." He was greatly interested in the details I gave him of Lumholtz's Aus- tralian experiences.

Sunday, February 9, 1890

W. got his trip out-of-doors today, the day being fine, though chill. Suffered somewhat from the cold, and made his indulgence slight. Says he is reluctant to tempt the weather. "The sitting posture makes me eligible—opens me—to all the external agencies."

Monday, February 10, 1890

5.30 P.M. Spent half an hour with W. in his own room. Had just finished his afternoon meal; now sat reading the local papers. I did not think he seemed exceedingly well. It having been quite cool, even cold, he had not ventured out today. His first question to me was about the temperature. "Pretty cold—isn't it? Too cold to be out?" And yet when I told him of Harned's sickness and my belief that much of it came from too much in-doorness, he averred: "I can see it well: one must in a way, live with out-of-doors"—for—"How much of all disease comes from the stomach—how much if not all! And the stomach is in direct communication with the sun, the air, the rivers—" &c. Then he amusedly asked me—"You have not seen my new mittens, have you?"—after some search pulling them out from under a pile of papers. "There—see these! Ain't they fine!" And then he went into child-like playing over them. "What struck me most was their seamlessness—their one-piecedness." And he enlarged on the wonder of mechanism through which they had grown. He spoke of his "growing sensitiveness," to the cold and that "these aids are not to be sneezed away"—though there was a time when his "blood flowed that freely" he "could almost have dispensed with covering altogether."—"Mary got them for me—they were recommended to her there in the city as policemen's mitts. So," laughing, "you see the new category I am included in!"

Said he had "a long letter from Sidney—from Morse." Then: "I have not given it the careful reading I want to yet; when I do you shall have it. He sends along two newspaper bits—one about his own doings, goings-about—the other an old clipping about our dinners here." Then the mention of Morse seemed to arouse some other matter. "Did you ever meet Leonard Morgan Brown when he was here? It was several years ago—Morse was with me at the time—a fine fellow. We all liked him—Morse did—and Mary, too: he impressed her. He was Ernest Rhys without Rhys' articulateness—strangely reserved—a strong, unspeaking, patient nature: had not the literariness, the discursive power, of Rhys—a rather sickly fellow, having trouble with his body—a constant contending as I understand it. I hear from him from time to time. He is now in London—teaching. Today his letter contained a five-pound note—I shall probably have you get it changed for me." &c.

He advised me: "I have been thinking today about your mention of my birthday. If you decide to take any notice of it, it appears to me, the best thing to do would be to make it 'the young people's compliment to Walt Whitman.' That would tickle me—I am curious to know how much the young people count—and it would better answer your own plans, perhaps. And then, have the girls there: it is not a little in my mind, how the girls are appealed to—it has, oh! a great significance—a great!" And in the course of remarks that followed: "Oh! 40 is not old! I consider even some centurions young! See Bob—why, Ingersoll is young to the core—heart, speech,—his vivacity inextinguishable—a child of the modern—if the modern can be so talked of as young—and I guess it can."

J. L. G. Ferris wrote in Sunday's Press (in connection with the Academy Exhibition): "Mr. Alexander's portrait of Walt Whitman should be taken notice of. The picture, without a doubt, has been painted only for that purpose. Nothing else will excuse the personal liberties taken with the bard." W. said: "Yes, liberties! Damn their lights—the whole kit of them! These artists are spoiled by the iniquities of the time. The drift of art everywhere—literature—have the vice common to theology, the clergy, churches—what they call *religion* (what impudence to call *that* religion!)"—"The belief that things are explicated in parts—portions—details—prettinesses: as if nature ever in anything took the *small* way of communication!" And then: "I want you to go see it—to tell me frankly—I know you will: I hardly need to say that—what you think of it—the whole story of it." I said I had met Boyle at the Club last week and asked him what he thought of Gilchrist's Whitman, Boyle replying: "I don't like it at all—I don't like anything he does—I don't like the man!" W. smiled and asked, "Are they his words?"—and to my assent—"It is important to know what such a man thinks,"—though very cautious as I could see, not to say a word in the direction of endorsement.

Tuesday, February 11, 1890

5.35 P.M. I found W., his hands folded, a towel upon his lap (he uses a towel for a napkin; always washes mouth and hands after a meal)—contemplating the hazy, dampened western sky. He greeted me in his wonted way—"Ah! it is Horace!"— hand extended. Said he had been out—more than an hour.

A letter on the table from McClure, of the newspaper syndicate. "He writes that he has somewhere a department for young folks—in his charge to fill—wants something from me. I am not at all certain I can move myself—or will be moved— to some utterance, reminiscence, statement. We shall see: see what we see," he continued.

He was quite "riled," as he said, "to see that Charles Emory Smith's place as Minister Plenipotentiary to Russia is assured." Adding: "Minister Plenipotentiaries are humbugs anyway—thorough shows, shams, superfluities—undemocratic. A good *charge d'affaires* would serve all the purposes of such a minister: the ornamentation could very well be abated." And he instanced "Marcy's pronunciamento, so to call it, 25 years ago or more—I forget who was President then—Marcy absolutely directed that our ministers were not to wear dress suits on reception days." &c. And he told of one of his own friends, a diplomat, "who went to the King of France in his dress suit—to France, the best of all with the right to be called *proper*, if propriety can anywhere be predicated." Ministers were "remnants of our older era—survive because they had been known for a thousand years and no one here was brave enough to attack it—as [also] the electoral college, which rose out of fears of the populace. But America is assured, apart from politicians, pro or con—or ministers— or bluster. In the masses [there is] no want of virility—sanity—that is America's hope."

W. asked amusingly: "What would we do without the sinners? Take them out of literature and it would be barren."

He had taken much interest in the accounts of Sherman's 70th birthday. Spoke of Johnston as "still a youth, though grey: a characteristic American of the sort that never grow old—are intrepidly young to the end." Gave me Morse's letter, which he had laid aside as promised. I read him a letter received from Brinton today in which B. spoke of the various requests to print his Bruno essay as a pamphlet—that he had resolved to do so—and wished through me to ask W. for a line or two to go along with it. W. said: "I shall keep that in mind and do it if I can—if the spirit moves me. You see how my Quakerism persists!"

"As with a child—so with America: so much consists not in what is going on today, or tomorrow—but in a man's, a nation's genesis—what he brings for thousands of years back— what natively enriches, buttresses, him."

Wednesday, February 12, 1890

7.20 P.M. W. reading the local papers. Out today, "an hour or so." Weather perfectly clear. Has not yet done anything practically as to Brinton's request.

Morris asked me today, how an extract from a recent letter from W. W. to Rhys, in which W. said his life was "ebbing slowly away" or something to that effect—had come into print. It seems it appeared in one of the Sunday papers. But

W. said: "I know nothing of it—did not see it: yet I read the Press—the Times. You had better ply Morris for specifications. We ought to know."

Referred to the great murder trial now on its way in the Camden courts. "It is a long, draggy event—a horrible matter all through." Yesterday he saw "Tom Harned has been announced to speak before the Camden County Medical Society tonight.—Now," he said, "I see no mention of Tom in the accounts—he could not have been there."

As to Morse's remark in his letter that Latchford had written something for the Tribune apropos of a report that Gladstone had predicted the laureateship for Swinburne: "To make Swinburne the laureate would complete the operation of getting all the fat in the fire!—perhaps complete the laureateship! Yet the question arises, if not Swinburne, then who the devil shall it be, anyway? There don't appear to be anyone, the best light you put it in." W. said he had been "much interested to learn" that Latchford, according to Morse's letter, was greatly impressed with the Morse bust as found in my book. "There are none too many who penetrate to the genuineness of that work."

Thursday, February 13, 1890

5.35 P.M. W. sat by the bed-room window, his dinner just done, his attitude pensive or musing. I returned him the Tennyson book. His questions were many and curious, without committing him, yet indication of the lines in which he had himself hoped. "Is there any weakness? Does he show any sign of failing—even a slight sign? No? How does it average? *Has* it an average?" And on my remark that Tennyson certainly expressed more strength than—for instance—was expressed in Whittier, W. assented: "That is so—thoroughly so: Whittier has very few strings—very few—to his harp—only three or four—though, to be sure, these are pure and strong."

Gave me Poet Lore for February, with the remark, when I told him that Prof. Seidensticker (represented therein by an essay—"The Relation of English to German Literature in the Eighteenth Century") was a friend of my father's: "I have read the article—it is quite good—suggestive." These were really the only pages of the magazine cut.

Brinton said in the course of a letter I received today: "Thanks for conveying my wishes to W. W. In whatever shape he is moved to express himself, prose or verse, as a letter or a prefatory remark, brief or lengthy, it will be welcome to me, and appreciated by all lovers of the strong men of history." W. exclaimed upon my reading: "That is certainly fine—fine—fine! I shall do what I can for him—certainly shall do *some*thing if the spirit impels me—and I always wait for that, as you know." And when I told him of a judgment I heard the other day—that W. is "the only writer in America now of the first rank," W. jokingly and laughingly said: "If that is so—if I am in any danger that people will think so of me, I had better watch myself more closely—for fear my house of cards may be shaken, shattered—should collapse utterly."

He made some reference to the murder trial still going on up the street—but thought the story "horrible—lacerating" in its details. Spoke of a proposition now to bridge the Delaware. "I was out a long time today—it was mild—sweet: we went to the river—saw it go past—the sky above—across there the big town." And "how sad" the prospect that the islands were "doubtless to be torn away!" And yet would they not be necessary if the bridge project now in Congress came to a head? "Oh! the bridge appeals to me—it should come: a grand, expansive undertaking it would be! I am always in favor of great bridges—great roads. Fifty years or so ago—or forty—there was a scheme to connect all America by noble roads—the west to the east—the north to the south—and some of them were even commenced. There are said to be several great roads—roads that will compare with the Roman,

295

the best so far known in history—out around Pittsburgh. But the scheme came to nothing—for soon we had the cars—the great railraods—and then such a thing as a turnpike became vulgar—no one would hear to it. And yet a great road is a great moral agent. Oh! a great road is not the stone merely, or the what-not, that goes to make it—but something more— far more!"

Friday, February 14, 1890

5.30 P.M. Buckwalter was on the step as I arrived. Mrs. Davis admitted us. I went right upstairs where W. was reading the local papers, B. staying in the parlor till W. told Mrs. D. to send him up. Buckwalter had brought along a basket of oranges which W. duly appreciated.

On B. expressing his pleasure that W. got out of doors, W. said: "I got out yesterday—today it has not been possible. Yesterday's jaunt—and it was quite a jaunt—was a fine one. The sky, the river, the sun—they are my curatives." B. gave W. some account of the Bonsalls, saying that Bart's Colorado Springs trip, though doing him some good, was undertaken too late. W. thought: "A mere change of air is apt to do a fellow good—whether by excitation, what, I don't know—by something that cannot be put in a word"—and then that Western air was itself sanitary—"and I don't know but eventually the Pacific coast—a thousand miles of it—up and down—will be the choice out of all America for the properties of its sanitation." "Even up in Oregon." And "I have heard Puget Sound above all." For "many, many years ago, I knew an old sailor—broken down—in New York then—talked with him often. He had spent 50 years, sailing—gone to all parts of the world, all lands: and I asked him a question—of all the lands you have ever traveled to, out of all the ports you have entered, is there one that stands preferred about and beyond, all the rest? And it was to my surprise, too, he replied that

296

there was—and when I asked its name, he gave me, Puget Sound. Then I questioned him about it closely—he saying they had been cast up there by some accident—the old brig, cutter he had gone off in met with some disaster—went down—needed repairs,—something." And then W. spoke of sky and water &c. as given him by this narrator.

Buckwalter left in a little while and we sat together talking some time longer. W. made some allusion to the elder James Gordon Bennett: "He was not at all prepossessing—had a decided squint, cross—to his eye." And as to the marriage debate Tucker is reprinting (Greeley one of the parties)—"That is very old—is certainly to be decided against as a chestnut. I read the letters many years ago—I should say 25 at least. Whenever anyone takes to talking of divorce or religion, I am reminded how little any one can possibly say about either, and how the deep currents flow and flow and flow and flow—achieve their ends, in defiance of all that is often called good sense, good morals. Every new case is the continuation of a thousand—of tens of thousands, of streams that pulse on away from human sight or even human imagination. Why explain?—how?—or chain the sunset—the glow we see there to the westward now"—pointing. "People think an event consists of itself alone—but what event is there but involves a thousand elements scarcely dreamed of?"

Saturday, February 15, 1890

7.50 P.M. W. reading the paper. Referred to the weather at once, questioning me—"Is the moon up?" &c.—and explaining that though the day had been "beautiful" he had not been out, Mrs. Davis being away, and they not wishing to leave the house alone. W. said: "I have had a card from Mrs. O'Connor. She is quite melancholy, saying that she don't know which way to turn for difficulties. It seems that the man—or one of the men—to whom William loaned money—

is not paying up according to promise. It is a sad plight—and yet I suppose she will come out it *some*-way—as a fellow from the very nature of the case must."

W. was considerably amused by an announcement in to-day's Press that preachers would tomorrow discuss the question, why so many pews were empty. "It seems to me a very plain case," he said, "a case easily explicated to any one who cares to see. The simple truth is, from time immemorial theology has built itself upon mythology—and now the time has come when that mythology can no longer be believed—believed by any one of any account. We need a reconstruction—*are having* a reconstruction in fact—of theology, so to call it—perhaps properly so to call it. I have heard it said that the church and genius are divorced—the church and the masses, too—and when we ask why, the preacher will say, from pride in the genius, stupidity in the others—that contrarity is at fault whatever. Damn the preachers! what do they know or care to know? The churches have constructed a god of moral goodness—wholly, solely, moral goodness—and that is its weakness. For if there is one thing that is *not* true, that is the thing: not but that moral goodness has its part. See what we get out of science, democracy, the modern—on this point! According to such a standard of moral goodness—the standard of the churches—probably nine-tenths of the universe is depraved—probably nine-tenths denied a right in the scheme of things—which is ridiculous, outright: might have satisfied an older intelligence, but will not ours. Our time, land, age, the future—demands readjustment—demands the fuller recognition of democracy—the *ensemble*: these have hardly been recognized at all in the old theology. What can science have to do with such a spectre as the present church? All their methods are opposed—must be opposed—utterly opposed: for one means restriction, the other freedom: the church—illadjustment, science—harmony." He referred at one point to "the smooth-faced, self-satisfied preachers."

Sunday, February 16, 1890

9.45 P.M. Saw W. in his own room, where he was reading the Press. Said he had "greatly enjoyed" his breakfast. Looked very well. "I hope to get out today." Temperature splendid—morning absolutely unclouded. Said sometimes he felt with the papers "as the house-lady with servant girls: I won't hear to having them about."

Called my attention to a score or so of prints, [illegible] heads from Appleton's Cyclopedia of American Biography. He had "much enjoyed them"—they were "so delicate—so unique." I did not stay more than five minutes. He spoke of the photograph on the mantel as that "of one of my London Socialistic friends—admirers."

Monday, February 17, 1890

7.40 P.M. W. reading papers: had several on his lap. Hugged up close to the light.

Morris had brought me in today a copy of the Press of Sunday week [Feb. 9] containing the following:

A Letter from Walt Whitman.
Special from the Dunlap Cable News Company.

London, Feb. 8.—A private letter from Walt Whitman to Ernest Phys [Rhys], dated January 22, says that he feels no very marked change is happening to him, but he is slowly but surely ebbing away.

"America," he continues, "is still busy all over her vast domain, talking, plodding and making money. Every one is striving to get to the top, but there is no special individual signalism. I guess it is just as well."

This I gave to W., who said: "That's curious—how that comes around to us! It sounds much as if I might have thought it—yet I doubt if I said it just that way. Still—I don't know. How could it have got out? How did Rhys come to give it out—or did he? No—there must be some other explication. It's curious how inevitably the things we would wish published are sedulously hidden, and things we would not are hurried to the light!"

Spoke of Harned's having come in yesterday—"the first time for weeks—yet looking the same as ever." When he learned I had seen the Alexander picture at the Academy yesterday he was very curious, like a boy. "Sit down," he said, "tell me about it—tell me all you know about it!" I gave the opinions of others—he then: "And now, what did *you* think of it! That's what I want to know." I spoke of it as better than Gilchrist's at the head; G.'s trunk better—but described the picture as a whole as inadequate—the head not badly painted, but *pinched*; the coat black or very dark blue—the neck scarcely more full than the fashionable neck—the hands faulty in extreme—hair back of head rather good, and forehead notably so—but beard wooly, defective: something in the expression rather good, but the general appearance meagre—head too large for body—coloring good throughout—as a piece of art, probably a good one. W. laughed out: "I see—I see—and that is bound to be the case—they'll have it their own way—the *art*-way—, whatever occurs. You would think that if an artist wished to make a picture of me—of anyone—he would seize upon me just as I am—skin, bones, hair, coat, pants, all—but no—somehow that does not satisfy them—nature can be improved upon—and so they improve and improve and improve, till all the nature is improved out of a picture." I said something about the necessity of knowing a man inside as well as out in order to paint him. W. thereupon: "That is so—that cannot be questioned: yet the artists all act by a contrary rule." And to my further saying; "It is not everybody who can paint you—" W.—"No—you are right: but then the statement can be much enlarged: we may just as well say: it is not everybody who can paint anybody." Then he went into some interesting details: "I am not surprised at the result you speak of. Alexander was here—came several times—made some sketches. He came originally at the instance of the Century Company. I don't know how it was effected, but it appears his pictures were not satisfactory—were never used there. Perhaps it was because things I said at the time were somehow heard there. This is all surmise, to be sure: but I clearly remember that the sketches did not impress me—took no hold on me—on the contrary were unsatisfactory—and I was free to confess this—did confess it to several. I don't know whether anything I said was carried to New York—probably not—yet possibly it was. And I am sure neither Gilder nor William Carey, my friends there, would refuse to give some weight to my words in that connection. Oh, the failures and failures and failures of artists!—the *deliberate* failures of artists! They bring us perpetual disappointments: though in a way we can be said to expect just what we get. Think of Eakins' picture—of Sidney's bust—by contrast! Sidney had a curious genius for carrying images—would seize something in you, and hold it forever—work it out, be you present or absent. And Eakins! How nobly he conforms to the Carlylean standards!—the standards which declare: you will come to this first in doubt, chagrin, perhaps: but here is an art that is nature—that will grow, grow, grow upon you: develop as you develop—is finally all opened to you as a flower! Who can look at Eakins at the start and be satisfied?—but looking longer, revelation comes—little by little discovery, discovery. Oh! there is no doubt Eakins is our man!" And to my phrase "brutally natural" he said—"I like it said that way: it takes us back to the elements."

Tuesday, February 18, 1890

7.30 P.M. Only briefly in to see W., who questioned me jokingly for "news," as he always does, and said when I told him I had been reading Johnson's little book on "The Worship of Jesus": "It must have a pith: I can fore-feel it, as they say. There seems to be propensity in human nature to worship some person—to tie to some person, ideal or actual: in the case of Christianity to Jesus. It is a marked, an irresistible— tendency. Whether this is a second sense, whether it origi- nates as the taste for tobacco, rum—not from innate first in- stincts—is a further question which might well be debated."

I had narrated how O'Connor, the day I saw him, had often in the rush of speech, choked—apologized—saying his weak- ness took that with many other forms. W.: "That is new—it was not so before—it was a torrent—broken, often, but never stayed."

I said my impulse had been, after seeing the Alexander picture Sunday, to send a note to the Press critical of what had there previously appeared. W. urged me to do it. "Too often it is the tendency simply to accept such a thing—to not inquire of its merits—how it meets its pretensions. A word that calls order is often the best word to be said."

Wednesday, February 19, 1890

5.10 P.M. W. reading the paper. I had quite a long talk with him. Just after his dinner he always seems in rising humor— the blood flowing to more animation, speech given a conse- quent freedom.

Developed considerable talk of old actors. Jefferson said in his January Century talk: "There are many good actors that have this peculiar raw quality who have been on the stage for years; and it is because they begin their careers by acting leading characters. Mrs. Mowatt and James H. Hackett were examples of many in our profession who have committed this fatal error." W. objected: "That would give an entirely false idea of Hackett. I doubt if Jefferson knows—doubt if he ever saw him. At any rate, while I read these articles—and some of them have an interest—it is all superficial—gives none of

those significant side-lights and deep touches which are almost necessary to the true understanding of old dramaticism.
Hackett was not appreciated by some, as the best things *always* are not appreciated by some. He may not have been
popular after the modern sense, but he was a man who could
hold his audiences—and high-class audiences they were, too.
He and Henry Placide and Mrs. Vernon and Charlie Fisher—
these were the true creatures of the time—the highest-born
of all to their work! Yes, I knew Don—Sir William Don: he
was a tall, slim fellow—with an irresistible comic power. I
was going to say genius—and genius it was, of a sort. I more
and more question if the modern men can enact such comedy
as had the boards in my young days. There is a new sense of
humor abroad—the Byronic taste, that craved for whiskey of
vitriolic intensity—whiskey that bites the throat as it goes
down—not whiskey that laves every spot as if balm. Such
men—men formed on such a taste—could not repeat the old
comedy. I know people will say, yes, the old is best, is *always*
best to the *old*: but no—no—I think there is more than that
to the story—I feel sure I am an exception to the rule of those
who declare, feel, that all goes with age. I never think of
[Emma] Alboni but I think of the finest voice, organ, that
ever was. Her contralto—what a purity! what a range! And
whatever her change of pitch, there was no loss of power, of
integrity. After Booth was Forrest—a masterly man, with a
voice strong and true and musical beyond all about him. Forrest was a man of parts, too: there was a time when he was in
much demand—was a sort of social *elegante*, and proved his
right to be thought it; and again, was in demand for
lectures—what we call addresses, now. Of all the persons,
events, of those times, Jefferson's perspective is full of defects. His writing is much less interesting—true to the life—
than Siddons', or Fanny Kemble's—yes, even than
McCready's."

Asked me where I was going. "Up to Tom's?" But no—I

was going to Philadelphia. He added: "I intended asking you to bring me more whiskey. I am quite out of whiskey and Tom's is the bestest ever was! Oh! it is genuine stuff. I know nothing near so good anywhere else."

Thursday, February 20, 1890

7.30 P.M. In at W.'s only a few minutes. Found him in the parlor. Had not been out today. I said it seemed like old times to see him down stairs in the evening. He asked: "Ah! it seems like a step forward, does it?" And then quietly—"Well— maybe it is!"—But his tone was of doubt.

Still he was very cheery. When I spoke of the beauty of the river at sunset he remarked: "Ah! it is good to be with the river—good: the river mends us: is good for many things more than one thing!" He was in a tender mood. I kissed him as I left.

He said: "News is scant: nothing comes up but the Le Coney trial." And he said as yet he had felt no impulse to write the Bruno lines for Brinton.

Friday, February 21, 1890

7 P.M. W. in his room, reading the local papers. He laugh- ingly said: "Tomorrow is Washington's birthday—so our loyal Camden papers (the great patriots!) have no issue!" And after his laugh—"We all abuse the papers, but what would we do without them?" Asked me about those in Philadelphia.

We talked of the adjacence of his own birthday. "Yes," he said, "it is coming near again"—and then dreamily—"Who knows? who knows?"—adding tender comment on the birth- day after-clap, 1888, and the "wonder that things have sur- vived so to date" after what had been gone through, with doubting and watching. He admitted that his own "looking forward" was "to but one issue"—and that—"who can tell how soon?"

He talked somewhat of Alexander's picture again—in the old strain of dislike. "He took a few sketches here—I thought them wonderful meagre at the time—to my mind they seemed to come to nothing—arrive at no effect—no statement. And then he went home and did the rest in his study. What could be expected different from what has appeared? The devil with all the artists—or most all—is that they lack veracity—seem to feel under no obligation to produce things as they see them but rather to color up and up, till the public eye is properly titivated. How can there be true art on this basis?—first-class art by first-class men?"

As I sat there Warren brought in a rose and some leaves which he said had been left there by someone from the Third Street Church for W. W. thanked him—went on with talk— Warren leaving the room. By and bye, when I got up to go, he asked, as he often does: "Are you going straight home?"— upon learning I was, taking this flower from the bunch which was in a mug on the table and saying—"Take this to Aggie— give the dear girl my love." When I went downstairs and Warren saw I had the rose, he was quite indignant, remarking: "He don't care for flowers anyway: he don't care a fig for 'em!"—not appreciating that W. *did* care devotedly for them, and because caring, would share them with his friends and make them the coin of his good feeling. The day before W. had asked me the same thing: "Are you going straight home?"—then saying: "Take a couple of oranges along with you—one for your mother, one for Aggie."

He thought—"most of all do the reporters lack veracity: oh! for a true tale from a reporter! How vivid that would be, could we but have it! But no!—everything with them too is in the dressing!"

305

Saturday, February 22, 1890

Out at Germantown all day—went to see [Edwin] Booth as Richelieu in the evening: saw nothing of W. W. Worked a little on the Whitman article for the New England Magazine. The day too cold for W. to get out.

Sunday, February 23, 1890

9.45 A.M. Stopped in but briefly. W. just done breakfast. The letter-carrier especially favored him by bringing in his mail. A letter from Bucke and a copy of the Osceola Gazette.

W. asked me about my seeing Richelieu (Booth) last night. Then of actors in general. "I don't think this matter of acting absorbingly important. I don't feel as if civilization, progress, life (American or other), hangs in any way upon the existence of theatres, actors. There was a time when the stage held a rarer place in human life, but now other factors enter in—share the feast, the gifts."

Expressed gladness to learn from the papers that Tennyson was better. "It is good to hear."

Showed him a short article headed Walt Whitman—on obverse traces of a cut, inscribed WALT WHITMAN. "A sweet poet and true." We could neither of us imagine from what paper.

WALT WHITMAN.

Walt Whitman, a descendant of an old Puritan family of Long Island farmers, but on the mother's side of Dutch ancestry, was born on May 31, 1819, at Huntington, in that island, thirty miles from New York City. He was brought up in the town of Brooklyn, where he learnt the trade of printer in a local newspaper office. He was much in the great city, employed both as printer and newspaper writer or editorial assistant. In 1850, with his brother, he went to the Southern and Western States, working some months at New Orleans. Returning to Brooklyn, he edited the *Freeman*, a daily and weekly paper, and produced a volume of poetic rhapsodies called *Leaves of Grass*. The contents of this singular book are neither verse nor prose, but a series of ejaculations and aphorisms presenting many original ideas, and appealing to the common feelings of mind in favor of the natural enjoyment of life, the healthy exercise of the active powers of mind and body, and the frank reception of wholesome influences. It was designed, he says, "to emanate buoyancy and gladness"; and it soon became a favorite book with many readers in England, as well as in America. But we doubt whether its author would have obtained a firm and wide reputation if events had not associated him with some thrilling incidents of the great military struggle that went on from 1861 to 1865. He volunteered, in the second year of the Civil War, as a relief agent in the army hospitals, which he joined in Virginia at the end of 1862, and worked indefatigably during three years, making over six hundred tours or visits, and personally attending on 80,000 or 100,000 sick or wounded soldiers. Experiences like these, in camp and hospital, in the field and on the march, could not fail to be instructive to the poet and philospher, who learned more with his heart than with his head. Yet he was not the man to seek in such terrible miseries of his fellow-creatures the materials of literary effect. His notes or diaries, part of which were published, give many touching anecdotes of the brave sufferers, who were of both sides in the war. After this, Walt Whitman held a clerkship in the Attorney-General's Department at Washington, till in 1873 he was stricken with paralysis, and retired to live at Camden, New Jersey, his home from that time. Dwelling with friends in a farmhouse, and spending most of his days in contemplative repose among rural scenes, he has been a minute observer of Nature, studying the trees and flowers, insects and birds, like Thoreau, with the affectionate intimacy of a comrade and disciple.

Walt Whitman's merits are entire sincerity; an intense love of nature, including human nature, in its broadest, homeliest, and commonest manifestations; a genuine patriotism and love of freedom; a manly individuality which rejects all compromises with fashionable prejudices and mere conventional assumptions; and a spirit of benevolence, which shines through his life as through his writings.—(See page 5.)

Mrs. Burleigh, from whom I got it, had received it from another and was herself in the dark. W. laughingly said—"It is very tantalizing."

I stayed out briefly. He looked ruddy. Complains of his sight.

Monday, February 24, 1890

7.45 P.M. I received a letter from Brinton this morning, saying the Bruno matter would be in type the last of this week. Not having time to go down to W.'s I sent him a note by mail. The first thing now after shaking hands (he was in his room as usual, reading) he said: "I had your note this morning, and"—putting his hand into his inside vest pocket and drawing forth an envelope boldly addressed "Dr. Brinton"— "here is a word or two—probably 5 or 6 lines—impromptued today. They may do—may not: I can hardly say: you will know, I am sure. Send them to the Doctor if you think they will serve his purpose. I am sure I feel it an honor to be asked, and am glad to have my word go in there, for I feel it is in good company." I met Davidson yesterday and he told me his own speech was to go along with Brinton's. "And he tells me Walt Whitman is to write the preface." I laughed at the idea of "preface," though sure W. would write a few lines, as now he has done. At first he was going to sign simply "Walt Whitman"—but his final thought was to write—"Impromptu words of Walt Whitman"—and so it stands. "I must have proof," he further said. I put in—"I'll tell Brinton you want proof and plenty of copies!"—to which with laughter—"Yes, that is better still: that is a point we must not forget." Said he was sure he "would like Davidson." Davidson well knows Jeff. W.: "Jeff is a good deal about New York: you know, he *debued*[?] there!"

Felicitated over a paragraph in the Press describing a still further improvement in Tennyson's condition. "They call it— 'a shade better'—that's the way they put it. Well—he's an old man on the last edge of life. And there's the wife, too—the mate of him all these years: how it would *treat* me to see her—I don't know nearly but as much as to see him." Spoke similarly of Gladstone's long wedded life.

Said he had heard nothing of the flash picture taken in his room. "And having heard nothing, I suppose nothing resulted. I had my doubts from the first." He asked me suddenly, with amusing color: "What do you know of Bok"— spelling his name—"the newspaper writer? He has lately come into these parts—gone on one of the weeklies. What do you know about Dr. Allibone, the quotation man? Bok is much such a man. Allibone was a sort of chief-cook-and-bottle-washer in literature—a hunter after dates,—made up of curioish tendencies—a searcher after hidden lines, useless origins, ridiculous gossipries—a sweeper of the literary floorboards—how many editions—and how bound—and where was the cloth bought—and who printed: a literary branch leading mostly into lies—not artificiality merely, but downright lies. Bok has proved a most assiduous man—as assiduous as Humboldt's Albany correspondent, who wanted an autograph, a sentiment: I believe letters two, 3, 4, 5, if not more came, and all to the same effect—kept it up for years. America is still very young, and yet seems able to support quite a number of such fellows—a crop of them. They are called *literary*, but God help literariness if they are literary!"

The mention of Humboldt caused the remark that Humboldt, Macaulay and [Washington] Irving died the same year (1859)—"And Humboldt head and shoulders above both the others" W. thinks—"easily—easily. And the brother, too— Wilhelm—a great man by all my means of knowing. Sometimes they hunted *double*—in pairs, I think." Bok has not yet been over to see W.

Tuesday, February 25, 1890

7.45 P.M. As I came up to the house I found there was no light in his room—and sure enough, as I found from Warren, he was lying down. Had not been out today. Said he felt "so-so"—and no more.

Remarked at once his "interest" in the fact that the fair was given by Congress to Chicago. "I wonder if that is irrevocable? I suppose so." And then laughingly, "I wonder what the New York Herald says of it?" Then went on to speak of the Crystal Palace "long ago". [This was a building at the New York World's Fair of 1853, which was destroyed by fire in 1856.] "I found it a mine: what I delved for and found there—who can tell? It was a wonder of [?] thing, beaming, joining, grooving—a delicate, sufficient mechanical wonder. I contemplated it often on that side with the greatest joy: it so filled and surrounded me. And yet when it burned it all went up in a puff."—"Not least of things there were great art-products sent from abroad—fabulous in material value—great in values of any sort."

Referred to the electoral college as "a remnant of aristocracy—a reminder of an old distrust of the people."

Wednesday, February 26, 1890

7.30 P.M. With W. 15 minutes or so. He was reading The Long Islander. Talked very freely. Out today—the weather very mild. He said: "Jenkins appears to be orating up the street [at the trial] at a great rate. It is the usual confusion. One side is determined to prove certain things happened—then the other side gets up and shows that these things never could have happened. Out of all of which I question if much or any truth is extracted."

I had a letter from Brinton today asking if the manuscript I sent him had really been in W.'s own hand. W. smiled. "Yes—

that is the very hand—the critter's own," lifting his hand to suit the words. Brinton had also referred in the letter to W.'s "sonorous verse," W. thereupon: "That sounds good: I hope the verse *is* sonorous: I have my many many doubts."

When he heard I was going out to see Peter Montgomerie tonight, he would have me take papers—putting into a package as I stood hat in hand, copies of the Inquirer, Woodstown Register, Pall Mall Gazette. "Take these—mere reminders—with my remembrance, my affection." He alluded to having sent "A Twilight Song" to the Century and added—"Today the check came. It was only a little piece—the 'Twilight Song'—and now, when will it appear? That is another matter. Gilder is very well disposed towards me—a great deal better disposed than we have any right to expect, considering him as the literary man he is—the magazine—all." And to my questions: "I should not object to appearing in Scribner's if they paid me for it. Still I am a little afraid to send anything—to approach a person I do not know at all. I have been so often cuffed—met not only incivility but downright and cowardly insult—I must pick my way. The Century folks are kind throughout. This piece is not formidable—it is merely a song in memory of dead soldiers—oh! the many! many! many!—unknown!"

Thursday, February 27, 1890

7.20 P.M. W. lying on the bed. I do not like the new tendency—which is in fact a relapse to an old. He complains of some weariness, oftener recurring.

I asked him about the birthday. Whatever is decided upon, would he prefer Philadelphia or Camden? He would express no preference. "If you can get a light carriage—an easy one—do that: with that I can go almost anywhere. I am in your hands. Whatever you do, you will find me consentaneous—willing to connive. All I would urge is—no high-falutin!

Whatever comes, let it be your spontaneous product." Last evening in West Philadelphia, I came upon a personal in a Flint, Michigan, paper: "Walt Whitman has at last come down to a wheel chair." When I told W. he laughed with great heartiness.

He remarked again: "What a hornet's nest President Eliot seems to have pulled about his ears in going for newspaper unveracity—the reporters. Yet the truth of the matter is all with Eliot—all he said is true—every word—and the wonder is, why everybody don't admit it. It is well enough known to us, so to say it, on the inside, that the average reporter (of course there are exceptions)—the average reporter has no more notion—no more intention—towards veracity than if veracity was never called for. The lyingness of the news is most astonishing—brazen: I should think no one would for a minute take up cudgels against the Professor for his frankness." Another moment he said: "I see Thayer is to write a paper on Bruno for the Atlantic. Thayer is a very likable young man—has been here. He is in one sense a Whitman man: that is to say, a Whitman man under conditions. He won't accept the critter just as he stands—yet has a kindly disposition our way."

Friday, February 28, 1890

Did not see W. at all: worked till late (6.45), then direct to Germantown, there working with Clifford &c. on the Johnson manuscript. W. did not of course get out. The weather decidedly inclement—raining.

Saturday, March 1, 1890

7.50 P.M. W. reading the Century—Jefferson's piece. Seemed in good trim physically, and said he felt so. As to the May dinner: "If I am as well then as I am now, I shall be glad to put myself in your hands. But you must tell the boys, I make no promises: I am not in a condition to be certain of the future—even of tomorrow."

Said he had had "a good long letter from John Burroughs" which he had "sent off to Doctor Bucke this evening"—explaining—"He speaks of you; wishes to hear from you when you are inspired to write. He is back again at West Park, prepared to go into the new season—to dig and dig away again. The letter is very good—but in the pessimistic vein. It seems the onus of the poets of our time—the literary fellows everyway—writers, thinkers, what-not—to turn everything into pessimistic explication—everything. The writers in the magazines—to question—to exclaim—what a devil of a monotony is life!—and such like. The public wants it—it seems to be the tendency of the time. Even Bryant was touched by its poison—seemed to like to write of death—to dwell upon it." But was there not a Greek calm in Bryant's dealing with the subject? "I suppose that can be said of Bryant—he felt it was a natural fact—as such to be noted as you pass. But the average drift is not a healthy one: it goes downwards." It was "hard to account for even a hint of the tendency in John" but "there it is."

I read him an article Chubb had sent me today—a supposed conversation between a visiting Englishman and a native American. W. listened—enjoyed. Then he said: "That is all to be said—but this cat of democracy has a very, very long tail, not to be all unfolded in a few questions and answers. I don't remember whether I said so to Chubb when he was here, but I know it was my feeling to say of our American life—some of it—that it was all tapering off into gentility—that *genteel* was the word, that everyone, striving to be something, thinks there is no something but as it is found in gentility, respectability. It is a bad sign—it augurs ill—yet augurs *not* ill, too—according as we look at it—from what side we regard it. I have no despair—I am free to say that. Since the war, I have no longer had the least fear but an eventual issue of freedom was secure. Since the war I have sat down contentedly, convinced that we were to be righted at last. Oh! there is no doubt of it! And not the most to this end is to come of the civilizee himself—the man of cities, knowing as he is, and prosperous—for civilization, cities, are also a great curse. I know in the armies the clearest-brained, cleanest-blooded, of all the soldiers—were the farmer-boys. In them was the future—democracy—America."

Sunday, March 2, 1890

W. at home all day. Kept busy at his papers, "writing some and dozing more." He complains of "the great alike-ness of these days indoors." I question him from time to time again about the hospital proposition, but he will give me no encouragement. Must now write to Bucke on the matter. His question put to me some time ago—how does W. take my question?—not answered because I have wished to say something conclusive. For the present I consider B. answered negatively. Shall so write.

Monday, March 3, 1890

7.45 P.M. Night very cold. W. in his room. Not reading. Fire brisk—room hot and close. He asked me immediately about the weather. Not out of course today. He said of his own occupations: "I have written a long letter to John Burroughs, which I sent off tonight—a letter to Dr. Bucke, which also went off tonight—a postal card to Mary Costelloe. These things serve to keep a man awake. Letters coming *this* way have lately been few. The letters I have received have been mostly of the autograph kind: asking by media of subterfuge. One letter that came was the funniest, the damnedest—. A woman, in the west, in Iowa, Kansas, somewhere, said she had heard I gave away copies of Leaves of Grass: which proving so, would I not send a copy to her? That seemed the damnedest I ever heard." And he laughed most heartily.

Asked after Dave McKay—then of authors and publishers—instancing Emerson's "wise management of his own plates: ordering a thousand printed from time to time, and so keeping track of his affairs on his own book. John Burroughs thinks *he* has been most horribly swindled by the publishers. He has not said anything about it to me lately but that used to be his idea. John's books have a wide currency—seem to go pretty much everywhere—and there ought to be some income from them."

Referred to the Le Coney trial—L. acquitted today. "The main notion seemed to be, to get somebody badly licked: for the truth, no one seemed to care—no one."—"Looking at such events, we seem to breathe in a world of lies."

A letter to me from Williamson (N.Y.) today, asking after W.'s condition and if he could stand the fatigue of sittings for Sergeant, the painter, now from England, if he came on here. W. said: "I don't know what I think, if anything: I have no inclination any way—for or against—except, perhaps, against." But I questioned—"What shall I tell Williamson? I shall write to him." W. then: "If you write him say, yes, let Sergeant come—I will give him all the help I can. Visits—occurrences—of that kind, break in somewhat pleasantly upon the dreary, monotonous life we lead. I cannot promise any great help—perhaps to give him two or three half-hours. When Eakins came, he would spend from half an hour to an hour—and he was a man good to have around—possessed of marked peculiarities. There are pictures and pictures. That Gutekunst picture that your father threw into that great scale, with such noble results—it would be hard to beat that. I can easily see how that should be our final pictorial counterfeit. It thoroughly fills and satisfies me. I suppose we all have a little vanity," &c.

315

He said he had been reading Jefferson's memoirs in the Century "carefully" and was "bound to say" he was "not much impressed" since "Jefferson seems to know remarkably little of events that you would think naturally his own by right of profession." And then: "There are some writers who, knowing the character they have in hand to like corned beef and cabbage, will argue for pages the reason for such a sympathy. Jefferson does so with Forrest—argues elaborately upon points the public cares nothing whatever for—need not know about. I have seen Jefferson act many a time: he is an ad captamdum man—a man of the school of men who, having a character in rags to portray, piles on the rags to the point of suffocation—till the whole affair becomes farcical." As to Sir William Don: "He was not a man of the highest talent, but in the range of his art (to use a very loathsome word) he had certain gifts not to be denied."

Tuesday, March 4, 1890

5.30 P.M. W. had just finished his dinner. Spoke of Harned's having been in. Asked me if I had written to Williamson, and learning I had, said: "Let the man come—the artist: I will do for him what I can—give him, say three sittings of half an hour each—which will probably be enough."

Advised me that I "should write to John Burroughs"—for— "he spoke of you in the letter yesterday (which I have sent to Doctor) and said he would be glad to hear from you any time you felt moved to write." Laughed somewhat over Boyesen's lectures on American Literature at the University. "We have plenty of books in America—but about the literature?—oh! I have my doubts!"

I had with me a copy of the Moss process engraving catalogue. W. thought: "Perhaps these new methods will thoroughly democratize art. To an artist, so-called, art is a very narrow thing indeed—he always puts the narrower meanings upon it." I suggested "as the theologians upon religion"—to which W.—"Yes—exactly: it is the same thing. Art is to paint a picture according to a mode—but there is more to the story than that!" A picture of Whittier in the book attracted him.

He remarked the various little paragraphs about Carpenter that nowadays creep into the newspapers. "He is a man who shares the view of Jesus, of Bacon,—who says, don't let us talk of faith any longer—let us *do* something. Any man can jabber, tell a story—any fluent-tonguey man can do that. But the man who can live the virtues, needs no courier, announcers—*is* the fact other men only dream of—he is the man we want—the man to *absorb* morality—to *become* it! Carpenter has the keenest sense of all that. He has been here, I have well seen him, he is very sympathetic towards America, very democratic—a great advance on his countrymen generally— even the cultivated men—scholars, artists, we see—who come here."

He asked to "step in upon Melville Phillips" some day at my leisure. "Ask him about my proofs—why I have had none. He proposed to make the March issue of Munyon's Illustrated World a Whitman number. I wrote him something—but what I wrote was very scratchy—scraggly—and I would not have him put it through without giving me proof. But having no proof I presume they changed their minds about the March number." One of his comments: "I constantly hear people call for the new—for new pictures—and yet that call has no seduction for me whatever, for the oldest are often the newest to me. I find some of the pictures I came upon as a boy first are still fresh to me—exhale perennial dew."

Complained that the weather was too severe and he could not get out today. "Had a letter from Rhys about a week ago. He remains in substance the same man: strong, quiet, serene." Spoke of the odor of wood—"its exquisiteness. I remember it at the great New York Exhibition—a whole room given to it. To me it was a constant delight—a perfume better

317

than all perfumes." I described how in my boyhood I had used to watch the pump-maker outside Camden—a Mr. Vautier—and what to me then was the woodsy experience. W. exclaimed—"Oh! I can realize it. I had just such experiences when I was a youngster."

He gave me a copy of a Camden paper—the Courier, asking that I read editorial therein "taking exception—almost violent—to the Le Coney verdict." I did not think he took that much interest in the trial.

Wednesday, March 5, 1890

7.15 P.M. Found W. in the parlor in the dark—alone. He greeted me cordially, said I should "sit at the other window—see out-of-doors." Said he felt very well, but the weather continuing as it had, he had been closely confined. Inquired after the sleetiness—if it was at all improved &c.

The electric light at the corner threw a strong glare along the street and he remarked the changed systems of lighting cities—questioning me how far the electric had become the general light in Philadelphia and "wondering if the lights along the bank of the river—up and down"—did not "make a rare touch pictorially—with all that follows?" He referred to "democratic" streets—such a street as Columbia Avenue—in which the masses came out nights to do their shopping—and the fact that such a street was being "duplicated in Camden—in Kaighn's Avenue." Such thoroughfares had always had an especial interest for him—"especially in the older days—in New York, when I was free to wander as I chose"—and "*did* wander."

"What of politics?" he asked me. Adding—"How far do you assent to the feeling that it is said Cleveland and all his entourage holds, that Cleveland is bound to be the Democratic candidate at the next Presidential election?" And to my opinion that the feeling was prevalent among private Democrats, whatever of public I did not meet, he spoke of C.'s "good bearing" and his own conviction that we had "not heard the last of him." Much amused over Puck's cartoon of four representatives of the Party of Moral Ideas &c.

No proof yet either from Phillips or Brinton. I had a short note from Morse today. W. informed me of a short note in from Kennedy. "He says he gave the Danish piece to his man at once upon receiving it, but that some one of the man's family died about that time and he went away and was not able to attend to it at once. The man reports it as very favorable. No doubt he'll render it for us."

Thursday, March 6, 1890

5.45 P.M. W. in his room. Day extremely cold. Boys out-of-doors skating on the pavements. Some snow along the streets, but not much. W. discussed the new appearance of things—his own "imprisonment"—yet "delights in the gift to see, if not tread the earth."

He asked me about the dinner. Young Hughes had been in to see me today, stating his grandiloquent plans. I told him of our own intention as to a dinner on W.'s birthday and he thereupon had nothing to do but drop his own plans. He had had one Wagerman (?) of Brooklyn—to write a poem: "He is the greatest poet of the age"—after a pause—"excepting Walt Whitman." To my incredulous looks—"but he has not published much: he is atheistic" &c. When I told W. this he laughed—then said seriously: "Better not only to have that postponed but dropped—dropped flat, without compunction!" And further: "My fear is of a deluge of soft soap—that I may go down in the flood. No—no. I think what you did was the best thing *could* be done. Above all we must avoid flattery—the tendency in anyone to pile it on and on till a fellow no longer shows his honest *self* at all! And you must see to it—see it is not done." I said my plan was to have a

319

gathering of W.'s known friends,—no formal speeches: speeches if anyone was prompted to speak—but none otherwise— everything spontaneous and free. W.: "That is an idea—a good one—it commends itself to my mind at once. The birth- day at Harned's!—how *au fait!*—I shall not forget it—it was *sui generis*—as in fact all true dinners or celebrations of what- ever kind should be." And then he said again: "It was a good idea to sit down on display plans: keep it in your own hands— the hands of those who know me. I shall wish to be good- natured—to assent to everything if possible."

Friday, March 7, 1890

7.20 P.M. W. sitting in the parlor. Complained that it was not as warm as his own room, though there was a strong coal fire there and it seemed amply warm to me. But he admitted: "I am more and more sensitive to the cold: my inanimate limbs." Left with him Morse's letter.

Morris today commented on Alexander's picture sharply— called it "a bag puffed up by the wind." W., after his laugh over my repetition of this, added: "I am not surprised: no doubt I should disfavor it myself had I the chance of a look— as I haven't." And then—"A simon-pure artist cannot do it— cannot trust it!" Referred to Phillips. I had not been in to see him yet, but proposed it tomorrow. W.: "I had from Munyon yesterday a proof of the autobiographic piece, which I read and at once returned. But nothing else has come. If you can, go in to see him—give him my reiterated request for proofs— tell him I must on no account be missed. No man has suffered worse than I have from editors who insist they can read my proofs better than I can and printers who insist that they know the location of the commas better than I do." And he thought: "It is always the particular error you don't want to happen that *does* happen, anyhow."

Speaking of business men's mid-day religious meetings in

New York: "Business piety is always to me an anomaly—it is as if made to test how much a man may smile and smile and be a villain. I suppose it is a sin to say that—I suppose that is severe: but the humbuggery of business piety has always impressed me—given the significance of the situation. And now, in old age, something confirms me as forcibly as ever in the notion." As to the weather: "I keep to my old habit—and not only in this thing: I listen to all the prophets—then wait till I see the weather itself!"

Asked me Ingersoll's address, which I had partly forgotten. I asked, "Have you sent him the book yet?" And he replied, "No—it was for the purpose of sending it that I asked you for his address. I should have done it long ago—I feel some embarrassment in my neglect—for it is a neglect." Reference having been made to Williamson as a collector (as known by fragmentary paragraphs in the papers)—W. said: "But a real Shakespeare manuscript!—what a find that would be! And yet not a shred—not a sign—of one of the greatest of history's great—the writer of plays that have now become a necessary part of our civilization! Had there been a collector to collect *that*—it would have made the whole race of collectors illustrious! As I say of Emerson—he somehow seems to justify the whole literary class. How the collectors would in a like manner profit! Out of such a preserve to go forever into sacred estimation!"

Saturday, March 8, 1890

7.45 P.M. W. in his room—again reading Felton's lectures. He returned to me Morse's letter, with a letter from Dr. Bucke containing enclosures from Mrs. O'Connor which he wished me to read. I gave him Ingersoll's address.

Harned came in while I sat there—and finally we went out and to his house together. Just before H. had come in W. had given me a whiskey bottle to have H. fill. When finally we were to go, W. asked me if I would not "bring the bottle back tonight" as, "I am all out of it—feel like a little nip before I go to bed." His talk very full and clear—so much so as to excite H.'s remark. W. referred as often before to the story of the miller: "I don't care by what road you brought the wheat, so it is good." And added—"That is a sockdologer for the preachers, ain't it?"—laughing heartily.

He had read a story in this morning's paper—English news—: "A preacher there—in one of the royal chapels—a somebody or other—made a reference to the Queen, who was present, which made her blazing mad. He was a man probably knowing somewhat of the part preachers played in the reign of Louis XIV—fellows who would rebuke the nobles—even the Kings—from the very pulpit. This man said—or is said to have said—'And as for you, madame'—and then gone on with his sermon. After all was over the Queen called him—gave him what the Irishman would call, 'a piece of her mind'—told him he should never preach again in a royal chapel, or something to that effect." W. had been "interested"—yet put in finally: "I suppose the whole story is doubtful—it has a fishy smell. For somehow the Queen has always impressed me as one possessed of the greatest tact." And then he instanced the Buchanen reception episode again: "That is undoubtedly authentic—it made quite a ripple at the time—and is proof to me of the Queen's tact—a possession which in women—as seen in women of even ordinary make-up, often—is the biggest thing in the world."

Clifford lectured in Camden last evening on the French Revolution. W. referred to the subject—Carlyle's exposition of it—illustrated by a story out of his own experience—then: "And so with this—I wonder, not that it was bloody, but that it was not bloodier. The capacity of the true man for turning upon his oppressor is one of the glories of the race—its security, in fact. I remember Mrs. Ernestine L. Rose—the big, noble woman!—when speaking of the Revolution—the

Frenchmen—and it was one of the very few things which ruf-
fle her out of her beautiful placidity; her eyes would flash—
and she would exclaim—'What!—to be trod down and not
turn! Do you take the people to be of wood or of stone!' Oh!
her eye, her cheek, her way, her half-rising from the chair—
it was all fine. And the words are as strong, I put them there
in my note-book—have kept them all these years. Perhaps I
missed in giving them just now, but that is their substance.
And that is one reason why I never went full on the nigger
question—the nigger would not turn—would not do anything
for himself—he would only act when prompted to act. No!
no! I should not like to see the nigger in the saddle—it seems
unnatural; for he is only there when propped there, and prop-
ping don't civilize. I have always had a latent sympathy for
the Southerner—and even for those in Europe—the Cava-
lier-folk—hateful as they are to me abstractly—un-demo-
cratic—from putting myself in a way in their shoes. Till the
nigger can do something for himself, little can be done *for*
him." He spoke of "the line of social demarkation in the lower
orders" as "very much more obvious than that higher up."

W. spoke of Washington—the cost of living there as high:
"Yet no city I would better like for living than Washington—it
is so open—so little crowded—so unrestricted. Yet Washington is no longer the place for the Capital: fifty years from now
the Capital will be elsewhere—off towards the great West—
to the Mississippi or beyond. There'll be a devil of a row, but
it'll be done."

He spoke quite warmly with Harned about the Le Coney
trial. "Was it not rather a trial of lawyers?—a tournament of
legalism?" And yet—"though I believed the man guilty, I
should not have convicted him; there were turns and turns in
the evidence which preserved an air of doubt straight along."
Yet he questioned Harned closely. "The thing that impressed
me deeply was Jenkins' statement after the trial—several
days after, that he believed Le Coney guilty if ever man was."

Harned put in—"I heard even the judge on the bench say that—Judge Garrison." To which W.: "That is even more significant—of vast moment in the making up of my own mind."

Could not find Phillips at the Press office today. He is never there on Saturdays.

Sunday, March 9, 1890

W. had a quiet day—reading. Weather remains cool, preventing him from going out-of-doors. Says he maintains his health however—"at least at what it was."

Monday, March 10, 1890

5.50 P.M. W. in the parlor. Still light. The room comfortable. Still, he had his big shawl thrown over the shoulder nearest the window. He looked really well. Went into warm and fine discourse of "the grandeur of river sights—sounds: the waters, skies, the big town over there"—and his hope that "as spring comes, we can have our regular outings, and *long*." Alluded to "the scarce events"—saying: "There seems now what they call an interregnum—in everything—or, perhaps not that, but in literature, certainly." Adding—"The Critic this week suggests it to me: the dullest number for a long time."

I had but such a hurried glimpse of him, then home to supper.

Tuesday, March 11, 1890

8 P.M. On my way to the Club: University Extension debated tonight. Professor Adams from Johns Hopkins and Pepper of Philadelphia. W. spoke of the subject: "A little dubious," as he said, whether it "could be so termed as very decidedly to enrich the masses." Somehow "our democracy

needs something no college can give it." But he took "no ground *against*" for the "full proportions and even the kind" of scheme afoot had never been deeply thought over by him.

Sent his "general love" to any who might ask (as some always do)—and special remembrance to Dr. Brinton."

Wednesday, March 12, 1890

7.15 P.M. W. sitting by the open parlor window. Had been out today. "Enjoyed the airing—it was a great benefaction." And—"The evening has its own beauty, too—here, as I sit close to its best effects of rest and quiet."

Boyle had told me at the Club last evening that Wilson Eyre had been over to the cemetery in Camden and made some sketches for W., but W. told me now that Eyre had not been in to see him. "And if he makes a design, the question will still remain, will it suit me—what are its impressions upon me. And then there are practical matters to be considered—to raise the money to pay for it." He said: "I hold my negative, to be used if necessary." Boyle has put the matter in Eyre's hands, as belonging properly to him. W. admitted— "Perhaps it does rather come into the province of an architect."

Asked me specifically about the Club meeting. When I spoke of after-features—"the chat with the boys," as he put it—he added—"I've no doubt that is the best part of it—the part I would most enjoy—a royal feast, taken as it may be." And then he added: "If I could come—perhaps some day I can—I'm sure it would be a great enjoyment to me to simply sit there, and see all of them about me." I laughingly put in— "Why not come over some time? If you will come, we will provide you the lightest carriage we can find." He, taking it more seriously—"That is a proposition to remember—I shall train [?] it in my memory."

We made arrangements at the Club for Clifford, Williams,

Morris, Harned and I to meet Brinton at his house next Monday a week to discuss the Whitman birthday. Brinton will send us 50 copies "and more on demand" of the Bruno pamphlet when out. W. "glad he so well remembers—is so disposed." And Brinton said further—the reason it is not already out, he is waiting for a reproduction of the Bruno statue at Rome.

W. said Thayer—"W. W. Thayer—from Cambridge—was here today. We had a good talk. He is a man Brinton should meet, and who should meet Brinton. He has a great notion of the value of Italy to modern life—says it is vastly underrated. He seems to be commissioned by somebody or other to write a book about Italy. He says of the Papacy, for instance—that strange as it may sound to say it, there is no country in the European-American world in which so little is made of the Papacy as in Italy. I have often wondered myself how strangely religious forms, conventions, stupidities, orthodoxies, persist in America—in this land." He alluded to Garibaldi: "I have seen him and I liked him; he always interested me, though I cannot say I ever was enthused. Thayer talked of Italian things in a way that interested me."

Thursday, March 13, 1890

7.25 P.M. W. in the parlor. Raining heavily. Chadwick said in a recent sermon: "And it would be far less absurd to hold Chaucer responsible for Walt Whitman or vice versa than to hold the earliest writers of the Bible responsible for the latest or the other way, or the whole responsible for any special part." W. was interested in this—thought it "rather more to be respected as an opinion" than Savage's classification of him with Tupper as an example of the artificial in literature. "If that was delivered to a Boston audience, it must have brought a ripple to many a lip."

Pepper had said at the Club the other evening that the only mistake the founder of Johns Hopkins had made was in not putting the college at the national capital. I told W. the thought struck me at the time that as the capital would no doubt before long be moved West, such an objection was *nil*. Said W.: "You are right: I can see nothing else but the removal. That it will come I no more doubt than that it is in Washington now. There will be a hot fight over it—someone will make the proposition—others will oppose: there will be much pressure each way—a surging of opinion, popular and official: finally the West will have its victory. That is one of our topographical questions which I consider settled."

As to a stupid postal law: "I can see no suspicion of a reason for it; the fact probably being, that some fellow had a kink: some others were bound to abet him for the sake of being abetted in their own kink—and the law was made. That is the history of laws. I suppose if there was such an industry as that in glass eyes, and someone proposed to import a great assortment (or little) of glass eyes, a great howl would go up for a law to protect domestic makers of glass eyes: indeed, I don't know but there is one already. There is no limit to law when the argument is once granted."

Says this weather leaves him only so-so.

Friday, March 14, 1890

7.30 P.M. W. in the parlor. Raining hard. Had his shawl drawn closely about him. Room dark. Gleams from the electric light out at the corner would play on his beard occasionally. Brinton sent me proof but was dubious of matter that had not already gone to the printer. Gave to W.

We read an essay of Edward Carpenter's at the meeting last evening. W. asked about it—then, to my remark that C. had no striking literary gifts, was acquiescent—adding—"The best thing about Edward Carpenter is always his noble demeanor. You will find his spirit always right—that he's in earnest—that he is not playing his life away."

He suddenly asked: "When did you say was the next meet-

327

ing of the Contemporary Club?" And learning, the second Tuesday in April—"Well—I had been thinking it was. That makes the day the Lincoln anniversary. The thought occurs to me that if you would all like it, I would come over that night and read my Lincoln address—read on that 'My Captain.' That is, if you folks were perfectly in accord about it. This will be in the line of the silvern 25 years—this a silvern-funeral if not a silvern-wedding. You can put that in your pipe—proceed on it as you choose." He expressed his hope that we would feel open to it, "not that I would impose—the point coming rather out of a sentiment that I ought never let that day pass without a word hailing it—*this* word, if may be."

I promised that I would get in communication with the President at once on the question.

Saturday, March 15, 1890

7.50 P.M. W. again in the parlor. Says he likes the change of getting downstairs. Speaks of not feeling well—attributes the disturbance of the last 3 or 4 days to the weather. Was in good voice, however. My father was down to sketch the chair today for Mrs. Fels' picture. W. "glad" he had come.

Said he had examined Brinton's proof. "There was nothing to change but, perhaps, a comma—and for that I wouldn't send him word now, at this late hour." W. then laughing at "printerial dogmatism"—he having had much of it to contend with in his time. "They do not proceed by general rule—rather, a professional caprice—and they make the most sudden reversals—some of them too funny to credit."

He had "sent a bundle of papers to Nellie O'Connor today." Some reference to the "gloom" of her last letter and "letters in general." W. thinking: "How different William was!—the prince of company! Jovial after the very highest sense! A man of superb emotionality—of great mind—or stupendous character-significances. There was no company like William—I never met another, man or woman. When we were all in Washington together, it was always 'Walt' and 'John' and 'William'—the choice of the easiest, freest, comradiest way!" He was amused that some objected to his friends' calling him Walt—thought that in me, for instance "nothing but 'Walt' could be excused" despite our different ages—for "our relations are such as to enjoin the nearest appellation."

As we talked, a noisy drum and fife corps came along the street, trailing a mob of boys and girls after it—playing vociferously—and stopping directly across the way, seemingly to serenade somebody. I looked to see if the noise disturbed W. but he only laughed with great heartiness and said—"I wonder if they are traveling about with the notion that that is music?— tub-pounding as I call it." He thought "very much of the virtue of charitable organizations" was lost "by the blind partizanship that reigns in all—in their management. It nullifies a thousand things. And I do not know but this poison runs all through our public life."

Promised me a motto for The Conservator "if so be one hits me."

Sunday, March 16, 1890

9.55 A.M. W. in his bedroom reading the Press. Consulted his watch and remarked how late he had got up. Just finishing breakfast.

Left with him a copy of the Peacemaker containing Clifford's address. "It is wonderful," he said, "the amount of special publications there are springing up—fads, so to call them. Yet I endorse this matter of arbitration—everything that can be said for it. I have no doubt the time will come when this will be looked upon as a barbarous age, incredibly stupid— hopelessly throat-cutting. Yet there is an instinct in man—in our America—leading inevitably forth from this—yes, inevi-

329

tably. And these men are that far ahead—have taken the step."

I picked up a piece of old and stained manuscript from the floor—one sheet only—and called W.'s attention to it. He said: "I have no idea in what connection it was written—it was long ago—long, long ago. Yet that writing is the critter's, without a shadow of a doubt." He added—"Take it along—see what you can make of it—it is a waif."

Then away—only there briefly. Day cold—blowy—he thought he would not get out, as proved to be the case. A review of "Gems from W. W." in the Critic W. has not seen yet.

Monday, March 17, 1890

5.30 P.M. W. just finished dinner. Reading Poet-Lore, which had just arrived through the mail. He remarked— "Pretty thin, ain't it? I have been looking it over." Then gave it to me. "If you have any curiosity at all, take it along." As his own Critic had not yet come, I left mine with him.

I had a letter from President Macalister expressing delight at W.'s suggestion of the Lincoln evening. Committee meeting tomorrow afternoon. I inquired of W. if he had any particular notions to give me—and he said—"No—but to tell them I will (being alive) come. I will have to be given a light, easy carriage: the rest I will attend to or it will take care of itself!"

Gave him a bill for $4.15 from Ferguson. Though it was old, remembered and would pay.

Tuesday, March 18, 1890

7.30 P.M. Just over from a meeting of the Executive Committee of the Contemporary Club. Members "delighted" at

W.'s proposal. Matters concluded—meeting for 15th April. Effort to be made to have Dr. Furness and General Sherman come, to add to W.'s utterance. W. seemed gratified. "It is a sentiment with me, to keep this day sacred for Lincoln." And then—"No—it will not hurt me: I am nothing to brag of—but it is a great deal to get out of the monotony of this chair-life. We did not know—were doubtful—of the dinner last year, but all passed off well—*better* than well. You know, even if a fellow is badly battered he's not bound to parade his batterment—nor will I." And as to the essay itself—whether he would wish to touch it—"Very probably: there is always something. It is a short hour's delivery: the essay, piece, elastic—can be made more or less."

Wednesday, March 19, 1890

7.25 P.M. Though it had snowed all day (the snow going to slush) and was now chill, though not cold, W. sat at an open parlor window. When I entered he got up on his feet and struggled to pull his shawl up over the neck nearest the window. Laughed: "As the writer says, 'I wrap my mantle about me,' and sit down to pleasant thought!" I was in but for a glimpse. He reported "nothing momentously new with me."—"Letters coming every day, of course" but these "mostly for autographs." Dr. Bucke, however, "writing assiduously" still.

"The most important event in the world today perhaps—is Bismarck's resignation—now really given, taken—as before only rumored given, taken. I suppose his work is in fact, done. After all he had his part to play: he stood for unification, condensation, compactness, nationality—not provincialism. Roughly, no doubt, to a great extent—but powerfully, irresistibly. Finally, at the worst, a factor in our democracy—an abettor—a man believing in union, in his own way." I was sorry to have to rush off—for W. was in humor to go on in this line and I wished to hear. He was very affectionate—on my leaving took my hand—"Good-bye—bless you, boy!"

Thursday, March 20, 1890

6.50 P.M. W. in his room, reading the evening paper. On a chair near him a pile of papers—Camden's Morning News—containing a ¾ column article "Whitman's Old Age." W. had secured a number of them—made up 15 or 20 for relations and friends. Called it "pretty reliable: for a newspaper report, remarkably so!" Adding: "It was a young man named Kake who came—or Cake—the son, he told me, of a minister somewhere hereabouts; and this was his first 'take'—he had made no reports before of any kind. I encouraged him all I could." And afterwards: "But as you say, Jeff (meaning Charley Jefferis) was no doubt there at his elbow when he wrote it up, making good suggestions—putting it together, joining it." Kake was with W. last evening. W. put on an incredulous look at the point [which] mentioned that he had read "The Wound-Dresser" aloud to his visitor—but however I tried, I could not get a yes or no from him whether the statement was true. His whole look, and every probability, said "no".

W. gave me a 5-pound note—the one spoken of some time ago, to get changed for him in Philadelphia—I should pay Ferguson out of it. Thought there should be "an international money—there *would* be, when the right solidarity of man" was "accomplished."

He expressed curiosity to see the changes in Philadelphia architecture. Had sat in his chair here on the river bank and noted across there great buildings new to his eye—"undoubtedly not up in the days I traversed the streets." And he asked: "How would it do the afternoon of the Club meeting—to have the carriage come early and give me the glimpse." But then he remembered—"perhaps the fatigue would be too great—

I should have much care. But we'll see, anyway—we'll pin the idea up for consideration." Thought I might give a copy of the News to Morris—"though there's nothing in it—hardly a word, if that—news to my intimate friends or to those who, like Morris, know my intimate friends."

Referred again to Bismarck. "Only time—50 years—a hundred—can tell the wisdom of this move—perhaps explicate the peculiar place of the man. The man among our public men whom he most resembles is Stanton. No doubt Bismarck fitted well to the years of his service—was the needed man." And of von Moltke and Bismarck—"their wonderful reserve."— "Oh! the wonder of silence in those men!" And he added: "The great man is not only the man who conceives an idea but the man who can incorporate that idea into practical working human life—of a nation, class, what-not. Bismarck was such a man. Others may have dreamed the unity of Germany—he fulfilled it. We might say as well of Luther—his great fight against all the devils of earth. No doubt thousands before him had inwardly lived his protest against the Popes: but with him it was death to be silent: he seized the idea— saw that it was concretely realized. He, too, with the greatest, in his own way. It is curious to know how Frederick's diary threatened Bismarck's laurels. I do not know but Frederick did first officially conceive [?] the idea. I place less importance to that than others are apt to do."

Friday, March 21, 1890

6 P.M. W. sitting in his big chair, close up to the fire, seeming to enjoy himself against the wet weather out-of-doors. Has now been kept at home days. I gave him the change for his 5-pound note. Had paid Ferguson's bill out of it.

I had a letter from Williamson in which he said as to Sargent [letter missing]. W. remarked: "All right—let him come:

I have no doubt I shall sit for him if he gets here—persists in his determination. It can be managed."

We talked of Emerson's personality. Salter read an essay in Philadelphia last evening and took occasion to speak of Emerson's "flinty" personality: that it is the books, not the man, that are supremely great etc., and that E. was lacking in mobility, imagination etc. I took exception—saying to Salter that Whitman's picture to me of Emerson had been of another character. W. assented: "I am glad that you did object. That was a great mistake—a great: there is no worse error to surrender to about Emerson. As a man, a companion, an intimate, he was impeccable—a character of essences, elements—no man ever lived more so: a certain stateliness, dignity, reserve—of course he had it—but none too much—not more than was required. Who more, who ever so much as, Emerson, demanded, was entitled to, a reserve? *Every* man needs it. I have found even in myself the call for care, circumspection. I cannot go to Philadelphia—or could not when I got about—without guarding myself against questions, comers, strangers, reporters, writers, intrusions varied in kind. Emerson, much more subject to interruptions, bore himself grandly before them all. Emerson fulfills his work—more than fulfills it—Emerson the man glorifies Emerson the writer. I know no one of whom this can be more fitly said—no one: in fact, none *so* fitly. Wherever you are you can say this for me—I authorize you to say it, wheresoever. I am glad you were on hand last night to say your word of dissent, and *my* word in the bargain." I said I wished he had been there to speak for himself. "I wish I had been only ten minutes. But from what you say you delivered the right message." As to Emerson's being "unapproachable," I insisted—"It is according to how he was approached, whether he was approachable or not." And W. asserted that "just there is the gist of the case." Adding more fully: "Emerson was of course himself—he was not all types but one type—including all, but combin-

334

ing himself into one. He was not hail-fellow in the sense of the good general, the old sailor—the sailor put in earliest years before the mast—roughing it in that line a life through—but he was a man, every inch of him—as I may say it again, using my old story,—he was a font of type—a genuine letter—only set into a new text. The wonder is, considering all, that he maintained his phenomenal sweetness. I should wish everywhere to bear my testimony to him. The noteworthy fact is, that all our modern men—the late men—have been eminent fellows as men—in the great humanities—in personal radiance of habit, demeanor,—in pulse of comradeship: Walter Scott certainly was—and Tennyson: oh! I am sure of *him*. And here in America among our own men—take Bryant, for example—cold, exteriorly, in a way—marbeline—to coin a word—yet superbly true on all sides. And Whittier, too—a circumscribed nature in some ways—with an unquestioned streak of fanaticism, yet pure, human, secure—his very fanaticism no doubt his necessity."

Saturday, March 22, 1890

8.10 P.M. W. in his room reading Frances Willard's "Glimpses of Fifty Years"—of which he said: "I don't know who sent it to me—perhaps she did. It is a curious book—the book of the smartish American woman—prohibitionist and other ist—bright, quick, cute, "but not a volume to go much distance into."

He referred to the Bermuda lilies on the table—"They have, it would seem, no fragrance at all—but they are a wonderful inspirer of a fellow's indoorness." They had been brought by Miss Ingram, "the daughter of our old friend—a doctress—or doctor: I believe Horace Greeley would not have the other."

Who had written the Critic notice of the Whitman "Gems"? "It is by some expert hand—I should say, at Jennie Gilder's

335

choice: I hardly think Joe would have invited it—perhaps Jennie's own—but hardly: I thought, *Kennedy*"—but to my dissent, "it carries no such ear-marks" he objected—"That is the very point: I think they do: they are the sentiments of a man who has read books—knows books—goes to the heart of books." And yet—"We can scarcely know—I only put that out as an idea: it may miss the mark badly." But however, "It was generous, good: it was a large and open word."

Hoped to get out within a few days and to see my father's picture, now in Newmayer's window, framed. "I have lately come across a son of Newmayer—a young son—met him several times—once on a jaunt in my chair—once at Odenheimer's: and there is a girl, too." And so on, in that strain of kindly geniality.

Sunday, March 23, 1890

Did not see W. this day. Out at Germantown. He did not get out: weather fair but very windy.

Monday, March 24, 1890

5.45 P.M. W. reading the local papers. In his bedroom. Said at once after greeting me: "We have had a wonderful jaunt today—several hours of it. We have been at Newmayer's—looked at the picture there: and to your father's, there to see the second version. How nobly fitted your father seems for that work! These two are all in all probably the best Whitman pictures extant—oh! the best! Warren liked the second one even better than the first. I don't know if time and my own thought will justify that opinion—though it is not improbable. And the frame there at Newmayer's! It is a surprising inspiration—they tell me it was yours? I know none more fit—wonder only that they are not more common." His "jaunt" had "all been a great treat—the look-in on your father and his work—the turn to Newmayer's—the glimpse of the peopled streets again."

I had a letter from Bush today. He is now back in New York. Among other things (wishing to send some) he asked the question—"Does Walt Whitman drink champagne?"—a smile playing upon W., who asked, "Does a duck swim?" and laughed heartily. "Yes—let him send a sip or two—it has a wonderful lift for a man!" Adding—"This Bush is evidently a genuine man: he serves us right and left, with the greatest generosity and willingness." His wife still in Stuttgart: he may come on to Philadelphia soon.

W. spoke of a visit from Harned yesterday. "He came with Mrs. Harned." They had convened about the dinner, which we are to talk over informally tonight at Brinton's house. W. said: "I think I made it plain to Tom that so far as I am concerned there must be two factors not excluded—women, wine. The Camden dinner was such an unqualified success in all ways—*sui generis*—that one would not dare raise a word of criticism. But this is a new affair—there is time to steer it right—let us do it: or do *you* do it! I know there are two sides to the wine question, but this time we'll try this one!" But he warned me: "Let us have nothing high-falutin'—let everything be done in temperance: a good hand-shake there together." Yet he was in our hands—"and what you do I am sure I shall assent to."

My invitation to attend some sort of Whitman meeting, uptown [Philadelphia] Wednesday—residence of Adams, 20th and Green—W. looked at seriously and urged me to go. I expressed some fear, lest they would call on me to say something. Whereupon W. laughingly: "Well—you can easily evade that. Tell them you will wait till you have heard all the others—then if anything needs to be added, and you have it in you to share, add it for them." I mentioned the literary dinner at which Emerson was called on for a speech—reluctantly rising—looking around upon the company, serenely

337

smiling, sitting down again, no word at all said. W. remarked: "That is exceedingly fine—that is one of those natural impulses—the happy inspiration of a moment—by which men are marked for great things. I can think of Emerson so situated—the lift of the body—the poise—the smile: then the finale: all his own. Stupid! oh no! but a difficulty sublimely escaped! I know how a man often exceeds himself in such an act—surprises himself. One of the last times I was in New York some of the boys toted me around to see things—meetings, what-not. Perhaps I have told you of this. They took me one day into a meeting of infidels—horrible heretics, all—but tip-top fellows—and right up front. They were discussing blue glass: it was the time of the *up*ness of that theory, and lots was being said. By and bye I was called on to say something—and at first I refused—but next [to] me was the good fellow who took me and he wanted me to get up—whispered, 'Get on your feet—show yourself, if no more' or something of that sort—so up I got—my full length: and put in a word or two—about to this effect: 'As long as you seem to insist upon it, here I am. I get up, the better to see you, and to be seen, face to face. As to the theory of blue-glass, I know nothing about it and shall not therefore add anything to the general fund of misinformation by attempting any share in the debate with you today.' It seemed to take them by storm: they set up a great applause. I was surprised at myself, that I so well acquitted the hour. Now, these impulsive incidents—off-throwings of the moment, would not suit men like Edward Everett—or our own Lowell—to whom elegance and care and propriety is the first consideration: the big-wigs: but to some of us, it is a solution of the whole difficulty of natural vocal expression."

Tuesday, March 25, 1890

7.25 P.M. W. belowstairs, in the parlor. Said he had received the Review of Reviews today—Stead's—"and something was said there about an article written by Sarrazin, of Walt Whitman, in the Universal Review of February 15th. I don't know if it is the old article or some new one. If you can't find it in the Mercantile [Library], let us at any rate keep note of it, track it up—perhaps send abroad for it."

At the meeting at Dr. Brinton's last evening, there were present besides Brinton himself, Harned, Morris, Frank Williams, H. L. T. Considerable discussion: finally settled upon a dinner for 40 to 50, to include women, the nucleus of the list to be asked for from W. himself. Dinner to be in Philadelphia. I was appointed committee (with Harned) to solicit such a list. I now explained to W., who consented—would do it tomorrow. He supposed a list I would make up, "and the others," would "about include all the names"—yet he would "put them down explicitly." Expressed satisfaction that we had "avoided high-falutin' plans" &c.

My sister sent him an angel cake today "over which much joy was mine." Half expressed a hope of going to the church concert tonight (Unitarian)—"but no—I see it will not do."

Wednesday, March 26, 1890

7.40 P.M. W. again in the parlor. Very cordial. Room dark. Spoke of the concert last night. Thought "it must have proved a success."

Again said: "The Lincoln night is a sentiment with me: I must not speak that speech but on Lincoln's own day. It has a sacred import—a sacred origin: it is a fire on the altar."

No list yet. Had forgotten it. "It is amazing—or at least tantalizing—how many important matters slip my mind. My memory for new things is becoming less and less dependable—markedly so." No letters today "only a few papers: the papers always come."

On my way to the Whitman meeting in Philadelphia W. advised me, upon my questioning: "Should you feel moved to say anything, tell them, you came here this evening, found

me here on the lower floor, in my chair, a blanket drawn
about me, cool, not braggish, cheery, happy—having had a
good outing, propelling, today in my chair. That soon, between nine o'clock and ten—nearer nine—I shall have my
daily rubbing—a first-rate, vigorous, massage—by my young
friend here"—he will never say *nurse*—"who knows well how
to handle me—knows to do it wonderfully well!" And he said
further: "Tell them I am well cared for here—with good
friends—and Warrie to serve me—to lift me, even, if I will:
for he is tremendously strong—can take me up in his arms,
so"—straightening his arms out—"which is a feat with one
having a corpus 200 pounds in weight." (Does not seem to
think he has lost weight, as he undoubtedly has.) This was his
"personal" message, as he called it. Then he added of his life
work in general: "I have no axe to grind—no philosophy to
offer—no theory to expound, in Leaves of Grass: all I have
written there is written with reference to America—to the
larger America—to an America so inclusive, so sufficent, no
phase of life, no nationality—can escape it. As you know,
Leaves of Grass is made up of six or seven stages of life, three
of which—the first three—have had that inestimable benefit
which comes of being fought against, bespattered, de-
nounced. I have not worked according to any elaborate plan:
have tried rather to fill in the gaps—wherever a gap was
left—wherever a gap appeared—I started out to put something in it. In what is called poetry—singing—the fellows
who go on singing the same old songs, again and again and
again—but of the most ancient, worn, poetic stock—get mad
as the devil at any suggestion of changed modes."

"Leaves of Grass," he added, "has had this advantage: it has
had a stormy early life. Nothing could make up for the loss of
this—it was a priceless privilege. Ease, comfort, acceptation,
would have ruined us. Even now the storm is not all down—
perhaps better *not* down. However, we will not let the new
kindness spoil us: there's yet to see! there's yet to see!"

Said again: "I should like to be within convenient distance—in the next room—back of some arras—so to hear the boys as they go on tonight—hear what they think to say; though I don't know that it would benefit anybody much. How little the universe worries, whoever questions it! And as men, we ought to be as unmovable."

Thursday, March 27, 1890

7.30 P.M. W. in his parlor. Had not yet made out the list. Lamented his memory again. Clasped his hands together in most unusual fashion when I asked him about it. "What a fellow I am! After the most faithful promise, doing nothing! I must! I must!" And so promised another time.

Asked me about last night's meeting, which sat till after 12—about a dozen men (most of them young) present. A rather unique experience. W.'s questions very scrutinizing. Particularly interested to know the comment of one on his use of foreign words "and inaccurate use"—W. laughing heartily, exclaiming—"That pulls a fellow's pride down many a notch! It is a good foil to our conceit!" And "most unique of all, the explanation!" laughing heartily again—the explanation being that W. affected blundering Americanisms in order the better to hold to his character. W. wished me to tell him more but I was in a great hurry and had to leave. But he would not let me go till I had promised to "go more fully into it another time—perhaps tomorrow?"—Cordial—and said he was "happy" in his "own way"—though "the weather is too varied to do much to exhilarate."

Friday, March 28, 1890

5.45 P.M. W. in his bedroom, having just finished the local papers. Said he had "started out today—but was forced

341

quickly home again." A terrific gale and storm at 3.20 in the afternoon. Just preceding it W. had been out in his chair. Warren, pushing him, was dubious, but W. said, "Let's push on to the river." But by and bye, meeting a couple of men whom he knows, one of whom said to him—"Old man—you'd better be going home"—he consented to a return. Thought this trip had given him some cold.

"Not a letter for two days," he reported. "There seems a lull, even with the autograph people." No list yet. Exclaims aloud over his memory. Commented on Bismarck's weeping over demonstrations of the populace in Berlin. "Bismarck has his position [?]: history will pay a big account to him." Punch's cartoon—representing the Emperor as dropping his pilot overboard, W. thought "exceedingly happy—keen; and it is not wonderful [that] it has created a stir in Europe."

W. entered upon further questions about the Whitman meeting the other night. The affair seemingly had a unique interest for him. There was the subject of "Calamus," which had been much discussed—Sulzberger questioning the comradeship there announced as verging upon the licentiousness of the Greek. W. took it seriously, saying thereto: "He meant the handsome Greek youth—one for the other?—Yes I see! and indeed I can see how it might be opened to such an interpretation. But I can say further, that in the ten thousand who for many years now have stood ready to make any possible charge against me—to seize any pretext or suspicion—none have raised this objection; perhaps all the more reason for having it urged now. 'Calamus' is a Latin word—much used in Old English writing, however. I like it much—it is to me, for my intentions, indispensible—the sun revolves about it, it is a timber of the ship—not there alone in that one series of poems, but in all, belonging to all. It is one of the United States—it is the quality which makes the states whole—it is the thin thread—but, oh! the significant thread!—by which the nation is held together, a chain of comrades; it could no more be dispensed with than the ship entire. I know no country anyhow in which comradeship is so far developed as here—here, among the mechanic classes. It is for the possession of this that I own such a warm affection for the Russians—*comeraderie* [*sic*.] has gone a great way with them— yes, and with the German—anywhere under the History [?] influence—though I don't know why I should say this, for in Oriental countries there is an ample expression of the same spirit. The American is not demonstrative, as a rule, but I have seen the boys down in the war, in the hospitals, embrace each other, cry, weep."—But he still admitted: "It is fortunate we may have these strictures—not veneer, did you say?—no cynicism? That was most extraordinary. I am all the more convinced I should have been near—to overhear in a way. These young men (or old) are certainly on the right road. A great man—somebody, has said: in trying to judge individuals, we are continually balked, but in judging men in masses, things adjust themselves, which is the substance of his judgement. Leaves of Grass is an iconoclasm, it starts out to shatter the idols of porcelain worshipped by the average poets of our age—not ruthlessly—not wantonly—but to do it seriously, as having a great purpose imposed. I love to go along through the land, taking in all natural objects, events,—noting them. For instance, watching the cow crunching the grass—I can hear its melodious crunch—crunch—its bovine music: the lips, soul, of song as much there as anywhere. And the mother at home knitting her children's stockings: not forgetting the yarn—not omitting the needle. The poet would not have that—it would lack in sound, elegance, what he calls poetic evidence. But for me it is my necessity—it is all music—the *clef* of things—to discriminate—not so much to produce an effect, or that at all—but to state the case—the case of the universe: to seize upon its typical phasings."

This was all said with a great vehemence as if it came of deep and long rumination.

Saturday, March 29, 1890

7.58 P.M. Found W. sitting in the parlor with Harned—talking about the dinner, concerning which H. was questioning him closely. W. had not yet made up a list—indeed was "feeling bad"—explaining: "If I had the Club Lincoln reception to be asked about over again, I should say *no*; for I certainly have the grippe, and am in no humor for speech-making." I asked him how it affected him. "Chiefly in the chest—with a chokiness—down here"—placing his hand at the opening of his shirt—"but worst of all, in the head and at night: it disturbs my rest." His voice somewhat husky, and he coughed some. Yet talked cheerily and freely. "I shall try to weather it out: probably two or three days will show me how I stand, if standing at all—as I guess I will."

I asked if he had received the Critic, and he answered affirmatively. In it was this: "In her lecture on 'The Literature and Religion of Ancient Egypt' at Chickering Hall last Friday evening, Miss Edwards said that the poetry of the Egyptians, although singularly regardless of rhyme and metre, like Walt Whitman's verse today, is true poetry of a high order." W. liked this—it was "warm feeling from an unexpected quarter": and when Harned recounted one of Miss Edwards' heroisms—"After all the women lead—seem, the fine samples of 'em—to justify themselves." And by way of general comment: "I should not wonder but in 10 or 20 years we would shift our ground—that we would date no more from the Greek culture, but the Egyptian."—Harned dissenting—preferring the Greek, but W. continuing: "But no matter, Tom: it's not what we like but what is—it brings in our Colonel Ingersoll's question again—*is it true?*—how about its truth?" And further—"I have for some years noticed that trend in scholars—at least in some of them."

The reference to Ingersoll brought on questions of pulpit orators: W. remarking: "Have either of you read Talmage's

344

sermon on *Angels?* It is a most remarkable performance: it is the funniest thing I have read this many a day: why, yes—not only hears the flap of their wings—as much as knows what they have for dinner too! You ought to see it: I shall probably somewhere come across two copies of it, which I want you both to read: it will show you your own straying: for here is one on the most intimate terms with the unknown!" And W. laughed with the greatest heartiness. "I suppose Talmage has some sort of power—yes, what they call oratorical power—a transcendent audacity—a determination at all hazards to ram his doctrines down your throat. Has had immense congregations." Yet Talmage was "by no means the right man"— "Brooklyn—New York—now offers the biggest field to the equal personality—*the Beecher and more*—the man who can grasp the situation—who has the tongue of fire, the burning heart—who *flows* out, not *reads* out: who fills any platform without notes—who has a message for struggling humanity." Beecher had been "a great man"—yet "not *entirely* free, still somewhere, or several wheres, manacled. But the new man must be free, must have an untrammeled spirit." Very specific as to Beecher's power in the pulpit. "He spoke with few notes—and that, by the way, is a matter of habit; start with notes and it's all up with you—but start young impromptuing, as it is called—though it is *not* that, as you have just shown in the case of Professor Adler—and all is right." And then he added—"I notice Salter is cutting a great swathe in Boston— seems to be getting a great hold there." Salter only in Boston on a visit: spoke at Harvard. I had a note and some MS. from him today.

W. said Gilchrist had been over this week "one night. Herbert comes late—generally when I am about to go to bed— though I am glad to see him, of course—he is always welcome." Immense storms (floods &c, chiefly west) in the country. Vessels missing—the great "City of Paris" had a long passage but today was reported arrived in England. W. said he had felt intense interest—"and it is good news to know it is safe."

He thought the truly great preacher ought to have "enough money but not too much"—and explained—"I mean, ought to be limited—say, to two or three thousand a year."

Sunday Morning, March 30, 1890

9.50. Saw W. in his own room. Reading The Press. Just up—late—later breakfast. Complained that his cold (much affecting the eyes) was severe and had disturbed his sleep. But after his wash had felt refreshed. Gave me a letter of Bucke's in which B. inquired if W. was to speak anywhere April 15th, B. proposing to come on. W. then inquired after my own reading—also concerning the New England Magazine piece—was it not about time I had sent this? "Only nothing is improved any by undue haste."

I have an idea his cold comes from his sitting on several damp nights last week at the open parlor window.

Monday, March 31, 1890

7.15 P.M. W. in the parlor, his blanket about him. Coughed considerably—reporting his cold "not a bit better"—denominating it "undoubtedly a case of grippe." Said it left him little comfort. "If I keep this way I fear for my promise to the club: still, I guess I won't: I guess there'll be a turn from this."

Asked me what I knew of Wells, the new editor of The Press in Smith's absence. "The Press threatens to be the type of the misfit in journalism: I know no paper which more surely exemplified mal-apropos-ism." There was "a vein in it so narrow" he could not forego his hate of it.

Spoke of Mississippi floods—of his own experiences in New Orleans—"the wonder and delight of the levee there: a place of places, picked out of the offerings of the world." Not what the Seine "might be imagined to be"—Paris at the Seine "probably resembling, or being resembled by, our Cincinnati, more than by any other point." But the levee at New Orleans—its own type—curious among river fronts—certainly in America." The whole Mississippi valley subject to floods—"the country low—yet with a lordly look, too."

No list yet. But had "felt too unwell for thought or application" in any direction.

Tuesday, April 1, 1890

7.30 P.M. W. in the parlor, securely wrapped in a blanket. Better? "Not much!" But wasn't *some*thing much? "I suppose it is: do you notice it in my voice? I suppose the weather will eliminate it, with much more." I said, "Yes—time and the weather." To which W.—"That is undoubtedly a great cosmic combination—the most powerful we know, against which [there is] no appeal."

He remarked: "The Century came today," evidently desiring to turn from continued talk of his condition—a habit of his—"and it has quite a fat pouch of things good coin in the literary market—things that seem demanded. Among them, with the most excellent engravings—exceedingly fine, true—specimens of that single abomination which always makes me gag—Madonna and Child—exquisitely engraved. You and your father would enjoy the technique of it—but of all the outdated creations: it is that, surely."

And again: "Several of the pictures in Jefferson's piece are of a high order. But the more I have seen of Jefferson himself and now see of these pictures, the more convinced I am that he is not the man to personate Rip van Winkle: Hackett was the man who could do it." And he swelt upon the joy of those early days in his own life "when stage-people were my daily bread" &c. "I think I must some day before long pick myself together and write out remembrances of the old Park Thea-

tre. Rayner was one of the men there—an English gentleman. Sir William Don, later on, was a character, too. I was
only a boy, but all that there was in me of the aesthetic, the
musical, was stirred by their impulse. I did not know them
personally. Hackett was too great a man in his way to be so
obscured as he is now. Nobody seems to know of him: he was
perhaps *too* first-rate for preservation." I urged him to the
writing. "You think I could do it offhand—impromptu? I don't
know if I have the faculty for making the statement called for.
There is some hint of it all in Specimen Days—the early
part—but only a casual hint. I want to do it—yet I am afraid
to undertake it. I am not up to exertion nowadays: what I do
I must do at my ease—not with bonds upon me."

I told him I had a note from Brinton asking how many of
the Bruno books we wished and that I had replied, 50 or 75—
for both our uses. W. then again spoke of the hope that Brinton would some day meet Thayer "on that, if not some other,
common ground. Thayer has a special Italo-American knowledge—perhaps such knowledge as Brinton would enjoy rubbing against: I don't know—persons are hard to predict! Brinton would have to be on his guard, lest he be driven off by
the first evidence in Thayer of extreme scholarship, culture,
worldliness. Thayer is largely dominated by such an element,
although beneath that sympathetic, emotional, to a degree,
too. This quality, however, intervenes—is to be counted on.
No—not as necessarily the part of the scholar. Take Sloane
Kennedy—although this was inextricably mixed in his composition—as I should want it mixed,—scholarship in him and
all that it implies—yet his spirit is not so mixed: his spirit is
free, freeing." And there was O'Connor, too—"he was the
universal democrat—a man of our own make-up. Kennedy
comes by right to his scholarship: yet his spirit—the personality—is with him the first fact; the prevailing impulse. Even
in his espousal of the Baconian theory, O'Connor maintained
his individuality untouched—unhindered. The glory of the

348

Bacon–Shakespeare plays—and O'Connor recognized it, in-sisted upon it—not only in what he wrote but in what he always said to me—was in the fact that they started out to make the statement of feudalism—the life of it, its persons, what-not—and made it, letting all else to take care of itself. That is art at its best—at the point where it is nature. If my own work tallies with less than this, it fails of the hope I set for it."

Wednesday, April 2, 1890

7.25 P.M. Found that W. had been having rather a serious day of it. In his room, lying in bed—where he had been nearly all day. "Last night," he said, "was one of the most dreadful of nights—probably the dreadfulest I have ever spent; and this morning I had a chill—a rather severe one." No doctor—nor would he hear to my sending for one except upon worse developments. Voice very husky—chest choked—spoke with effort and coughed much. This cough had ha-rassed him the night previous. Complained also that it af-fected his head. I did not stay long. Told him of a long letter I had had from Bucke, prospecting for a trip this way within a few weeks. W. interested—questioned me. Afterwards I consulted with Warren: instructed him to call Walsh in on the first sign of a worse turn and to send for me at any hour of day or night—at any time of a serious development. Hope tomor-row will show a return to comfort with W.

Thursday, April 3, 1890

7.30 P.M. W. on his bed. Had spent an improved day. Voice still bad, however, and chest choked. But looked well. Fire in stove burning lustily, through the half open door throwing about the room fugitive gleams of light—sometimes in the direction of his face and hands. He was rather facetious about

Good Friday (tomorrow). Was it a holiday? And upon *yes*, adding—"Well—that is one thing religious traditions do for us anyhow—or theological."

I left with him a big bundle of Bruno books sent to me by Brinton. He smiled upon the bundle. "It is a liberal one, anyhow—no doubt a plenty; and we will try to do justice to it."

Spoke more hopefully of the probability of appearing before the Club on the 15th; and of getting out of doors. "I should think, looking out, taking it in visually, this has been a great, great day!" As it had—mild and sunny to wonder. A great relief to find him and it so much improved.

Friday, April 4, 1890

1.30 P.M. With W. but briefly—in his room. He reading Bruno. Spoke of his condition. "It is a persistent cold: and it leaves me very weak: I am hardly able to blow my nose." His face [?] paled. Warren says he is very weak—has almost to carry him to the bed and from it. Hard grating cough.

W. said he had looked over the Bruno book. "It much gratifies me: even to the way I appear there. It seems all wisely planned. I had no idea Dave could accomplish such good work: the book is worthy of him, of Brinton, of Bruno."

Dr. Furness has consented to speak with W. on the 15th. Furness nearly 88 years old. W. exclaimed: "Oh! what a wonderful sight! Such an age and still such activity!" And—"It is a hale continuance packed full of suggestiveness."

Saturday, April 5, 1890

5.30 P.M. W. had just finished dinner. "See the cookies," he said, pointing to the table—"take some of them: they will please you—they are Mary's."

Informed me he had "sent off a number of the Bruno books

350

today." On the table a blue-pencilled memorandum that he had done so to Tennyson, Symonds, Rossetti, Dowden, Sarrazin and some others. He offered the mem. to me. "Suppose you give it to Dr. Brinton to show him how we are bestowing the books." I suggested retaining till next week—he might have more to send: which he acquiesced in. One copy addressed to Dowden and endorsed, "Walt Whitman America," he asked me to put in the P.O. as I passed.

Coughed much and complained that the cough hurt his throat and head. His color better than for some days: a trace of paleness still visible. Amusedly, showed me a new pair of shoes—the first shoes to the ankle he had worn in several years. Straightened his leg out so I could inspect them— thought them "a bargain at 3 dollars" and laughed at the idea of *his* "hunting bargains."

Said that Jim Scovel and Charlie Jefferies had been in today. Jim "was sober and looked well." Somehow having something to say of policemen at large, W. remarked: "I am under the impression that the London police are the best of all— more human, more knowing, better calculated for their work. I know we often hear of their brutality—brutality in the face of mobs; but then, in the case of mobs, the brutality is probably on both sides."

Sunday, April 6, 1890

10 A.M. W. in bed still. Said he felt "rough." I did not go up to see him—only sent up Kennedy's letter containing the translation, which arrived yesterday.

———————

Later on, towards evening—having passed a bad day, his cough violent, hacking him much, he sent out for some good whiskey, got off the bed, and made up a stiff punch, which helped him, and cheered him into some conversation, as had not been the case in the earlier hours.

Monday, April 7, 1890

5.30 P.M. W. in his room, on the bed. Insisted on getting up. I helped him to the chair. Is stronger than for several days. We talked together for half an hour.

He returned to me Kennedy's friend's translation of Schmidt. I showed him an extract from "Point of View" in the current Scribner's which I had copied out: "If Walt Whitman, for example, were what his admirers' defective sense of style fancies him, he would be expressive." W. laughed and said—"Let him go to hell: that's all I have for him!" I exclaimed—"*That's* 'expressive,' anyway!"—to which, after some further laughter, W. explained that the writer probably did not know what he was writing about and for that reason was trapped. Much and anything might be said against W. W., but this sentence was put together "ignorantly." W.'s cough quite violent but loosened greatly.

He would have it, (upon my reminder, that he was going to send Brinton his book): "I'll give it to you now." So I got a copy of the Complete Works from the box and W. inscribed it with Brinton's name and "from the author." Upon my saying that Brinton's stock was Quaker far back, W. said: "Ah! that explains in part why he likes me, likes the book!" And upon my remarking, with the heavy book in my arms—"It is a great institution"—W. continued: "It ought to be—it takes up a tremendous period—assumed an immense task—essayed to glimpse 50 of the biggest years in history: and if it only here and there hits the life it met, it has its deserving. I often reflect, that one ought to have been glad to be born into such a voyaging—such a series of giantesque circumstances."

W. asked me if I had found the postage correct on the Dowden book the other day, and to my "yes" he laughed—"I supposed it was—but like the fellow who pops the question to his girl—he knows she will say 'yes'—yet finds it essential to hear her say it!"

Questioned him if he was inclined to abandon the Club exploit next week—but found him determined *not*. "No: I doubt if even you or Doctor Bucke know just the egotism that backs me in such an undertaking as this. It is in part the explanation of my work—of Leaves of Grass. There is a chance I cannot come, but on the whole I shall fight it out: if I can get there I shall. I feel pledged to it—not to you but to myself. It will probably be its last deliverance. I hope to be identified with the man Lincoln, with his crowded, eventful years—with America as shadowed forth into those abysms of circumstance. It is a great welling up of my emotional sense: I am commanded by it: only a severe chastisement could hold me from my contract." So I was to "tell the boys—if Walt Whitman can hold his head up he will be with them."

Talk of abolitionism—W. saying: "The abolitionists have always exaggerated the importance of that movement: it was not by any means the beginning or end of things. It was a pimple, a boil—yes, a carbuncle—that's it—out of the nation's bad blood: out of a corpus spoiled, maltreated, bruised, poisoned. The Southerners, by acts of folly—acts like that of beating down Sumner—added to the fuel. That was the subject of *one* of my differences with O'Connor: he was hot for abolition—would not hear to my objection that a man should save some heat for something else. But something besides the abolitionists brought the matter finally to success. I was close to the life [?] of the mechanic truth [?]: I could get at its first notes: I knew it well—in Brooklyn—in New York. And although at one time four-fifths of the country was for slavery, yet slavery seemed doomed. A great something, uncaught yet by writers, explainers, expositors of our history, worked out the great end." It was "a case of bad blood: it had to come out—and out it came: a great flood, leading upwards!"

353

Gave me some newspaper Whitman scraps. I suggested: "Bucke might come down and read your Lincoln."—but he quickly said: "No, not Bucke—nobody: it is a mass of notes—broken—and no one could handle them."

Tuesday, April 8, 1890

Went to W.'s at 5.30. Up to his bedroom. I entered, closed the door: he on the bed, clothed, fast asleep. He was breathing heavily: flat on his back—his hands folded across his body. I stood irresolute in the middle of the floor: he moaned and moaned—said half-audible things—"Yes" "Who can say?" "What a sight!"—things aside from these undistinguishable. I half started to go out—as I did so, a violent fit of coughing came to him: he woke: looked up: saw me there: smiled: extended his hand. "Ah boy! and what news *your*-way-wards?" Shook his head over his own condition. "It is little to brag of—hardly any change: none at all." When I spoke of the Club—"Ah! we live in hope: we must not give it up—*yet*." Saying however again—"But I confess it is a dwindling hope. This is much misery: I am half killed by the phlegm—uncomfortable—hacked: hard-breathed."—Which I found afterwards to be the substance, too, of the message postaled to Bucke today, W. giving me the postal to read and then to mail.

Very particularly inquired if I intended delivering the book to Brinton this evening—also, that I should not forget "to show him or give him the list of Bruno men." What should be announced at the Club tonight? That he could not come? "No—give my love to them all: tell them Walt Whitman is here, remaining in this grip of a grip—not despairing, but owning up to a serious doubt of possibilities. I should not say more: in fact, more cannot be said now: I am disinclined to yield entirely: there are still seven or eight days of hope!"

Eats little, though more than on previous days.

Wednesday, April 9, 1890

5.30 P.M. To W.'s again on my way home. He sitting up, looking out northward—rather weak in appearance—"still discomposed—banged and badgered"—in his own words.

Spoke of "a short letter from Dr. Bucke: probably 7 or 8 lines: and he likes the book—says he sat right down and read it." I delivered the big book to Brinton last evening. W. "pleased that the Doctor is pleased."

I told him of MacAlister's announcement of the dubiosity of W.'s appearance next Tuesday, and said for myself—"I am now doubtful of it myself."—He thereupon—"and so am I— though I still hold up some hope." Still coughs violently, but throat is clearer. Advised that Bucke come down—stay at Cape May. "I know a place there—the Aldine Cottage: several of my nieces stayed there a season: it is good—I know from them—and sufficiently democratic to suit the Doctor."

A letter from Rhys. W. thought the Times matter of Sunday "undoubtedly Jim Scovel's."

Thursday, April 10, 1890

5.30 P.M. W. in room. Very much better in appearance. But said: "I spent a bad night—the worst yet: all tickling, tickling, choking, from the mouth to the diaphragm. But there is ease today,—comparative ease." Then: "I have had visitors today— two: old Dr. Furness, Horace Howard, the son: and oh! the grand, good, old man! He is quite an antique, but a [physiognomy], too. A wonderful spectacle—an old man, at such an age men are rarely given: to me a breath from divinities!"

Again—inquiring what papers I had in my hand, he looked at Harper's Weekly and Young People—remarking: "I feel each week almost, a shove forward in this sense—a marvellous step. Even in the daily papers. Why, in the Record, yesterday, was the head—the head of a murderer—and how

355

good it was! A distinct advance certainly, in ten years. I watch it: it gives me hope: it means the democratizing of art along with other things." Then happening to turn on to the editorial page, a passage caught his eye—he reading to me—"President Harrison has written something in favor of the removal of the tariff on art,"—adding thereto: "Oh! I did not think the little man had spunk enough to do that—or sense, even. We are indebted to our friend Tom Donaldson in good part for the imposition of this tax: he mainly lobbied it, I think. Though how a fellow can be a Leaves-of-Grass-man and fall into such a ditch defeats all my explanations. Tariffs and Leaves of Grass! No-no: there is an inevitable, implacable, antagonism!"

Then back to art improvements again. "I have thought, how much can be done with stained glass—how much has been done: have thought of my own head, with an idea of having it so produced. Think of it—some method by which nominally to produce these heads—give them currency! It has color, radiance; color is such an element in me—red, white. Think of a window in some lofty dome—far up—fronting the strong light"—gesturing, lifting head and glance—"and there our giants—a head here, a head there. Take the old Doctor's—take Hedge's—how they would serve the hunger of the eye! I should suppose it might be made an inspiration—a democratic inspiration. I did not say this to the Doctor today—they did not make a great stay of it. I was not well—feeling like the devil—a bad night arguing a bad day, of course. A fellow could not stand many such nights!—they would break the last cords!"

Once again he remarked: "I have been looking further into Brinton's book: it is a simple, direct, story—bears repeated consultation. I think Brinton our man—achieving effects after a natural way or none at all!" He had sent a copy to Kennedy. "I shall send one to John Burroughs—but I had some doubt whether it would interest Stedman."

356

Talked definitely of next week. "I think your plan of waiting till Sunday the best one: I should like to have the benefit of it. It is no trifle, which I want to resign, but a pledge I want to make good. I must of course, judge well of myself, I must not go—so be-devilled—worn—to be put on the stage in a half-comatose condition"—he laughed heartily at the ludicrous picture—"flaccid—to slump. That must be guarded against. I want to come—it is part of my duty yet while living, if I can. No one can know the will, the egotism, that bears me on to this—not you, even—nor Dr. Bucke. My hope has been diminishing little by little, but not yet to a total negative."

Called my attention to a copy of The Universal Review—wondered if I could get him another copy in Philadelphia. The Sarrazin piece there evidently in full, in the French. "I think it is the same old piece—there is every evidence of it—except the reading evidence. I do not think the magazine of a very high order, though that number certainly has things to recommend it. If I had Morris right here, I would ask him for *viva voce* renderings: that would give me clues. But it is not worth going to any trouble about."

When I left, he said to me again: "Let us hold Tuesday open to events: say Saturday or Sunday—they will safely indicate: we will be guided by what they argue—bad or good."

Friday, April 11, 1890

5.40 P.M. W. again in his room. Sits up rather more than in the early part of the week. Certainly looks some degrees better. Reading the local papers. His cough nearly gone—color better. He will not give up the Club yet, though his resolution is undoubtedly shaken. Wrote Burroughs, however, thought he would have to, much as he regretted it.

He sent the Bruno book today to Burroughs, Bertz, and others. W. alludes to Brinton as "of the school of the great modern scientists and progressive metaphysicians." He so

357

writes to Burroughs, as he has said it to me. The last few days has habited himself to my reading his postals and mailing them for him. "They'll give you about the kernel of my health affairs."

W. received today a copy of Psyche, London. Advised me to give it a look. "It has a considerable cover"—and—"I think it a palpable imitation of The Universal Review in the way of shape." Called it "Esoterism"—how "little it interests me." And then of George Chainey—"He is the Jim Scovel of religion—he has been everything, but nothing long. It is surprising how many of these fellows are thrown up by the current— spirits of water blown skywards, then quickly fallen, subsiding. Chainey is a plausible man—something of O'Connor's build—but that's where the resemblance ends. He is handsome—is what he is by virtue of intellectual attrition. Chainey has been here—was cordial enough—perhaps markedly so. Like Conway, I think he started out by being a Methodist—then went from one thing to another—touched every string—at one time was in Boston, an infidel of the extreme type. London seems a great place for the accumulation of cranks—men who hardly have ideas, who have conscience, rather. Chainey is one of these, wonderful glib of speech."

I left with him a copy of The Ethical Record. He wished to read Morse's "My Grandmother's Religion." Examined the Bazaar I had with me, commending all the pictures, even the fashion plates.

Saturday, April 12, 1890

5.45 P.M. W. sitting looking out on the western sky. Day delicious—he could not get out, however. Spent a bad night last: face pale and he complained of being much possessed with "nightmarey thoughts." Even now would not entirely yield on the Club matter. "I will give my ultimate in the morning—wait till then!" Though improving, he felt "it won't amount to much till too late for the 15th." When I told him Warren thought him much better, he smiled. "Warrie detects finer shades of difference than I do."—"The point about the Club is, I know I could get there—but after getting there, what?"

Reported having read Morse's article in the Record. It is wonderfully light, cheerful, fine—helpful to an old fellow like me—very Morsean: I read every word of it." Showed me a photograph (landscape) sent him from Denver by some one there, Rushton by name. Admired Blake's Easter card— called it "very fine: very unique."

Read him a card I had received from Mrs. Fairchild. He was much touched. "Oh! the good woman! and does she say that? Read it again."

191 Commonwealth Avenue
Dear Mr. Traubel,
    Enclosed is cheque for April: I am sorry to be late again!
    I wish I could be with you for the celebration I shall be in heart. On the 14th I always read the Lincoln poem and the description of the murder aloud to my grandchildren.
    Greet our dear poet from his faithful friend, and believe me
Very truly yrs.
                                    Elisabeth Fairchild.

And then: "Multiplications of multiplications of things pile upon me these days: a much too great kindness, care, consideration, in friends. Yet not so much but I believe I respond to it all."

Morris wrote this, as found on the Editorial page of today's Bulletin. W. said with a smile, "He seems to speak by authority!"

It has been for several years past the reverential and touching custom for Walt Whitman to read his lecture on Lincoln on the 15th of April, the anniversary of the Martyr-President's death. At the desire of the Contemporary Club the venerable poet will this year give his reading before its members and guests on Tuesday next in the galleries of the Art Club. There is an especial fitness in the address from such a source on the events of the war, and especially on the greatest of modern American characters. Whitman, by association and sentiment, through personal recollections, and a loving and profound regard for Lincoln, is the chosen laureate of his memory. His elegy, "When lilacs last in the door-yard bloomed," takes its place beside the three or four great death-chants of the English tongue; while his shorter poem, "Captain, my Captain," which he will also read, is a pathetic tribute to the same noble name. Walt Whitman's lecture will be followed by addresses from the Rev. Dr. Furness, Dr. S. Weir Mitchell, and Mr. R. W. Gilder, of the Century.

Phila. Bulletin, April 12, 1890.

Sunday, April 13, 1890

Went down to W.'s about 10. The day exquisitely clear and mild. W.'s room shut—in bed yet. Learning I was there, he sent down for me. He received me cordially, apologizing for "the closeness of the room"—not markedly so—"as I must screen myself from draughts of whatever character." Said: "I have spent a fine night—slept well—spent the best night for a long while: and now I feel so refreshed, I determine to take the leap. You can so report me." (As I did, later on, to the President and Miss Lanigan.)

W. said, "Tom Donaldson was in Friday night, after you left."

Monday, April 14, 1890

5.30 P.M. W. in his room: had just finished dinner. Out today—a new suit on: had had the cloth there (the finest) but just now made up. A shawl wrapped about his shoulders. Spoke of his improvement from the outing: "It was a struggle, but went well—very well."

Had been working on his Lincoln. There before him—new lines in blue and black pencil. "I shall not read it all, I'm afraid to attempt it: I shall shorten it—a passage here and there: but not cut it deep—not to make an actual incision." Was writing a few new notes. "This will be my last public appearance, without a doubt: it is not in me to make a trial again: at least, that is as I feel now. Oh! I feel greatly blessed *now*: If Providence continues, within 40 hours more, we'll be out of the woods—out of *this* woods, anyhow." He keeps the Lincoln in pasteboard covers—some of it in ms. some printed. He said again: "Tom was here yesterday—spoke somewhat about a carriage. I want Mary to go with us—she will want a seat: and you? yes, you. And of course, Warrie—and that will make us full! I am sure about the carriage—but the man? We want a humane fellow—a trusty, careful man, having due regard for his burden." He told Mrs. Davis she ought to go along, as it was doubtless to be his "last public appearance"—just as he states it to others.

His cheer wonderful. "I have written Dr. Bucke—in fact have written him every day the past week—now, saying I have after all undertaken the leap. Oh! where will we land?"

Referring to the letter I gave him yesterday from Brinton, thanking him for and applauding the book sent, W. said: "I forwarded it to Dr. Bucke: I know he will take to it—penetrate it: oh! it has a deep deep! Brinton is one of the big men—the progressive scientists—the top of our civilization's heap. After all is said—after the full story is told, the future will read, acknowledge, in these men our best specimens—America's. In my own work—in Leaves of Grass—I have known no anxiety greater than to keep abreast of these results—not, at least to contravene them. I never knew them specifically—never could make any direct statement of them. Yet, as years go, I felicitate myself that I have voiced no silliness—have made no impeachment of them. Oh! how it is to keep in touch with them! I have no doubt that is one of the secrets of Bob's power: he keeps in touch with big men—with the great progressive, serene, scientists—their searches, results: biggest of all, their spirit. And from such a mine a good digger can't but draw treasure and treasure!" And this reminded me of word coming as to Ingersoll's ill health the winter through, W. expressing solicitude and saying: "No—I have never sent him the big book—but now would be a good time, wouldn't it? The great Bob!"

Spoke particularly of "wishing Agnes [my sister] to be present—and Mrs. Harned, too." And added—"I shall not write to Dr. Bucke tomorrow, I must save all my strength." He signed about eight cards for the Club—Clifford, Mrs. Baldwin, Anne, Mr. and Mrs. Ed. Burleigh, Kemper, etc.

As I left W. said: "Come down early tomorrow—on your way home—and see if all is right. We will brace up to the last strain!"

Tuesday, April 15, 1890

In at W.'s on my way home, at 5.15. He sat close by the fire in his room, his shawl about his shoulders (the day cooler than yesterday)—ruminating. I shook hands—asked him how he felt. He said: "Not as robust as yesterday—not so sassy—but still stupendously determined." Jastrow had come in to tell me today that Higginson was in town and would come. W. exclaimed on my repeating it—"Oh! damn Higginson!" And when I said further, "He is staying with Miss Repplier I believe,"—he added—"and damn Miss Repplier—damn 'em both: that's my compliment to *them*!" And yet with a laugh—"Let him come: it can do no one harm."

W.'s manuscript there on the table, tied up in the covers. He has been writing a few words of new introduction—one of the discarded sheets of which was on the table and he had me read. Asked me about the carriage. We will take the 8 o'clock boat, in order to get W. there late, and have him start at once:

it is his own desire. "No reception," he said, "you do quite right, boy—Horace. Keep 'em off! No gush, no heat: a sacred act—entrance: a word of reverence: let that be its spirit, its dome, enclosing all!" He asked again: "You are going with us? We want you."

Down again to W.'s at 7.40 —he in his unlighted room, asleep. Carriage at the door. I gave the driver his directions. Overhead, cloud: the air chill—but neither mist nor storm. Things so far reasonably auspicious.

Warren and I proceeded at once to W.'s room, Warren lighting a candle. W. was roused by our entrance—got up instantly. "I was fast asleep," he explained, "but am ready—just as you decide." Inquired if the carriage was there—and "is it a closed carriage?" then—laughing—"Well—if we go overboard we'll all be drowned! It's an ignominious death!" So we helped him on with his hat. He suggested taking the blue wrapper. It was rather dilapidated—Warren looked at me— urged the shawl instead and I reinforced him. So the shawl was pinned about his shoulders. Once, trying to stand up, he fell forward, only restrained by Warren's hand and my own from falling. Weak. The downstairs trip was rather unsteady. "I still feel queer in my smooth new shoes," he explained; but there was weakness, too, of which he took no regard. Had he the manuscript? "Oh yes! it is here—in my pocket"—clapping his hand there. Downstairs he stopped in the hall half a minute, to further adjust the shawl—then with us into the carriage: unevenly down the step, across the pavement—leaning heavily on Warren. He and Mrs. Davis sat in the back of the carriage, Warren and I opposite. Walt at once inquired if the windows were open—learning that they were, was satisfied.

I had received a letter from Bucke today—very dubious about W.—the "instability" of things. I wrote instantly, describing W.'s improvement. Now I told W. of Bucke's probable early visit—then that B. had promised me a piece for the Conservator on "W. W. and Modern Science." W. was much struck with "the pungency of that question"—said it brought back Brinton to him. Then wondered—"Has Brinton much [use?] for poetics?" I replying—"Modern men of science look for something in literature which they rarely find: Brinton is one of these men: he sees much in Browning, espouses Leaves of Grass." W. thereupon: "That is very significant: there must be something in Browning, when such fellows hold to him: to me it is an unread—not necessarily a flouted story." Electric lights everywhere on streets and boat *blinked* him. "They are too strong for my old sight." Yet on the boat a sign on one of Strawbridge and Clothier's wagons—a small line of letters, 10 feet at least distant—he saw with precision. We thought his sight not so bad as he imagined, but he insisted—"It is going—it is going: I know it—feel it." Talked of the beauty of the wagon, its mirror: then upon Warren's reference to the current of the Ganges, questioned him definitely of details. At the ferry he waved his hand to several of the men—"How are you, boys?"—no incident, however: I did not press talk. He thought the river "a trifle coolish, but refreshing."

We drove out Market Street to Broad and down Broad. W. talked little. Said at one moment reflectively, touching Bucke's complaint of health: "Doctor has waged a long and heroic fight: it is in his mould." Occasionally peered out at some object. "Things look familiar." Coming off the boat, laughed—"Yes—here are the gin mills, all in place!" The Broad Street coaches attracted him—especially the people on top. "It is a reminder: it stirs up memories."

As we drove up at the Art Club (8.24), Harned stood there, the first to greet us, calling out word: then Frank Williams—Morris—and quickly Talcott Williams from indoors. It was a laborious task getting him upstairs to the 2nd. floor (the elevator inoperative): W. insisted on walking: which was done, slow-paced, several supporting him, but Warren mainly. At the summit I gave him a chair, on which he fell heavily, much exhausted: "I feel dazed: my head is in a whirl: let us pause here." He left hat and shawl with us—waved his hand to several standing about the doorway: greeted Morris. Then, when recovered in port, was led by Warren to the stand: a low platform, 2 feet high. Morris and Frank Williams had placed some lilacs there on the table. A little whispered collocation with the chairman and with Tom Dudly, who greeted him, then—first regarding the lilacs, had them put aside—so as to command the table. Read preliminarily a few written paragraphs of introduction, then the lecture as known in print. W. sat with his legs crossed—his arms on the arm of the chair— the body resting to the left. His position was easy, however: he seemed to read with difficulty—or to see so. A light brought him did not better the situation. His tone strong, melodic,—at times rising to great eloquence—as when treating of the battle fields—then of Lincolnian meanings. His figure—background: all grand. It was an extraordinary gathering—from 3 to 4 hundred. A victory his, after 3 decades of scorn and slander—brought into the very citadel of literary fashion and bequeathed the hour's (and future's) triumph. He was applauded several times—once responding with a wave of the hand. At times he would throw his body back in order the more sharply to define his emphases. After he had finished the address, he read "O Captain!"—with greatest effect—power and pathos.

Nor did he hurry out at once when done: stayed for Furness' talk—occupying about 10 minutes—rather inconsequential—applauding him, pushing his own chair back on the platform. His going was much as his coming. Everybody rose spontaneously with his own rising. He greeted some by name—H. H. Furness, for one. Halted in the hallway a minute, sitting—we adjusting his coat and hat. Would he have something? First he rather thought *yes*: what had we? But again: "I guess, nothing. No, Horace—thank you. You know the old saying—silver is good, but gold is better: it would be nice to have some, but nicer *not*." This the briefest sketch of a memorable, impressive evening. His voyage to the carriage laborious: he took the flowers with him. I did not take the return trip with them. "Thank God for the open air!" he exclaimed on getting outside. How did he feel? "Oh! all right! I'll stand it!" And so good night!

Wednesday, April 16, 1890

5.10 P.M. W. in his room. I found him engaged, writing a piece which he had headed—"Walt Whitman address night"— part of it on opened envelopes, part on brown paper, and part on good cap: 4 or 5 pages (small).

I inquired at once how he had weathered the night past. "Oh! we got home *trim*: it was a good ride, both ways: such an easy carriage! And then our human man who drove us! We held our chin up very well. The thing we ought to felicitate ourselves on, is, that we didn't give out altogether—that we came out of it alive! It was a good trip: I enjoyed it: it was a full breath—a new aroma. . . . Why! you certainly got together there a tony crowd—such handsome women: I looked about—saw so many: young, older—even the old ladies! And so many in what they call evening dress—gaiety, light. My own feeling was, that in such a place, on such a platform, where the usual man comes, grammatical, accurate, literary, polished, elegant, a dash of the un-couth, of the un-elegant— a strain from other altitudes—from open-airs, I hope—the light and shade of woods, our river, the sea—comes well— comes appropriately—may fill in a need, expedite social evolution. Oh! it was there the emphasis laid itself—I took it all in curiously." He confessed that his eyes troubled him, and inquired—"But did you hear? did they all hear, do you think?"

He had not yet seen the portrait (his own) in the Illustrated American—current number: now I called his attention to it—

showed him a copy. He asked—"You will leave this with me?"
And then: "It is the Sarony picture: and look here—he has
put a harp on it! I should say, heave all that away—the harp,
the wreath, this line"—indicating a plain line about the picture. Then, consulting a little 3-inch article inside,—"They
asked it from me and I sent it—but this *facsimile* I intended
for the portrait page: well! well! it don't seem to matter what
you tell these fellows—they go about it their own way anyhow! Certainly it's pretty good: he has the idea of the hair—
makes it in wave, not curled—and the shadows not so deep
as in the original, and better not." Said something vehemently again about editors and their habits.

Spoke about his writing. Had felt well enough to go at it.
"I slept well after the storm: all seemed well-ordained. I
promise you the additional matter in manuscript—a copy of
it, someway: I think I may in a day or two have it all printed."
Said: "Dave reports to me that this paper will not thrive—
does not—cannot live. But perhaps that is only one side of
the story—the side of outside business judgment—by no
means always correct." I gave him a mucilage bottle, self-
sponging—which seemed to attract his attention amusingly.
Had asked me for it the other day.

Dwelt again and again on the significance of the meeting—
his own presence there—"in-elegant, not clothed by a mode,
rugged, old, a long fight back of me—what ahead?" Was altogether unscathed by his experience: his color strong, his
amusement (a great deal of that in his impressions) jovially
explained. I urged him to write his reflections. Told him of
Montaigne's cat, whose playing induced M. to remark: "She
amuses me: who knows but I as much amuse her?" W. exclaimed: "I don't know whether that is new to me or known
once and lost—I incline to think, never known. But however,
and simple as are its words, I am moved by it: oh! how deep
it cuts! how centers in the heart of things!" And so—whoever
the cat, the man,—we were to hear W.'s version. "I remem-

ber that a long time ago, down at Timber Creek—I would go along the stream, looking, singing, reciting, reading, ruminating—and one fellow there—a splendid sapling—I would take in my hands—pull back—so-so: let it fly, as it did with a will, into position again—its uprightness. One day I stopped in the exercise, the thought striking me: this is great amusement to me: I wonder if not as great to the sapling? It was a fruitful pause: I never forgot it: nor *answered* it. I suppose—this is a new strophe—Montaigne in other dress."

Thursday, April 17, 1890

5.30 P.M. W. just finished his dinner: reading local papers: several of them on his lap. Returned me The Illustrated American: "I have sent for some copies. It is a very good picture—one of the best in its way—that is my verdict. It is very interesting, that just as I am about to step out, I am like to be applauded: just as the curtain is about to be rung down I am saluted. But that is fate, providence, whatever—not to be explicated."

Laughingly told me McKay had been over a few days ago—"paid me royalties between 50 and 60 dollars: think of it!—for Leaves of Grass and Specimen Days both! It is a long story of woe—a catalogue of impecuniosities—this record of my printed labor!" But there were other ways in which he was "compensated,"—"in best friends: friends, few, but the *better* of which the world never saw."

Had sent his piece about the meeting to the Boston Transcript, and I could have the manuscript if they sent it back. W. said the way he went through the other night and his good condition since, surprised him greatly. Whatever his "determination"—he had not "anticipated so radical a process—one so safe. We ought to congratulate ourselves we were not *hors de combat*—let alone, coming out with flying colors, so to speak."

Friday, April 18, 1890

5 P.M. W. in his room. Looked rather pale, and on my remarking it, said: "It is true, I guess: I am not feeling well: these are not good days for me—bad days, in fact. Yet I have just eaten quite a good dinner—half a dozen raw oysters—and fine they were, too! What finer than a good oyster! But I am not well—am weak—do not sleep well,—gain no strength."

He afterward said: "I had a long letter today from Australia—a literary letter in part, personal, too—affectionate—and all that"—from an Irishman, Bernard O'Dowd—Melbourne—a clerk there. A curious letter (dated 3/12/90) starting off—"Dear Walt, my beloved master, my friend, my bard, my prophet and apostle"—. Enthusiasm abounding. W. said: "Take it with you, read it: then let us send it to Dr. Bucke." W. had answered briefly—gave me the letter to post. Said he had also put together several pictures in a big envelope to send but "was staggered to find it needed a dollar and 24 cents postage—have it here still." Left with him a copy of Harper's Weekly.

Will he write a Lincoln life? It seems a tempting proposition, to which he alludes only briefly. But how can he? "The strength that I have is easily played out." A picture of Rudolf Schmidt just received: placed on the mantel—a large head. W. asking: "Don't you see the Yankee in it? Schmidt is a marked man—intellectual—radical—progressive—advanced. His life these five years has been almost tragic. He was married some five years ago, and after he was married—not long—his wife went insane, and so continues, I think."

Said he had not noticed Furness' critical judgment the other night in asking [making?] high mention of Grant's book, the Hay–Nicolay Lincoln, and Joe Jefferson's autobiography as "the great books—at least the great biographical books—of the time." "I should say it was ludicrous," W. laughingly replied. "As to Jefferson's book—it is dry, not supremely good-

369

natured, not knowing at all in things of the past 50 years—things he should know or pretends to write about pass him by utterly—in much he writes he gives but thumb-nail glimpses, if that—the sun, the elements, the real firmament, beyond his reach, his sight. No great book was ever made of such lack-gifts. It may be I am harsh because I have not looked far enough into the book—yet I am sure this is not the whole story. There was probably some touch or event in Jefferson's book that moved the Doctor—and at once his adherence was assured. Of the Century books—the war pieces—of Grant's—all those special articles, what-not,—the mania of this decade, I feel—their importance lies in the documentary evidence they collect, preserve: all to be recast by the right man, when his time comes and he assumes the field: but not that any one now, so far, has come with insignia to know, to tell. The historian is not yet born: the voice of these times—the historic voice—[has] not yet spoken."

Saturday, April 19, 1890

7.55 P.M. W. in the parlor. Cordial. I sat at the Western window, W. at the East. Talked for half an hour and more. Mrs. Davis in the room part of the time—W. questioning her—"And how is it with thee, Mary?"—signifying after a great interest, by sundry turns of talk, on all she said.

W. thought: "Now is the time for the American newspaper. Some doubts might be, if one is called for—if it would be upheld in appearing. But the right paper, the right management, man, would assure that, I have no doubt. But it must be for Americana: not in a strict literal sense, but in the larger sense of that ultimate democracy for which America stands—which it points to, prophetically. I have thought in reading the Bruno book, how autochthonous Brinton himself seems to be—a creature of our life, soul—large, in mass unposing, frank, courageous."

Had received a copy of Liberty today—"but not opened it yet." Had he seen Childs' new book—recollections? "No: it has not been sent here. I can see Childs' quality: in its way it is of the first order: large-measure,—a heart of gold at its center—a true pulsing nature—full of generosity, response, to all human influences." He said Childs' "personality" accounted for "his power to draw aliens near and make them his own"— and it was a power "large for human issues."

Laughed again over Furness' "literary acumen," as he called it drolly. "It would seem to outrage even the common sense of criticism. All we can say of it is, that some people prefer boiled cabbage, baked codfish, pork-and-beans—and these are undoubtedly legitimate dishes, however we differ in our taste for them."—"But after all, the Doctor's judgment smells of his age." But all in the best humor—referring repeatedly to Furness as "that grand old man—that spendid specimen."

Freely spoke of International Copyright. "No—I do not think it would raise the cost of books. But then, however that be, I do not think it the primal question: before that, is the question of justice to the author. I have not entered into the details of this subject—but my main conviction is clear. Oh! mankind—one side of him is a big rascal—has no conscience!"

No word from the Transcript yet. The matter he has sent in is very brief: written in the third person throughout. "Perhaps they will not care to print it. I have asked for papers."

Sunday, April 20, 1890

10.15 A.M. Mrs. Davis just taking breakfast in to W., who looked well, and had been reading the Press. He said as we came in: "I was quite staggered here—it knocked the breath out of me—to read a headline—'The Death of Peter Doyle'— here in the paper: but it was not *our* Peter Doyle: it was some old man, somewhere, given the same name. Oh! our good

Pete—a rebel—not old—big—sturdy—a man, every inch of him! such a fellow—and health!" Said he had not read more in the paper. "This stayed me: it was a shock!"

Said he was promising himself to go out today. Thursday evening, upon my questions, he had said: "I *should* have gone out, to be sure—but was stagnated, after all." Yesterday he *did* go: now he says to me: "I promise to go today—unless a [illegible] lassitude overcomes me again, as it has so often before."

Returned him the Australian letter, which he said he would send to Bucke. I stayed but for ten minutes. He asked where I was going. Very cherry. But still says: "I gain no strength."

Monday, April 21, 1890

4.50 P.M. W. in his room. Looked quite ill and said he had been so. Not out, though the day beautiful. "I am doing very poorly—very: I keep so weak: weak beyond words."

Said he had had "a couple of visitors: Stoddart of Lippincott's and Melville Phillips. They came to ask if I would not write for the magazine. Phillips is a type of the literary man, semi-attached in several quarters—but doing good work of its kind." But how had the Illustrated World panned out? "Oh! the portrait was terrible! Haven't you seen it? There is one here"—searching for it in a pile of papers—"take it: it is damnably abortionate: I know nothing worse."

Frank Williams came in to tell me today of a letter he had seen, written by an intimate friend of Tennyson in which Tennyson was reported as recently saying—talking of literature— that he [Tennyson] considered Walt Whitman among the greatest of living poets—after some further reflection adding—"I don't know but I might say the greatest." I repeated this to W., who had me go over it several times (his wont) in order to make himself sure possessor of its significance. Then he said: "That is very happy—strong, helpful: that is a cooling breeze after a sultry day—after tired, sluggish, hours of pain: relief, hope! And he asked—"And you say Frank thinks it quite authentic?" Yes—he had come in, quite "tickled" over it. W.—"And so are we tickled." Laughing—"And if Tennyson takes to saying such good things of us, we'll have to adjust ourselves accordingly." I put in—"you *are* adjusted—your *adjustment* is what has captured Tennyson!" W. smiled—and to my hope that T. might somewhere have put himself so on record in his own hand, W. remarked: "Yes—it would be very desirable so: yet he seems wonderfully loath—chary, to make pledges, give written judgments. Oh! Frank is right: what you have brought me, if it prove confirmed, must be taken as of moment: it may have an importance, too—as well as a power to please us here, hearing it in this casual way. Tennyson is not only artistic—he is *art*: in him, art is *person*: all our modern impress is upon him: and there the wonder, the significance of his word for us."

Received from Kennedy yesterday, manuscript of the Transcript piece.

Tuesday, April 22, 1890

5.10 P.M. W. in his room, making copies of the Post to send right and left to friends. "At my instance they published the Transcript piece: I shall send out a number—some at home, some abroad—Sarrazin, Dowden, Symonds—others. I take it for granted they like to hear." He thought copies should go to Clifford, Brinton, Frank Williams and Morris—and I engaged to take them. Health still very poor: continues weak. "It is a continuation of the old story: chapter after chapter the same: no variation in the monotony."

"It is singular," he said by and bye, "how I seem to grow in demand: I am myself astonished. Today I had an application from the American Press Association. What for? A specialty? Oh no!—*any*thing, I suppose—prose or verse. O the mutations of years! Only a few years ago—five only—I waited for just such orders—wondered, and was willing, able, still with a modicum of strength: but no message came—the world did not want me. *Now*—hardly half a decade after, comes a multitude: comes cry and cry—after my power to respond is gone: after I am wrecked, stranded, left but to look for the end—or near end! And yet there is a sense of satisfaction even in this—though how much of such satisfaction is legitimate, justified—who knows? Can it be a passing fashion?" O the music and solemnity of utterance, as now he looked out upon the bronzing Western sky, then at me—then closed his eyes as if in self-communion! Subsequently he followed with words of sweet cheer: "You will see Frank Williams tonight? Tell him I am waiting to have the Tennyson extract authenticated. It is not yet published? No? Well we must have patience: and who should have it more than I?—for I have waited, worked, even through long years of hesitating faith." And again: "Tell Frank I have thought a good deal over it—that it has touched a chord—that it has a prime significance, once authenticated, that no man can impeach."

Left with him a copy of the American containing Frank Williams' comment on the Contemporary Club meeting. Would send it to Bucke. Spoke of word from Bucke and Kennedy today—with gift-box from K. not yet opened.

Visitors today, Colonel Forney's daughter and a friend, but he was too ill to see them. Referring to pictures again—Tennyson's in the Illustrated American—"After all, your father's—the two—are the best I know: they seem to summarize all that art can say of me."

Wednesday, April 23, 1890

5.15 P.M. W. in his bedroom: dinner just finished. Stayed about half an hour. He was reading the local paper. Said he had been out for about 2 hours in the chair. "It has been a delicious day. I enjoyed the fresh air—the change from much in-doorness."

Left word with Warren in the early morning that he wished to see no one—no one to be admitted. Said he had "sent off a great number of Posts: a good score and more abroad." Laughed when he learned I had secured seven. "It will get circulated!" Returned me Harper's [of?] last week.

I urged the matter of the dinner list again. He promised to give it some attention. It's a tiresome job, getting such a thing from him, between his "lassitude" and his "bad memory" (his own words). Said he felt much better than for many days past.

Much occupied with the account I gave him of a debate over oysters at Boothby's, the night before between Morris, Frank Williams, Jastrow and (myself) after the Club meeting. As to the point there discussed, that W. lacked *humor*, W. said: "That charge is not new—even so high an authority as Ruskin has urged it. And I think it ought to be urged, if for no more than eliciting the truth. It has its part to play in the drama. O'Connor should have been there with you—he would have enjoyed it—a five-minute charge would have satisfied him: a rush, a sabre-thrust—and then? He would have proceeded somewhat in this way—would have instanced a colored woman—a negro—we knew in Washington: I have heard him quote her often—the mother of a brood of children—superb in body, in health, vigor—no flaw in all her physiological being—He would have declared: see her,—see her body—see the ludicrous phases of it all—her absurdities, perhaps of gait, depth of color,—the side of her provoking risibility—all that: see it—note it! Well, I would not say Walt Whitman does not see it, too—does not even make allusion [to it]—but he does not allow it to obstruct him—he is occupied with the larger purport: the whole being, man, woman—*this* woman. It is true that he sees that quality, component—knows it exists, recognizes, includes it—but he knows, too, after putting it to its minor uses, that it is subordinate—that

375

after all humor, however largely construed, is a very small part of the cosmos. Besides, suppose he takes you out to see a sunset—the gorgeous panorama—the waters of a flowing river—the forests between: you go with him, you look—your business then is with the sunset, the stream, the waving trees, he indicated these—their meanings, signs, prophecies, and nothing else. It is along such a line William O'Connor would have argued. He, at least, would consider it conclusive: I have heard him urge it with his vast fiery speech in its torrential potency, all going down, surrendering. More than once, more than a hundred times, I have known him meet criticism of this sort, other sorts, readily, magnificently—at least for *him*, however *I* came out of it."

And then: "To know me to the full, they must not know only the poems, but the story there in prose, too—'Democratic Vistas,' certainly, if none other."

Hunted up a letter from Garland which he said "smacked of a significance" and he wished me "to see—to take note of"—but in the debris of the floor he could not trace it. "Let it go," I suggested, "it will turn up of its own accord—looking rarely benefits in here,"—and he laughed heartily: "I see you have touched one of my frailties." But he did let it go, saying again however—"I want you to see it—measure it."

Thursday, April 24, 1890

5.30 P.M. W. in his room, reading. After his afternoon meal he usually takes a course in the local papers, getting two— the Post and the Courier.

Brought him from Frank Williams the letter containing the Tennyson matter as spoken of several days ago. Written by John C. Trautwine, Jr., to some-one in Philadelphia named Suplee. W. advised me to keep a copy of the paragraph—also to send one to Dr. Bucke. "I wonder if Frank will print it entire? or perhaps not." It would be safer to copy. "It appears on the face of it quite authentic," said W. Here it is—

"Speaking of Browning, do you know that Walt Whitman is enthusiastically admired in England? Mr. Harrison, for instance, is quite devoted to him, and says that Tennyson says that W. W. is one of the greatest, if not the greatest, of living poets, or words to that effect. Mr. Gordon, you know, surprised me by manifesting the greatest interest in him. Verily a prophet is not without honor, save in his own country. In this, too, I must want training. There are fine things, in W. W.'s writings, but I can't help wishing he had put them into prose, instead of into such rocky verse."

W. smiled somewhat over this, but made no comment.

I took a fat letter to the P.O. for him, addressed to Stoddart, of Lippincott's, and not only duly sealed but additionally tied with a string. Garland's letter not yet turned up.

Friday, April 25, 1890

5.10 P.M. W. reading a letter. Had found me Garland's letter.

Dear Walt Whitman

I feel like writing at once about something that has delighted me. In talking with Thomas Sergeant Perry last night we fell to discussing your work, and to my delight I found him a great and unequivocal admirer of your work. I was pleased beyond measure, for Mr. Perry's opinion on your work is more valuable to me than that of any man in America—with one exception. Mr. Perry is a man of vast learning. He is a historian of literature. He knows the development of all Western literature, he is just finishing a large volume—very radical—on the Greek literature, he has written on German and English literature. His criticisms are based not on personal feelings but upon principles—he looks at any man from the *comparative standpoint*. He is the leader of that school of thought with us here. So you see this has value—this opinion of his. He has been abroad for some years studying and now is writing on various historical lines. Mr. Howells and he were two of my most honored friends.

"It seems to be to the same purport as the letter you brought me about Tennyson. It is a straw—they both are straws—to be taken note of. Are we like to become popular in our old age—in our retirement from the stage? Who knows the issue of all this? After all that is gone before—the abuse, defamation—unknowing hatred—this a rebound—but—" and so he ended the matter in a smile—adding, however, again—"Let me send this letter to Bucke when you are done with it. But in the meantime do you turn it over well—take its full measure—for the day may come when you if not I will need to record all the details of this story."

I proposed sending a copy—extract—about Tennyson to Bucke. W. thought it "a good idea," but added—"The thought strikes me if we had not better have a few of them struck off— say 25 or 50. Curtz down here would put it into type and give us the copies for 25 cents or so. We may want a few: there are several I even now think of who ought to have copies—Burroughs, Kennedy—some even for abroad."

I asked him if he had any curiosity to see Bucke's piece sent me—but he laughingly shook his head. "No—I can wait till it is in type: as I grow old, I am less and less to be figured in that direction: I never was any too eligible." Left with him a copy of Scribner's containing an article on Millet by T. [Truman] H. Bartlett. W. much drawn to it—pleased with Carroll Beckwith's portrait of Millet. "I should say the fellow who drew this has a future: his method is justified in this hair, if nowhere else—but *else*where, too." And—"It is wonderful, the fellows now at work, making for new ideas, fields—laying out fresh schemes—in art, everything."

I told him Morris was somewhat solicitous, lest what he had said of W.'s lack of humor should have evoked feeling. But W. said: "No—it was all right: he does not fully under-

stand: why, I am as much as anybody a weigher, investiga-
tor—questioning significances—anxious to get at my meanings." I said: "Very few know how fully you objectify yourself.
I am often asked by persons who have been here if I thought
you were offended at certain things said: I tell them they do
not quite measure you." W.—"You are right—they do not: I
hope the time will never come when I will sit [in] stupid de-
nial upon criticism: I welcome all—welcome even the lying,
slander."

Morris had looked over files of the Democratic Review—
1842 or thereabout—stories there signed "Walter Whitman"—
were they W.'s? W. now said to me: "Yes—I guess there's no
doubt of that—they're mine, if I want to claim them—as I do
not! I don't think much of 'em—they're better forgotten—
lain dusty in the old files." He had no copies, so far as he
knew. "Except a stray one, here and there, kept out of forgetfulness."—"The Democratic Review was quite famous in
those days—started in Washington by a young man—Sulli-
van, I think was his name: I knew him well—a handsome,
generous fellow. He treated me well. Hawthorne published
some of his famous tales through the Review."

Saturday, April 26, 1890

5 P.M. W. received me cordially. Eating a baked apple—
the last of his dinner. Read him a passage from this week's
Critic by "The Lounger"—about the Lincoln address, evidently surprised by the Transcript piece—the writer apparently not suspecting this to be by W. W. "'Twas cordial," W.
said. "I don't know who that 'Lounger' is. I asked Melville
Phillips when he was here, and he did not know—knew no
more than we do. He did make a guess—guessed it was Jennie or Joe Gilder—but I am seriously in doubt—doubt of its
being either. To come from either one of them the warmth
would surprise me."

Returned me Scribner's: had read Bartlett's article on Millet. Yesterday had doubted if it was his Bartlett or a son: now he said: "I think it is *our* man—that he must have spent some time there. It is only passably interesting—does not impress me deeply." Gave me Lippincott's also. Still further a letter from Bucke—received today—on which he had written "for Horace." All these he had tied together in a string.

Sunday, April 27, 1890

10.15 A.M. In at W.'s for about five minutes. Sat in his bedroom: W. just finished breakfast. Warren making bed &c. W. said, "I feel very well this morning—have made a good breakfast of fish." Adding, as I edged towards the door—"Give my love to any of the boys you meet: tell them I still sit here, confined but not unhappy."

Left with him Garland's letter—also copy of the Tennyson matter for him to print. Learned of Frank Williams' mention of the latter in America this week but have not seen it yet. Laughing interest expressed to me by some who learn the origin of the Transcript piece in W. himself, that he said there—"W.'s voice and Magnetism the same." But W. had said to me the day after the meeting: "I see I can hold a meeting as of old: I was not sure of it till I got there—till I had commenced."

Monday, April 28, 1890

4.50 P.M. W. had just finished dinner—was reading the American. Frank Williams had sent him a copy. Said he had enjoyed it. Morris has an article there, which W. had read. "It is quite pessimistic," he said, "decidedly so. Tell Morris for me that he'd better look out: it'll do him no good, and may ruin him. It is a dangerous fire to fool with. I know there are things in Morris' life which may account in part for this: but not wholly—rather, he is in the line of the ages' tendency—the Occidental tendency, as I call it. All the literary fellows, almost, take it—assume it, breathe it in as a fashion—are affected by it even when they do not know it. But Morris is too good a boy to go down that incline. I think it the bane of our civilization—the Western civilization—Europe—as distinguished from that which we call Oriental—that this drift bears all on its crest. The age must take a turn from that—eventually take higher courses. Even William O'Connor, who, of all men, you would think protected, exempt, bore traces of it, from head to toe." I said, "But O'Connor was so powerful, so native and strong, I think this was merely an incident in his life." W. then: "Yes—you are right: I should have qualified what I said without being prompted to it: O'Connor was marvellously gifted, for music and battle, both."

I should thank Frank Williams for his American note—"Tell him it is just what I could have hoped for—to the point, not piling too much on." Wished papers particularly sent to Dowden and Rossetti abroad. Williams in to see me about newspaper friends of W. W. I gave him addresses of Kennedy, Baxter, Walsh, Habberton, Chambers. W. commended.

W. was out this afternoon for half an hour or so. "The air was a little pungent—champagney: but strong, pleasant." Harned had been in "a couple of hours ago," and "he brought me the deed of the cemetery lot. So you see" laughing—"I am now sure of a place to be buried in—if that has any importance. Was't it Hamlet who said it had *not*?"

Further: "Jim Scovel has been here today also—tries to prove to me that I ought to attend the planked shad dinner: but of course I declined." He thought it "would be very fortunate" if he "prove able to attend the birthday dinner on the 31st of May"—for he "had considerable of dubiosity, even as to that." His condition now he realized "at its full gravity" and knew he "must take greatest care."

381

He had a letter from Stoddart today. "He is quite willing to pay my price for the poems, pieces, I sent him the other day, but suggests that he would like to use them, one a month rather than in the way I suggested. I thought I would like them to go in—fill a page—perhaps under some common headline. But I have written him I am quite willing he should follow out his own idea. I should like it better the other way, but it is not a point that presses upon me either side." He characterized Stoddart as "a man no doubt fully qualified for his place—and enough of the conventional literary man to fit with Philadelphia: perhaps the better fitted for *not* having strong quality. Philadelphia wants the Allibones—editors— pickers—dilettante—the slighter natures—daintier vessels. No—Stoddart is by no means the man Walsh is. It never struck me to ask myself that question, but now you ask it, I can see how far more keen, penetrating, Walsh must be."

One of the "points of value" in Williams' paragraph was "the quite evident kindliness—the willingness, in a quiet way, to have the world know where Frank stands."

I left Bucke's "Leaves of Grass and Modern Science" with W. in proof. He was glad to have it. Ingram's daughter had been here. Card on table. "Yes, she is a doctor and quite a fine girl, too. Ingram, himself is true blue: a sample at its best of the middle-class Englishman, pervaded richly with the instinct to good—to extend the circle of brotherhood."

Tuesday, April 29, 1890

Did not see W. today. An absurd article turned up in the North American—signed Fred Dayton—copyrighted by the American Press Association—using a drawing from one of the hatted pictures of W. for illustration, and not a bad sketch of the house. But the text ludicrously stupid when not vulgar.

Forgot to add to notes yesterday that W. in speaking of

Philadelphia characteristics in literature, said: "And there's Bok came over—B-O-K—a fair sample—the Brooklyn man—one of the Jim Scovels in literature, absolutely characterless and irresponsible. And Philadelphia cleaves to *him*, too! He has gone with Curtis, there, with the Home Journal." Curtis, whom W. recalled as one of the objectors to Ingersoll's presence at the dinner. This leading W. to say of Ingersoll: "All we hear of him as a man is tuned to a clear key: I have no doubt he is a man pure and strong—with eminent qualities of heart—demonstrated in his family and outside: one of the men we look to for futures—for America to thrive by."

Wednesday, April 30, 1890

5.40 P.M. Talked with W. in his own room about half an hour. Had been out today. Written some—a postal to Kennedy, in hopeful vein. Got $60 from Lippincott's for four small poems. He speaks of them as "Poemets": "After the Argument," "The Unexpress'd," "Sounds of the Winter," "To the Sunset Breeze."

Showed him the North American piece. He had not seen it. Read some of it to him. Exclaimed—"A fool—to be sure! Will you leave it with me? I couldn't stand it all in one dose." And then: "I remember one fellow who was here—a bad, bad speciman—poor reporter—who came in and announced that he was here for a long talk—which I dissented from—passed him out in short order—I hope courteously, kindly. But this man—Dayton?—and Mary says he was badly *rummed*?—Yes! I remember him: but he was a little better than the other. Certainly these fellows have a marked faculty for going wrong if there's the least loophole that way" &c.

Returned me the proof of Dr. Bucke's "Leaves of Grass and Modern Science"—saying of it: "Certainly the Doctor is developing a striking idiocratic style—one superbly his own—

strong, direct. This article is very gratifying to me—very satisfactory." Then remarked that Bucke was due here on the 12th: had so written Kennedy.

Was surprised to learn the newspaper had already got hold of "A Twilight Song"—printed in the Ledger yesterday—from the forthcoming Century. He took up his roped package from the table—gave me 3 copies of the Curtz-printed poem—minus the phrase added to the magazine headline "(For unknown buried soldiers North and South)." "That," he explained, "was added at their suggestion to meet a magazine exigency. It don't hurt or hinder—neither does it help. . . . But," he added, "as this is a good paid-for piece, let me follow out my custom—credit the poem where it belongs"—taking pen and writing "Century N Y May 1890" on each one, at foot, and putting on one for me "for Horace Traubel from the author." I was going to a meeting of the Club at Sulzberger's tonight—so one copy was to go there.

Said he had a letter from Dowden, about the Bruno book and other matters—"and you may show it to Dr. Brinton for me: it probably would interest him." But in the heap of disarranged things on the table he could not find it. Showed me a list of those to whom the Brunos had been sent: which might also go to Brinton.

I called his attention to a portrait of Bonnat in Harper's Weekly—a bust from Dubois—fine—of what he said first— "The engraving is superb" and afterward—"and the bust itself must be a great one—truly made after the larger methods."

He picked up the Cemetery deed from the table (enveloped)— and said: "I wish to give this to Tom to keep safely for me."—And after a pause: "But first I want to find my 'last will and testament'"—laughingly—"it is here somewhere, lost in the confusion." This his first word on the subject since the day in December 1888 when Harned took it along with him and put it away in his safe. So now I said—"As to that— Walt—I think Tom has always had it in a secure place"—relating to him the circumstances of the taking. He was perfectly satisfied. "Why—that is a relief; then it has always been stowed snugly away! Good! I thought it still here." And—"You were right—Tom was right—both. And now I am saved ferreting for it."

Called my attention to an English catalogue, rehearsing rare and autographed Whitman books for sale—prices varying up to 11 and 12 pounds amused him. "I wish I had a few hundred of the books myself now—they would set me up! When I *did* have them, no price was low enough to persuade the world that they were to be desired!"

Left a copy of Current Literature with him.

Thursday, May 1, 1890

5.30 P.M. Stayed with W. about half an hour. When I came in he was reading the Boston Transcript. Said he had read all Dayton's piece last night. "It can be explained, I suppose, by the statement that he probably had to fill out that space, and not having the material from his visit here, added enough to make an interesting and a foolish article." And he added—"It was all utterly stupid, too." Done with Current Literature. "I have read it pretty well though: it is a good table—a well-filled table: probably the best table for public appetite, which carves a solid meal of plain grub."

The Century here. Morris has a little poem therein. W. made no direct comment on it—only—"I should say of that as I do to the boys who wish to learn to swim: go to the water again and again and still again—finally the skill will come."— Added however after a pause: "But Horace, you should remember that there are many portraits painted—thousands and thousands and thousands of them—and yet *very very* few of them that really *are* portraits: they are rare enough—*great* portraits—to count on a few fingers." He afterwards added in a similar strain: "I have read my own Century piece over today, and like it very well—am thoroughly pleased with it: for one thing, pleased with its absolute unliterariness: as if I had utterly, disdainfully cast it aside, would have none of it at all! This is not a new sensation. I have always been best pleased with what seems most to disregard literariness: the artistic, the formal, the traditional aesthetic, the savor of mere words, jingles, sound—I have always eschewed: language itself *as* language I have discounted—would have rejected it altogether but that it serves the purpose of *vehicle*, is a necessity—our mode of communication. But my aim has been, to so subordinate that, no one could know it existed—as in fine plate glass one sees the objects beyond and does not realize the glass between. My determination being to make the story of man, his physiological, emotional, spiritual, self, tell its own story, unhindered by artificial agencies." Some one had said, on reading the Century poem, that W. was evidently more moved by war subjects than any others—but W. demurred—"I do not think that the case: what I have just said is rather the explanation."

He took up another theme: "There are certain literary traditions, and the man who violates them is quickly advised—'Damn you! cut none of your capers *here*—no kicking in the traces!' One of the things that has tickled me of late as I sit here—right in this line of thought—is the major-generalship, with pay, given Frémont. He must be an old man now—probably 80: but he was always a come-outer. There was a time in the war when everybody was willing to damn him. In the West, in Lincoln's time, he proved too previous. Lincoln, with his wiser, clearer eye, seeing so much farther, having regard, as Frémont had not, for the enemy in the rear as well as the enemy in front. All Lincoln's life was turned to a generous key. When he went to New York, as I have described it, at a time when men's hip-pockets abounded in knives and revolvers—the men only looking for a chance, a pretext, to whip them out, to set the town ablaze, to murder Lincoln, others: at this time, at all later times, Lincoln's policy was, not to offer this opportunity—not to strike this spark. Who can measure the value of such a personality—in its way all-seeing—to America at that time?"

Friday, May 2, 1890

5.15 P.M. W. reading the paper—in his own room. Just finished dinner. Not out today—"not extra well"—yet, as he says, "I am mad now I did *not* go out!" Writing—this afternoon—verse—under the headline—"Go forth, ye jocund twain!"

Paid him 5 dollars for the copy of Leaves of Grass delivered to Edelheim. Told W. E. had also given me $15 towards the fund. He exclaimed—"God bless him! the good man!" And then: "I wonder if this would in any way have cast light for Elias Hicks? Elias had a bitter question to put to himself, especially in later years: he would say—speaking of the Bible—'When I think of the misery it has caused in the world, the carnage, the wrong, on the one hand, and then of the good on the other, I am at a loss on which side the balance lies.' But," said W. "I am not: to me it is a perfectly clear proportion."

Spoke of the suspension of a bank in Camden—and I thought a little anxiously—of "that at Second and Market." Adding—"If that should go up, my world would go up with it." Aldrich had a poem in the Century. W. spoke of him as "almost poetic"—enlarging, however, to the effect—"there is fire in him—something more than ordinary." He had read "Baby Bell" and other bits of A.'s work. Dowden's letter has not turned up yet.

Talked of historic reputation. The value of history I thought often in counsel of what to avoid rather than in measures to adopt. W. thought: "That is so: and history is interesting when it shows what contemporary men thought of events—how deceived they mostly are. Mirabeau was a good instance: in his own day and for 40 years after, adored, almost deified—yet now known for a man who would have rivalled Tweed in political debauchery—a most consummate handler of bribes." How, for instance, about the current reputations of Darwin and Emerson? "They will last—they in a way justify themselves—are sufficient unto themselves." This led him to say of Emerson and the charges that he was "dignified to excess, and icy of exterior, at least."—"No"—shaking his head—that is a mistake—at first glance, Emerson was a little timid—some would call him finicky: but soon all the impression of that flies, and there remains the solid enduring qualities. Emerson may have seemed distant to those who were absorbed in literary finesse, in gossip, in commonplace affairs—because he took but little interest in that direction; but on the world's field he was a master—a man. He had not O'Connor's conversational power, to be sure—in the first place, he would not have wished for it, then had not the right training. O'Connor was a powerful talker—eloquent—of widest interests, sympathies. He set out for such possessions."

A picture of Bonnat in the Bazaar by Dubois excited W.'s admiration. First he commented on the engraving—then on "the marvellous expression of the sculptor's own work."

Saturday, May 3, 1890

7.15 P.M. Only in for a look at W., whom I found in the parlor, with hat and coat on, and a blanket superadded by Mrs. Davis.

Left with him Bucke's proof, received from B. today with a number of changes. W. wished to look it over—would return to me in the morning. Did not think "anything could in its way beat the statement the Doctor has put there."

Curious when he learned I was on my way to Philadelphia to hear Von Bulow play. "So that is the famous Von Bulow I have heard of these 30 or 40 years almost?" He had an impression somehow that Von B. though "sufficiently alive to technique" was yet not under bonds to it: that he gave much for *expression*—"in a sense is lawless"—and this impression had excited in him respect.

"Had a good outing today," he reported—"weather so mild—the sky, even in its cloudiness, so gentle and serene." Said he looked forward with pleasure to Bucke's visit "now so near."

Has not made our list yet. A difficult pull!

Sunday, May 4, 1890

Stopped in at W.'s 10.10 A.M. W. just up—breakfast untouched so far. Replying to my query, said he felt "damnable."

Had read Bucke's proof, which he returned to me. I did not stay. Later I found he even felt worse as the day progressed. Weather showery. He did not of course attempt to get out. Probably a cold from sitting at the door awhile last evening—and later by an open parlor window.

Monday, May 5, 1890

In at 5.40 on my way home. W. on bed asleep, but waking, spoke a while with me; looked very bad—said he had spent "two horrible days"—"but now I am better—have eaten something this afternoon for the first time."

Asked after "news." Then advised me to take the cemetery deed to Tom, saying afterward however: "You are sure he has the will? Suppose you bring it up to me some day—I should like to look at it: shall only want it for a glance. Of course Tom's office is the right place for these things."

Did not prolong talk. Mrs. Davis thinks W. perceptibly growing weaker—as, indeed, does he himself,—complaining, as he does, of pains in knees and ankles.

Monday, May 5, 1890

7.55 P.M. In to see W. again for a few minutes. Had left the cemetery deed with Harned. Told W., Harned would some time bring the will around to him: just now it is buried inaccessibly in his safe. W. perfectly satisfied. Was in the bedroom still and still lying down, though not asleep. Had had chicken broth, he said—and some minor things. But "the pull tough." Things not looking up in a way to cheer me.

Talked with Harned about the idea of having the birthday dinner at his house, using the parlor, and all hands to chip in for costs. Brinton's idea, too. T. quite acquiescing—pleased. W.'s condition so uncertain, [it seems] inadvisable to go to formal preparations.

Tuesday, May 6, 1890

5.50 P.M. W. sitting—not reading in his room. A posy of flowers—pansies &c.—in a little glass on the table, which he frequently applied to his nose—expressing joy thereat—"the first fresh spring flowers—oh! how blessed!" As to his health: "Oh! I am much eased! There is certainly an improvement—and I have eaten some."

Curious—how he always questions—like a child. "What have you got there?"—questioning about a package—"What is all that mass of paper?" I laughed and he did too. He handed me a copy of O'Connor's Donnelly book from a chair. "Didn't you ask me for it? No?" and then—"Oh! it was Tom then? Well—take it to him: I knew somebody about here asked for it. Take it to him—I have it here—back from John Burroughs. And here is John's letter, too: it came today: take it—when you are through we will send it to Dr. Bucke—the good Doctor!—and he soon to be here, too!—just about a week now! Oh! it is a great comfort to see *faces*."—ending as if in reflection.

I talked with Harned last night about dinner on the 31st. W.'s condition so dubious, we hesitate to make public preparation. Resolved therefore, to have a limited number at H.'s home, using his parlor (to be freed for the purpose) expense to be borne by a group. I explained this to W., who said—"I like it far better as arranged that way. Even so, Horace, I feel it is a little doubtful whether I shall be able to get there. I should say, limit it to 20—not more than 20 at the most—make no effort to do [have?] more. This last flash of the comet's tail has been a severe one—has badly damaged me—has left me way up on shore. It is true, I have a way of coming about. As a usual thing, however great the impedimenta, I come out at the last moment, perhaps scarred, but not ruined. And it may prove so again. Napoleon always found an exit—could always extricate himself—until the last, until his Waterloo—which was the end of the narrative. I shall have my Waterloo, no doubt soon, but till then?"—As to having Bush and others who have never met him come to the dinner—"If I were asked my own preference, I should say, *no*—I'd rather they did not come: I do not like to make my first appearance in such condition as I enjoy now—especially as I have been now for several days—weak, broken, disabled."

Has been writing some today. I alluded to the Century poem—to Harned's high opinion of it: used in touching upon it, the word "latest," as treating style &c. W. then: "That *is* literally my latest work—it was written within the past 2 or 3 months—sent to the Century—paid for. They sent me proof—said they wished to use at once—asked for a sub-title, which I gave them. I did not like the idea at first, nor after the idea the actual line, but now such objections as I had (they were not positive at all) are mostly gone. I sent it, complied, because"—laughing merrily—"because I usually send what I am paid for." I interrupted—"You will do that, but you will not alter or deduct?"—"No: oh! I am exceedingly touchy about changes—will not hear to 'em—hate to have even a comma go wrong. But the Century folks treat me well—very well; I find they humor all my eccentricities."

He wishes 50 copies of the next number of Conservator, desiring "to send them far and near—many abroad." Bucke's article appears there—"and it is so satisfactory, strong, virile." I brought to his attention the bill received today from Ol-dach—balance of between 40 and 50 dollars, now standing nearly a year. "He has treated us well," W. said, "we must pay him, and at once."

Joking about my increased salary: "You must look out—you will be in danger of growing rich: riches are so many threats!" Of Aldrich—"He has there in the Century, a dainty sonnet"— ["I vex me not with brooding on the years"]—"Yet more than dainty, too: the best thing I have known from Aldrich."

We spoke of indications of health—how far *out*, how far *in*. W. "You are right: it was not the big burly partly rosy fellows to whom our officers looked in the war days for the best ser-vice, but to agile men—men of long-enduring sinew—often small, but lithe." And—"In the hospitals, pain, horror, was best sustained by the smallest men."

Wednesday, May 7, 1890

4.50 P.M. W. just finished dinner. A strong odor of soap in the room, of which he said: "They have been making a show of cleaning today, if it can be called that: scrubbing, washing, dusting, arranging, in a general sort of way." As to his own health? "I am improved, I think—so to call it—but my im-provements as a rule are not very radical."

Gave me a copy of The Author—dated February—contain-ing a Whitman passage: extract from the Philadelphia Times (probably one of Jim Scovel's farragoes). "It may interest, if not instruct, you." Looked rather better, but weak. Said his sickness did not trouble his eyes. Writing some today: a couple of sheets there, with freshly-written fragmentary lines of poems.

Asked of Philadelphia and of the big speculations in buildings now remarkable there—commenting: "Years ago, when I was a young man—I knew a man in New York named Holt: a curious, interesting man who excited my curiosity those years. He had come from Cold Spring, Long Island—where, by the way, my mother might be said to have come from. He was an expert in preparing fish, eels, the like—at least his wife was—together working—succeeding wonderfully well—accumulating 12 or 15 or 20 thousand dollars. Eventually he got the bee in his bonnet: he wanted a big place—built one: down on Fulton Street, near the ferry, as you cross over to Brooklyn: a good place in its day, and standing yet, I believe: he called it Holt's House, or hotel, or something signifying the same. And here was his struggle, in which he finally went down. He put all his own money in cash on the place—then on top of it a mortgage of a hundred thousand dollars. I stopped there a number of times, when I had been out in the country: it was not expensive, [was] clean. But Holt had it in a crisis year, could not continue—was sold by the sheriff. The old man was heroic: he was grey then and not extra strong—but the two bravely went to work again—started another little restaurant—Holt, however, before long dying. He was too old, stupid, worn out, to make a decided stand against fate. The moral of [all of] which is, not to over-vault what is innately possessed—not to build your buildings too high!"

He sat with his hat on—the air chill outside and damp.

Thursday, May 8, 1890

4.40 P.M. W. in his room, finishing dinner. Said: "I have been making a meal of strawberries. Mrs. Davis brought some in, unhulled—said that was the fashionable way to eat them: to take them up, one at a time, in the fingers, dip them in sugar, then swallow. But I returned them to her—told her I had no doubt that was a very good way—perhaps the best way—but that I had been brought up under the old dispensation, to eat them sugared, from a dish." Then he spoke of a great liking for berries: "Perhaps New Jersey gives us the finest berries known in the world today." Liked all—blackberries, raspberries, strawberries—"perhaps blackberries best of all"—the raspberries better when "mixed with currants—white or red"—"I have a sweet tooth—find it appreciates all but things of cloying sweetness: confects of that order." Adding: "Guava jelly was at one time an established confect: in grandmother's time—grandfather's time—it was a great dish—exists still, for that matter—though as I have said, whether imported or not is still a question with me: it can still be bought—a brand I think even better than the old."—"The cultivated blackberry beats all I know in this way: it deserves to be apotheosized!"

I returned him Burroughs' letter, remarking a pathetic vein. W. affirming: "It is so—a sort of *passé* vein—as if of a cloth, all wrung out. And yet this is evidently written out of some cheer—in a mood reflecting joy, brightness—for John." Among W.'s further reflections were these: "In spite of all, John has been dealt with by literariness—very few but have been so affected—however slightly: though John would indeed be the last man you expect so actuated—participant of out-of-doorness—the minks, foxes, fences, woods, new moons, the paraphernalia of nature—but even upon John the branches hang over, they are full of moisture, he cannot wholly escape the woods yet. But somehow all the great dons seem glad to know somebody who has come out if they cannot shake it all off themselves. There was Emerson, here—not wholly rid of it, yet rejoicing in every sign of delivery—and Tennyson, more radically comprehending even as he grows older—Tennyson, who, if he lasts long enough, will be wholly free at

last! And John—though I should not call him a don, yet is my
friend, seems unaltered towards me. I know I have sometimes asked myself, whether Burroughs' attitude towards me
has changed: but no, it has not: I am sure of John to the last.
I don't think even you have any idea—so full an idea, anyhow,
as I have—how natural some of the feeling about John should
be. I seem to see the tendency in him towards literariness
grow stronger with age—yet I remember that even so keen
and cute a man as William O'Connor—so born critic he was—
warned me in those early years in Washington, to put my foot
down on John's book about me—to have nothing to do with
it—even allow it. Oh yes! William was one of the first to
change—to recognize the gold in John: I only mention it now,
confidentially, as we sit together here, to illustrate. I cannot
imagine anybody doubting John—every page is fresh and
juicy—juicy as are few pages that teem about us. When I look
about me—realize how the best fellows have strayed off, in
greater or less degree—I wonder at myself, that I, near the
72nd year, have not pulled the same building down on my
head: have escaped the danger, by almost miraculous ma-
nipulations—gone free of the taint, and rejoicing and even
rejoiced with by others."

There was a Gutekunst picture (one of the bad versions)
which I picked up from the table. W.—"made of express in-
tent, to produce a good picture: it is destined for the fire,
where the others have gone—is only spared because for the
present it is used as a paper knife. It indicates well the mov-
ing-forces of what is called art: how the elements are feared,
the compounds [?] courted." I wished to show this to my
father. W. would only let me do it on promise I should surely
bring it back. "I design it for the fire," he said again. Showed
him an article from a stray New England weekly about Elizabeth Porter Gould—with whom W. was much coupled. He
thought: "These are of use, I suppose, to show what is in the
air—how we have changed it at last: and to show that even-

tually even the citadel itself will be penetrated, through some chink or other. For the air is all-reaching, permitting no denials."

Wished me to find out for him date of Queen Victoria's birthday. "My friend John Reed, himself an Englishman, used to pass here daily, but now that I want to see him, I never find him passing at all." Spoke of "Annex to Annex" of L. of G. Said: "I have thought of getting out a little book—a special volme—a part of it to go in in future annexed to November Boughs, a part to Leaves of Grass—perhaps all to November Boughs. I am speculating about it now. Perhaps before long we'll get to work on it. It will of course be uniform: will contain the Century prose piece, the poems, memoranda, odd bits, not printed."

Had forgotten about Oldach's bill—would write check tomorrow. Thought I should take Schmidt's portrait also to show my father. "I do not like it much myself, but most do. He has had almost a tragic life.—The European fellows beat us— their climate, what-not, are superior. That picture of Symonds—it is unsurpassed, if reached."

Friday, May 9, 1890

5.40 P.M. W. just concluded dinner. Looked very much improved and *was*. Not out today: wind rather high and chill. Looked at the Bazaar I had with me, admiring Baude's [?] engraving. Had written a postal to Mrs. O'Connor, which he asked me to mail.

I returned him the portrait by Schmidt and the Gutekunst Whitman spoke of yesterday. My father had asked for the latter but I would not leave it with him, regardful of my promise to W. Now I explained—at first W. laughing and saying: "No—it is destined for the fire—irrevocably: look at the formal pose—the expression, too, a damnable one!" But finally relented. "Well—if your father really wants it, take it to him:

it hardly becomes a fellow to be stubborn on such a point."
Regarded Schmidt's picture intently. I spoke of it as "the
head, rather of thinker than poet—intellectual." He assenting: "That's just it—just what it is: the head of a Yankee. Oh!
he has had an almost tragic experience, and borne it well, I
do believe!" Of art and artists—literary or other: "There are
some things unknown if not unknowable: art—what is it?
Who can tell? An ineffable something, defying speech."

W. asked: "Have you found out for me yet when Queen
Victoria's birthday is due?" I think he is writing about it but
did not ask. He spoke of Harned's address before the Unitarian Club last night. "It is wonderful how the world is getting
flooded with speech: yet all seems somehow to work out for
good!" Expects Bucke next week. He is to bring part of his
family with him—go direct to Cape May.

Left with him a copy of the February Atlantic which I had
with me. He never sees it—thought he would like it to read.
Said the more he thought of the dinner "the wiser seems the
conclusion you came to the other night." Suddenly said:
"There! no check for Oldach yet! I never thought of that from
the moment you left yesterday till just this second ago." Then
deploring his memory "which plays me crooked more than
ever it did before."

Saturday, May 10, 1890

7.50 P.M. W. on his bed—not asleep, however. Talked well
and freely. Harned came in after I had been there about 15
minutes. We stayed till 8.15. The gaslight being low when
Harned came in, W. invited him to turn it up. W. had forgotten the check. He advised me that he would have it for me
tomorrow. "I cannot find my loose checks." Gave him memoranda about Queen Victoria's birthday. "Curtz," he said, "was
here today, and he told me: the 24th. He is one of the curious
characters, full of the odds and ends of knowledge."

I had a letter from Bucke this evening. Starts Monday: will reach Cape May Tuesday, stay there Wednesday, for rest: will come to Camden Thursday. Wishes to meet me then. W. said: "I have not written him for several days, from knowing how near he was to the day a coming."

Father Huntington speaks in Camden tonight. W. knew somewhat of him, then of his interest in the Single Tax—adding —"and that to this day goes beyond my understanding." W. when questioned said: "I feel very well for me—though not out yet, to be sure. But then one can never tell; night before last I spent a good evening—easy, bright—yet suffered the night through—could not sleep—was as wakeful as I am now, talking to you and Tom. It is a dreadful sensation, to be awake and in any such condition."

Urged Harned not to work so hard. "Do not smash the golden egg," he put it, "take good care: now is the time to do it. I used to think it was a grand thing in old Brougham that though born sickly, or made so, he accomplished much because he dared to allot a part of his time absolutely to rest—to say, I'll work like hell for 9 months in the year, but for 3 I'll lay low—do nothing. And how his sleep was (even the night of [Queen] Caroline's crisis), a blessed sleep—the dream of life to weariness!" I asked, had W. himself some such power? "Yes—*some*—but no such remarkable development of it as Brougham."

Gilchrist in to see W. last evening. "He told me of a move—today I think—to Long Island. He has found a place there—he calls it Paradise: in reality it is called Center Point, I think. He has got hold of some farmhouse there—in an orchard—and rare sights I understand—and" with a laugh—"he has invited me up there for the summer. Yes, he evidently will stay longer in America than he intended: must in some way have come into a heap of money—perhaps from his brother. I think that after the publication of his book on his mother, his brother must have realized that the identity of the Gilchrist name rested with the mother and with Herbert—and he may have been constrained to more generosity. Mind you, this is only surmise. I have not had anything told me: it is plain however, that Herbert has come into money—perhaps he has sold his picture, in part or whole. He even speaks of keeping this home for two years. Five thousand pounds from a man like his brother (it would seem mountainous to us) would not seem particularly much."—"Perhaps the sister would come over too."

Had had a visitor today—a man he had known well when young on Long Island. "Yes: I have seen him off and on—but now, poor fellow, he is all wrecked from drink." Spoke of women and intuition: "Yes, by that faculty—that divination, which in the best women makes them superior to all philosophies."

Learned that Clifford would be at Harned's for tea tomorrow. If a good day W. would try to get up. "Is Clifford sure to be there? Well—I won't promise—I'll hold it open: in advisement. You remember the story I tell—the mistress and her hired man, to whom she offered a drink. His refusal was very diplomatic—'No, mistress, I'll not take any now.' . . . Leaving it to be well understood that he held it open for any future choice. So with me: I'll look upon the hour as eligible—upon Clifford as eligible—if no more." And to Tom's description of the larder—laughed—"That alone almost makes the argument conclusive."

Several visitors today. Said to me at one point: "The *litterateurs* of our time are after the artificial—mix everything: fear elements—the air, the wild storms, the sea. Even I often take a drink of wine in preference to cold water. It all indicates a deflection from the line of truth."

Sunday, May 11, 1890

5.20 P.M. To W.'s with Clifford and Harned. W. reading over a package of old letters, which he carefully re-tied and laid away on the table. Looked well—but had not ventured out—the day too chill. Greeted Clifford with special cordiality. Tom talked about Scovel's audacity in inventing interviews &c with himself. W. saying: "Oh! Tom! you mustn't mind that: he not only invents interviews with *me*, but writes letters and signs them Walt Whitman!"

Tom happening to pick up a copy of Munyon's Illustrated World, noted W.'s Osceola poem, which he had not seen before. This aroused W.'s memory, causing him to say: "The poem is given almost word for word out of conversations I have had with Catlin: Catlin, the great Indian man." Then, directing us to the picture of Osceola on the wall—the lithograph: "That is from life: a fine spectacle he makes, too! But Osceola was like a great many of the niggers—like Douglass—in being of mixed blood, having a dash of white, not pure Indian. His grandfather—a Scotchman or Irishman—with a dash of the rover in him, at one time either married or lived with a squaw—then the parent! And the parent disclaimed all his white stock heritage—kept up the chieftainly character. Osceola himself taking it all in as a part of the common air." He spoke of "the days when I loafed about the Brooklyn Navy Yard—knew the fellows there—tens of them—scores. And first from Osceola's surgeon, then from others, I learned that he literally died of a broken heart—died of the confinement, imprisonment." This brought up reference to O'Meara, Napoleon's surgeon, whom W. spoke of as "faithful, but not overmuch faithful"—part of his espousal of N. coming from hate of England—"which an Irishman imbibes as they say, with his mother's milk."

Had not yet found his checks. Returned me the Atlantic—in which he had read several things, among them an instalment of Holmes' "Over the Teacups." Not much impressed. Clifford's Hilda had remembered the apple W. gave her on the visit some time ago and now sent a message, that her love should be given him and another apple asked for! W. laughing greatly at the statement of it by Clifford.

400

Said that "Nowadays Mary will not let Jim Scovel come up at all—he is in disfavor!" Laughing—"Oh! Mary is invaluable to me in such matters—and Warren, too—but Mary, invaluable! The fellows come—they must see Walt Whitman: if only Mr. Whitman would see them for a moment! But no, Mary is inexorable—the Doctor has ordered that nobody see Mr. Whitman: Mr. Whitman is too sick, feeble, to be wearied by visitors, &c.&c. And that is her reception to interlopers." Spoke of Bucke's coming—that he had found his memory verified—"the Aldine at Cape May, and the man's name Mueller."

Monday, May 12, 1890

5.20 P.M. Stayed and talked with W. until 5.42. Had just returned from what he called "a fine jaunt" in his chair. Said he felt much eased: "I do not know what is the signification of the legal term 'easement,' but it seems to me a very good word for my own case. I certainly am eased: and the jaunt was indeed a fine one: remarkablest feature of all, too, that we have all this sun and balminess with a north-east wind which means usually to be cold, raw, perhaps damp, rainy. I was tempted often on the route to sit still, bask in the sun—though Warren protests—I don't know but rightly: for these or things kin are cause of my woe—at least according to my suspicions if not belief."

Addressing a letter to Bucke at Cape May, he started it—"Dr. Bucke of Canada." I said I was "sorry" he had not got up to Harned's yesterday—the dinner so good. He replied: "And I am sorry too, and mad. But I solace myself with thinking, well, now it is all over, I am safe here: if I had gone, eaten, I should perhaps have eaten, drank, too much, and suffered for it." This led him to say further: "Alice [Alys] Smith was here today—and I told her about the dinner—inviting her to come. She informed me Mary Smith might be here by that time—that some legal necessity would probably force Costelloe here before long—that they may pack up any minute—perhaps arrive within 10 days. How delightful! And the women!—that is one of my special points—to see them there. I would not enlarge: set a limit, then limit that limit!" And he said that "Now for the first time I feel as if I should be there with you—as if the dubiosity had been dissipated."

Referred to Vaux' candidacy for Congress in Philadelphia in re Randall, dead. "I have always looked upon Vaux as *outre*: a dare-devil fellow facing current customs—especially the customs of Philadelphia, in some respects the rigidest known in America: I can well imagine that a man born in Philadelphia—a man who *is* a man—looking about upon these restrictions—hating them with his whole soul—rebelling—should break bonds, dress as he pleases, as I understand Vaux does—more at his will, say his say, defiant to the last word of tyranny. And then in Vaux this independence is perhaps aided by money. I have never met him."

Refers to his "new lease of health"—doubts however "if for long"—but it "invites new tasks"—perhaps the Lincoln after all? But "the day is gone by when I dared any great task." Though the Lincoln not immense, he was doubtful if he was not "warned against it." The Critic spoke of Lincoln as *next* to Washington in the hearts of Americans, &c.—but W. objected: "We cannot really speak in that way: we should say, rather: there are two stars, two streams, two flowers, one not to be set against the other, both to be measured as fitting their spheres." Said he had "observed with pleasure" a notice of Brinton's new book in the Critic.

Had me mail notes for him—to Bucke, Gilder and his sister in Vermont.

Tuesday, May 13, 1890

5.15 P.M. W. sitting in his room—unoccupied. A black coat on. Greeted me warmly—saying then—"I am trying to recover myself: I have had an experience." Then: "I have been out—startled—dazed: but now am better: have had my meal—strawberries, chiefly, which have quite set me up." Then he continued, in more detail: "I have had a visitor—see—here is his card"—handing me however a card in W.'s own hand—this:

> "David L. Lezinsky
> 1607 Post
> May 13 1890"

"I wrote that off by way of remembering it. He has been here several times—four times, I think: he came twice—I did not see him—then again last night, again today. These times we talked together. I am very careful instructing Mary about strangers—yet never wished to turn them away harshly, having in mind always the possibility that they may buy a book"—laughing. "This man has proved himself in one respect by buying several books and paying for them. But he went on at such a rate about Leaves of Grass, I thought he was turned—he was wrong here"—tapping his forehead. "But when I put the question to Mary, she said, "He is sane as you or I." "The tone of the man—his startling propositions, all confound me. As I understand, he comes from California, must have money, has become possessed of ideas about Walt Whitman. Today he went off to Washington, to be back again in several days. Why, Horace, you have no idea of the exuberance of the man: he talks of buying all my books, of buying a share in the copyrights, paying me several thousand dollars, having me write no more but by consultation with him: a series of surprising stipulations. This afternoon he came in a hansom—quite a nice turn-out—insisted, the carriage was at the door—would I not ride a few minutes with him—and instantly we got in, he talked like a house afire—keeping it up, a constant stream. Between that and the flutter of the carriage—with a driver who evidently wanted to show off what he could do—I got completely dazed—my mind in a whirl. It was this I spoke of when you first came in." The coming of this stranger was quite news to me: we talked of it for some time. W. said: "I am quite willing to sell him my books: that is what they are here for." As to the man's insanity—"He is perfectly sane, however effusive." Adding in a humorous vein: "He seems to be badly bitten—the worm has got into him: it is a fire that has burned at least 8 or 10 days, I should judge. He seems to be Hebrew: what do you make of the name? I shall of course do nothing with him. First of all I want you and Doctor to meet him if he returns—to talk to him closely: it may develop the case more fully—explicate it, rather." Again: "He wants every book: even speaks of going over to Dave's to buy every copy he has—the complete stock. It is an amazing notion."

On my way to town this morning, I had met Bucke at the ferry, waiting for the Cape May train. Talked together 20 minutes. W. exclaimed—"Well—I want to know!" Adding: "And so you have seen the Doctor—the veritable man! That is a confirmation, an assurance, of the best order." I said, "One of Bucke's first questions was 'Will Walt write the Lincoln?'" W.—"No, I will not: I do not think I should dare undertake it." Adding: "Oh! that grip *has* grip of the worst sort: it is true I am to all intends rid of it, but I am not sure what development it is preparing me now." Said his letter to Bucke at Cape May had not been much. "Its main message was an enclosure of the last letter from Ernest Rhys."

Gave me Contemporary Club cards for my sister Agnes. W. also asked me to get him cords from Oldach—3—wished to send a big portrait to Elizabeth Porter Gould. Gave me a little note "to read to Oldach."

Wednesday, May 14, 1890

7.55 P.M. W. reading Scott: sitting with hat and coat on, the room very warm, a great rain out of doors pattering on the roof: his red handkerchief at the throat: using the gas towards the west instead of the usual bad chimney jet on the table at the other side of the room. Very bright—said his feeling of comfort continued. Had a letter from Bucke (as I had), who would not be up till Friday.

I had brought him the heavy paste-board for the photos. He inspected—was pleased. "That will take Elizabeth's picture to her, safe and sound. She seems to have some sort of collection of photos—a penchant that way. And this is one of the war photos—the hatted picture—1863: not the one you have, but the one Mrs. Gilchrist chose as the best *she* knew."

Check-book not turned up yet. Will give me the check "without fail" for Oldach tomorrow—"if I have to write it out. I have no prejudice against writing it out, but it is more regular the other way." Further said: "I have been out today—four or five miles down the pike: my unknown friend, or stranger-friend, it seems, left an order in Philadelphia that I should be so provided: so over it comes today—and I was glad to avail myself of it. I went down to the Cemetery—Harleigh: I want you to go there, too—see my lot. Ask for Moore, the superintendent. He will treat you well: he is an Irishman of the better kind: I like him. And curiously, he is the first man of the kind, in such a position, whose views coincide with my own. He is eager to keep the trees—to keep nature out there in her own character—not to have her spoiled, deflected. I think they wanted me to go in the open, in some prominent place, conspicuous—but I went deep in the woods. Moore is not bitten with the art-side of life: not sacrificed to that bane of all literary, artistic ambition: elegance, system, convention, rule, canons. In that respect he is our man."

Reference brought us back to Lezinsky. Said W.: "He has not appeared again: when he does, I intend putting him into Mrs. Davis' hands. I want in some way to fix it, too, that you and Dr. Bucke ply him in a long talk. No—no—I do not think he is anything but what he appears—my impression was a good one, favorable: the explanation of it all is, it is a bad case of Leaves of Grass. He seemed to have astounding ideas, plans, propositions. Not only asked to buy my whole stock of books—but the copyright as well. I told him I could not see that the copyright was of any value to anybody—though it might, after a long while, in many, many years, come to something. That I would not care to sell it anyhow. I am willing to sell books and books—but my freedom?" And yet he seemed to be in much self-questioning [as to] what the stranger was up to. Warren thought there was more to it than appeared, but W.—"No—I do not. He is perfectly sane—has a good clear straight eye."

Thursday, May 15, 1890

7.20 P.M. W. on bed—a low light in room—but not asleep. Greeted me cordially: said he was "wearied." "I was out today—the carriage came again: we went along in the rain: but I do not think it hurt me." Had not written the check for Oldach. Said: "I should be cuffed for my forgetfulness."

I do not like W.'s inclination to lie down so much. The warmer weather is evidently playing on him. A reporter from the Press came while I was there. W. would not see him; advised me to go down and talk to him, which I did.

Did not potter about at all. W. expectant in regard to Bucke's coming tomorrow. Said he had written him [B.] today.

Friday, May 16, 1890

5.20 P.M. Found Dr. Bucke in the room with W. W. Talk was animated. W. did not look over-well, but seemed thoroughly awake—not at all reserved.

We talked of the stranger—"the unknown," as W. sometimes calls him. "The coachman—the hansom man—calls him Lindsy." And—"That is just as he wrote the card—'1605 Post'—though what it means—whether army post, post-office, or street, I don't know." This in answer to our question. Then further: "I haven't the least doubt in the world but the case is just as he represents it: he has Leaves of Grass on the brain—it is a bad case. I did not of course ask, but if, as I suppose, he has fortune—and he spoke as though he had: had the manner of a man of the kind—a mere matter of more or less—the proposition he made to me—was nothing to him. If I am mistaken in him—if my experience of human nature leads me astray now, in a case of which I am so confident, then I shall never set up to judge again! The hansom came again today. I went out—but after we had got about half way to where I intended—the mist seeming about a foot thick—the rain falling—I advised him to turn back—though not making any feint or sign that way himself, he did turn back. Warren was also with me. The cabbie told me he had coached Lezinsky, Lindsy, off and on for four or five years. He comes in, making flying trips—as he did from Washington the other day: in Philadelphia to meet an engagement late in the after-noon, then back to the depot again and away to Washington. That is a sample of his methods." Again W. assured us: "I told him the other day I wanted him to meet you—also, Horace. In some way we must arrange for it. All my inclinations are to trust him. You fellows can get a shy: see how he measures up to you."

Subsequently W. said, half-seriously, half in mock-despair: "I have had unwanted news today—bad news—almost star-tling news: the Century has rejected my poem—the poem I sent the other day"—turning to me, because I had mailed it for him: "Ye Jocund Twain" &c.—"It comes with this note, which you might as well read"—handing to us a page and a half note—"My dear Whitman"—from Gilder personally—reciting that previous poems sent by W. would "help" him and were not so markedly personal &c. W. said: "You might take the poem along with you if you choose—though you must bring it back, as I never like to give matter away in proof—especially as it may still be sold—that somebody may buy it." We discussed the note, somewhat, W. saying laughingly—"It is bad enough to be rejected, just that alone—and by the Century. Yet they are not all friendly to me even there—Roswell Smith, for instance: he never has been. But Gilder? I have always counted on Gilder. I guess he wields a controlling hand—possibly, however, not an absolute one." And again: "I do not see that the poem is any more personal or subjective, though it is both, than others, many, perhaps all—which they have paid for and used. It may be that someone there has now woken up to the fact! This may be somewhat involved, too, but I guess not markedly so—not more so than others. All my poems require to be read again and again—three, four, five, six times,—before they enter into the reader, are grasped—filter their way to the undersoil." Bucke argued somewhat that the publisher knew the small comparative quota of Whitman readers—perhaps a few out of three-hundred-thousand—therefore from their standpoint were justified—but W. shook his head: "No—I do not see the weight of that: it does not appeal to me—does not explain the situation."

I suggested that he try the poem with Scribner's—but he looked dubious. Bucke urged it—then both—but he still shook his head. "I should get it back." Well, suppose you do, &c. "You mean that if I do not expect acceptance, it would be so much fat?" And again—"I shall not promise." I put in— "We don't want you to promise, so you send it!" And yet—"It will do no good—no good: they would not take it: I will get it back!"

Should Bucke come again in the evening? "Yes—say at half-past seven—for a little while."

Saturday, May 17, 1890

5.30 P.M. W. sat in his black coat, in his own room, reading Symonds' book on Dante, of which he at once spoke to me. "It is a new edition: Symonds has sent it to me. Look at the print—don't you think it handsome? An alluring book: personal, strong—a bit out of John's own big heart. After I am done with it I want you to take it and read it."

Doctor not down to see W. after I left with him yesterday afternoon. Too tired last night. Went to bed at Harned's immediately after supper. This morning gave me a few lines additional to make up his piece for the May Conservator. W. asked: "So you think he has gone away? gone home? [i.e., to Cape May]. Well—I have been sitting half expecting him all day."

I left with him a copy of the Critic. Curious about some Carlyle anecdotes I told him were there. Also left with him a copy of the Conservator which I had. "When will you bring the others?" he asked. And then: "Bring them in the morning—early as you can: then I can put them up at once: there are a lot I want to send off." Out today again. "The carriage was here: we went along up to Pea Shore: you know Pea Shore? And there I got out of the carriage and sat down awhile, looking over the water. Oh! it was a great day! I enjoyed it—breathed it in—bathed in it!"

I told him Doctor thought he [W.] ought to write something for my paper. He laughingly said: "How should I dare? After this, I shall not aspire to write anything—to assume that anybody wants my handiwork. After the Century has gone back on me I must take new bearings—see where I stand." Had he sent the poem to Scribner's? "No, I have done nothing with it." Wished me to point out the new paragraph in Bucke's piece, which I did. Then: "Doctor puts it strong, don't he? But then, as someone has said, when you have a statement to make, make it with full vigor, with all its implications: and Doctor seems always able to do that."

Of Rudolf Schmidt and American humor: "He considers it the raciest in the world, and so, often little characteristic bits I come upon I put up and mail to him." I asked W. if he had seen the piece in yesterday's Press. "'Walt Whitman's Grave,' you mean? O yes! It startled me when I first looked at it: I wondered if I was dead and buried!" The idea that London contested for his remains amused him hugely. I told him the fellow had said the lot chosen by W., which he had seen, was thoroughly "characteristic." W. then—"Probably it is: if his article had as much about it that was characteristic it would pass well!"

From Philadelphia Press . . . May 16, 1890:

WALT WHITMAN'S GRAVE

The Aged Poet Picks Out a Burial Lot on the Outskirts of Camden

Walt Whitman has chosen a spot for the final disposition of his body, when his life is ended. The place is characteristic of the man. It is located in Harleigh Cemetery, about a mile from Camden, and in the prettiest part of the grounds. It is a natural mound, beneath majestic oaks and chestnut trees, while about 200 feet below a stream of water flows over a precipice from an artificial lake. A driveway, which leads through the woods, winds within a few feet of the spot, and the boughs of the gnarled oaks are spread like arms over the hillock, and touch the greensward on the sides. Back of this piece of ground is the woods, where a footpath leads to the entrance gate.

Walt Whitman has been in poor health of late, never having fully recovered from his serious attack of the grip. Yesterday he was able to take a drive, but upon his return home he was prostrated with the exertion, and was unable to see any one last night. He confirmed the report of the selection of the site and the informant said that many persons had called upon him to make his selection of a burial place at Washington, Philadelphia, New York City and London, but he preferred to rest under the trees in New Jersey, where his friends might visit his grave unfatigued.

Harleigh Cemetery is a picturesque plot of ground on the Haddonfield Pike, beyond Kaighn Avenue. The grounds are level, no mounds being visible where bodies lie. Mr. Whitman was attracted to the spot and became attached to it while driving by during his recent convalescence.

Word from Kennedy, he said. "It was addressed to Doctor, but marked, 'Walt open,' which I proceeded to do. Nothing new: he speaks of the birthday—will not be able to get here: is working under great pressure—expects release for a while in July—then will be here for a day or two." I said I thought Kennedy was perhaps injuring his higher powers by this work. W. saying at once in the most earnest way—regarding me intently—"Tell him that! tell him that!" Adding after a pause—"I wish you would: the thought has struck me, too."

As I had not read Thoreau's "A Week on the Concord and Merrimac Rivers," W. thought I should. "You should take my copy—it is on the other side of the table there." I found it. "Though a little mutilated, it will give you the best of Thoreau—which is *best* indeed."

Gave me a portrait—the Lear—for Jacob Lychenheim: promised him many months ago—but forgotten till today, on my reminder. Had not yet sent the poem to Scribner's. Nor had the check-book turned up yet—I should bring him a National State Bank check from my father.

Sunday, May 18, 1890

10.10 A.M. W. had finished breakfast and was reading the morning papers. The day perfect—sun fine, air balmy. Would he get out? "Yes—but not in the carriage: the man is off today." Said—"I feel quite well: have eaten a good breakfast, with relish."

411

Left with him 50 copies of the Conservator. He said: "I shall send copies to Symonds, Sarrazin, Rossetti, Dowden—" pausing—"these, at least." Adding that he would keep a list, so I should know who had them. Remarked with considerable vehemence: "This starts my ire again: I think, here these papers will go to the ends of the earth for one cent—a mere sign [song], you might say. As a nation's (yes, an individual's) hearts are shown large in little things, the miserable pretense of our freedom is exploded by our patent meannesses. Yesterday I got the Symonds book—notice of it: had to pay twenty-five cents before it was delivered. Yet I can send a book straight through to Europe on the single postage: it goes direct to my man, unquestioned. And this tariff this time was very small, too—probably because they had no idea of the real value of the book. A while ago I had to pay a dollar and a quarter on a volume sent me from England!"

Spoke of the Critic as "a most interesting number—especially the Carlyle part. Which I have not been able to say of it for a long time." Expressed pleasure with Bucke's added paragraph. "It is very good—very: I read it last night. The Doctor is certainly developing a style—as direct as a blow, each movement of it. This piece impressed me as fine—finer than I had thought—frank, very radical. Yet as if saying all along 'I've more than this in reserve: this is not the end of my string.'"

I had brought him a blank check on the National State Bank which he filled in for me for Oldach.

Monday, May 19, 1890

5.45 P.M. In with W. about 15 minutes. In his bedroom. Black coat on. Told me he had been out in the chair yesterday: today in the carriage—in the latter "we went down to Gloucester—to Billy Thompson's. No, I did not get out: not a drop to drink." But of Lezinsky as yet no sign.

Returned me the Critic. "It is an interesting number—for the Critic: but not great: only above its average—especially the Carlyle matter." Gave me a list of 23 to whom he had sent Conservators—a curious list. "I shall send more—perhaps many." Admired its printing.

I spoke of my interest in Thoreau. Had read "Concord River" and "Saturday" sketches. W. remarked: "I supposed you would be seized: it is a seizable book. Keep it as long as you choose—forever if you choose. I don't believe I shall ever be moved to read it again." And then he said: "The mutilations are mine: I must have used the pages for something—it was long ago: I do not remember *what*. I liked Thoreau very much: yet there was something in him, as in his books—a superciliousness, a disdain, of civilization—which was extremely offensive to me."

Referred again to what I said the other day of *pressure* upon Kennedy: thought I "ought to write him about it—tell him frankly: it is fully as important as you think" &c. Particularly admonished me—"If you leave a note for Doctor at the ferry, with Ed Lindell, tell him in it to be here sharp at 2 tomorrow"—they having arranged for a drive together.

I told him our later idea of the birthday was this: to have simply a supper at Harned's for a family of us, and a reception later in the evening to which anyone could come. This would save seeming *selective*, &c. To which W.: "That is a piquant consideration: I like it, the best yet. An elaborate dinner is not like us anyhow—does not accord with Leaves of Grass. We must save ourselves [from] ridiculousity: that our friends may not misstate us." After the Club meeting tomorrow we have arranged for an informal talk between Brinton, Bucke, Morris, Williams, Harned and Traubel. Brinton acquiescent— Bucke to attend Club with that in view. W. said "I cannot promise to be present: I am not in the condition to promise anything: but if I can I will. So you can make your invitation cards contingent."

Referring to Gilder's letter again: "I did not send the poem to Scribner's. That letter is not all cleared to me by any means. Yes, it is a personal poem: but what have I ever written that was *not* personal? That is our meaning—that is the task we set—the journey we set out to make! I have the letter here still. Sometimes I wish I had kept that other letter—the letter from Holland: quite a long letter it was, too—covering several pages: superfluous and impudent and offensive in the extreme. In a fit of impatience—the moment's impulse—I threw it into the fire." Had it been kept, would it not have thrown some light? He thought so: but "there is no use discussing it now: the milk is spilled."

Gave W. receipt from Oldach.

Tuesday, May 20, 1890

5.20 P.M. W. in the parlor with Bucke, whom I found animatedly talked to by the printer Curtz: Curtz descanting on the history of American brands of pills. Bucke much amused. W. paying no attention—looking out the window, questioning and talking to me—except at one point when Curtz recited a pill poem, W. exclaimed—"Oh yes! that beats Leaves of Grass all out!" Just returned from a drive with Bucke. "We have been out to see my lot. Doctor likes it very much—but says he has a far better scheme of his own: another place where he thinks I ought to be buried." Which I found out afterwards, to be a grave on some knoll near W.'s native place, with no monument but a big granite boulder.

W. had told Bucke while on the road, that he designed a cottage somewhere out of the city, but near it. Only "nebulous," however. Spoke to me again of Thoreau. Only there briefly. Then away with Bucke, who thinks him somewhat improved. To meet B. again at W.'s (to go to the Club) at 7.30. Bucke staying with Harned.

414

Evening, 7.30. To W.'s just in time to see Warren helping him in from his chair. Bucke says, while supping at Harned's, a ring at the door apprised them, on opening, that W. was there. They then went down together. We went into the parlor: with us, a Miss Cline of Westmont, who brought W. a bag of bananas. W. talked with us freely—speaking of "Execrable names of towns," &c.—mentioning New York State's—then of "Glendale, Rosemont, Rosedale and the like—thousands of them—glens this and that—of the least consequential order." Thought we "secured no benefit by a desertion of Indian names."

Not feeling any the worse for the much outing. Threw up the window and put his hat on. His "Lincoln" not yet touched—"nor like to be," he says. Either feels or plays to feel much chagrined over Gilder's note.

With Bucke to the Contemporary Club; after the adjournment of which, Morris, Williams, Brinton, Bucke, Harned, Harry Walsh and H. L. T. went on to Boothby's, where we had our discussion and arrangement of the dinner. Decided to hold it at Reisser's (Phila. 5th St. between Market and Chestnut)—$3.00 a head.

Made up a list of guests; H. L. T. made secretary—Brinton to see caterer. To be held at 6 P.M.—our list including 25 or so; to be extended if need be or thoughts of new names arise.

Bucke gave some examination to W. again. Says though W. is comfortable—perhaps rallying some—that his pulse is unusually poor. But thinks he will easily be able to get to the dinner next week.

Lezinsky has gone west—W. expected the coach to stop but it continues.

Wednesday, May 21, 1890

4.50 P.M. W. eating his dinner. Appeared quite well. The hansom here today again and he out to Pea Shore. Speaks of how often in the old days he went out there in his own carriage. "I liked to drive down into the water—stand there: contemplate the sky, the city, the ensemble of things."

Enjoyed his meal, especially, as he said, "the berries and the rice-pudding." Wished to know if Bucke had seen my father's W. picture. B. much impressed—thought it reminded him of Eakins'. W. said: "I never thought of that—but I endorse all the rest,"—and then—"The great strength of both—as I have always said of Tom Eakins'—is, that the point taken insists on the truth—the utter truth—the damnablest: that the subject is not titivated, not artified, not 'improved'—but given simply as in nature. It is a healthy statement, coming after Herbert's, with the Roman curls, and the like." And then he asked my father's opinion of Eakins' picture. "He thought it a fine work?" Yes—"Very fine? Very?" And then to my father's one criticism—that the complexion did not do W. justice, his being the finest he had ever known, so pure and strong—"That is a point that never happened to me. But there is another—I have waited a long time to see if it would be remarked—if it was not only a fear—surely a mistake. But neither you nor Bucke nor Tom have said a word about it. Did you never feel impressed with the *blindness* of the eyes? It was something that came to me at the very first." And to my "no"—"Well, I guess there's nothing in it. Tom has a very keen eye and has made no sign of seeing it, nor Bucke, who is quick enough to see the ends of things."

Bucke has gone to Cape May. Will be up Friday afternoon. Mrs. Davis has been at W. to take tea with Bucke downstairs and has asked me in—W. consenting: 4.30 Friday, a doubtful hour for me. But it would be a rare day: he has eaten but few meals downstairs since June 1888. I detailed to W. the results of the conference last evening about the dinner. He questioned me closely—said: "No doubt I shall be there. Yes, if I keep as I am I may very easily get over the river."

I gave him my list—suggested several new names. "Do not

forget Johnston," he counselled—"and tell him to bring his wife or daughter." And "Melville Phillips, perhaps, though that is not imperative." Advised keeping the list down. The Flower Mission sent in a bunch of flowers while I was there, which W. took and scanned with joy, remarking especially "the daintiness of the mignonette."

Gave me a copy of Poet Lore for May. Had read Brinton's piece therein—"The New Poetic Form as shown in Browning." Had been "interested today in the accounts published of men sent, deputed—commissioned, to investigate cave-dwellings in the far west. It ought to be a fruitful theme—great in results."

Thursday, May 22, 1890

5 P.M. W. in his room, finishing his meal. Expressed his "comfort." Had not been out. "The carriage did not come to-day." Yet wished to know about the weather. "I am just now preparing to go—to take a trip in the chair."

I supposed he felt pretty certain of holding up to the dinner? But he laughed mildly. "I *expect* to get there; but there are 9 days yet, and I am not prepared to say I may not get one of my worst set-backs in the time between." Adding however—"But we won't work with that in view—rather, with the other." Expects Bucke up tomorrow.

Described to me a letter from Stedman—then gave me the letter itself. "You will like to read it! The good Stedman! What a revelation of depthless friendliness! He sends along with it a check for 25 dollars. I don't know whether he intends this for me or you—for me direct or for the fund; but I shall keep it this time. He says in there when we need more you should send him word—'nudge' him—but don't nudge him soon: I should not do so for some time. I have written him but did not say anything about the dinner." I read the letter—said the money was undoubtedly meant for the fund, but it produced

417

no effect on W., who simply said—"You think so, eh? Well, I shall keep it"—to me another bit of evidence to that partial parsimony which I observe in him of late—for he knows as I know that he does not need the money for his own personal use—that all the real heavy expenses attached to his present life are paid out of the fund. Yet, curiously, this parsimony does not extend to things. He not only tells me to "keep the Thoreau book—it is yours," but, today—on my commenting upon a big 1871 portrait on the table, said—"I have not many but you must take that one," signing my name to it at the same time.

I showed him plate-proofs of our Johnson book, which he looked at "with admiration," as he said—adding—"they threaten to make a handsome book." I read him an amusing passage from a letter from Morse over which he laughed with great heartiness.

"Tell Sidney," he counselled, "that we are not that poor, and have not yet made up with the dog." Adding—"It is interesting, how reporters go wrong as if by the most studied deliberation."

Friday, May 23, 1890

4.50 P.M. I came later than his dinner-hour (4.30), so as I entered the front door (usually unfastened for me) W., sitting in the kitchen, called out: "Here he is now! Come right in Horace—here is your place!" A good hearty meal then of chicken, potatoes, peas, strawberries, &c. W. partaking of all, helping me, appearing in the most cheery mood.

Had been to town this afternoon—in the hansom—with Bucke: going as far as the park and spending several hours on the trip. Bucke says W. gave the driver a dollar. W. himself much enjoyed [it]. Had noted changes in Philadelphia—the new big buildings which had "struck me with admiration"— and "The grass even more than the trees out there by the

418

river—oh! how they possess us! It is a gorgeous panorama!"

Bucke asked W. what he "had done with the poem"?—meaning the Century rejected piece—to which W. replied—"Nothing—it is upstairs, untouched." I told him: "Harned says he don't see why you are so damned thin-skinned these days, after what you have gone through, to care anything about it." W. laughed, Bucke said—"And a very keen remark, too,"—W. then taking it up—"I see. I did not take it to heart. Only it was pleasant to think I had at last got a medium—a means of communication—and the loss of that is what touched me. I suppose I should not have calculated upon it: Gilder there in New York is surrounded three, four deep with literary dogmatists—men who won't on any account consent to be dethroned, to give way—especially when by some uncouth fellow who comes lounging along, with less than a title even to a hearing." Yet he said again: "We are too sure of the throne to fear to be deposed by success or neglect. And trial by fire is not bad—it is not a thing to be got rid of. We may as well abide by it."

At mention of Ingersoll's possible coming to the dinner—"How good that would be! That would be a clincher—I think Bob would bring everything to a head."

W. talked of cable cars, electricity as a motor, &c. After the dinner we adjourned to the parlor, where Bucke and I stayed only a few minutes, Bucke asking—"You have had a full day of it, Walt?" "Yes—I think I have—very full." "That is what I thought: Horace and I will go now." W. said: "I did not mean that: I had other things in mind." He sat down by the window and we left.

Saturday, May 24, 1890

7.50 P.M. W. in the parlor, hat on—a shawl on his lap—the window closed, and he remarked the coolness of the night.

Spoke of his poem and "note" to the Queen in today's pa-

419

pers. Had appeared in the Press and the Ledger. He said: "I sent it to the World and Herald, too." Had it appeared in them? "I wonder?" He did not know. "The papers printed them quite accurately. Yes: I have them on slips, too: you shall have slips if you choose." And further: "I have wanted for a long time to say something to this effect of the Queen to bear my testimony; for it is a sentiment that involves a good deal. Not many realized to the full then, or could now, as I did, the gravity of that situation, the tact and excellence of the Queen in relieving it."

We spoke of the dinner. I had received a letter from Johnston today saying he could not come. W. said: "I had a visitor today, introduced by Johnston. In the note Johnston told me the same thing." Josephine Lazarus wrote me to the same effect. W. regretted. She said (to my question) she could not tell me who "The Lounger" was in the Critic, nor who had written the favorable Whitman reviews: she thought the main part of that routine was done by the Gilders themselves.—W. exclaiming: "Then 'The Lounger' must be Jennie Gilder, who has experienced, perhaps not a change of heart, but a new dispensation, an awakening, a fresh birth." He continued as to the dinner: "I would not apply to anybody to attend—have it quite in bounds—only 15 or 20. I take it, this dinner is a good deal like my Lincoln lecture, which I did not write because I thought I had anything new to tell, any striking antitheses to set up, but because I felt the world needed a reminder, that I needed to write it—the [?] right to read it. And so it was done. The dinner's importance is in there being a dinner: we want to hold it—to confirm our preparation, our attitude." Said he was particularly sorry Johnston could not come because he "wished to see Kitty," and hoped Johnston would bring her.

W. remarked again: "Our fellows must make great, big, generous, comprehensive, satisfying allowance for Gilder— for others like him, there in New York—crowded upon by a howling mass of literary fashion, who hate Walt Whitman from their toes up—will have none of him—would stamp him out, stay him, tread him down, as a growling fire. This feeling has no doubt protested with Gilder, pressed him. He is situated there as Emerson was in Boston."

Mrs. Davis was in the room, and W. desired her to "go upstairs—bring me the red book on the foot of the bed for Horace." After she had brought it, W. said: "Yes—I have read it—a part of it—very carefully, especially the Heine. The Heine is not as good as Arnold's—both are good but Arnold's the better. In fact I think the Heine the best thing I know of Arnold's,—though on the whole I don't think Arnold has any particular message for us—for America. This is the book of a young man—a college man—not of an old stager. The Whitman is very good—at moments very penetrating, having flashes of pure insight. It is not all through the same—here and there he fails." Bucke had thought Ellis put W. "the top of the heap," but W. said: "I do not think so—I rather feel that in America he gives Emerson ascendency, if he indicates it anywhere—which, belonging anywhere, belongs to Emerson. But he don't speak of it that way—brings it into other connections, rather." And he added: "But read it—read it well: see what you make of it." Adverting again to Heine— "He is not done justice to. If only we could get a life of Byron and Burns and Heine in which all is told—bad and good, light, shade, everything,—there would be a biography worth while. We have such a life of Burns, in a way—he tells everything himself—but of the others not." Morris had told me of a guest at a dinner, who, between John Foster Kirk and Horace Howard Furness, asking judgment as to what constituted as accurate biography, received for Kirk's answer—the absolute truth, every fact; Furness', that the shade should where possible be left out. W. considered—"Kirk has hold of the varmint's tail."

Asked me about the portrait he had given me other day.

421

Did I not see an intellectual cast to it? "And is that me? I am inclined to doubt. It is more in position than anything else." Had read Stoddard's paper on Boker in Lippincott's. "It is full of venom—not venom against Boker but others—and in that spirit. I don't think he understands Boker or turns his good side out with the bad. He is like one who makes much of the piano tunes in a man's life—of his fingerings of things, and failing to mention the supreme strophes, the essential ingredients. Biography cannot be written that way."

Thought "William Cary and Robert Underwood Johnson, of the Century, might be invited to the dinner if several more names were required to fill up" because "I count them good friends." Am to take down to him in the morning Morse's medallion of George Eliot.

Sunday, May 25, 1890

10 A.M. On our coming I went upstairs (I had taken Morris Fels with me) and found that W. had stayed up late last night talking with Warren—therefore later in rising than usual, only now washing, and no breakfast yet. So I went down and we waited in the parlor. Shortly he sent word down for us both to come up. We were there with him for 15 minutes.

Showed him the George Eliot [a bas-relief clay medallion]—which he held at full length of his arms and commented upon admiringly. "That certainly must be very fine. How clean cut! It is a beautiful piece of work. Morse is surely improving and improving. How Dantesque the features! It is clean, pure, strong, through and through." Laughed about "Professor" Morse. "It is a strange sign in Sidney's career, to be sure!" The other day he had exclaimed laughingly—"The simple Morse, dubbed 'Professor' at last! It is a spectacle to be cherished!" Asked about the weather—does not expect the carriage today. Gave us slips of yesterday's *Queen* poem.

Today's Press contains paper of Gladstone on "Labor." I

asked W. if he should read it—knowing he would not. He said: "That is one of the questions I carefully avoid—rarely any more read anything about it. There are ten thousand solutions, but I don't know of one solution out of them all that in any way meets the hour, shows the way out. This question is like the Irish question—there are two interests conflicting—strings pulling two ways—the one all Ireland, all for Irishman, who know nothing but Ireland—the other for the British Empire—that compact of vaster interests touching all parts of the globe. Indeed, it is our Indian question repeated—which has interests purely for the Indian, interests then of the whole body of states, leading to the largest results. In the meantime the poor aboriginals, so to call them, suffer, go down, are wiped out."

I remember this further of what W. said to me of Ellis' book last night: "What is the significance of descanting of Emerson and Thoreau under the head 'Whitman'? Why not with heads of their own?" And again—"He speaks of some Burroughs piece on Thoreau: I wonder if I have ever read it?"

We left shortly: his breakfast ready. Mrs. Davis just preparing to bring it up—she had come into the room as we sat there. He at once asked her about some headache she had suffered last night, adding to her smiling rejoinder—"Well Mary—I'm glad it is gone."

Monday, May 26, 1890

7.55 P.M. W. in his room, reading Lippincott's: light high up. Not very well: said he had had "a bad day"—had "caught cold."

I had for him three beautiful dark roses, out of our own ground, sent by Agnes. He held them in his hands, smelled them, regarded them, a long time—remarking: "They seem to me the most beautiful I have ever seen: as specimens absolutely perfect. The thought will come, did they just *happen* so, or have they deeper, deepest reasons for being? Yes—yes—that is the seat of all our questions—the wonder that makes us all our mysteries." And by and bye he would have it that I take an orange to Agnes as "recognition and remembrance in turn."

Spoke of "bad news"—viz. "a letter from Alys Smith, who tells me she cannot come Saturday—that her examinations are near, her studies imperative, and so on." In a little he continued: "The thought has come to me, if we had not better abandon the whole project." But why? "Well, you must not be Socratic—must not ask why." Further on, however, explaining: "I confess that the thought arose out of Alys Smith's letter. And between you and me, I don't think that letter quite satisfies me—no, it does not."—"I had quite calculated on Alys, and her default—the default, anyhow, of most of the women—excites my reflection—may prove to have a significance." I could see he was disappointed—he had made such a point of it. I explained that Bush would come over from New York. This appeared to cheer him. Adler had written that he would be far west by Saturday, (en route to Denver) else he would be with us—W. saying: "Whatever comes with the yes and no of others, I feel the truth and honor of Adler's: I trust every word he says." As to some of the "boys" in Philadelphia who might attend—"If there are vacant chairs, let them come: it would be well." No word yet from Gilder, Stedman or Ingersoll. "I guess we will get on all right—reach the end of our voyage *some* way—it is a thing I leave in your hands."

Bucke comes down tomorrow from Telford. I had a note from him today. We referred to Ellis' book. W. remarked: "The thing that most impresses me is the daringness of the man: he has his beliefs and will say them. And if I may say it, besides the scholarliness they betray, they have a mathematical quality—a tendency to figure everything out into evident outlines. The Heine essay is of the same order—more mark-

edly so, if anything—the mathematical exactness there, too."
I said the essay had to me strikingly set off the Sarrazin essay,
to which W.—"I can well see how it should—how it does to
me also." And further—"The great point is to have judgment—a new point of view, as this undoubtedly is. And this
is a vigorous man, too."

Found on the table another Washington photograph, unmounted, which he said I should take if I cared to. "Mount it
on cardboard—get your father to—then bring it back to me
and I'll put my name on it."

Tuesday, May 27, 1890

5.10 P.M. W. in his room. Just concluded dinner. I took him
the local papers from the hallway, for which he expressed
gratefulness. He was out today in the chair—the carriage for
the present having ceased coming. "Bucke came at half past
twelve: we left him here when we went out. He is now on his
way to Washington. It seems to me that Bucke, who came
here to rest, is not resting at all—that he is driving things
harder instead of easier—what is more, shows signs of it. As
I look at it, it would have availed him much more had he
settled at Cape May—taking advantage of all it has to offer—
and it has much to offer—is a paradise of a sort. Now he goes
to Washington, to con over O'Connor's manuscripts! God save
me from such work! It is awful work to piece together another's manuscript. The writer himself has an *idea* of connections which a stranger has to study out, *worry* out, through a
mass of appalling discouragements, difficulties. To me it is a
bête noir. There are several reasons why I should never have
it to do—in the first place, because it is intricate and laborious, in the next because it is just this black beast." And yet—
"I suppose after all it is part of the Doctor's purpose in being
here to know how his irons (and he has many in the fire) are
coming on." And further: "We have not seen particularly

much of him this trip, though today our talk was rather more full than any others: mostly of Ellis and what his book brings up—Arnold, Heine, and many other such matters."

I wondered if the other essays in Ellis' book (I have only so far read the Whitman) would not help me to an understanding of Ellis' point of view? "No—I don't think so: it is all there in the Whitman—perhaps the Heine would help you some, but no others."

Suddenly he asked me: "Did you see the Record this morning? According to the Record I am dying. I suppose I am, in a sense, dying: but I have been pretty sick these past six years, and the past two badly sick: so that I do not see that it needs to be remarked upon now. I have had many ups and downs—usually an up for every down—though I suppose some day I'll get a down from which I shall not recover. But so far I have escaped fatal harm, the sun has inevitably come out after the clouds—and here I am. It's all Adam Sloan's work"—as I understand, based on the Camden Telegram article of yesterday afternoon—"and of a piece with Sloan, without a doubt. And yet even he ought to know better. He has been here half a dozen times—knows my friends, atmosphere, *entourage*, (or should) and a thousand and one of those indirections by which a story is known better than by what are called direct testimonies. Yet he writes this way!" At one point the report says: "Whitman never was of a robust physique"—W. laughingly saying: "What stuff! Why, that is the very point we travel on!" Already two reporters had been here today, to one of whom—"a large-eyed, nice looking youngish boy, from the Times—I have talked. God knows how it'll turn out—one can never say!"—"To the ordinary reporter—the lower orders—the samples we mostly meet with here, the word that Mary may have said to Sloan, or Tom, was sufficient, with the money impulse in the office, to fill a column. Sloan probably plead[ed] very hard to see me, and Mary no doubt was quite decisive as to my condition."

WITH WALT WHITMAN IN CAMDEN

From the Philadelphia Record, May 27, 1890
WALT WHITMAN ILL
The Poet Succumbing to Old Age
and Feebleness
HE'S CONFINED TO THE HOUSE
A Familiar Face Missed in the Streets of Camden—
Preparing for the Final Scene

That Walt Whitman, the "good, gray poet," is failing—and rapidly, too—is a fact patent to all of his intimate friends. Yet the fact is being kept from the public through regard for the aged poet. Whitman is extremely sensitive on the point of his own physical welfare, and any allusion to his condition brings forth confidential expressions of his buoyancy of spirit, yet ill-concealed admission of weakness.

The weather during the past few weeks has been particularly distressing to him, and he has been unable to leave his house to breathe in the sunshine and the light he so loves. His rolling-chair became a familiar object on the streets of Camden for a few weeks this spring. Every day or two the picturesque figure of the great, shaggy beard, blowing in the breeze, the huge white hat and the limbs snugly incased in a heavy woolen shawl, was pushed along on the sunny sides of the streets by the sturdy young man who acts as the poet's body servant. On every hand the wheeled chair and its famous occupant was greeted with great respect, children whispering to each other as it passed:

"That's Walt Whitman."

The chair has not been seen on the streets for weeks, and inquiry at his residence on Mickle Street is met with the answer that Whitman is suffering with a severe cold, and that he is not at all well.

71 YEARS OLD

Whitman will be 71 years old on Saturday next, but it is doubtful if he will be able to attend the quiet little dinner arranged to take place as a celebration in this city. A few of his most intimate friends and admirers have arranged the affair.

Lawyer Thomas B. Harned, the poet's close friend and counselor, reluctantly admitted that Whitman is failing rapidly, that a marked physical change has come over him, and that his friends are

427

just beginning to realize it. Whitman was never of a robust physique, and of recent years he has been feebler than ever. Dr. Buck [Bucke], his biographer, is spending a good deal of time with him now, and he, too, admits that the famous man is nearing the end.

Counselor Harned has at his office in Camden Whitman's curious will. It was drafted by the poet a year ago, and has been regularly attested by Mr. Harned. It is a singular-looking document, and no one save the poet himself—not even his counselor—knows what it contains. The paper upon which it is written is ordinary foolscap, one sheet pasted lengthwise on the other, and the whole tied with a piece of common wrapping yarn.

But "whatever all this," he had been down to the river, and felt "already set-up from yesterday's cloudland"—adding: "It makes me less inclined than yesterday to call the dinner off!" I had a letter from Ingersoll, saying he would come over "if possible," and would let me know positively in a day or two. I should write to Ingersoll, telling him not to regard these reports if they reached him—W. advising me: "If you do so— say to him: 'I was an hour ago with Walt Whitman—we had a good talk together—he sends his best love and affection, and hopes you will come over'—or something to that effect, putting it as near my way as you can." He supposed Ingersoll would "finally say *no*, as all the rest are doing,"—adding however—"I know if he does, it is from necessity, as being a very busy man." I had a letter also from Arthur Stedman, stating his father's absence from the city &c.—for health—had left even before W.'s letter of last week arrived. W. spoke of Stedman's sons—then of how he "always liked the wife." He was also intensely interested in a letter I had from Mrs. Fairchild. "She always moves me deeply," he said. Appearing to be rather serious from the number of those who refuse to attend the dinner.

Again—in a tone full of music—"You have no idea how much good Agnes' flowers have done me: I want you to tell her so: I have taken them up again and again. They are singularly beautiful specimens in themselves; they came at a very opportune time. Last night and this morning I was not feeling well at all: and these—color, odor, all—perfect it seems to me—appealed to me direct. It is interesting, the little things that will serve to overlay a man's troubles. Beecher, they say, had a resource—he loved gems—at times when he felt blue, despondent, he would look at them, handle them, and they set him right. They were in a little pouch or box, which he carried with him:—and he was known to stop in at some house on the road—the house of some intimate—ask for a room—explaining that he wished it for rest, and for only a brief space. One such time his host, after 20 minutes or so, went into the room, fearing something was wrong—and there was Beecher—sitting: his chin on his hands—the gems spread out before him—intently regarding them. Then he explained. The story came to me in that way— is perhaps not strictly true—yet is illustrative—not improbable. These roses from Agnes have had an effect like that upon me."

Warren brought in some mail—for one thing a couple of copies of the Springfield Republican. "I guess they have the Victoria piece," he said, "I sent a copy to them." As turned out to be the case. "The Republican has always been friendly to me. Talcott Williams hails from Springfield."—And then by some reference to T. W.'s connection with the Press: "Of the man Calvin Wells, and that other, Charles Emery Smith, I care little—I think they amount to little." Remarked that "the lyingness" of the average reporter "invites the application and adoption of the Tennysonian epithet—"the reporters in a loomp are bad!" Mrs. Davis told W. she wished for nothing to do with them. W. putting in—"Nor do I."

Having made some reference to the Broadway Tabernacle in New York W. said: "Though it is gone now—torn down— destroyed—and no sign to place it any more, yet for me it lasts, will last, as one of the most emphatic memories of my early life; I had much time then—little to do—and was often there. It was the speech headquarters of the abolitioners of

the time—of come-outers of all shades—I delighted to hear
them, they were so dead in earnest—many of them such fine
specimens of men—Phillips—and there was Clement M.
Clay—and others. Yes, Burleigh—him I remember well—a
grand looking man—hair parted in the middle, curls. Often I
would hear the roughs, the enemy, in the meetings there;
they would say, 'Here he is! here is Jesus!'—in derision. No,
it was not imitation in Burleigh—it was his own natural physiological self, expressed in perfect port."

W. said he had been making his meal "off of strawberries,
mainly" and "good they were for an old fellow—and a young
too?"—looking at me and laughing. Adding: "But I had a mutton chop, also—and that reminds me: I had among my friends
in Washington, many curious fellows, whose habits and ways
were a constant study, entering by more ways than one into
the sinew and marrow of my work. Gebrowksi [Gurowski?]
was one—but I do not mean to speak of him now: I have in
mind an old commodore—a peculiar old codger—he took his
meals in a restaurant I knew well: was given to mutton
chops—liked them—yet, never at one time ate more than
one. His directions to the cook, or waiter, were singular, emphatic: he would say, 'Now, I want you to bring me a mutton
chop for breakfast—mind what I say, *one* mutton chop—not
more'—here W. raised his finger admonishingly, looked at me
over his glasses—"*One* mutton chop—*one* mutton chop—not
a fibre more!' And then in the morning the man would after
all bring him a good full plate, three chops instead of one,
and the old man, his ire up, irascible to the last tone, would
cry out, 'What does this mean? Did I not tell you to bring me
one chop—but *one* chop?' 'But Commodore, this is the system of the place, the way of the kitchen: you would be
charged just as much for one as for three. And, Commodore,
you are not required to *eat* the three if you don't want to!'
But the commodore was not appeased. 'Damn you! it's not
the one or the three, but I want you to obey orders!'" W.
laughed in great humor, then: "Nowadays, when Mary brings

me up my chop, she will say—'I remember Mr. Whitman: *one* chop!'"

I read W. a letter I had received from Burroughs. The last sentence, "I am fairly well, but not buoyant," excited W.'s smile. "That is characteristic of John as he is these days—a lugubrious output, of a certainty." And then: "You are right, he has no right to such a humor: John has grander eligibilities—basically is of better stuff: this is the new crust of him. Oh! there is no doubt but that he has been tossed thick by that New York crowd—however little he knows it himself, tossed thick: very few escape it. I know what it is—know it well: most of my years were passed in some sort of contest with it. And I know that the bitterest enmity I have had to contend with is there in New York. O yes! there has been a change in John, and that is the reason. I think, know, O'Connor realized the change but not the reason. It is the change that will come over a poor girl of finest impulses, cast into the society of gossipy, mean-minded, libidinous women—effected, not knowing it—though that is stating it severely. Or like the case of the nobler men who study theology—whose religion goes well till it comes upon that rock of a damnation for most of the earth—is then wrecked—then itself goes to hell: *hell*, the lie of ages and ages, to me the impredenliest[?] horror dared by men's lips. I do not know that we are right to such comparisons with John, but I give them as in a way illustrative. Probably John's change does not manifest itself in his writing"—I put in—"Perhaps only in subjects—more literary and theological." W. then—"Yes, that John should take account of—especially the theological, which is enough to damn any man!"

Wednesday, May 28, 1890

7.30 P.M. W. on bed—dressed, of course—but not asleep. Not out today. Felt bad. "If the dinner was tonight," he said, "it would have to to on without me"—but he smiled and added—"But it is *not* tonight—these are usually *not* bad bad nights: somehow I seem to crawl out in season every time."

Read him notes I received from Julian Hawthorne and John Boyle O'Reilly. "They are fine!" he said, "both fine! They sweeten an old fellow's bones, ease his aches!" And perhaps they would be good "paragraphs" to print "sometime" if "the spirit moved." Though W. was perceptibly disappointed at the many "impossible" friends, he now said: "If Ingersoll comes, he will make up for all the rest: but I suppose he won't." I refused to give him up. "To not hear is a good sign: he is thinking about it!" I said. W. then: "I guess you hit it there—and we *will* wait." Asked if Bonsall was home? Then answered himself—"No I am sure not. He might come."

Said he had sent Warren over to Weir Mitchell, "to get some points on massage, or learn from Mitchell of some one who could give it to him." Adding, "Warren is rather set upon learning it, and I encourage him. There are none too many massagers, as I call them—especially male massagers,—nor good male nurses, for that matter. Yet no men are more needed, more important."

I expressed regret that the Springfield Republican had enclosed the Victoria piece in other matter, and managed thus to weaken it. W. said: "What you point out is true, every word of it—it is the ineradicable habit of editors to make things different from the way they are written. The point anyhow was, to print the poem on the 24th." Spoke definitely of his condition. "This seems the turning-point—whether for the grip or not remains to be seen: I feel on the borderland, not knowing which side I may be faced."

Referring to Ellis again and expressing some disappointment in the Heine essay, W. asked: "Did you say you had read Arnold's Heine? No? I have it here—you should take it—read it." The Times note had turned out [to be] an inch, no more. "Which does no harm anyhow. My theory is, that the boy wrote it out fully enough, but [it] was not accepted beyond this length."

432

Thursday, May 29, 1890

5.45 P.M. W. in the parlor—had been out in the chair today. Looked much better and felt better. Had with me a copy of Story's "A Roman Lawyer of the 2nd Century"—which W. said he had "never seen" but would like to read. I therefore leaving it.

Knowing I was reading "Diderot," from Ellis, he shook his head. "It is not deep—not penetrating." I expressed the feeling that the book as a whole did not reach my expectations— that it was too literary—not enough above average criticism. W. thereupon: "That is a just view—I share it fully: except at points he does not rise to the occasion. It is the rock upon which some of our best fellows split—the too-literariness of structure, tendency. These things can never mark our men— the Leaves-of-Grass-ers—those who believe in primary human emotional qualities first of all—the elemental juices, so to call them."

No word from Ingersoll yet. W. said: "It is too much to hope for a good word." I put in—"No—the delay itself proves to me that he is trying to come." W. then: "That is the hopeful view, anyhow: let us hold to it!" I specified to him the list of names as so far known and he appeared well satisfied. "The whole drift of things as you have managed it—described it— appeals to me: it is an expression of youth, of hope, of trust, of belief in our future, our cause—oh yes! all that and more!—Brinton and Bucke old? No! the spirit of the dinner is all young—as such commands me! For my pleasure it could not have assumed a better form." And further: "As I have been sitting here the last few days, the thought has come: 'What can *I* do for this occasion—what word, utterance, idea, feeling, express, contribute? What can *I*? Tell me?" Further— "This will undoubtedly be my last public appearance—" I interrupted laughingly—"Like the farewells of actors? You always seem to come around again, whatever your fears." He laughed very heartily and after being composed again—

433

"That's funny—but Horace—you little know how near my consciousness it is that what I say is true—that this is my last—that there comes an end, and here are we, *near* the end! And I know you would say then, all the more reason why we should retreat gracefully, with the best force and tact that is in us! Now, how shall *that* be?" I had suggested the other day, his writing some lines, printing and distributing them, if the spirit moved him: but he has not done that—"My condition has been against it." Now he asked: "How would it do for me to select a couple of lines—print them on cards—enough for the diners—signing and dating them myself?" Which idea after discussion was decided on. "I cannot promise it," he explained, "I cannot bear to be urged—but we shall see." And as to what two lines—"*any* two lines—they are easily found— the only point being that they are not *in*appropriate."

Gave me a copy of the big book to give to Jennie May— just married to Sam Fels—which I transferred with Anne's and my greetings added.

Later Thursday, May 29, 1890

Down to W.'s again at 7.25 P.M. About 10 minutes after leaving before, Warren had rung our bell to hand me from Walt—a telegram just received, to this effect—

"Will be with you Saturday evening. Tell Mr. Traubel." This [from Ingersoll] took me to W. again, whom I found gone to his own room, sitting with hat on, a fire started in the stove. He admitted he was very much pleased. "It is the best news of the week don't you think?" he asked—and further—"With Bob will come a whole host: he never goes unattended!"—a high estimate—and—"What is in a man will come out—if not in one way, then in another. In Beecher it came out in ecclesiasticism; in Ingersoll, in much higher form, in anti-ecclesiasticism—in both, naturally"—and—"The good Bob! He has us in his soul, too! It is a triumph we have scored—who knows but a triumph for *him*, too!" He thought: "This will tickle Doctor and Brinton, I guess—particularly Doctor, who longed for it but did not expect it." Bucke will be up tomorrow. I did not stay longer. Left with W. the June issue of Current Literature.

Friday, May 30, 1890

10 A.M. W. eating breakfast. But shortly up. Not looking well or seeming well. Thought he had had a chill last evening. This the explanation of the fire there in his room. But better now. Said: "I do not despair of the dinner even yet. Yet it is not impossible I shall be kept away." And—"Ingersoll is our best card—it is marvellous the way the prospect of having him here sets me up!" And further—"The evidence seems to be accumulating at last in our favor."

Why did the Russian government not touch Tolstoi? "It would start in the whole civilized world a cry of indignation. Those fellows, who dare everything, would not dare touch him." He "endorsed" "every word" I said of Ellis &c. "I don't feel [drawn] to the Diderot at all: it is an indifferent piece of work. Ellis is not our man, though his evidence is significant."

I went to Germantown in the afternoon. Discussed with Mrs. Baldwin, arrangement of the table, which Bucke endorsed in the evening, in our talk at Dooner's. Bucke over to see W. today: thinks that a good deal of W.'s present trouble is from incaution in diet. Left with Mrs. Davis some instructions.

W. said that if the dinner was tonight he could not attend, but that he "always has a way of coming round to events"—and expects to this time as at other times. I have entire faith in his presence tomorrow.

Saturday, May 31, 1890

Day cloudless; temperature mild. I did not see W. till his arrival at Reisser's at 5.30. Had arranged with Bucke for him to come over with W., as he did, Harned and his wife along. Morris and I met at Reisser's preliminarily at 5.25. Gutekunst would have prepared to take flash picture had he not been notified too late (today). We put cards on the plates. The table spread almost the length of the big room.

The first to arrive were Brinton and Frank Williams. After, the hosts floated in, one after another. Ingram with Johnson's daughter, Bertha (who late in the night, on going, W. kissed)—&c. &c. By and bye Bush, who did not know anybody, but asked for me—a fine, strong, youngish man—whose coming and whole trip was a refreshment to me, as to him.

When W. himself came, the Chef and his big German assistant put their arms about him and literally carried him upstairs, he with his arms slung over their shoulders. A picture not to be forgotten—his face, with its rich color, strikingly set off by his light hat and garb. Brinton remarked—"His legs are not much use to him any more." W. went into the cloak-room at the back—sat there and held a sort of informal reception, one after another coming forward to be introduced, or, knowing him, to say a good and familiar word. W. extremely glad to see Bush, when I introduced him. Mrs. Baldwin brought in some wild flowers from Germantown—which I put in water and placed directly in front of W.'s plate, he much enjoying, and taking them home at the end. Later on, standing near the doorway, I saw Ingersoll come up, looking about curiously. Addressing him and introducing myself—he regarded me—saying heartily: "Is this you, Traubel? I'm glad, happy, to meet you Traubel!"—we chatting awhile there—Ingersoll going then with me to the back room, passing to W., who was very hearty. "Well Colonel—I am glad you came over: it was good of you" &c.—passing some courtesies of that order—Ingersoll then floating about the room. Corning, introduced to Intersoll as a Unitarian minister, I remarking, "I go you one better."

There were no formalities anywhere—perhaps one or two dress suits—(Ingersoll's open vest notable) but no more. I suppose there was a pretty acquaintanceship struck before we sat at table. In arranging the table, my idea was, to get those together who knew each other and would adjust well. Then, when the time came, we suggested to Boyle and Frank Williams, that as a committee they support W. to the table—this being well done, and causing the easy transition of the diners to their proper quarters. The tables looked well. The full list of diners was 31—4 of them women—W. much applauding this "tinge"—as he called it. W.'s appearance at this juncture rather weakened. I questioned him—had his "yes"—then ordered him champagne. (It must not be forgotten here, that all W.'s provisions were furnished from the money sent me weeks ago by Mrs. Fairchild.) The champagne revived him much—exhilarated him. He joked about its not being enough—yet would not have more when asked. There was on all sides quick geniality. Soon all were conversationally grouped. W. had at the start much talk with my sister and to Morris, his proximate friends at the left—afterwards to Frank Williams, at his right. Ingersoll for some time discussed affairs with Bucke—then Mrs. Baldwin exchanged cards with him and he turned her way, proving just as free one as the other. As might have been supposed, this was the center of the room. For a long time I could not hear what W. was talking about across the table. He and Ingersoll were simple as two boys in their ways. I heard W. at one moment speaking of the "damnability" of something in a raised voice—then again damning something (laughing, too) outright. Ingersoll's damns happened also. No one else would have dared, yet in these, the tone &c. seemed to justify. Ingersoll had much to say of Shakespeare—W. finally getting interested and himself participating. At one time Bucke and Ingersoll fell into a loud discussion—Bucke intense, Ingersoll quiet, smiling, positive. W., to some of his assertions—"Do you say that, Colonel?"—

and—"Oh Colonel! that is very striking—very profound—and [well?] said, too! I have never heard it so well said before! But is it true? is that all?" W. after "that hidden something back of the plays—unwritten: what is it? I know it is there, yet I do not know what it is." Ingersoll, however, taking the simpler explanation of their spontaneous narrative—but W. shaking his head—"No—no—no: I feel something below all that: I could not outline it, but I am aware that it exists." Ingersoll not liking Epictetus for "I do not like the slave virtues, and he preaches them." W. much interested in that.—Conversation just so free.—Three or four times in the course of the evening there were sorties of this kind, at which speech at other parts of the table lapsed and attention was general. Ingersoll and W. discussed Bacon—Ingersoll not inclined to put first value on him, W. rather assenting to such tribute—whereat I.'s strong explanation and W.'s assent that "they *are* strong—great," yet did not fully convict him. Several hours went in this sort of colloquy.

After the food, when the coffee was on—I suggested to Brinton to call for remarks—perhaps Ingersoll at once? Brinton proceeded opportunely, after a little—rising in his seat, gracefully alluding to the informality of the occasion, and asking Colonel Ingersoll if he did not have something to say. The Colonel was quickly up on his feet—pouring forth then a talk of 55 minutes (timed by my sister—though Walt thought it 40 or so)—rich in warmth, eloquence, grace—and simple. While he spoke W. pitched his chair back, folded his hands across his stomach, regarded him intently. The scene was memorable—sometimes touched by a ripple of laughter, again by tears, again to awe-filled admiration at some powerful stroke. The Colonel's voice was melodious in the extreme—his words simple and direct—his illustrations vivid—the whole speech cast in form of poetic cadence. Several times W. interrupted him. "Do you say so, Colonel?" And—"Great! Great!" It was a striking enumeration: after each quick point of review, Ingersoll facing W. direct, throwing out his hands, and saying—"And I thank *you*, (or *sir*, now and then) Walt Whitman, for that!" It was an apostrophe to freedom, an appeal to Whitman's democracy, a plea against respectability, a picture of spontaneous life as contrasting with artificial methods in letters and thought. W.'s interruptions were free—to one—"Do you say so, Colonel?" Ingersoll responding "I do, and I say further" &c.—this flowing into the speech as if a part of it. After he had sat down, there was a few moments' hush—a benediction: it had been a wave of great influence passing over us all. Then Brinton stood up— said some brief word and called on Bucke to follow. Bucke, however, full of feeling, doing no more than respond that he was no speaker, that in Walt Whitman's presence and after such a speech as we had just heard, it was not fair to call upon him. W. very hearty—had exclaimed when Ingersoll sat down—"Oh, thank you, Colonel! that is the greatest summing-up I have ever had!" And when Bucke was called up— "Yes, Doctor—let them hear you." Subsequently came Harned, Talcott Williams, Weir Mitchell, H. L. T. W. greeting each one in a simple characteristic way—"Yes, there's Tom: get up, Tom"—and—"Talcott: Talcott ought to say something"—and nodded Mitchell's way in *his* turn, and to me gave an approving "Tell them what you can, Horace," as I rose. In the midst of Harned's speech he interjected five minutes of his own talk—saying at one place (as to Harned's reference to last year's celebration)—"I recognized that for all it was worth—it was a great occasion, a testimony, word, from near friends, from neighbors—the man next door, across the street: an offering of affection. It was great, great—surpassed all that had gone before; but as that surpassed others, this surpasses that: especially"—looking across the table and waving his hand towards Ingersoll—"especially counting in with this the Colonel's statement—the fullest I have so far known—the most generous, unforgetting." And later he gracefully said to Ingersoll again—"Since the great ticket the Colonel over there has given us."

When Brinton introduced me (I hoped he would leave me out, but my fear that he would not was justified)—I spoke to this effect: I could have little to say—I felt as though this was a battle we were in; I had remarked to Bucke the other day, that while the battle is on, combatants do not turn historians. The time has not yet come for me to bear my testimony to Walt Whitman. When it did, I hoped to do justice to the magnitude of that influence, both as it touched the world and affected me. At the mention of "testimony," W. waved his hand across to me. "That's so, Horace—the time has not yet come. Soon I will be gone, will be in my grave, passed away—then in many, many years you will say your say, deliver what remains out of these present stores." And then, while I stood up, waiting—he went on, depicting his own aims. "Often," he said, "it is by the things unsaid, rather than the things said, that give importance to speech, to life. I have kept the roots well underground. Leaves of Grass, be they what they may, are only in part the fact—for beneath, around, are contributing forces, which do not come out in the superficial *exposé*,"—and so on generously, to effect such as my notes day to day discover. After he was done, I said, "No one knows better than I know, Walt Whitman's admiration for what he calls the transcendental spirit of modern science, and in no man in America is that spirit more generously embodied than in Dr. Brinton, who sits at the table here with us tonight. I therefore call on Dr. Brinton to say something direct," &c.—as so far he had not done, only moving others forward with exquisite delicacy and himself keeping in the background. Brinton thereupon spoke. I should not have forgotten above, either, what was said by Morris and Frank Williams—both greeted, as were the others, by W. W. on Brinton's call. W. W. halted in one of his own talks to say:

"But I must not be garrulous—this threatens to lead me far away."

Then when all hands were at their ease, the speaking done, Ingersoll and Whitman got into a famous colloquy about immortality—the heavens—the purpose of life &c.—in this Brinton joining to some small extent: Bob brilliant, eloquent; Walt firm, picturesque—oracular. "Oh Colonel! Colonel! Colonel! do you say that?" he inquired at one time. The Colonel if not negative, doubtful; W. affirming—giving his illustration of the locomotive (see the account in the Camden Post of June 2nd.)—the talk in noblest temper on both sides. Some of the retorts famous—as when T. Williams turned in his speech to Ingersoll and said: "Perhaps in the future world our friend will be surprised to find himself in agreement with Christ," or words implying that—to which W. quickly—"Perhaps Christ will be as much surprised to find himself agreeing with me." And when Brinton was skeptical, [as to] whether the animals fear death, Ingersoll instanced the roach— "Which, when chased and in fear, will never pause, if pausing at all, on the light spots of the carpet."—W. seemed most drawn towards the Shakespearean and Immortality controversies, questioning and speaking freely enough himself. At one point in Ingersoll's speech, when Ingersoll spoke of his preference for the love of pure womanhood above the love of God, W. said half under his breath, yet so we could all hear— "Bold, bold, bold!" It was a striking picture, as the controversy on immortality seemed warmer, the chairs moved closer, till clustered about Ingersoll or Whitman all sat with chained attention within a closer circle. In the end Brinton went back to his point of the table—and declared the dinner adjourned.

After that Walt was not long in getting away. I slipped around and asked him how he was. He had talked till he was hoarse. Some of his friends pressed forward and shook him by

441

the hand. Sulzberger, whom I introduced, said he thought he was a veteran, and all the others were young, for he had read the first edition of Leaves of Grass in 1855. W. turning to me as he was led off and saying—"And he is, too." At the door he turned to me—"Where are my wild flowers, Horace?" I going back to the table and getting them. On the way to the door again, Ingersoll put his hand on my shoulder. "I want to see you a minute, Traubel." "I'm going to take these flowers to Whitman." "I know it, and that's why I want to see you"—drawing me aside—taking a roll of bills from his pocket—counting out 5. "Does that make 25 dollars? Yes? I cannot see without my glasses." And then when I put in my "yes"—he added—"Give them to the old man and tell him they'll help him out of some of his scrapes." I hurried downstairs—W. already halfway—plodding. When in the carriage I gave him first the flowers—"The exquisite wild blossoms," he called them—then gave him the money with Ingersoll's message—to which first he laughed—"Did he say that?"—following [with]—"Oh the good Colonel! Good to the last!" Further I asked him how he stood it—how he felt. "Well, here I am: I feel tip-top—more alive if anything, than when I came." Soon was driven off. Several fellows came up to the carriage for a final hand-shaking—Ingersoll, Talcott Williams, Bush &c. Finally the carriage drove off, Harned and his wife, with Bucke, along.

I went upstairs, got my hat and went to the cars with Mrs. Baldwin. With fine intuition she said: "I won't let you go home with me Traubel: you ought to be back there with those men: I can get along very well." Had this not been her wish, and had I not gone back, a great experience had been lost—for when back, though Ingersoll had at first thought of going home in the midnight train, he was there with a cluster of fellows (had been persuaded back) in the back room: Morris, Brinton, Ingersoll, Bush, Traubel, Buckwalter, Sulzberger, Smith, Frank Williams, Edelheim, Schelling making up the

party. We were there till 12.30, some smoking, others drinking, some doing both. Ingersoll took a nip of whiskey, but not
much, going most for Apollinaris. Insisted likewise in give me
5 dollars for the dinner. We sat there till nearly 1—amid the
happiest fire of social wit and wisdom I ever knew. Ingersoll
evidently in his element—communicative, free, eloquent.
Here was all his secret: to talk on his feet as he did to us at
his ease sitting here. Anecdote, theology, what is idealism—
what is poetry &c.—all up. Many of Ingersoll's bits stick to
me—among them this: "Every true poet must keep his stern
within six feet of the earth: all true poetry is winged somewhere between Shelley's skylark and Burns' daisy: go above
the skylark and you get among the gods and angels: and no
human heart was ever moved by them; get below the daisy
and you come into the region of dragons and devils: and no
human heart was ever glorified by fear." To Ingersoll Walt
Whitman was great because he stuck to the human &c. Much
discussion of immortality. While we all sat there, near 12,
who should come stalking back but Bucke! He threw down
his hat, took his place in the circle naturally—was there till
we all left.

Ingersoll gave some marvellous Shakespeare quotations—
analyzing differences between French and English drama:
the French the drama of *type*, the English of *character*. Also
recited the first three verses of Whittier's John Brown poem
in a way that made Morris exclaim—"I never thought much
of that poem before, but you make it sublime tonight." A brilliant fire of question, quotation, analysis. He did not think
much of Tennyson—"he is a one-tone poet: if I were to express him on color, I should say he was grey"—and when "In
Memoriam" was instanced, he shook his head—"it is all on
one string: all good-byes, I'll see you again, farewell" &c. And
so was Whittier such a poet, in one color. Shelley to him "a
vast sea"—Keats' Grecian Urn ode "a perfect bit"—but Byron, after all, the greatest English writer since Shakespeare—

443

and so on—impossible to follow. As we were about to go off together, Ingersoll said—looking around the circle that sat there, easy and composed—"Boys, I believe it has done the old man good to come over: it has probably done us all good to meet each other face to face. It has been a great night—a night none of us can forget." We then all sauntered up Chestnut Street together, Ingersoll going in at the Girard House. He shook hands separately with us all—in saying "Well— good night to you all," adding—"I live at 400 Fifth Avenue: there's not one of you would not be welcome in my home at any time. If you come to New York, do not forget me." And so it was good night: a night fervent with comradeship, under fair skies and happiest results. Who could have arranged it all? It came because it must. My efforts had all been to get the diners there—all else admirably took care of itself. We all parted in such happy enthusiasm.

Bucke's coming back happened thus—he got on a Market Street car at the Ferry—at 5th Street Frank Williams got on—had to take the train. Bucke, learning we were there yet, got off at 6th Street.

W., enviably unforgetful: when leaving the room asked Weir Mitchell about *massage*, which Warren is wishing to learn scientifically.

Sunday, June 1, 1890

10.10 A.M. Down to W.'s with Harned. Bucke already there, as arranged for with me. Had come in to say good-bye. W. appeared to be what Bucke called "all tuckered out." Voice hoarse, eyes rather heavy, in a state of general lassitude. Still, he reported himself "all right," spoke of last night as "a great night"—and "Bob was our feather: he beat the record." Bucke remarked to me [afterward?] that nothing better manifests W.'s weak condition than this result (passivity) of last night's event.

We talked of many things—W. of the dinner mainly—called it"the greatest happening of a line of happenings" &c. His farewell to Bucke very manly, quiet, pathetic. To me "Good-bye for the present, boy."

He has not abandoned the idea of getting up cards for the guests—"We will talk that over," he said to me; but to have got them up yesterday would have involved too much of a hurry—I cannot be urged." There was a reasonably good account of the dinner in the Press, which W. had read—better in the Inquirer. Times account accurate in the main, but brief.

After Bucke had left W.'s with me, we went to town together—the Dr. to his hotel, I to a meeting—coming together again at 12.20 at Broad street depot, Bush there and going to New York with Bucke.

A good-bye that touched me—for I feel it will not be long before B. is summoned for the last act.

Monday, June 2, 1890

8 P.M. W. by the parlor window, which was closed, though the evening was very warm. After he had greeted me he said, "I can't get over Ingersoll's great speech: it was the culmination and summing-up of all." And again—"I could not get over it, therefore wrote about it—and what I wrote is in today's Post: I sent it there." Then advised me to "see that the boys get copies." Further—"I should like it myself—and of course it might just as well be known that the piece is mine"—which, though unsigned, does not need this telling.

Asked how Ingersoll was to be addressed in New York. Then spoke of the champagne at dinner. "It was the finest I ever tasted—but I feel short of my measure of it—some one of the waiters must have confiscated it, or a part of it. Some rare brand, stowed away somewhere for select ends!" Yet— "I suppose I got as much as was good for me—am probably in better condition for not having all that was my share!" Said he was "recovering" his "poise somewhat"—had been "shaken" by the event—"but I feel a sort of triumph in it."

Would think over the matter of the cards. Spoke of Leaves of Grass as "under ban in Russia"—"perhaps blacked out, as Kennan describes it"—which was "not surprising—would be surprising were the case other."

The Ledger today contained a notice of the dinner.

The account from the Camden Post of June 2, 1890:

INGERSOLL'S SPEECH

He attends the Celebration of Walt Whitman's
Seventy-second Birthday

Walt Whitman is now in his seventy-second year. His younger friends, literary and personal, men and women, gave him a complimentary supper last Saturday night, to note the close of his seventy-first year, and the late curious and unquestionable "boom" of the old man's wide-spreading popularity and that of his "Leaves of Grass." There were fifty or sixty in the room, mostly young, but some old or beginning to be. The great feature was Ingersoll's utterance. It was probably, in its way, the most admirable specimen of modern oratory hitherto delivered in the English language, immense as such praise may sound. It was 40 minutes long, in a good voice, low enough and not too low, style easy, altogether without mannerism, rather colloquial (over and over again saying "you" to Whitman who sat opposite,) sometimes impassioned, once or twice humorous, amid his whole speech, from interior fires and volition, pulsating and swaying like a first-class Andalusian dancer.

And such a critical dissection and flattering summary! The Whitmanites for the first time in their lives were fully satisfied; and that is saying a good deal, for they have not put their claims low, by a long shot. Indeed it was a tremendous talk. Physically and mentally Ingersoll (he had been working all day in New York, talking in court and in his office,) is now at his best like mellowed wine or a just ripe apple; to the artist-sense too, looks at his best, not merely like a bequeathed Roman bust or fine smooth marble Cicero-head, or even Greek Plato; for he is modern and vital and veined and American, and (for more than the age knows,) justifies us all.

We cannot give a full report of this most remarkable supper (which was curiously conversational and Greek-like) but must add the following significant bit of it.

After the speaking and just before the close, Mr. Whitman reverted to Colonel Ingersoll's tribute to his poems, pronouncing it the culmination of all commendation that he had ever received. Then, his mind still dwelling upon the colonel's religious doubts, he went on to say that what he himself had in his mind when he wrote "Leaves of Grass" was not only to depict American life, as it existed, and to show the triumphs of science and the poetry in common things, and the full of an individual humanity, for the aggregate, but also to show that there was behind all something which rounded and completed it. "For what" he asked, "would this life be without immortality? It would be as a locomotive, the greatest triumph of modern science, with no train to draw. If the spiritual is not behind the material, to what purpose is the material? What is this world without a further Divine purpose in it all?"

Colonel Ingersoll repeated his former argument in reply.

Tuesday, June 3, 1890

5.30 P.M. W. in his room. Had not yet been out—though he "hoped" to "get out in the cool of the evening." On the table a big bundle of Posts which he wished me to send off for him—tied up by a fatty string. Also, a postal to Ingersoll, thanking him for "coming over" for his "speech" for "the money." Said he had "sold a book to one Sears," at some distant point: writing, as precaution, for acknowledgement of receipt of the book. Returned me Current Literature of which he had read Gossip of Authors and all corresponding matters. As per my promise to Bucke, I urged W.'s preface to O'Connor's book. "I have not started yet, but I shall do it—I feel it a religious duty."

Again and again he said: "I *enviges* you your after-talk with Ingersoll"—and when I gave him some specimen blocks of it again—"It must have been great—it has a significance I cannot evade." Adding then—"He is a child—a child of nature"—

447

and again: "I hardly supposed Ingersoll was such a fine sample of a man—a fine physiological as well as spiritual fellow." And further: "And after all that is the whole secret—to *be* a child—to be simple—to take no intricate ways to accomplishment."

Had kept a list of those to whom he sent copies of the Post—which he showed me. "They are most of them abroad"— explaining—"I shall probably send off a good many more— add them to that list." Was "perfectly willing to stand by the record given Ingersoll." "The whole evening" was to him "an astonishment—a revelation. Such a spontaneity—such good heartiness—and climaxing all, such a speech—oh *such* a speech!"

Laughs repeatedly over "the minister, Cake"—who "out-Heroded Herod in coming here"—proposing—"communal marriages, in a way—in my parlor—the profits to be divided between poet and priest!" And he laughs over it with great zest.

Wednesday, June 4, 1890

6.10 P.M. W. reading. Had "had an outing today"—"Lezinsky's carriage appears on the scene again!" Had written Lezinsky at Butte City, Montana—sending him also a copy of the Post.

Bertha Johnson and Ingram in to see W. today. W. wrote postal to Bucke. Is to select for me the lines for the card. Day very warm—in the eighties. W. would not "confess judgment," he said, on his health!—"and yet it's not what it might be cracked up to be." As we sat there he suddenly lifted his hand, as if to catch its first indication—"Ah! I feel the just palpable sign of our early evening breeze—that sweet after-balm of our hotted days." Adding that "it is very sweet to me—I enjoy it here, out of the tops of the trees"—pointing at the trees out of doors.

"The run of things these days," he said again, "is to monotony—don't you find it so?" Gave me a little bundle of mail
matter to take up to the Post Office. Will let me get out the
card my own way.

Thursday, June 5, 1890

5.30 P.M. W. not out today—had not ordered the carriage
over—too warm. Complains that he is at too great discomfort,
going out in the hottest hour—prefers his chair "in the cool
of the evening—by the river" &c. Warren in the room when
I entered, explaining to W. the result of some experience with
a massager in Philadelphia whom he is consulting for instruction. Had seen Weir Mitchell—W. very much interested—
repeated the result to me.

Laughingly referred to Ingersoll's picture of current poetry—"little birds twittering on boughs"—called it "mostly
right," but added—"There's more to be remembered, too.
Sometimes the truest notes are struck by the smaller tribe—
the thrush, surely—I don't know but even the canary—the
imprisoned canary." And so also of Ingersoll's distaste for
metaphysics: "I can realize that—sympathize with it—but
there's also another side: whether the metaphysics, taking the
true not the formal sense of it, does not finally filter down and
down, through the mass, till all the race is impregnated—
enriched—farther seeing."

A picture in the Century of Ford's Theatre—as decorated
on the night of Lincoln's assassination—took W.'s attention—
inducing W.'s extensive comment on the Museum that now
works the structure. "I have not examined the picture critically: I don't know just how accurate it is—but I know the
place well. I have had a drawing of it, made by the architect
Bloor, New York. I remember well how angry he was with
me for passages in the Lincoln lecture—passages in which he
thought I did injustice to actors, theatres—which he con-

449

tended were always and anywhere as good influences as any."
Then W. spoke of the "high value" of specimens in the museum. "The government got hold of it—it has been faithfully
held to its object" through the "rare fidelity of the doctors"—
who, as he knew them in the war, "were a rare class." I questioned, "How rare? Markedly above other?" "Yes—without a
doubt. No one knows better than I do the importance of those
men. I fell into that sort of intercourse from which nothing is
withheld."—"We hear much of the generals—nothing, practically of these men. Of the usual city doctor class I do not
think much, but of these special men, sifted for the great purposes of the army, time, I have the biggest admiration. I
could illustrate by a case: the case of a young fellow suffering
from diphtheria: it was a serious case and a serious moment.
I urged it on one of the doctors there, a young man, to bathe
the patient's throat with a mixture of sweet-oil and chloro-
form. What did I know about it? It was an uncommon,
homely remedy. 'I know nothing about it,' said the doctor,
but added—'No matter for that: I shall try it at once'—which
he did and relieved and finally recovered the man. It was to
me a rare example of receptiveness. The typical good doctor
of the army, than which I know of no better, probably on this
globe, united rare sacrifice with deep emotional, sympathetic, qualities—would adapt himself to conditions—was
never a medical dogmatist. It is a beautiful thought, the history of which has to me a spice of sacredness—a glimpse of
high, however unheralded and unpretentious achievements."
And again—"Speaking of those war-surgeons—the thought
arises, if situation does not sometimes make a fool great." And
he spoke of "their more [?]al quiet records, known only to
professional men, and not enough to them. Oh, the doctors!"

Friday, June 6, 1890

5.20 P.M. W. just finished dinner. Weather continuing very
hot, was not out today. Had a copy of Pall Mall Gazette con-

taining the Victoria poem. W. liked "its appearance there much."

As to physicians spoken of yesterday, said: "I have often resolved I would some day record my testimony: I feel it in me to do so. I have already by brief passages hit the thing—but no, not satisfactorily. I must in the end find a fuller statement. There is no class—from their very quiet and reserve—which we are so like to forget, pass over."

Examined Harper's Weekly which I had with me. "It is a great sheet—each picture a wonder: a dish for days and days. And the best of it all, a dish which the masses can afford to order. It leads inevitably to the democratization of art—a tendency very marked, a democratic extension already seen on every hill top."

Said to me: "I had a letter from Ingersoll today—a good letter, called forth by the paper I sent him—a manly letter, full of him as he speaks, simple, throbbing, big-hearted, direct." And adding that he "supposed the signs were palpable," that W. W. had written the Post piece, "by the statement of qualities, one on another—cataloging they call it—if no more." But he could not find the letter, look as he would—across the table, on the floor &c. Finally gave it up. "I will save it for you when it turns up—it's here somewhere. Not a new letter anyhow, in the sense that it adds anything to what the Colonel said yesterday." Then he went on to tell me that he had selected the lines for the dinner card—turned around—took a "complete" W. W. from the floor—opened the book at a place marked—laughed outright—"Why—here is Ingersoll's letter, turned into a marker for the book!"—as it indeed proved to be. "Put it in your pocket," he said, "it will appeal to you—the great Bob!" And—"Here are the lines. How will they pass?"—pointing to the two last stanzas of "Salut au Monde!"

Salut au monde!
What cities the light or warmth penetrates I penetrate those cities
    myself,

All islands to which birds wing their way I wing my way myself.
Toward you all, in America's name,
I raise high the perpendicular hand, I make the signal,
To remain after me in sight forever,
For all the haunts and homes of men.

He thought the best report of the dinner was in The Inquirer, of which he had got a number of copies and sent away.

Weeks ago he had inscribed a soft copy of November Boughs for Buxton Forman—missed it among his papers and did not send away. I have seen it a number of times on the floor. Today he asked me to mail: had packaged it. Also gave me papers for Gilchrist. Has sold several books this week. Complains of the day, that "it has been a bad one—not one of my worst, but a bad one decidedly."

I had mounted the portrait he gave me last week, which he now autographed. "It is the original of the Linton," he explained. I liked it better in some ways. He affirmed—"And by a true instinct too. In a copy of the sort the hand of a master may get much—strike in a few bold lines here and there—enrich, expand. But for all this he loses something, too—the photo has somewhat that he fails to retain—this has even befallen Linton, master though he be." Then—"The photographer was George C. Potter—I think he is now in Philadelphia—not a Leaves of Grass man, but friendly to me. I liked his mother much—he was a young man then." Advised me to go to see him.

W. has a postal from Bucke. Bucke sent me a diagnosis of W.'s condition.

		Insane	
Mem	*Private*	Asylum	Lindon
		Ontario	London, 4 June 1890

Within the last three weeks I have seen Walt Whitman five or six times. Had not seen him before since Mch '89. I find him a good deal aged within the past fifteen months. His general health remains very much as it was at the earlier date, and I do not think his paralysis has increased but he has lost strength—and especially the organic functions (those presided over by the great sympathetic) have failed. His increased weakness makes it appear as if his paralysis had increased, but as I say I do not think it has. His pulse is not nearly as good as a year ago and he is not able to bear as much in any way—both mind and body tire out more easily. His general condition is such that it is impossible for him to rally from his present feebleness. He may remain a few months or even a year very much as he is now but his life hangs on a thread which may break at any moment and it is about certain that should he live another year his condition at the end of that time will be much worse than at present. It is not likely that he will see another 31st May.

R M Bucke

My dear Horace

The above is of course *strictly private* not to be shown to *any one*—if I did not *know* that I could trust you as to that I would not write it—I reached home at noon today in good shape and find the folks here all well. Write me very soon and tell me how W. has got on since I left him—has he rallied from the dinner?

Your friend

R M Bucke

Saturday, June 7, 1890

Not in Camden—did not see W. Weather grown finely cooler. Good for W.'s condition, always lowered in days of extreme heat, as those past.

Sunday, June 8, 1890

10.10 A.M. W., after finishing breakfast, sat reading the Sunday paper. Had a pansy—yellow—in his hand, which he passed to his nose repeatedly. "Oh the beauty!" he exclaimed, and asked me—"Do you know what the wise men call the prevailing cosmic color?" And to my response "Yes—yellow"— he assented—"Yes—a yellow, with a tinge of brown." Then

"And I can see why it should be that."—"The wonderful intricacy, yet simplicity, too—of this little flower, passes all one's sense, leaving him only awe." Said he had been out twice yesterday—once in the carriage, once in the chair.

We advised about the birthday card. He endorsed my plan—to print his verse and signature on one side of a big green card, and on the other—menu and list of guests—writing between these latter the name of the particular guest to whom each card is sent. He said: "Let us follow your idea—make the obverse of the card simply statistic—say, with this line at the head"—dictating carefully—"Birthday Dinner to Walt Whitman by his friends, May 31, 1890, at Reisser's, 5th Street, Philadelphia."

W. then gave me "a circumstantial event"—as he called it, laughing. "It is the phrase of some one."—"What an incident Warrie had yesterday! Did he tell you? Well, I will tell you. It was on the boat—the ferry-boat—he met a fellow there who took him for a greenhorn, which he is not: a fellow not of very bad size—not of good, either—who came up to him—offered familiarities—passed himself off for a pugilist—had backed this man and that &c &c. He asked Warrie to feel his muscle, which he did, good-naturedly—finding it anyway utterly flaccid. Then the fellow asked him about the time. Warrie had his fine gold watch with him—(he has two, this the best)—with a sailor's freedom, took out his watch and complied with the man's request. So they talked and sat together—tete-à-tete—it was a curious episode altogether—Warrie not at all fearing—yet, while not deceived, not thoroughly suspicious, either, though not to be taken off vigilance unawares. By and bye, looking down, Warrie felt the chain dangling against his legs, no watch. With a flash of intuition he knew instantly *why*. Warrie quickly asked the stranger—"Where's my watch?" "Why, in your pocket, of course." This, however, appearing to justify Warrie's suspicion, now full up in arms—it was confession. Warrie instantly, no time lost, took the scoundrel by the throat—planted a blow between the eyes—knocking him over—then giving him a few violent choice sailor-oaths. As the man fell the watch slid out of his pocket. Instantly a crowd collected—advised him to arrest the man, but he said, 'No—I have the watch, that is enough.' The admirable thing about it all is its spontaneity, its inspiration—illustrating a sailor's concrete insight, instinct. You know Bruno's maxim? It was: Doubt, doubt, doubt—but Bruno in this case would have been out of place. But Bruno spoke for other conditions. I endorse Bruno—he is my man— our man: his maxims, too. But the beauty in Warrie's case was, that it was a swift result—came of something deeper than self-debate."

Monday, June 9, 1890

5.50 P.M. W. in his room—reading the Post. Out in his chair today. "A bad day," he said, "a bad headache the day through." Looked dragged out. No carriage yesterday or today: had directed the man to come Tuesday or Wednesday.

Times half-column yesterday (evidently from Jim Scovel)— made up bodily almost from the birthday book. W. explained: "There was ten dollars in it—that was enough: those fellows need no other inspiration."

I got the menu from the *chef* at Reisser's and left manuscript for card at Billstein's. W. "curious to see how it works."

Looked over the German Democrat one-and-a-half-column printed on his birthday (I had it with me). Questioned me with respect to its tendency: "Is it good? Is it favorable?"

Tuesday, June 10, 1890

5.40 P.M. W. reading Scott—poems. Very much better today, though not out. Weather warmer. Warren brought in a couple of letters and a paper while I was there. W. read the former, one of them being from Bucke. "Doctor writes, but nothing new. Still speaks of 'Harrington,' which Mrs. O'Connor

gave him—is reading it." Was it true, as Bucke put it to me—
"I am more and more convinced that O'Connor gave up all
for Leaves of Grass." W. was dubious. "O'Connor had a great
deal more individuality—his own *self*-ness—than even Doctor knows. Yet in O'Connor there was doubt, too—doubt of
his own performances—and this was a deterrent force."

Expects Kennedy here "after the 7th—he shakes off his
shackles on that date." Left with him Scribner's containing the
2nd. instalment of Bartlett on Millet. "Everything about Millet draws me—is a magnet. Even the simple ingredients, out
of which came such wonderful results."

Gave me a pamphlet by Schelling, containing two essays
on Browning, which he had "looked into but not read."

Wednesday, June 11, 1890

5.20 P.M. W. in his room. Not yet out. Very warm—up in
the 90s. Looking over his own big book—open before him on
the table. Had read Scribner's—"much attracted"—and "Mrs.
Davis has it now—I wanted her to read the story 'Jerry.'"

Showed him proofs of the card. Was perfectly satisfied with
my arrangement of it. Some defects in the verse, for which
another proof tomorrow. Left him Harper's Weekly. "I shall
like to look at it: I am always anxious to see all that is written
and done, not so much to read, investigate, all, as to know
what is transpiring."

I had a letter as follows from Ingersoll this morning, written
in reply to a request the other day.

LAW OFFICE
Robert G. Ingersoll,
   45 Wall Street,

                          NEW YORK, June 10, 1890.
Horace L. Traubel. Esq.,
       Camden, N.J.
My dear friend:

   Most people have peculiarities. One of mine is, that I cannot recollect any speech I have made. It would be impossible for me to give even an outline of the remarks I made at the Whitman banquet.

I can write out an address, putting in as much as I remember in making up the balance. How would that do?

With regards to yourself, and to Walt Whitman, I remain,

Yours very truly,

R G. Ingersoll

W. read and was much taken with it. "You told him to give you *that*? Good! That is the right word in the right place. Anything from him, to the effect, would be a crown for us." I had said to Ingersoll, "not for publication," but W. insisted— "I should not have said that—there are very many who would like to see it. I have just had a note from Kennedy, asking for some full report. There are glimpses of it in the Inquirer— but how poor, how thin, all that to the reality. I do not suppose the Colonel would object to our using it." "Ingersoll was our Kohinoor: he topped our gems." And then: "It was a great event. I was much—most—interested—in the marvellous spontaneity of the man—how his speech bubbled out, apparently by no effort, yet to sublime results. It has always been one of my chosen delights, from earliest boyhood up, to follow the flights particularly of American oratory. I went into the courts—when there was a good preacher about, went to church—heard all the best specimens of Southern speaking— the big lawyers, Senators—Congressmen—but none of them brought such conviction to me as Ingersoll—the speech that night at the table—such suavity, ease, suppleness, capacity— such power to say, yet not to appear to know all the gravity and wonder of his power. It was a revelation—brought me conviction of many stray thoughts, observations—was in itself confirmation of my philosophy, if I may be said at all to have a philosophy—of the doctrine to keep close to nature. Nature follows close upon the mood of the mind that contemplates her—is moody as it is moody, bright as it is bright, laughs in its laughter, weeps in its tears. And this, written large in Ingersoll's manner, established for me his pre-eminence—justified him as it did us."——"It is a vast gift—too vast a gift for mathematicians to measure. Great speaking, what we call great speaking, is plenty—we know it in many peculiarities—the Websterian grandeur—all that; but speech like Ingersoll's—this gravity, linked with such joy—holding the worlds at tongue's end—is a divine gift, a divine fire." Then he said smilingly: "Doctor writes me here," motioning towards the table—"questions me—'Who wrote the Post piece?—was it Horace?'—he laughed—"perhaps it was *finesse.*" But added—"No, not that—Doctor is not that kind of a man—not a finesser." Here seemed suddenly reminded: "Now that I think of it, Horace, and you are here, I want to ask you: it was on my mind last week. When I was in the midst of my talk with the Colonel—the talk I touch up in the last paragraph there in the Post—was coming upon my close—reserving for the end my sally, my big guns—as the Irish carter, who kept his beasts slow, that he might end up roundly—before I could free myself, deliver the word, Weir Mitchell came up, put his hands on both shoulders, so"—indicating—"and said—'Well, I'm going to adjourn the meeting now'—as Brinton did at once. Was I breaking up? did I show signs of a collapse?—or what was it? It sat down without mercy on my Irishman's spirit. I have wondered and wondered what Mitchell meant." Perhaps Mitchell's *fear* had something to do with it; W. was grown very hoarse. But as for anything else—"I was not conscious of it myself—I felt on the contrary strong to the end." He had not noted Bucke's discomfiture that evening. He added: "The whole thing was an act of grace—the table itself was arranged with great art." When I told him my trouble in doing this—"Well—it was well done at last, which is the important point. Yes, yes, as you say, no such event could be planned—it can only be hoped for—as Burns wrote it, it is certain a child will be born, but whether to be a saint or a damned scoundrel remains to be seen."

I told W.: "O'Connor said to me last year—'If you ever meet Ingersoll, you will find him a great big eloquent child.'"—W. putting in now—"Ah! he said that? So it has proved. This dinner, great in itself, was cemented by Ingersoll's presence, took historic place."

Thursday, June 12, 1890

W. in his room, just finished dinner, which he said he "enjoyed." Not feeling strong—weather severely warm—"melts me out." I showed him proof of lines on a card. He asked, "Should something be added here to show they were written to people of foreign lands?" And to my negative—"It has no difficulties to me," he said, "I see it is *hyper*critical: let it go as it is—I am satisfied."

Returned me Harper's Weekly and Scribner's. Reading the latter today again, had "read part of Stanley's article" headed "The Emir Pasha Relief Expedition"—but not all—for it was not all out. "I can hardly say I am much interested, much less enthused. Stanley does not move me—perhaps because I have not looked into him enough—if I looked deeper, I might see more." But Bartlett's Millet article had "appealed." Terrible storm last night, of which he spoke. Bodings now, from cloud and sultriness. Not therefore out.

On the floor a pile of books which I found to be the Centennial edition of Leaves of Grass and Two Rivulets. "It is a new batch—I have just unearthed them—they are a recent discovery. I thought those on the table—fixed up—autographed—were all. I must set to work, get these in shape." I should say, probably 10 or a dozen sets.

Friday, June 13, 1890

Stopped in at W.'s on my way home at 5.30. He sat fanning himself—the day very hot. Will not go out in the heat of the

day. Says his condition is "well up—yet nothing to brag of."
Ate a good dinner. My newsman gave me a copy of the Atlantic (specimen) of December last. W. expressed some interest and I left it with him.

Yesterday he had me mail for him an envelope of pictures to Aldrich, of Iowa (Librarian) and a letter to Pearsall Smith—and today he had made up a copy of the pocket edition to send to Ingersoll and a paper for the Smiths again, England. No further word from Ingersoll yet. Frank Williams has given me his banquet speech.

I met Frank Williams today and he gave me in brief, the argument of a little paper just accepted by Lippincott's. There are two contending or different forces in literature—the one static—the one dynamic: the first to preserve (as Lowell &c), the second to add (as, in America, Emerson and Whitman). Between Emerson and Whitman Frank makes comparison thus: Whitman reveals man, whole, in a flash, illuminates the whole being; Emerson in side-paths, here and there, in glimpses. I explained this to Walt who smiled as to the comparison. "We will have wait till we read that," he said: the important thing is, how does he argue himself there." Were such comparisons dangerous? "I think so: but whether this is remains as I have said."

I urged him to go out and *to the river*, by all means—and he assenting—"as soon as it is a little cooler, we'll try it."

Frank Williams has a great deal of feeling on the point, that Ingersoll, in his speech at the dinner, tried to argue into Leaves of Grass his peculiar religious and philosophical views. I said it had not so impressed me. Williams' speech as he gives it to me, all correct except that part in which he bitterly speaks of the "narrowness" and negation of agnostics, which was not uttered but is after-word if not after-thought. I argued with Williams that an agnostic *could* not deal in negations, as he says—that his whole temper is one of suspense, not deciding either way on the question of phenomena, &c.

460

Finally he admitted my distinction, and further that he perhaps did Ingersoll injustice.

At 7.20, hurrying to the ferry, I came across W. in his chair at 2nd and Federal streets, Warren pushing him. He had been down to the river. I told him of Talcott Williams' note, saying he had a report of W.'s own talk. W. said quickly—"I wouldn't give a cent for that, but would give a good deal—Oh! a good deal!—for Ingersoll's!" I said, "We'll get Ingersoll's"—and he at once—"Do you think so?" Saying again of his own—"I am a little curious after all to know what I did say." He had a flower in his hand—some blossom of grass. I hurried on.

Saturday, June 14, 1890

8 P.M. W. not at home—had gone to the river with Warren about an hour before. I sat at the door waiting and in about 10 minutes he came wheeling along. Cordial and bright. Sat out in his chair and talked. Yet quietly disposed this evening, too—and I did not disturb him except here and there to say some occasional word.

I had a note from Buxton Forman today, which I read him. "You should send him a book," W. said—adding—"I acknowledged the 25 dollars he sent me—also sent him the books—expressed them: they made too big a package to mail."

"Not extra well," he replied to my query about his health, "only as well as the law allows." Saluted (as they he) most of the people that passed: "Good evening, ladies," to some—and to a child—"How do you do, dearie,—little dearie"—putting out his hand and receiving its own timidly offered, the child shyly looking at him the while. Then it was, "How do you do, Uncle Danny," to the ferryman that passed, and "Ha! Frank! is that you?" to some one that I did not know; and then a word now and then to a neighboring child, with a piece of ice in its hand. Then he had his chair turned around to avoid the glare of the electric light, sitting in the shadow of the tree.

Harned met Scovel today who admitted he had made the Times matter up complete out of the birthday book. W. would say no more than "the great Jim!"—and laugh.

I reminded W. that McKay had never been invited to the dinner—that till today I had not even thought of his name. "Oh! that *was* unfortunate! It did not occur to me either."

Sunday, June 15, 1890

10.05 A.M. W., his breakfast finished, was reading the morning papers. He spoke of Emerson, "the questioning Emerson"—of the young men who saw him and whom he "profoundly questioned"—explaining—"This was because he had nothing to tell that he thought would interest them, while everything they had to tell would interest him." He confessed this was often his own attitude of mind "in contact with fresh youth."

"Is it like to rain?" he asked me, and said he "promised" himself to get out if it did not.

Advised me to "send book to Forman—and write him, too." Thinks I should write to Symonds, also. "I cannot write long letters—you can tell him all about affairs here."

Monday, June 16, 1890

5.50 P.M. W. in his room, writing a postal to Buxton Forman, of whom he at once said: "The package arrived all right—the cost"—specifying, out of the letter which he lifted from the table—and which afterwards he gave to me.

I showed him the final proofs of cards from Billstein, of which he said—"I am perfectly satisfied that you have seen all things adjusted. Look out that all our names are right." Speaks again: "I must see if 'The Beauty of the Ship' has not been forgotten in late editions." Said his foreign mail is quite large"—including "several letters and papers"—a copy of the "Celebrities of the Century," containing H. B. Forman's Whitman biographical notice among them. Called my attention to it—then to what Forman said of it.

He had seen the paragraph in today's Press headed "Whitman's Greeting to Victoria," extracted from the Lady's Pictorial—reading as follows:

The Queen was much touched by the numberless tokens of affection and loyalty which reached her on Saturday from every member of her family and all classes of her subjects. The King of the Belgians' graceful act of courtesy was much appreciated by Her Majesty, who is keenly sensitive upon matters of personal chivalry, and the Queen was pecularly gratified by the tribute from Walt Whitman, which was promptly brought to her notice. The old American poet's birthday offering was very striking, coming from a Democrat of Democrats, and his tribute to the magnificent service rendered by the Queen in the "Trent" affair, in averting war between England and America, a remarkable recognition of the personal influence of "a woman and a queen."

Laughed somewhat over it. "She will probably send you a big draft in memory of the event—for ten thousand," I said—he putting in with great jokiness—"or *more*—oh! certainly *more*! But it has not come yet!" Was in doubt if the paragraph was "authentic"—but cared little either way. His point had been to "utter what was in me"—and "the rest must take care of itself."

Autographed a big book for Daniel Longaker—I taking it with me. Intends sending a copy to Bush in New York. Referring to a note in the Conservator that Clifford had read in church on Sunday "a simple but majestic group of lines from Walt Whitman," and I telling him that Sam Longfellow was present when Clifford did so, and C. thought him interested, W. remarked: "Sam is very gentle, sweet—very much inclined to be radical—but there's something in him"—I put in, "his extreme gentleness takes the edge off his sword"—W.

continuing—"Yes: I was just going to say that he is—let me see—we might call it, soft—a type of men who stop at the last point, hesitate, fail: it is the way of most we meet—it was the fate of Sam's brother, too. Henry always looked rather stronger—a little portly, though not much that, either." He would like to "read Sam's life of Henry"—had not done so. "They are, or were, both of them men of the old-school—Henry especially so, with something of modern dignity and manner added: and there is anyhow something in that old-school manner full of charm, which justifies itself."

This led to talk of ministers and ministers: I told W. of Ingersoll's exception of Talmage from much of his respect and W. said, "I might say I share that with him. I don't know anything about Talmage as a man, but if as a man he is anywhere near like the Talmage we know of in a public way, he must be a pretty mean cuss. Didn't I speak to you of his sermon on angels some three or four weeks ago? For sublime and audacious stupidity, it beat all I ever knew for depth of shallowness." I laughed: "A bull! a bull!"—he heartily sharing—"So it is—yet there's the whole truth in it for all that. But however we complain, disdain, there seems to be a constituency for him—he appears to be wanted—has a place—especially in Brooklyn, I should say." But why in Brooklyn? "Well, there are in Brooklyn a great diversity of market for just that sort of thing—that vulgar statement of life—for religious mountebanks, charlatans. There is a large population in Brooklyn of the 15[,]00[0] to 20,000 dollars-a-year people—for whom Talmage is just the thing: vulgar to the last degree—out of the meanest stock—wanting in lofty ideas, beliefs—a Baptist, Presbyterian cut by tendency—perhaps Methodist, too—though the Methodist comes out of ranker, deeper, richer soil, of greater promise, and has in America acquitted itself of higher performances." He had heard he was under ban with Joseph Cook—"But that is right: it would seem much the worser to myself if he smiled upon me"—and so with "all Comstock specimens." "We must not forget William O'Connor's priest, who took up Leaves of Grass, spent an hour over it, then in great rage threw it on the floor, 'Damn it! I hate it—will have no more of it!' Oh!" exclaimed W. "if you could have heard O'Connor tell it, throwing into the tale the unction he did, you would split your sides! It was a splendid exhibit of mock passion in William."

Read W. some extracts from Frederic Harrison's essay on Carlyle which he seemed much to enjoy.

Tuesday, June 17, 1890

5.20 P.M. W. had just gone out in his chair. Mrs. Davis reported him feeling very well. I had cards with me but did not leave them—having word to go along when I did.

7.20 P.M. Down to W.'s again—found him just returned from the river—sitting in the chair, directly in front of the step, facing east (to avoid the glare of the electric lights). Stayed about 20 minutes. He talked with extraordinary freedom.

Said he had had word from Ingersoll today. "He wrote a letter—then sent me the book called 'Prose Poems'—they came together in the first mail this morning—made me a good breakfast. Ingersoll protests in the letter against the title—'Prose Poems'—which he says was the choice of the publisher, not his own. But I like the title well enough myself—can see no objections to it. There seems to be a great collection in that book—mostly touches at this and that in a few lines—but some near complete: the Lincoln piece, for instance—I had read it before several times—today I read it again. It is a great statement—will bear reading *ad infinitum*. The vastness of Ingersoll is that he *is* vast—has no shams. I know no one who at his best flights can any way equal him. I find myself every now and then saying 'no' to his specific religious, historic, literary, judgments. But beyond and above all my objections are facts which make all of them slight and counting for little. After the mistakes are the higher qualities (or *before* them), qualities that place him far, far above us all, out of reach—qualities of character, background, atmosphere, out of which he emerges, into which and in which he flings and bathes, and plays a sublime melody through it all. It is a wonder, how he glorifies, almost justifies, even his mistakes: it is the grand manner of the man. Yes, he *is* the fat boy described by Bartol—then he is much more—and it is that 'much more' which the ill-feeling of the time fails to see. The book is in every way elegantly produced—covered with what would be called tree calf—every page elegantly pressed—too much so—too fine—overdone. But Ingersoll has probably no more to do with that than with the title—he has a worshipful publisher and that explains it. It is a book selling, I should say, for 5 or 10 dollars." Then he continued the subject: "I have read many of the small pieces today—then the Lincoln, then the Voltaire—exquisite rare work all. I know no one else in our day doing it or able to do it. Yet we are a nation of gabbers—all talking at once—probably for that reason to so little effect. The great wonder with Ingersoll is the art of it all—the superb certainty—ease—suavity—a direct simple quality of which I nowhere else catch a clue—the art of the lily, the rose, that grow because they must: it surpasses explanation—we only know that it *is*—like the sunset, the trees overhead"—looking aloft. Did Ingersoll say anything about his speech here? "No—not a word—I have no idea we will ever get that—it is gone, forever. I confess that I, for one, cannot say I am just as happy to have it lost as to have it. I am as greedy to have it as I was the night it was spoken. I mourn its loss. It was one of those superb bursts which gush from the push of the heart—that comes forth without a break—exquisite melody of speech, fire of life, possible only in fortunate hours, as if by some unpredictable play of elemental forces."

Had "enjoyed" his evening "profoundly," he said. "We sat by the river for a long time. It seems to be a quiet day on the river—less movement, activity—fewer boats—and I did not regret it: I enjoyed the peace, the serenity. And oh! the atmosphere, the haze, that bathed the water, the city across there, the sky!"

Advised me to write something about the birthday dinner and send it to the Boston Transcript. "They call it a tea-table sheet up there, probably in contempt, some of them—but it has more than that to be said for it on the whole—has quite a receptive nature for new ideas."

I left cards with him and he would sign them.

Wednesday, June 18, 1890

5.15 P.M. W. just finishing dinner. Looks very well—"maintains" his "standard," he says—"in a way—which isn't much of a way after all."

Showed me Ingersoll's handsome book, still in its box—but on the floor. "Almost incongruous with me," he smilingly remarked. Also gave me Ingersoll's letter on which he had inscribed "letter from R. G. Ingersoll June 16 1890." "Here is the Arnold book, too," he added—"it turned up today—and I want you to read him on Heine." "Essays in Criticism," 1865 edition, Bucke's name therein. W. then: "I don't know how or when I got that from Bucke, but here it is."

As to loss of Ingersoll's speech he said again: "I could not make it a matter of unconcern—any more than I can say of Sarrazin's piece that we would have been just as rich if it had never been written." He has several times in the past week alluded to this paragraph out of Unity—done so with laughter, as a usual thing.

The greatest American poet, if he is such, Walt Whitman, stands in much higher regard in England than among his own countrymen, who are more perplexed than pleased over this high praise bestowed on the author of "Leaves of Grass." Tennyson is the latest authority quoted as assigning our good, grey poet the very highest rank among his kind.

Later . . . In the evening, I met W. in his chair at the Post Office—Warren inside inquiring for mail, W. talking with a young man and woman. It was very warm—he had taken off his coat and thrown it over the back of the seat, and rolled up his shirt sleeves. No vest on. When I asked him if he was on his way home—he said laughing—"I am on my way to the river—which is as much home as any other place."

Thursday, June 19, 1890

5.20 P.M. Having "eaten a good dinner," W. said he felt well. We talked a little while together.

He described Boyle O'Reilly—"a really handsome man— not large, but giving evidence of attention to athletic things: handsome, with that Irish-Spanish combination of character which seems to establish the origin of Irish nationality. . . . Yes, I can think what Hawthorne looked like, though I never saw him—probably a man resembling Aleck Cattell here in our own place—but more than that, too." But "Thoreau, though pleasing, was too angular—did not suggest any athletic observance."—"Boyle O'Reilly is a man of warmest spirit, good to meet, good to know, good to have for friend. He has been faithful to us." Much of this called out by O'Reilly's item in the Pilot calling W. so far America's greatest poet.

W. again expressed doubt if Ingersoll's speech could be got. "The Inquirer report, bad as it is, is the best I know, and ablest, shows us what we lost in not getting the speech at the time." Said he had not yet written anything on the O'Connor preface.

Would go out later on, when it had got cooler.

Friday, June 20, 1890

5.30 P.M. W. reading the Camden afternoon paper, having finished dinner. Expected to go out later on.

I had a copy of the Bazaar with me—a picture therein "The Social Pipe"—by J. G. Brown—an old couple [the man] smoking,—indoor scene—the man evidently in the midst of some narrative, the woman looking, listening. W. much attracted thereto—regarding it after his manner when much interested—long and quietly. "It is very fine," he said, "it hits them to the life. And who is J. G. Brown? I am interested: what does he do?" Brown's Broadway sketches much appealing, till he said, "He is a man we should know." Looked the paper through. "Oh! the French!" he exclaimed—"the French excel us in all the things we call *fine*—in fine wit, fine art, what not: they are unequalled."

I was in to see Talcott Williams today at the Press. He thinks he will be able to give his speech, on the whole—though with perhaps a few things here and there varying with what he uttered. He seemed shy of Ingersoll—said Ingersoll "was not so aggressive that night as usual," it was true, &c. W. laughed when I told him this—"Oh! we don't share that. That would make a good companion-criticism for John's fear that O'Connor was too radical and hot." T. W. had a report of W. W.'s talk about immortality at the dinner. I asked W. if Ingersoll's part in that was not as necessary as his own—necessary to the play of speech,—and he said—"Quite; it was a part that must not be omitted. But it is Ingersoll's speech we are all after and probably will none of us get—that great burning scorching fire." T. W. thought the only way to get it would be to persuade Ingersoll to dictate it to a stenographer. But Walt insists—"He won't do it, I'm sure: if he can, he won't." Williams in favor of printing the matter together—very generously urging upon me, also, to let no *cost* deter me, as he would willingly share in all that was required. I said—I did

469

not so much contemplate printing just now, as having the matter somewhere preserved before it is too late. W. W., however, repeatedly says that "if we get" Ingersoll's speech, "we certainly must put it into type some way: I have already been asked about it from all quarters—all our friends—all the Whitman fellows—want to see it."

W. made up cards today to send to Mrs. Heyde, Pearsall Smith, Mrs. Stafford and others—and gave me to mail. Also a birthday book for one of the Johnston girls and a paper for Bucke.

Talcott Williams discovered to me that he had a high opinion of Eakins' picture of W.—W. now said: "I do not see how anyone can doubt but it is a masterly piece of work." But to T. W.'s regret that Eakins had not attended the dinner W. said—"I am more sorry about Dave—we should have had him"—though admitting that he had not thought of McKay any earlier than I did.

As to Ingersoll's preference of Marcus Aurelius to Epictetus—"Well—they are two lands to travel through: I accept both—they are essential to the voyage." I remarked too—that it was rare to meet a great speaker whose written matter had epigrammatic and classic value, as Ingersoll's. W. at that: "It is true, as you say: with Ingersoll it is a distinct and tremendous power. I have read all the pieces in the book [that] he spoke of in his letter—and much more, too." The box open again, at his feet: had been reading again today.

Saturday, June 21, 1890

5.20 P.M. W. reading the usual afternoon papers. Raining out of doors, mildly, in summer mood. "It is breaking," he said, "perhaps we will get out." Had he read Ingersoll's eloquent letter to vivisection in the papers? "No—I have seen a paragraph from it, but not the whole piece. I do not know that I am deeply interested in the subject. On the whole, I incline to believe in vivisection: it seems the necessary step to certain necessary ends. Science is entitled to some lee-way in investigation. I have often felt that I would give my body, my corpus, for dissection after death—would decidedly do it, but for the feeling of friends on the subject." How about the crueller forms of vivisection? "Even those—for reasons!"— He would not retreat. This led to some talk of cremation. "I am disposed that way, too. Why not? Our friend Ingram is a great believer in cremation. He had a friend die some time ago whose wish it was to be cremated—who stated very specifically that Ingram was to superintend it, which he did—coming to me a few days after—offering me a handful of the dust as a souvenir." W. laughed merrily—"It was funny, wasn't it? It seems a whole group of people wanted wafts of this dust as curios,"—&c. This led him to speak more definitely of Ingram himself: "He comes of Quaker stock—is thoroughly benevolent: a noble specimen of good English manhood—a mixture of the admirable Middle-ages philanthrop[y] and Eighteenth century deists, infidels: the generation of Voltaire—Cobbett—Paine infidelism. Ingram's particular fad is for the prisoners—he is what they call a prisoner's friend—goes into the prisons, smooths the rough beds of the fellows confined. He often comes to me for rolls of papers and magazines, which I gladly give him." From Ingram we moved to Adler's tenement-house experiment in New York—W. saying of Adler and his kind: "They are our pole-stars—they sweeten our way."

Enumerating those he called the "infidels" of the last century, he exclaimed—"Even Blake—yes—we ought to include Blake." Joking again about cremation—"It is a very handy way of keeping your corpses about you." Gave me a paper to mail to Ed Wilkins.

The Boston Pilot piece, of which we have several times talked together (printed under the date of June 7), was this:

471

WALT WHITMAN, the greatest poet America has yet produced, was seventy-one years of age on last Saturday. He is a poor man, but rich in the love and veneration of friends. He is known and honored in all lands as an illustrious American.

Sunday, June 22, 1890

9.55 A.M. W. rose this morning feeling and looking unusually well. I talked with him 20 minutes or so, he being in very easy and open mood. Kingsley, of the Continental Hotel, Philadelphia died yesterday—W. saying: "We have a friend of Leaves of Grass in the son, who seems to take charge now. I have met him several times—liked him."

Speaking of a paper in which he is "taboo"—his name even ignored—"It is one of the games played—but a vain game, as we know." Some one regarding Alexander's picture of W. at the Academy (Mrs. M. B. Earle)—had said—"It would have been more like him if he had been given a dirty shirt." W.—"That was a bitter dig: that hits us at the point of our greatest pride!" I said, "But the retort was, one person has no right to put his dirty shirts on another." W. thereupon, smiling—"That was a bitterer—that was a dig to the heart!" It had been "a frequent criticism" in older days, but one "not today so generously spoken, even if still felt."

Very applausive of Tucker, induced thereto by T.'s translation and sale of Tolstoi's "Kreutzer Sonata." "I have always had a strong liking for Tucker—far down in me: perhaps even an affection: he is heroic and frank to the last degree. Long ago he stood by us in a way I cannot forget. This act is characteristic."

Monday, June 23, 1890

8.05 P.M. W. sat at the parlor window, fanning himself: in his shirt sleeves, shirt open far down—a wrap over his knees.

Had not been out today, nor had he felt well. "It has been a bad day." Mrs. Davis explains—he was out till over-wearied yesterday—from 12.30 to 4—that when he came in he went to the parlor first, remarking: "Warrie—let us go in here: I don't know whether I'm standing on my head or my heels." Today resting. I did most of the talking—he questioning. He laughed over a new Leaves of Grass man I spoke of—"God help him!"—and of a book I sold—"God prosper you in all your good intents!"—To Longaker, a doctor. W. much attracted when I said: "I find medical men more open than others to receive the physiological Leaves of Grass." "Is it so? It is a thing I should like to make sure of." Amused at "the respectable army of Leaves of Grass-ers" I spoke of, and was "not surprised" to learn that a reader of L. of G. should be thought "queer" by his friends. Yesterday he "read all—or glanced through all" of Tolstoi's piece (translated in the Press) in defence of "The Kreutzer Sonata" &c.—but was "not ready to pronounce judgment upon it." Said he had had a letter from Bucke, "though it contained nothing new."

Referred to Sidney Smith's "Who reads an American book?" laughingly. Would it answer for this day? As to my "trinity of Americans—Emerson, Lincoln, and Whitman"— he laughed heartily. "So you said that at a meeting? How did they meet it? I should like to have been there and heard!" I had a postal from Kennedy today, saying he had not yet received his Mss. from Scotland. W. "much interested to hear." Bucke thinks Wilson holds it, thinking W. W. may die—that then would be a great moment to issue it. W. himself "cannot imagine any ulterior motive."

The room dark—no light in the hall. I shook hands with W.—went back in the kitchen to say a few words to Mrs. Davis. Soon we heard W. knock his cane on the floor, both going into the parlor, and he, as he rose, saying—"I guess I'll make a move, Mary"—Mrs. D. took his hand and walked ahead to the stairway—when, he staying himself on the banisters, she hurried on to light the gas in his room. He got up, not without labor, I going down for his coat. Did not linger. He asked me to close his door. Mrs. Davis says she is strictly observing Bucke's counsel (left with her) about W.'s diet, though he resents it somewhat, saying "I always have found it best to eat those things I like: I feel better for doing so."

Tuesday, June 24, 1890

5.45 P.M. W. at his middle bedroom window, fanning himself, looking north—coat off—complexion good—evidently in much better condition than yesterday. Day had been very hot. Would not go out till nearer sun-down. Warren came in—handed him a letter from Bucke while I sat with him. W. read. "He has received the card," he said, "likes it"—and further on he read aloud that B. was glad I still had hopes of getting outline of Ingersoll's speech.

I stated to W. that at the Contemporary Club executive committee meeting yesterday we had resolved for one evening next winter for discussing the question of revision of creed (at large)—with Ingersoll to open. I told W. that one member of our committee had spoken of Ingersoll as "too aggressive" and another of him as "not a scholar." W. laughing and retorting—"And the fun is, they are both true,"—looking at me, and after a comical pause adding—"Thank God!" He further said: "Both complaints are characteristic of the literary clan—of their eminent colorless quality, respectability." The Hegel night we had planned for November (with W. T. Harris to speak) W. thought "must prove a very fine one"—adding, when I said Adler might be there to combat him as a Kantian: "I wonder what is the difference? What Adler would say was the difference?"

I had met a Dr. Gould today who was rather (or a good deal) more favorably disposed towards Specimen Days than

Leaves of Grass—thinking the former "a great book" &c. W. said: "It is a good thing for a man to get that far, anyhow: that far, he will go farther. I should say, that anyone, to get hold of me,—the bottom of the big book—all I have written—would see that all my work is autobiographical—yes, and that this autobiography finds its center and explication in the poems— in Leaves of Grass. Of course it is in Specimen Days, too— but it is there by reflection—as the moon certainly, and prob- ably many another orb, is lighted, in what we see of it, by the sun. Leaves of Grass, with respect to our case, is that sun. The memoranda, bits, personalisms, what-not, in Specimen Days—even in November Boughs, have their place, but are aside to the general drift, as pleasant diversion in the plot of a play. Yet it probably is the autobiographical feature even here which attracts your friend—and it may be a good way, as Garland says, to begin with that."

Gave me a copy of The Writer: in which was a paragraph to this affect, about grace. Also returned me the Atlantic which I left with him some days ago. When I left, gave me several postals to mail. Said he was trying to get a particular brand of honey he much fancied: Luttzen's [Luttgen's?], at Hammon- ton—so writes L. about it.

Wednesday, June 25, 1890

5.20 P.M. W. asked me as soon as I came into his room— "Hasn't this been the hottest yet?"—as it had—though now, as he said, "there is a sweet breeze—I feel it on my head as I sit here"—gently stirring his long grey hair. Would take his daily trip in about an hour.

I left Harper's Weekly with him—he returned me the American I had left him containing Morris' poem "Oracle," the first from Morris I know without formal measure, and in blank verse. M. thought it would more meet W.'s pleasure. I

asked W. if he saw any reflex there of L. of G? But it was—
"No—I cannot say I made any such observation"—but would
not give any further view whatever on the poem. Questioned
me, then ceased talking about it.

Makes merry over Curtis' question in Harper's (in the
"Easy Chair"): "There is no critic living who can foretell
whether a hundred years hence our good friend Walt Whitman will be accepted as a great poet or have fallen into the
limbo where the vast throng of Hebbell's poets lie." W. laughs
and says—"that's a mighty ticklish question." When I dwelt
upon the *certainty* of remembrance—"Do you say so? It is
along way off—it is a venturesome prophecy"—yet not loth
to consider it possible himself, I am sure.

I received today this note from Talcott Williams, enclosing
another from J. B. Gilder:

> Ye Painte Shoppe,
> 1823 SPRUCE STREET
> PHILADELPHIA.

My dear Mr Traubel
  As you will see Walt Whitman before I can get over will you
see what you can do about this

> Yours truly
> Talcott Williams

> The Critic
> 52 & 54 Lafayette Place
> New York

> 20 June 1890

Dear Mr. Williams:
  Some time ago I sent to the surviving 31 of the "Forty Immor-
tals" elected by *The Critic's* readers in 1884, a request to vote for
nine successors to the members who had died. Nearly all have done
so. Whitman is one of the few who have failed us a second time. I
have written to him on the subject but with no effect. As I receive
frequent communications from W. W., showing his disposition to

be as friendly as I could wish, but never receive any acknowledgment of any note I send him, it occurs to me that there may be some defect in the organization of his household which prevents his receiving all the letters that are addressed to him by his friends. For this reason I should be greatly obliged to you, if, the next time you see or write to him (as I take it so near a neighbor has sure access to him), you would kindly inquire whether or no he received my letters on this subject. If he doesn't wish to vote, all right: if he *does*, I want him to do it. I can send him the names of some sixty men (native Americans, necessarily) who were voted for, besides the 40 who were elected, and he could underscore as many of them, up to nine, as he would like to see elected. Holmes, Whittier, Lowell, etc., and members living abroad have voted; but we shall print only the net result, without showing how any one person made up his list. Apologizing for troubling you, I remain

Very sincerely yrs,
Joseph B. Gilder

Have not yet referred these to Whitman.

Thursday, June 26, 1890

5.30 P.M. W. in his room. I took him up the Item and the Courier from the front door. "I hope the Item is not left for the Post," he said, "I should not so much mind if for the Courier." Looking through it—met the word "cinch"—speaking of it as "new" and wondering what it meant.

I read him Joe Gilder's letter. He laughed over it very much, but said, "My answer to it would be my answer to the telegraph boy—there is no answer." Thought the matter best dropped—cared nothing about it. Should *I* answer? I should do as I chose—he had nothing to say. As to anybody's interposing between him and his mail—that was "absurd"—"there is a clear road to me," he said.

Returned me Harper's—also, looking at [Harper's] Young

People I had with me, remarked the "beauty" of several of Hamilton Gibson's pictures.

Friday, June 27, 1890

Went down to W.'s a little before eight in the evening—but the house was locked up—windows closed, no one about, not even Mrs. Davis. I sat on the step 15 or 20 minutes but he did not come. Then went home. No sooner there, however, than he passed the house. I went along—sat with him in front of 328 for some time, talking. Voice seemed weak tonight. Day very fine—"Perfect," he said, "I can imagine nothing more luminous and mild." He stood the heat "pretty well" though not "without visible effect." Had been down to the river.

Speaking of a minister who took severe views of the Sabbath—would even stop a ship in mid-ocean but for the *necessity* to proceed—W. said, "You might have gone even beyond that—have asked why the laws of nature should not be suspended for the one day, the action of the heart, the organs of digestion. It is part and parcel of the same logic." Just the other day he was complaining of the restrictions against bathing along the river front, and now remarked that these things belonged well together.

Hicks writes me from Boston to get him an autographed copy of November Boughs, which he wished to give to Mrs. Helen Campbell, who, he writes, "has all W. W.'s other writings."

Referred to Curtis' Easy Chair comment again—W. asking particularly after "the drift of the article"—and adding—"I don't know but he has there hit upon the undoubted weak spot—and yet the question seems easily enough asked—it would not seem to be necessary for any ghost to rise from its grave to tell us that."

Saturday, June 28, 1890

5.30 P.M. W. in his room, with dinner just about done. Looked well—*was* well, in his way. Left Scribner's with him. "This modern printing excites my unceasing admiration," he said. Looked at pictures—took up his knife and cut pages. The Critic this week has a Harleigh Cemetery "Note," which excited W.'s laughter. The idea of a "precipice" near by his lot caused him to say: "It is a picturesque paragraph—just enough lie in it to make it travel fast." Gave me a letter received today from Bucke.

Referred to Poet Lore—which he did not read "greatly," yet was "glad to receive"—adding, "I think someone there has several times written me about it. I ought to be slapped for never having acknowledged. I would not swear I had *not* acknowledged, for sometimes my poor memory plays me tricks in self-condemnation, too—though I do not think in this case it has." Gave me November Boughs for Helen Campbell, which I had him endorse. Said it was his last copy there. Also, at my reminder, gave me a copy of the Gutekunst photograph for Hicks, autographing it also. Remarked that he supposed he often "replied to letters that deserved no reply and left unanswered letters that deserved some notice"—yet that this was probably always incidental to a man much-questioned and not "a correspondent by nature."

Discussed having some copies of the Elias Hicks picture struck off by Billstein. "The printing of that cut in the book was a failure." How easily men got the cut of their trade! "The undertaker: how soon he is as lugubrious as his business!" But a man must not be weighed and pressed down into a mould.

Sunday, June 29, 1890

9.45 A.M. W. just eating his breakfast, after having looked over the papers somewhat. I did not stay—went in mainly to

remind him of a book he was to do up for me. Very well—
but, the day so hot, not "exhilarated," he said. Hoped to get
out later in the day.

Monday, June 30, 1890

Did not see W.—being detained in the bank. But they told
me he went out late in the day, after the discomfort of the
heat.

Tuesday, July 1, 1890

5.15 P.M. As usually the case at this hour, W. musing in his
own room, dinner being over. We talked freely together for
20 minutes or half an hour.

He saw a book in my hand—questioned what it was—then,
hearing it was from Frederic Harrison, questioned me about
it. I read him from "The Choice of Books": "Balzac wearies us
by a sardonic monotony of wickedness; George Sand by an
unwomanly proneness to idealize lust." This excited W.'s indignation. "Does he say that?" he exclaimed—"I should say,
then—he has no right at all to put forth a word on the subject—not a word. Pfuff! 'Lust'—does he use the word 'lust'?
What does *he* know about it?—by what authority speak?" And
further, where Harrison names "Consuelo" with a mass of
Hugo's and Balzac's and so forth—calling them "books of extraordinary vigor," adding—"but it would seem to me treason
against art to rank even the best of *them* with immortal mas-
terpieces, such as *Tom Jones* and the *Vicar of Wakefield*." W.
insisted: "That is as poor criticism as well could be—he has
never read Consuelo—not read it in that sense which takes
its measure—gets at its meaning." My objection that The
Vicar of Wakefield and Consuelo were books not to be compared, "not to be classed together," W. assented—"I should

endorse that—it is well taken"—but felt that Harrison lacked in "deeper discrimination."

Kennedy sent me a short article for the Conservator—"The Quaker Traits of Walt Whitman," of which I spoke to W., who expressed so much curiosity I got on my feet and read to him aloud. I usually read to him, if at all, with vehemence—as, if I do not, he misses many necessary points. After I was done he exclaimed: "That is good—that is idiosyncratic—very good—a piece of Kennedy's self."

Speaks rather indignantly of the insistence of the papers that he has "gone out and selected his [my] grave"—explaining—"There's only enough truth in that to make it hold together—not a bit more—but I suppose that's plenty enough for the reporters." Returned me Scribner's I left with him the other day. Williamson writes me to know how much truth there is in the reports of W.'s serious sickness. Had been abroad, to London &c. I suppose this is an echo of the Record alarmist reports a month and more ago. W. W. little concerned.

Reference to Ingersoll's fight with the doctors over vivisection—W. thereupon: "That reminds me to ask you something I have been thinking about. What would you say of Ingersoll? Is he before all *sceptic*? I am not certain, but that seems the word for him—not denier, not affirmer, but one in suspense. Etymologically, is that the right use of the word? Ask Brinton, ask Alder—they are the men to know. I have had my curiosity aroused on this point. The more I see of Ingersoll, think of him, the more I feel that I can endorse him—endorse him even as regards immortality—for as I read him (these are great pieces he sent me) I understand him to mean mainly that what is to come we know nothing about—at least, that *he* does not—which is about what I would say myself." I said— "Ingersoll of course contradicts himself as often as you do—is in fact poet first of all," &c.—"speaking in pictures—the passing panorama." W. then: "I can say amen to all that—in fact,

481

it is indispensable to see it before pretending to an opinion."
And as to Ingersoll's aggressiveness: "After the conventions,
the formalities, respectabilities, such aggression clears the atmosphere. After Emersonism—(I do not mean *Emerson*, but
Emerson*ism*)—after Emersonism, the entrance of such a
positive force, knowing something, insisting upon something,
is refreshment: I applaud, love it: I think it is *our* voice, as-
serting its own."

Had not been out today. When I left, rolled down his
sleeves. "I guess we'll start out now."

Gave me mail—a couple of books for England, with postal
announcing their dispatch, a letter for his sister, Mrs.
Heyde—papers. The man in the post office said, "I never
weigh Walt Whitman's packages: I send them off just as he
leaves them." W. gave me a copy of the Boston Transcript
containing a letter (Paris) from Marchioness de San Carlos, of
the Nouvelle Revue, discussing American writers. "It will interest you: it is curious certainly—not profound—curious."

Wednesday, July 2, 1890

8.10 P.M. W. out when I arrived, but came, wheeled along
by Warren in 10 minutes or so. Sat at the door for half an
hour, talking. He asked after "news," saying he had written
postals to both Bucke and Kennedy today.

Speaking of the Century W. said: "I noticed John at work
there again"—a paper, "A Taste of Kentucky Blue-Grass"
(John Burroughs)—but—"I did not read it—perhaps shall,
yet." Touched also upon the discussion there between Henry
George and Edward Atkinson on the Single Tax. He questioned if the magazine would have discussed the question
some time ago—"but now it is quite the thing, therefore they
do it."

Spoke of the "delicious change in the weather." Rained very
hard most of the day, the rain leaving it much cooler. Asked

after Morris who is doing literary work on the Bulletin for a few weeks.

W. went into a long rumination—vocal—as to war. "One of the great lessons of the war was, to see the regiments go out fresh—then after a long, long, long time trail back—defile the old way once more. It was solemn, gigantic, in what it suggested." Of armies—someone had remarked the lusty appearance of the German army in the Franco-Prussian war. W. inquired [remarked?]—"That must have been by comparison with the French—I think it would be the French." And again, when I asked—"or the American?" "No—hardly that. Besides, the skillful recruiting officer does not judge by size, weight, flesh—but by grit, endurance—*he* knows what—the deeper indications." Friedrich Wilhelm's giants alluded to, W. said: "It is to that old man we owe the hateful hussar cap— damnable to look upon, damnable to wear. The modern soldier—the soldier of our armies—the soldiers of Sherman, our William Sherman—contrast, take-off, are as much as may be relieved of weight on the march—and in dress, *light* goods. The English soldier still sticks to his red coat, but that must go, too, and *soon*. The point is now, *no show*—make for simplicity—have the end of the march in view—have in mind the Napoleonic doctrine—battles are won by bivouac" &c.

W. remarked that Aldrich was to retire from the Atlantic and Horace Scudder to take his place. What did I know of Scudder &c?

Thursday, July 3, 1890

5.10 P.M. W. in his room, by the window, fanning himself. Good color. Complained however of the heat of the day. Raining slightly. Had been reading. Pointed out to me the Post. "I have been finding out here that Lord Salisbury has been offered a dukedom of some sort by the Queen for conduct she likes—perhaps for measures pushed—I don't know: but it interests me to see that he has declined—will not have the dukedom. It is almost as good as Carlyle's, if not better—perhaps more significant." But even Carlyle's expressed disregard for decoration &c. "not wholly disregard" for "I suppose every man—the most militant, antagonistic—likes to be recognized, appreciated—as I say it, made much of."

He had a letter from Ed Wilkins today. "He has had some sort of kick-up there. Ed is very undemonstrative—says little at all times—has a good deal of phlegm—and therefore I do not see just what has happened—but *some*thing, without a doubt. He speaks of coming down this way again—wants to— says he wants to be with me." I thought this singular. Why did he write that, knowing Warren was in the place today? I asked W.: "I suppose you and Warren are thoroughly adjusted?" To which: "Yes—thoroughly—and I may say further that not only in Warren but in all things mine these days I consider myself very fortunate—very fortunately situated"— with a smile—"even if my pieces *are* returned by the magazine editors—by the Century, Harper's, the Cosmopolitan, Nineteenth Century"—by the latter?—I had not known. "Yes—by it as by the others. I did not like the last Century note—Gilder's—it had something *covert*—like that last something sometimes in a dish at the table—I don't like it— it spoils the dish—but I don't know what it is,"—and then when I asked—"but what do you care?"—he said simply: "Nothing at all. I would not turn a finger for any one of them—not a finger. It is not for them I care, or their magazines, but the public ear—I wish to reach the public—to deliver my message." And further—"I do not object to your making all this as public as you choose—stating it anywhere— though not, of course, to lug it in." There were some objecting to his seeming preference for Ingersoll &c. "Well—if that is so, then I must take the first opportunity to clinch it—to make even more emphatic statement of my feeling. Ingersoll, like O'Connor—they call *mad*—but it is a great mistake. Let me see by what one word could I measure them? I am at a loss for a word: call them tower-like—standing alone—straight—an identity—vast—erect—not to be waived aside. There are plenty of men made up of a dozen influences—centers of scholarship, what-not—but these men are themselves, personalities, consistent, self-sustaining, identities." He wished no one to have "any concern about my friendships"—they would, "take care of themselves." When I took ground that "any life is as interesting as any other, rightly or faithfully told, he assented. "That is true to the bone—that would have tickled William O'Connor." Then—"I have by the way had a letter from Mrs. O'Connor—she is well" &c.

Friday, July 4, 1890

1.35 P.M. W. lying down, fanning himself. The day extremely uncomfortable—steamy. Had "not had his morning nap," he said.

I left the Ingersoll "oratory" interview with him. Last night expressed his wish to see it. Another of his expressions upon Ingersoll is this: "What does it matter for we can see all differences—his are his peculiarities—his own. Don't you remember that Shakespeare fellow—I think in Lear—Osric, wasn't it? He says when taunted for his dandifications—'Trifles, but mine own!'" W.'s gestures inimitable. "I remember how well Harry Placide rendered this—he played the character. There were several brothers, but Harry was decidedly the best. How inimitably he would act that character! It was one of the cases in which I enjoyed seeing the minor characters acted better than the principals—this was the judgment of all the wise fellows in theatricals then—though all this was well done, too. But, as I started out to say, Ingersoll's peculiarities are his own, to be respected as his own, as ours are to be respected—they are part even of his superb identity." &c.

I did not stay but very briefly. He asked if the mail had brought me any news—"None in mine," he reported. The Fourth very noisy: he did not like that, but it was a thing to be put up with.

Saturday, July 5, 1890

8.10 P.M. W. not in when I arrived but was wheeled along by Warren in about ten minutes. Sat in front of the step— then talked with me for full an hour. Seemed very bright. Was exhilarated by the weather—so much cooler. Night before last did not sleep at all—last night better—tonight expects "to do it handsomely." Had been down to the river. Hand cold—but would not let Warren bring a wrap.

Said Kennedy was now with Bucke—the latter had so written him. W. spoke of the Ingersoll piece on oratory—how "deeply" it had "struck" him. "It is very profound in many ways. For instance, while it is subject perhaps to criticism, take that part in which he says, there can be no more Decoration Day orations because men, to speak well, must have acted a part in the thing they speak [of]—that is profoundly so." And when I said, "And in that piece is practically an arraignment of modern average writing—that men are not speaking what they live—therefore do not move us" and that "No writing is good or of value that does not stir us"—he assented—"That is every word true—that is not to be sneered away." I quoted for instance the comparison made by Stedman and others, classing W.'s Lincoln ode and Lowell's together—and I objected that Lowell's did not stir me: "It is a thing built, not a current flowing: his is a structure, grown story by story: yours a limpid river." He said—"That is a striking distinction. I too, have often known them put together: but could never see the reason why—except, perhaps, as being upon the same subject." We lingered for some time in this talk, W. referring to Ingersoll's "gifts" repeatedly.

W. much amused over the Catholic priest who, having seen the Conservator, prophesied I would soon come to a recognition of the true faith &c. &c. "It might have been said that you already concluded you had the true faith," W. remarked. "It is the same story with those fellows: pork and beans is my dish, therefore you must like it—but no, we shake our heads at that—though we return them good for evil by not forcing our dish on them."

Spoke of Stedman as "no longer young—must be 60"—of the "bad son" and the good one—deserting him. "He is a man of worrying nature—does not take life calmly—is small and slender." Then of Wanamaker and the Brittanica [*sic*] suit—that it "ought to go against him"—of Wanamaker's lax moral notions, "pretended religiousness." I inquired today at Wanamaker's if they had Tolstoi's "Kreutzer Sonata." No, but I could get it at Porter and Coates'. W. commenting—"I hear they are considering whether to handle Leaves of Grass"—I saying—"That is worse than to instantly reject it—it is the attitude of the man with his hand on the knob of the door, doubtful whether to admit you or not"—and W. assenting—"that is a sharp way to say it—but it says!" Childs quite another man from Wanamaker—"He is a rare dish—there are numerous rare dishes—one for this and that—but all are necessary, and Childs is *one*." He knew Childs—knew his "generosities," rejoiced to hear incidents I could tell him. Childs' reminiscences "very simple"—this inducing comparison with Stoddard's—and W.'s: "Dick Stoddard is a poor mean cuss—made so, perhaps, in some part, by his ills—old age—the bad digestion, eyes, what-not." I suggested probably disappointments, too. W. thereupon speaking of the early poems: "'The Woman on the Town' impressed me most deeply—I read that more than once." But—"there was an acid in Stoddard—events, I don't know what, have stirred it up—the effect disastrous." This "reminded" him—"Did you read Conway's piece in the Press this morning—'Boccaccio in His Garden'—

That is a first-rate sample of what we have been speaking about. Conway starts out to write an interesting article and does it, no matter who suffers—but it is writing at long range, and Ingersoll is right—we must participate in the life of anything we attempt to portray." And—"Conway's proclivities are good: he wants to be all that is required—to be radical, liberal, even free—but with all that, he's such a hell of a liar, there's no knowing which part of him to credit."

When I spoke of Leaves of Grass and Specimen Days as composing "a remarkably consecutive life," he was evidently much attracted, questioning me very closely. "Do you say that? Do you think they hang well together?"—cementing it—"That is what ought to be."

Happening to mention Williamson, W. asked—"was he asked to the dinner?" then —"and Stedman?" Adding to this: "I am afraid we have missed some: there was Dave—we missed *him* and I never cease regretting it. Yes indeed, he ought to have been there—I was going to say he was almost *sine qua non*. You have been in to see him? You ought to go in—Dave is very philosophical—more so than you would suppose. He will take it all right. The way to do is, to put it all on my shoulders—that is the surest way out—I am the one who should have thought of him." I said I only knew Dave very mad on one score—Worthington—and I said to W.: "Dr. Bucke, who sees occult meanings to all you do, says, never mind, W. wishes that Worthington book to circulate" &c—as if with a wink. But W. only laughed heartily—"Yes, so much so I'd like to wring his neck."

Sunday, July 6, 1890

Day fine clear throughout. W. in good condition—got his outing. I did not see him.

INDEX

INDEX

INDEX

Cause and Cure," 264
Carson, Hampton L., 153
Carter, Susan W. C., 106, 110
Carus, Paul, 42
Cary, William, 422
Castelar y Ripoll, Emilio, 40, 269, 270
Catlin, George, 400
Cattell, Aleck, 468
Cattell, Alex., 113
Celebrities of the Century, 463
Celeste, Mme., 36
Century: 105, 145, 252–53, 280, 285, 301, 347, 482; publication of "Old Age's Ship and Crafty Death's," 105, 267, 274; publication of "A Twilight Song," 311, 384, 385, 391–92; publication of Whitman "poemet," 41, 47, 80, 105; rejection of "Ye Jocund Twain," 407–8, 419
Century dictionary, 164
Chainey, George, 131, 358
Chamberlain (*Boston Transcript*), 5
"Champagne in Ice," 32
Channing, Mrs. William F., 125
Chase, Salmon P., 38
Chiefs of the Six Nations, 56
"Child Went Forth, A," 157
Child, Josiah, 116
Childs, George W., 249, 371, 487
"Christmas Greeting, A," 95, 152, 169, 180, 214, 218, 220, 267, 268, 269
Chubb, Percival: 69, 145, 169, 199; visit to Whitman, 193–96
"City of Paris," 345
Clark, Henry, 267
Clark, Hobart, 25, 26, 27
Clay, Clement M., 430
Clay, Henry, 230
Clemens, Samuel, letter to Whitman, 106–7
Cleveland, Grover, 70, 318
Clifford, Edward, 35
Clifford, Hilda, 60, 92, 400
Clifford, John Herbert, 79, 93, 98, 157, 159, 399; letter to Traubel, 60–61; visits to Whitman, 193–96, 399–400
Clifford, William Kingdon, 178
Cline, Miss, 415
Coates, Edward H., 153, 218

Coates, Foster, 152
Coffin, Long Tom, 264
Cohen, S. Solis, 63
Colfax, Schuyler, 275–76
Conservator, 329, 392, 412; "The Quaker Traits of Walt Whitman," 481
Consuelo (George Sand), 481
Conway, Moncure D., 15, 112–13; "Boccaccio in His Garden," 487–88
Cook, Joseph, 464
Cook, Weda, 62
Cooper, James Fenimore, 35, 36, 41, 42, 250, 261
Cope, Professor Edward Dunker, 178
Copyright League, 138
Coquelin, 47, 159–60
Corning, J. Leonard, 131, 136
Costelloe, Mary Smith, 314, 401–2
Cranford, Kenneth, 114
Critic, 193, 218, 222, 324, 335, 336, 344, 402, 412, 413, 476, 479; "The Lounger," 171; "The Lounger," identity of, 207, 256, 379, 420; on Whitman, 61. *See also* Gilder, Jennie; Gilder, Joseph
Current Literature, 166, 167, 179, 220, 385
Curtis, Cyrus H. (*Home Journal*), 383
Curtis, George William, 476, 478
Curtz, Henry, 255, 397, 414
Curtz (house painter), 172
Cuttel, Captain Edward, 20

Daintrey, Laura: letter from, 74–75
Dana, Charles A.: *Household Book of Poetry*, 222
Dana, Richard Henry, Jr., 222–23
Darby, John, 219
Darwin, Charles, 41, 388
Davidson, Thomas, 308
Davis, Jefferson, 178–79
Davis, Mary O., 9, 11, 17, 25, 49, 174, 238, 266, 290, 361, 363, 370, 393, 401, 405, 416, 423, 426, 429, 473, 474
Dawson, Dan, 8
Dayton, Fred, 382, 385
Democratic Review, 379

491

INDEX

INDEX

INDEX

INDEX

payment of royalties, 51, 368
McKean, Thomas, 158
Macmillan Publishing Co., 261
Macready (actor), 140
Magazine of Art, 10, 73, 81, 250, 252
Magazine of Truth, 163
Mahabharata, 11
Mannahatta, 56
Mansfield, E. D. (English actor), 237
Mapes, Mrs. Mary E., 30, 159, 240
Marchioness de San Carlos (*Nouvelle Revue*), 482
May, Fred, 44
Mead (*New England Magazine*), 41
Michelangelo, 235
Millet, Jean François, 224, 456; "Angelus," 10, 180; self-portrait, 13, 73–74, 81; "Sower," 181
Milton, John, 254, 255
Mirabeau, Honoré Gabriel, Comte de, 388
Mitchell, S. Weir, 134, 188, 360, 432; letter to Traubel, 107
Modjeska, Helena, 2
Moltke, Helmuth Johannes von, 333
Montgomerie, Anne, 139
Montgomerie, Peter, 311
Moore, Ralph (superintendent, Harleigh Cemetery), 210, 405
Morris, Harrison, S., 29, 154, 280–81, 284, 320, 378, 380, 385, 483; article on Sarrazin's "Walt Whitman," 146, 148, 158; article on Whitman's Lincoln lecture, 359–60; essay on Browning, 9; "Oracle," 475; translation of Sarrazin works, 18, 181, 357; translation of Whitman works, 134; visit from, 257–60. *See also* Sarrazin, Gabriel
Morris, William, 275
Morrow, Rev. James, 285, 286
Morse: "My Grandmother's Religion," 358
Morse, Sidney B., 8, 80, 192, 217, 278, 422; busts of Whitman, 50, 52–53, 57, 63 (*see also* Traubel, Maurice Henry); "Camden's Compliment to Walt Whitman," 92, 96, 138, 294; letter to Whitman, 290
Moss process engraving catalogue, 316
Munyon's Illustrated World, 249, 317, 400
"My 71st Year," 101, 104, 116

New England Magazine, 41, 43, 46, 57
New Ideal, 180
New York Exhibition, 317
New York Exposition of 1853, 139
New York Herald, 11, 310
New York Sun, 235
New York Times, 243, 266, 270, 275, 355
New York World Building, 252
Nicolay, John George, *Abraham Lincoln: A History*, 230–31, 283, 369
Nineteenth Century Club, 17
Noel, Roden, 190–91, 198, 223, 245
North American Review, 163, 192, 223, 382–83
"North Star to a South, A." *See* Christmas Greeting, A"
Nouvelle Revue, 482
November Boughs, 43, 176, 396, 478

"O Captain! My Captain!," 328, 360, 365
O'Connor, Ellen M., 120, 142, 146, 151–52, 201, 328; financial problems of, 125, 297–98; letters to Traubel, 19, 124–25; letters to Whitman, 28, 129–30, 485. *See also* Whitman
O'Connor, William Douglas, 3–4, 6, 7, 28, 121, 131, 135–37, 197, 221, 243, 302, 328–29, 348–49, 375, 376, 381, 388, 395, 431, 447, 456, 465, 469, 484–85; and Bucke, Richard Maurice, 425; "The Carpenter, 31; "The Good Grey Poet," 5, 31; on Higginson, 62; on Hugo, Victor, 88; review of *Leaves of Grass*, 6
Odenheimer, F. B., 102
O'Dowd, Bernard, 369
Oldach, Frederick, 37, 41, 392, 397, 404, 406, 412
"Old Age's Ship and Crafty Death's," 105, 255, 267

INDEX

INDEX

birthday party, 325–25; proposes magazine article, 160; receives Whitman portraits, 117; tells Haydn story, 219–20; to U.S. Mint for Whitman, 187–88; on Whitman, 12, 16, 22, 146, 149, 180, 228–29, 233, 240, 250, 311, 418; on Whitman's hospitalization, 314. *See also* Gilder, Richard; Kennedy, William Sloane; Mitchell, S. Weir; Sanborn, Franklin B.

Traubel, Maurice Henry, 161, 164, 254, 255, 396; copy of Gutekunst portrait, 166, 213, 215, 232, 250, 253, 336, 416; copy of picture of Morse bust, 80; lithographs, 206–7

Trautwine, John C., Jr., 376

Trübner, family of, 116

True, Dr. O. W., 7

Tucker, Benjamin R., 472

Twain, Mark. *See* Clemens, Samuel

"Twilight Song, A," 311

"Two Mysteries, The," 31

"Two Rivulets," 241

"Unexpress'd, The," 158, 383

Unitarian Conference, 14, 97–98

Unitarianism, 103

Unity, 467–68

Universal Review, 339, 357

Vaux, Richard, 402

Velasques, Diego: "Head of Aesop," 105, 109

Vernon, Mrs. (actress), 100, 303

Vetta, Franz (Louis Newmayer), 8

Victoria (queen of England), 322

Wainwright, Mary, 141

Walsh, Dr., 349

Walsh, Harry C., 382

Walt Whitman cigar, 278

Wanamaker, John, 487

Warner, Olin, 44

Washburn, William T., 233

Washington Chronicle, 48

"Welcome to Brazil, The." *See* "Christmas Greeting, A"

Wells, Calvin, 429

Welsh, Rees, 285

Wheeler, (*Boston Transcript*), 201

"When Lilacs Last in the Dooryard Bloom'd," 359–60, 486

Whipple, Edwin P., 8

White, Tom, 16

Whitman, George W., 84

Whitman, Walt

  comments on people: Adler, Felix, 424, 471; Alboni, Emma, 303; Alden, Henry M., 95; Aldrich, Thomas Bailey, 163, 387, 392; Alexander, John White, 301; Arnold, Edwin, 32, 83, 84, 120, 271; Bacon, Francis, 127, 256; Baxter, Sylvester, 46; Beecher, Henry Ward, 163, 345, 429, 434; Bismarck, Otto Eduard Leopold von, 331, 333, 342; Blake, J. V., 177; Bok, Edward W., 309, 383; Boker, George H., 226, 234; Booth, Edwin, 99; Booth, Junius Brutus, 99, 175, 229; Boulanger, George Ernest, 20, 52; Boyle (sculptor), 231; Brinton, Daniel Garrison, 27, 28, 357–58, 361, 370; Brougham, Henry Peter, 202, 398; Brown, Leonard Morgan, 290, 291; Browning, Robert, 191, 195–96, 204, 206, 249; Bruno, Giordano, 40, 244, 246, 265; Buchanan, Robert, 245, 246; Bucke, Richard Maurice, 65, 94, 129, 132–33, 149, 167, 180, 281, 383, 384, 412; Bulow, Haus von (musician), 388–89; Bulwer-Lytton, Edward George Earle, 203; Burns, Robert, 263; Burroughs, John, 26, 27, 394–95, 431; Carlyle, Thomas, 39, 168; Carnot, Marie François Sandi, 20; Carpenter, Edward, 64, 65, 317, 327; Castelar y Ripoll, Emilio, 270; Celeste, Mme., 36; Chainey, George, 131, 358; Chase, Salmon P., 38; Childs, George W., 371, 487; Chubb, Percival, 145; Clay, Henry, 230; Clifford, John Herbert, 93, 157, 159; Clifford, William Kingdon, 178; Colfax,

INDEX

INDEX

INDEX

color, 453; cremation, 471; Crystal Palace, 310; current poetry, 449; dialects, 145; digestion and health, 288; disease, origin of, 290; dishonest publishers, 315; "divine average," 188; drawing lessons, value of, 278; editors, 367; Egypt, ancient, 344; elections, 118; electoral college, 310; environmental effect on character, 251; evolution, 196; false piety, 320–21; farce in theatre, 229; first impressions, 131; flattery, 319; Ford's Theatre, 449; foreign diplomatic service, 292–93; free trade, 20, 41, 62, 63; French national character, 127, 469; French Revolution, 322; gentility and respectability, 194, 231–32, 313; German engravers, 190; German "tendential" novels, 203; Gladstone-Blaine controversy, 223; Greece, ancient, 31, 32, 127, 161; health, indications of, 392; historic reputation, 387–88; hypnotism, 136; immigration, 82; immortality, uncertain faith in, 146–47, 165; insurance, 102; international copyright, 371; international currency, 332; Irish character, 166; Irish "question," 423; journalists, 15, 42, 43, 81, 163, 270, 304, 305, 312; judgment of impression, 69; judicial system, 126, 127; labor "question," 423; Lake Huron, 167; lawyers, 126; legislation, 327; libel in newspapers, 266; liquor tax, 64; literary critics, 119; literary formalists, 74; literary magazines, 200; literary traditions and techniques, 386; London, 35; London policemen, 351; Madonna and Child engravings, 347; marriage and divorce, 156; marriage for money, 13; metaphor, 243; metaphysics, 449; ministers, 186; mixed races, 400; modern dress, 264; monogramists, 90; morality, 26–27, 28; moving U.S. capital, 323, 327; music, appreciation of,

159; music, black American, 120; narrow reasoning, 284; Negro voters, 97; New Orleans, 167, 346, 347; new words in English, 164–65; New Year's Day celebrations, 223–24; newspaper illustration, 184; nurses, 171; old age, 189; *Open Court*, 36; opposition parties, 52; opulence of society, 234; oratory, 162–63 (*see also* O'Connor, William Douglas); "Othello" (Shakespeare), 173; Pacific coast, 296; Pan-American Congress, 102–3; papacy and Catholic clergy, 5, 12, 13, 70, 256; Park Theatre, 347; pessimism in literature, 258, 313, 380–81; "Phaedo" (Socrates), 66; physical size and heroism, 162; physicians, U.S. Army, 450; portraiture, 216, 385; postal service, 155, 210, 412; posthumous fame, 224; preacher's salaries, 346; predicting weather, 165; Presbyterian doctrines, 178; Presbyterian revision, 261–62; Presbyterianism, New England, 44; pride in aged, 285; printers, 17, 156, 167, 170–71, 238, 320, 328; Prohibitionists, 40; proofreaders, 267, 320; Protectionism, 115, 116; prudery and language, 186–87; prudery of society, 144; *Psyche*, 358; Puget Sound, 297; Quakers, 259; qualified compliments, 113; realism in fiction, 89; religion, 291, 302; religious holidays, 350; religious orthodoxy, 244; religious pictures, 252, 253; reporters, 36, 418, 429 (*see also* journalists, sup.); Republican campaign for governor, 97; restrictive institutions, 129; *Richard III* (Shakespeare), 119; roads, 295–96; Sabbath, practice of, 478; science and orthodox church, 268; secret societies, 53, 63; "sinners" in literature, 293; slang, 148; softbound books, 264; soldiers, equipage of, 483; Spanish Roman Ca-

501

INDEX

Whitman, Walt (*continued*)

tholicism, 31; stained glass, 256, 284; statisticians, 52; steam-whistle tones, 205–6; test of greatness in men, 55; theatre and civilization, 306; theology, 431; theology and mythology, 298; theology and religion, 116–17; tradesmen, 479; truthfulness, 286, 287; U.S. intervention in Russian politics, 144–45; Unitarian church, 31; Unitarians, 186; universal language, 17, 20, 21, 193; university extension education, 324–25; use of words "black" and "colored," 151; valet service, 217; vivisection, 471; war, 483; Washington, D.C., 323; Welsh character, 28; women and intuition, 399; women in Shakespeare, 175; women's use of married names, 226; wood-engraving, 66; Yankee character, 157–58

personal: "acceptance of universe," 201; actors, 155, 248; anti-Negro remarks, 323; autobiographical element in his work, 475; "autograph" letters, 139, 271, 314–15; biographers, 8, 167; biographies, accuracy of, 50; biography (unidentified source), 306–7; birthday dinner (31 May, 1890): 268, 291, 319, 337, 339, 390–91, 413, 420, 424, 433, 434, 445, 451–52, 454, 458; described by Traubel, 435–44; Brooklyn experiences, 141; Canadian trip, 185, 186; care in addressing mail, 93, cataloging in his poetry, 132; changing autobiographical note in proof, 167; contributions to "fund," 115, 119; copyrights, proposal to sell, 48–49; correspondence, 94; correspondents, 239–40; critical acceptance abroad, 166; daily meditation, 128; deafness, 6, 47; death, attitude toward, 136, 304–5; design of vault, 248, 249, 325 (*see also* Boyle [sculptor]; Eyre, Wilson); dislike of questions, 221,

226–27; dog, 114, 137; early financial hardships, 116; early stories signed Walter Whitman, 379; egotism and endurance, 284; evaluation of later works, 281; failing memory, 339, 340; fame in old age, 41, 368, 374, 378; favorable critics, 129; foreign cities, 210; free expression of emotions, 161; friendship with Traubel, 329; French translator, 89; grave site, 210, 212, 233, 405, 481 (*see also* Harleigh Cemetery); hospitalization proposal, 276 (*see also* Bucke, Richard Maurice; and Traubel, Horace); humor in his work, 375, 376; images in later poems, 284; impulsiveness, 23; inability to read French, 113; inactivity, dislike of, 139–40; insomnia, 398; interviews prospective nurses, 71–73; Lincoln lecture (15 April 1890), 330, 359–67, 379, 420; Lincoln lectures, 353; literary critics in New York, 421, 431; literary reputation, 295, 372, 373; Long Island, 228, 259; Long Island joke, 98–99; "love letters," 7; marking favorite books, 21; memorandum books, 227; metal works, visits to, 121; miller story, 322; mislaid possessions, 233; Montaigne's cat, story of, 367; New York City, 318; notebook, 12; nurses, 72, 73; observation of nature, 343; oratory, 457; owns farm, 176; personal philosophy, 457; Peterkin story, 97–98, 102; photographers, 287; physical condition, 22, 134, 169, 202, 282, 340, 391; portraits, 137, 143, 171, 190, 215–16, 232, 315, 366–67, 374, 452 (*see also* Alexander, John White); proofreading his poems, 267; prudish attitudes and word usage, 121–22, 133; public speaking, 338, 380; Quakerism, 293; receives deed for cemetery lot, 381 (*see also* Harleigh Cemetery; Harned, Thomas); re-

502

INDEX